THE UPPER ROOM

Disciplines

2021

UPPER ROOM BOOKS®

NASHVILLE

An Outline for Small-Group Use of Disciplines

Here is a simple plan for a one-hour, weekly group meeting based on reading *The Upper Room Disciplines*. One person may act as convener every week, or the role can rotate among group members. You may want to light a white Christ candle each week to signal the beginning of your time together.

Opening

Convener: Let us come into the presence of God.

Others: Lord Jesus Christ, thank you for being with us. Let us hear your word to us as we speak to one another.

Scripture

Convener reads the scripture suggested for that day in *Disciplines*. After a one- or two-minute silence, convener asks: What did you hear God saying to you in this passage? What response does this call for? (Group members respond in turn or as led.)

Reflection

- What scripture passage(s) and meditation(s) from this week was (were) particularly meaningful for you? Why? (Group members respond in turn or as led.)
- What actions were you nudged to take in response to the week's meditations? (Group members respond in turn or as led.)
- Where were you challenged in your discipleship this week? How did you respond to the challenge? (Group members respond in turn or as led.)

Praying Together

Convener says: Based on today's discussion, what people and situations do you want us to pray for now and in the coming week? Convener or other volunteer then prays about the concerns named.

Departing

Convener says: Let us go in peace to serve God and our neighbors in all that we do.

Adapted from *The Upper Room* daily devotional guide, January–February 2001. © 2000 The Upper Room. Used by permission.

Contents

FOREWORD

The lectionary, the three-year cycle of Sunday scripture readings, became more than an academic concept from seminary when I became a youth pastor at my local church. I was gifted *A Guide to Prayer for All Who Seek God*, edited by Bishop Rueben P. Job and Norman Shawshuck. Each week I was captivated by how Bishop Job would see a theme in the scriptures and beautifully describe how the verses built on one another, supported each other and the collective value and insight available by reading them together.

That same captivating wisdom, attention to theme, and profound writing that first drew me to the lectionary, is also what draws me to *The Upper Room Disciplines*. I have become convinced that I can trust the collection and flow not only of these lectionary texts but also the discernment of the authors to reveal something new about God and humanity, sin and grace, revelation and humility, individual discipleship and communal life together.

Ten years ago, when I chose a Sunday school class at my local church, I intentionally chose a class that reads and studies the lectionary texts each week. Many of the people in the class have been learning and sharing life together for close to thirty years—nurses and architects, photographers and ministers, stay-at-home moms and accountants, city planners and art teachers. As they have cycled through the lectionary texts together year after year, it has changed and shaped them, transforming them into compassionate parents, passionate citizens, tender servants in our community, and fierce advocates for justice in the world. I see them "being transformed into that same image from one degree of glory to the next" (2 Cor. 3:18), and I pray that I might experience the same persistent transformation into the image and likeness of Christ.

The book that guides and sustains many in that Sunday school class, and our local church, is *The Upper Room Disciplines*. The authors of this book have the same prayerful attentiveness of Bishop Job, the same love of scripture that calls my Sunday school class to gather each week, and the gift for writing that marks every Upper Room book.

The daily readings invite me to pause in scripture, rest in the history or parable or letter. The authors lead me around the edges of the verses, offering new perspectives and vantage points. They draw out a theme that is often brilliant exegesis but also a faithful call to live lives marked by works of mercy and justice. Daily devotion creates a vital life with God—daily comfort, daily conversation, daily calling "to act justly and to love mercy and to walk humbly with your God" (Mic. 6:8).

In all that has unfolded over the past year, I have found God present in the pages of *Disciplines*. Words written over a year before they were printed are yet inspired and perfectly apt for the season and week and day that they are read. I pray you find the same poetic beauty, awe-inspiring wisdom, and challenge to deeper discipleship that I have discovered in the lectionary and the pages of *Disciplines*.

So, beloved, I invite you to join me with *The Upper Room Disciplines* as our guide in praying the scripture in 2021 that we might be transformed as individuals and a global community from one degree of glory to another into the image and likeness of Christ.

KARA LASSEN OLIVER
**Executive Director, The Upper Room Center
for Christian Spiritual Formation**

God's Word Runs Swiftly

JANUARY 1–3, 2021 • MICHAEL E. WILLIAMS

SCRIPTURE OVERVIEW: These scriptures chosen to mark the new year give us a panorama of perspectives, from Ecclesiastes as a poetic musing on how life is measured out in seasons, to the vision in Revelation of what we commonly consider the end of time itself. Psalm 8 asks what the role is for humans in God's magnificent creation. At the core of these scriptures is a strong sense of God's presence and loving steadfastness in which we can rest.

QUESTIONS AND SUGGESTIONS FOR REFLECTION

- Read Ecclesiastes 3:1-13. In what season of life do you find yourself? What are you praying for in this season?
- Read Psalm 8. How do you feel when you read the psalmist's words that God has created humans "a little lower than God, and crowned them with glory and honor" (Ps. 8:5)?
- Read Revelation 21:1-6a. How is the vision of a new heaven and new earth described here good news for you? What do you see God making new in the world around you?

Pastor and storyteller; author of *Spoken Into Being* (1948–2018).

NEW YEAR'S DAY

Many people make resolutions on the first day of a new year, but what do you resolve on the first day of a new decade? (Though many herald a new decade when the year number ends in 0, the decade actually begins with the year ending in 1.)

You and I already may have made our resolutions, many of which we will break before the week is out.

I want to consider a different question: What would your prayers be for Christians across the world as we navigate this important transition? Let me share a few of mine.

First, I pray that we as Christians are more determined to live out God's commandments to love God and our neighbor than to make everyone believe exactly the way we do. Second, I pray that Christians include as neighbors every part of God's creation. Third, I pray that Christians would talk less and do more to respond in love to violence, poverty, hunger, homelessness, loneliness, and hurt. Fourth, I pray that Christians look for Christ in cultures and traditions different than their own. This practice may protect us from turning Jesus into an idol who simply mirrors ourselves.

I believe that if we, as followers of Jesus, will follow his example in these ways, we will transform our world into a place where God's love reigns. What are your prayers on this day?

Dear God, make me over into the image of your love. Help me to live out my calling from you as fully as Jesus lived his. Help me to make the world a place filled with your love. Amen.

A fellow who lived in the rural part of Middle Tennessee where my mother grew up responded in this fashion when people asked him what kind of Christian he was: "Well, I reckon I'm the regular kind. I cuss when I get mad and pray when I get scared." This kind of assessment of human virtue might lead one to cry out, as the psalmist does, saying in effect, "Who are we mortals that you pay any attention to us?"

Who are we, after all, here and now, two thousand years after the life of Jesus? We are certainly more technologically advanced than ever before, but is the world a more peaceful and loving place for having experienced two millennia of Christian witness and influence? Most people would say that it is not. Sadly, many of the conflicts around the world today involve Christians fighting other people or allowing other religious traditions to encourage fighting among ourselves.

Has the cussing or the praying of regular Christians had more impact? We have received blessing, but have we been a blessing to all nations?

Psalm 8 makes the radical assertion that God creates humans as little less than their Maker. Apparently the image that God holds of us is far greater than the image we have of ourselves. Let us pray that we will grow into the image that God holds of us.

Creating God, you made me in your image. Now help me to grow into the person you have created me to be. Amen.

Toward the end of Revelation, John receives a vision of God's future plan for the faithful. Throughout most of his vision, John offers a word of encouragement to followers of Jesus who are experiencing persecution. He does not claim to be an apostle or to hold any special position in the church. John's only authority for writing to Christians who are suffering for their faith comes from his having suffered too. He writes from exile on the island of Patmos.

The one word of hope that echoes throughout John's vision is that the future belongs to God. God's future promises the end of death and pain. The coming of the city of God will exhibit the festivity of a marriage feast. Those who have wept will have their tears wiped by the very hand of God.

As we begin a new year, those of us who have acquired many things and who hold positions of power in the church and the world may not hear John's warning that this world will pass away as particularly good news. Still those around the world who struggle to live from day to day and who suffer for their faith hear with open ears and hearts the good news of God's new heaven and new earth.

God, you wipe away all tears and invite me into a new creation. Help me to hear with joy your promises for the future. Amen.

God's Presence Amid Chaos

JANUARY 4–10, 2021 • J. DANA TRENT

SCRIPTURE OVERVIEW: This week's readings use both water and wind (Spirit) in a variety of ways. Water and wind are present in the Genesis story of God's bringing order out of chaos. Both the epistle and Gospel bring images of water in baptism and with the Spirit present. The psalmist invokes the voice of God thundering over waves and causing trees to shake. In the account of Jesus' baptism, that same voice breaks through to proclaim that Jesus is God's Son, the Beloved. Also, in the middle of this week, we celebrate Epiphany with Isaiah's inspiring vision of dawn breaking and the invitation to arise and shine because Light has come to us.

QUESTIONS AND SUGGESTIONS FOR REFLECTION

- Read Genesis 1:1-5. Where have you seen God bringing order out of chaos in your life? What are the situations in your life or in our world that seem formless or chaotic now? Can you see God working to bring order in those situations?
- Read Psalm 29. How do you respond to the powerful images of God's action reflected in this psalm?
- Read Acts 19:1-7. How would you answer Paul's question: "Did you receive the Holy Spirit when you became [a believer]?" How do you see the Spirit active in your life?
- Read Mark 1:4-11. Can you hear God saying to you, "You are my child, the beloved; with you I am well pleased"? How does it feel to imagine God saying those words to you?

Ordained Baptist minister, graduate of Duke Divinity School, and professor of World Religions at Wake Tech Community College; author of three Upper Room Books, most recently, *One Breath at a Time: A Skeptic's Guide to Christian Meditation.*

On this first Monday of the year, we begin at the beginning. The New Year is always a good place to start at the beginning. With its proverbial flip of the calendar and clean slate, we launch our 2021 resolutions: recalibrating the aims and goals for our lives. We often limit this recalibration to making order out of chaos in our bodies, homes, and routines. But how might we also re-center ourselves spiritually?

Today's reading is what biblical scholars consider the first of two distinct Genesis Creation narratives. In these verses, God demonstrates God's power by creating order from formlessness. Dark and edgeless, this mass of dis-order are the waters over which God's *ruach* (spirit or wind) hovers, preparing to create light. From this sweep emerges harmony: day and night.

Note that the creation of light does not deem the darkness "bad." It just is. The light, however, is called "good." In the ancient times in which this narrative was shared, God's "intrusion" of power and presence to create light from shapelessness would have been reassuring. It is even comforting to us now. Even where there is disorder, God is still at work.

We have all experienced confusion amid chaos. As on a moonless night at the ocean's edge, it's impossible to distinguish depth or boundaries. Where does one expanse end and the other begin? But God spoke order into being: "Let there be light," and there was. So it is in our lives too.

Even as baptized Christians, how many times do we doubt God's ability to shine amid a void? How many times do we miss the ways in which God is creating in what we experience as a formless chaos that threatens to drown us? How many times do we wish to be the creators of the world, rather than trusting the Divine Architect's ability to make something out of nothing?

God, invite us to be still and await your movement in Creation. Amen.

The psalmist describes an enormous storm with God as the source of the storm. This text resonates with the ancient Canaanite narrative of Baal, the God of Thunder, who tames chaos. From a historical critical perspective, it is certainly wise to exegete these parallel narratives. How might the ancient people have understood God's role as both instigator and peacemaker? Like in the first Creation narrative, God displays God's power in asserting tranquility over disarray. (See Genesis 1:1-5.) It's also worth drawing a parallel to Jesus' calming the storm. (See Mark 4:35-41.) But what do we make of God as the source of the storm before the calm? In Psalm 29, it is God who initiates the flood, earthquake, and fire. God breaks the unbreakable trees—and then God calls it off with a simple *shalom* (peace). What do we make of these mighty acts—the interruption and destruction of nature—followed by a declaration of power and peace?

In both the Genesis narrative and this psalm, God breaks through. God demonstrates mastery over each: the forces that cannot be harnessed nor tamed by humans. When we read these texts together, we are reminded of this resonance across testaments: an almighty, glorious God who commands calm from chaos.

We could certainly use a bit of peace. But we crave control—and we exercise it by relying on our own strength to create order. But this is not the nature of the revealed Ultimate Reality whom we worship. Our role as humans is to remain humble—trusting that God is powerful enough to create beauty from void and shalom from storm.

God, help us to approach you with awe, as in creation and storm. Amen.

Epiphany

In modern English, we use the word *epiphany* to connote a sudden revelation. This week, light has arrived in both the texts and liturgical seasons, illuminating that which was previously "dark" to us. During Advent, we awaited the sacred mystery of a baby, born to a virgin mother, who became the Son of God. At Epiphany, we gain full exposure to this prophecy: darkness had covered the earth—but the light has overcome it.

When my mother was a young girl, Isaiah 60:1-6 was among the first scriptures she memorized. It was her guidepost in times when she encountered darkness too dim to bear. "Arise, shine; for your light has come," was a beacon to which she could lift her eyes and be comforted in any scary scenario.

How does it feel to know that even amid darkness God's glory appears before us in Advent hope and Epiphany light? We only need "lift up" our eyes and look in order to "see and be radiant." But so often, we keep our heads down—enthralled with that which we think will make our heart "thrill and rejoice." We embrace the mundane and reject the very epiphany "treasure" that God offers because we are too preoccupied with temporary things that we believe will dispel darkness. Instead, we are invited to arise, shine, and look to the infinite Light.

When we feel dark and formless, chaotic and listless, Isaiah's prophetic voice reminds us to look up and consider the indestructible link to our Creator who has the power to create out of nothing and to incarnate as Messiah born in a stable.

God, empower us to arise and shine! Lord, have mercy on us when we keep our heads down, failing to accept the radiance that you intend for us. Amen.

Many coastal cities in the U.S. approach hurricane season with heavy hearts. The winds and water have broken them once or many times before—crushing homes and lives, washing away memories. This psalm demonstrates that power—but also the power of God for majesty. Like the psalmist who describes the natural event, our closest human experience is that of the raging storm, flood, earthquake, or fire. It's frightening, to be sure, but also majestic in its power and humbling in its strength. Consider the last actual storm you witnessed. Can you resonate with the psalmist's description of awe in a Creator whose voice "breaks the cedars," "flashes forth flames of fire," "shakes the wilderness," "causes the oaks to whirl, and strips the forest bare"? These seemingly chaotic acts of nature are not intended to incite a fear-based worship of God but rather to remind us of God's ability. In our human experience, we ought to look to that which we can see: hurricanes, fires, wind, floods, in order to understand a fraction of the strength of that which we cannot see: God.

The psalmist invites us to glorify God in order to remember that God's strength is ours too. It "thunders" just as I imagine it did in Creation. How often do we approach God with such a humble posture?

God, how incredible it is to know the majesty of your power. Help us to remember your strength—which, in turn, is our strength. Amen.

In today's passage, Paul is teaching in Ephesus, where he asks his students their understanding of what has happened at their baptisms and if they have yet received the Holy Spirit. When they reply, "No," Paul offers a pastoral tone. He doesn't berate, argue, or criticize; he merely teaches. We are invited to do the same.

Over and over this week, we have encountered God's presence in water: Creation, storms, and now baptism. But how is God present in baptismal waters—and ultimately—in us? What do our Christian denominations teach us about receiving the Holy Spirit at our baptisms?

Baptism is a sacrament—*mysteria*—a mystical experience that accounts for God's action (presence) in our lives. How does this manifest in your tradition and teaching? How might we all lean into Paul's urging, seeking to understand the ways in which the Triune God indwells us through this *mysteria*. In turn, how might revisiting our baptism unfurl into a New Year and Epiphany resolution of recalibration, re-centering ourselves spiritually?

God, help us to remember our baptisms. Urge us to consider what this sacred mystery teaches us and what it means for our communities. Amen.

Mark is the first Gospel written, likely circa the destruction of the Temple in 70 CE. It is the shortest of the synoptic Gospels, sharing narratives with Matthew and Luke—and it is full of the Greek term *euthys* which means "immediately." *Euthys* is used forty-one times in Mark, unlocking this Gospel writer's tenor and tone that stands in sharp contrast to Matthew and Luke, and ultimately—John. Like the New Year, Mark's Gospel begins at breakneck speed: launching itself into Jesus' baptism and then his wilderness journey.

After having completed Advent and Christmas, we are now hurled immediately into this urgent and profound opening. It demonstrates Mark's get-to-it-ness, while Matthew is eager to make an Old Testament-based claim of the lineage of Jesus from the House of David. Though we appreciate Matthew's pacing, sometimes we need a push from Mark.

The New Year is conducive to this nudge, and baptism is always an excellent place to dive in. It is the cornerstone of Christian theology. Therefore Mark's opening passage is pivotal to our faith, demonstrating the power and majesty not just of God but a Triune God—Creator, Christ, and Holy Spirit in one scene. This Gospel sheds light on a common theme we have encountered this week: the bold, mystical intrusion of God's presence. This is not intrusion in the negative sense of the word. Rather, it is a presence that is pronounced, the glory of which is impossible to ignore.

God, help us to remember the significance of the immediacy of Jesus' baptism and what that means for our lives. Amen.

BAPTISM OF THE LORD

Questions about baptism should abound this week. Why must Jesus be baptized if he is without sin? What is the larger message presented in his baptismal event? What does the baptism of Jesus mean for us as individuals—and for the collective body of Christ?

Depending upon the tradition and method, baptism has variations in significance and meaning. In its simplest form, baptism as "re-birth" into something new connotes turning away from something old. This is not in the binary sense of new/old, good/bad but rather, how is order created out of dis-order? How does God assert God's power and presence to tame formlessness?

From Genesis 1 to Mark 1, we've arrived full circle. We return to the early waters over which God's *ruach* (Spirit) hovers; and in one sweep, something new is created. In Genesis it is day and night. In Mark, it is the Christology of Jesus as Messiah. In Jesus' baptism, Christ does not turn (*metanoia*) away from sin in repentance (*teshuvah*). Rather, he turns toward ministry. His baptism is the cue to order the next three years of his life—the teaching and healing that will change everything on his way to death. "You are my Son, the Beloved; with you I am well-pleased" is a foreshadowing of the Good Friday and Easter Sunday fulfillment to come.

The image of God's voice hovering over the Genesis creation waters and Mark's baptismal waters resides with me and in me. On a moonlit beach walk, in my finite human brain, I see a sliver of Epiphany Light—and encounter what it may have felt like to be there to witness such majesty and mystery out of the ordinary.

God, help us to have faith in the mystery. Amen.

Knowing and Being Known

JANUARY 11–17, 2021 • KATIE RUSSELL HAINLINE

SCRIPTURE OVERVIEW: We read the stories of Samuel and the calling of Jesus' disciples in John, and it's easy to feel jealous. God spoke so directly into their lives that they should have had, it seems to us, full and unwavering confidence in their callings. Didn't they have an unfair spiritual advantage over us? However, the psalmist reminds us that God knows and sees us individually just as well as God knew Samuel and Jesus knew his disciples. God has plans for us, even if they are revealed in less obvious ways. The reading from First Corinthians is quite different in its message. Perhaps we can at least recognize that even if we never hear God's audible voice, through scripture God still provides guidance for our lives.

QUESTIONS AND SUGGESTIONS FOR REFLECTION

- Read 1 Samuel 3:1-20. Can you think of a time when you failed to hear God calling you? What helps you to listen to God?
- Read Psalm 139:1-6, 13-18. How does the knowledge that all humans are "fearfully and wonderfully made" inform the way you regard and care for others?
- Read 1 Corinthians 6:12-20. Paul writes, "All things are lawful." What does that mean to you? What are the responsibilities inherent in such freedom?
- Read John 1:43-51. Who are the people who invited you to "come and see" Jesus? Is there someone around you to whom you could extend that invitation today?

Graduate of Vanderbilt Divinity School; ordained in the Christian Church (Disciples of Christ); currently serving a congregation in central Iowa; married to Jacob, and together they tend a flock of house cats and wiener dogs.

Pastors are often asked to tell their call stories, but I often struggle to tell mine. The story could begin at my baptism when my parents and godparents pledged to teach me the story of God. It could begin when my college professors encouraged me to apply to seminary, or when the seminary's field education program placed me in a congregation, or when pastors I respected told me I had gifts to give the church. So many Bible stories describe callings that begin with burning bushes and blinding lights. I have none of those things, but I have Samuel.

God's call on Samuel's life began long before the sleepless night in our reading today. It began when his mother prayed for him and pledged him to God. It continued when he dutifully went to work in the Lord's presence, before he even knew what that meant. It was unfolding through Eli who interpreted the voice of God when Samuel did not know what he was hearing. Samuel's call did not just come to him in the night but followed him as he grew. The scripture says, "Samuel did not yet know the Lord," but it is clear that the Lord always knew Samuel.

What hope this story gives to those of us who stammer and stumble when we are asked to describe our call! What reassurance this gives to those of us who did not meet God suddenly through fire and light but instead came to know God gradually in the midst of daily life and work, who did not have a sudden conversion but grew into our knowledge of the Lord! While we have not always known God, God has always known us.

Dear God, thank you for knowing us and calling us. Help us, like Samuel, to grow in our knowledge of you so we too may be known as your trustworthy messengers. Amen.

Early in my life my parents and teachers taught me a valuable lesson: If your words are not kind, do not speak. I have not always followed this advice, but when I have it has served me well. I have avoided saying things I would regret. I have prevented myself from wounding someone else. At times this advice has even helped move a conversation from insult-slinging to constructive dialogue. I have learned that some things are better left unspoken.

However, this psalm suggests that this advice does not work with God: "Even before a word is on my tongue, O LORD, you know it completely." At times this knowledge is comforting; we are assured that when we cannot give voice to our prayers, God still knows them. But such knowledge is also convicting because it means God knows the unkind words we do not speak, the gossip we relish but choose not to share, and the injustices we witness but do not speak out against. God knows the thoughts in our minds even before we speak them aloud, even if we do not speak them at all.

We cannot keep secrets from God. God knows our inward parts and our inner thoughts. God's knowledge often exposes what we would prefer to hide or leave unspoken. While we may want to flee from such knowledge, the psalm concludes by suggesting we welcome it. It is God's intimate knowledge that has the power to correct and refine us. "Search me, O God, and know my heart; test me and know my thoughts. See if there is any wicked way in me, and lead me in the way everlasting" (Ps. 139:23-24).

All-knowing God, when I want to run from you, slow me down. When I want to hide, reveal what I need to see. Search my heart, expose what is sinful within me, and lead me on the right path. Amen.

In Psalm 139 the author marvels at all the things God knows. God knows our every step, thought, and word. God knows the heights of heaven and the depths of hell. God knew us before we even had a concrete form. God knows when we wake and when we sleep. God knows all our days.

At first, the psalmist seems overwhelmed by this knowledge, saying, "Such knowledge is too wonderful for me; it is so high that I cannot attain it." But the psalmist may be selling himself short. His knowledge may not be able to match God's, but he has certainly attained some knowledge of his own in his experience of God. In these twelve verses, the psalmist uses the words *you* or *your* over a dozen times, suggesting that in his experience of being known by God, the psalmist has also come to know God. The same is true for us.

When God forms our inward parts, we come to know God our creator. When God hems us in, we come to know God who will not let us go. When God knows when we wake and when we sleep, we come to know God who never leaves us. When God discerns our thoughts and words, we come to know God whose hand is always guiding us. When God knows us as Psalm 139 describes, we come to know an infinite God who is concerned with finite us. How wonderful that knowledge is! How good it is to know God and to be known by God!

Dear God, we praise you for your fearful, wonderful knowledge of us. Help us to welcome your presence each day, so that every day is an opportunity to know and be known by you. Amen.

The first half of this story will be familiar to most readers. Young Samuel is called by God in the middle of the night. But because Samuel does not yet know the Lord, he mistakes the voice for that of his mentor, Eli. But Eli understands what is happening and gives Samuel the instruction he needs to receive God's message. Samuel listens.

In Sunday school lessons, this story often ends at verse 10 with Samuel dutifully replying to God's call, "Speak, for your servant is listening." But when we press on through verse 20, we learn that God's message is one of judgment against Eli's household. At first Samuel is afraid to share what he has heard with his mentor. But Eli insists, and when Samuel tells him, he listens.

Eli and Samuel show that hearing the word of the Lord is often a communal effort. Samuel would not have known the voice of the Lord had it not been for Eli's wisdom and experience. Eli, who had lost his eyesight and his prophetic vision, would not have known that God was doing a new thing in Israel had it not been for young Samuel. Importantly, they loved and trusted each other enough to listen and learn from each other. Together they discerned the way forward.

Many modern readers may feel that the word of the Lord is rare in our days, since few of us awake in the night to hear God calling our names. But God is still speaking and is often heard best in community, as the example of Eli and Samuel shows us. Consider how God is raising up different voices in your life, church, and world to reveal to you something you could not know by yourself.

God, give us ears to listen to one another and hearts to trust one another, so that together we may hear you call us to new things. Speak, Lord, for your servants are listening. Amen.

Perhaps you played the telephone game as a child. While sitting in a circle of friends, one person would whisper a message into the ear of another. Then the message would be passed around the circle until it reached the end. If the message stayed the same, everyone cheered; if the message changed in its passing, the results often brought laughter.

The calling of the disciples in the first chapter of John's Gospel is not unlike a game of telephone. The message about Jesus is passed from one disciple to the next. First John tells Andrew, and Andrew tells Simon. Then in today's reading, Jesus calls Philip, and Philip tells Nathanael. The message generally stays the same: "Come and see!" But each person also spins it, giving Jesus a new name. One names him the Lamb of God, another the Messiah. One says he is the one whom the prophets foretold; another calls him rabbi. Each of these names says something different about Jesus' identity, suggesting that each disciple came to know Jesus in his own way. Yet each of them only came to that knowledge because they were invited by someone else.

Do you remember who first introduced you to Jesus? Like those earliest disciples, you have come to know Jesus in your own way; but someone probably made the first introduction for you. Perhaps it was a beloved Sunday school teacher who told you God's stories or a parent who taught you to pray or a church leader who showed you what a life of following Jesus looked like. Who, through their words or actions, passed the message "come and see" to you? Give thanks for that person today.

God, we thank you for the saints who have gone before us, making you known from generation to generation. Help us to carry on the gospel call, that Jesus Christ may be known in us and through us. Amen.

In this section of his first letter to the church in Corinth, Paul explores the limits of his message of freedom in Christ. Some in the community have interpreted the Good News as freedom to do anything they want, but others seem to be wary of adopting such a broad interpretation, especially when it comes to sexual morality. What is right is not immediately clear. Paul responds to the church's dilemma by modeling for them that freedom in Christ includes the freedom to wrestle with and to discern what we do not know.

Three times in this brief passage—in verses 15, 16, and 19—Paul asks a rhetorical question beginning with the phrase, "Do you not know . . . ?" By asking these questions, Paul invites members of the church to remember what it is they know with certainty. These include: that our bodies are members of Christ's body, that our bodies become united to other bodies through sex, and that our bodies are temples of the Holy Spirit. If these are things you know, Paul advises, you should choose your sexual relationships with great care because it is simultaneously personal, communal, and sacred.

Paul could have responded with a simple clarification of his message. He could have said freedom in Christ did not make one free to do whatever one wanted. He could have sent a list of appropriate and inappropriate behaviors. Instead, he reasoned out his response and gave the church a model for discerning the answers to our own sticky questions. Paul shows us that when the answer we seek is not immediately clear, we, too, can ask: What do we know with certainty? What beliefs do we hold with conviction? How do these inform our understanding of the issue at hand? How do they guide our faithful action?

God, in matters that I do not know, make my questions wise and my discernment faithful. Amen.

In God's world, what we think we know often gets turned on its head: The ones who cannot speak well are called to be prophets, the mighty and wealthy are cast down, the last are first, and the tomb does not end the story. What we thought we knew is reversed in today's passage too.

When Nathanael's friend Philip comes to him and says the Messiah is the son of Joseph from Nazareth, Nathanael says, "Can anything good come out of Nazareth?" Perhaps Nathanael's skepticism comes from what he thinks he knows about Nazareth, the small and seemingly insignificant neighboring town. Or perhaps Nathanael's skepticism comes from what he thinks he knows about who the Messiah would be, how the Messiah would arrive, or what the Messiah would do. In either case, Nathanael makes clear in his question that Jesus, son of Joseph from Nazareth, is not what he was expecting. Yet Nathanael allows his skepticism to turn to curiosity; he decides to take Philip's invitation to come and see Jesus. Jesus does not criticize Nathanael for asking the question but praises him for being without deceit. Nathanael's honest question led him to belief.

Nathanael is a great model for curious and questioning faith, the kind of faith that admits we do not have all the answers, is willing to let go of what we thought we knew, and is open to new revelation. When we embrace this kind of faith, we will be surprised and delighted by the way God turns what we thought we knew on its head. We will see God show up in people, places, and ways we would never have expected, like in Joseph's son from Nazareth.

God, help me to let go of any false knowledge or expectation that keeps me from seeing your revelation. Teach me to ask honest questions that lead me to what I do not yet know. Amen.

Trust and Respond

JANUARY 18–24, 2021 • DAVID J. FETTERMAN

SCRIPTURE OVERVIEW: Things are not always as they seem. To Jonah, the people of Nineveh seem beyond hope, so he runs away rather than going to preach to them. But God has other plans. To Jonah's surprise, the Ninevites turn to God. In our eyes, social standing and wealth may seem to divide people into different classes, but the psalmist declares that in God's economy all are equal. Paul echoes the theme of the temporary nature of all things in this life; they should not be our source of security. Jesus opens his ministry in Mark by proclaiming that God is breaking into history to overthrow what has been accepted as the way things are. Sometimes God's perspective is not our perspective.

QUESTIONS AND SUGGESTIONS FOR REFLECTION

- Read Jonah 3:1-10. Can you think of a time when you sensed God calling you to do something you didn't want to do? How did you respond?
- Read Psalm 62:5-12. How have you experienced God's "awesome deeds" in your life? What is your response?
- Read 1 Corinthians 7:29-31. What distracts you from focusing on God? How might you reorder your priorities?
- Read Mark 1:14-20. What might have led Simon, Andrew, James, and John to immediately stop what they were doing and follow Jesus? Are there things that make you hesitate in following Jesus' call to you?

Retired chaplain at Redstone@Home Hospice and Redstone Highlands Retirement Community in Greensburg, PA; Elder in the Western Pennsylvania Conference of The United Methodist Church.

LET'S TRY THIS AGAIN

Get up and go to Nineveh. Tell them to change their evil ways" (AP). Those were God's instructions to Jonah. But instead of obeying God, Jonah tried to run·away by getting on a ship to sail as far away as possible. He forgot that wherever he went, God would be there.

What a trip Jonah had! An awful storm, frightened ship-mates dumping him into the sea, and a big fish that vomited him up on the beach. And then God spoke again to a water-logged Jonah: "OK, Jonah. Let's try this one more time. Get up. Dry yourself off. And go to Nineveh to tell them that I said they are to change their evil ways." This time Jonah got up, went to Nineveh, and preached his short, powerful sermon—and lives were transformed because of God's word. Blinded by his own desire for revenge on his Assyrian enemies and his fear of this dangerous call, Jonah tried his hardest to escape God. He forgot that God is relentless in pursuit of us and that God's nature is love.

Like Jonah, we often forget the God with whom we are dealing. We don't always trust God. We fail to remember God's promise to always care for us. We futilely try to escape from God. But God's love and call pursue us relentlessly. Remembering that can make all the difference in whether we get up and go or try to run away. When God calls, remember that it is the God of Jonah, the God of relentless love and pursuit, who is calling you. Confident in God's steadfast love and trustworthiness, we can respond by going where we are led, knowing that the God who calls us will care for us and will equip us for any work.

Pursuing and loving God, give me courage and trust to follow where you call me to go. In Jesus' name. Amen.

WHEN LEOPARDS CHANGE THEIR SPOTS

There is an old saying, "A leopard never changes its spots." In other words, people don't change. That, however, does not appear to be God's attitude. God constantly calls for our transformation, showing us a new way—a way of love and peace and hope, a way that changes us and makes us new.

Today's story is one of many examples in scripture of changed lives. Jonah didn't believe that his enemies in Nineveh could change. In fact, he hoped that they *wouldn't* change. He wanted God to punish them for their evil, warring ways. His sermon, however, was more powerful than he imagined. The people came to believe in God, and their lives were changed. Their king told them to join him in calling fervently on God. God saw that the people's hate-filled ways had stopped. As a result, God rescinded the plan for their destruction and forgave them. These Assyrian leopards had changed their spots.

God is a God of transformation and forgiveness and love. The hateful can become loving. The liar can become truthful. The disdainful can become respectful. With God leading the way, transformation can and does happen. Sometimes we are the leopards who are called to change our spots. Thanks be to God for the forgiving love that relentlessly pursues us and gives us second chances. Because of God's mercy and grace, we sinful leopards can change our spots too.

God of hope and transformation, guide us to discern areas in our lives where we need to change. Lead the way that we may be transformed by your love. In Jesus' matchless name. Amen.

ABSORBED WITH GOD

Paul was concerned with what holds our highest attention: earthly concerns, or God. Essentially, he asks, "Are you consumed with things of this world: your marriages, your emotions, your possessions? Are you preoccupied with today? Or are you captivated with God and the new world that God promises?"

These questions are still relevant. What preoccupies your time, your thoughts, and your desires? Are you immersed in concerns that draw your attention to what the world offers—your own happiness and possessions? Or are you absorbed with God and serving God?

As a hospice chaplain I met a woman whom I'll call Florence. Florence was dying of cancer. We talked weekly for many months, and I learned much from her. Florence taught me that choosing God over temporal preoccupations is difficult because we have love and attachments. She also taught me that it is possible and necessary to make that choice. We talked often about her sorrow at the thought of leaving her beloved husband, children, and granddaughter, and how she chose God even while knowing the pull of earthly loves. Until her final breath, she loved her family; but she chose God as her ultimate preoccupation.

Paul acknowledges our temporal concerns and loves but reminds us of a higher, more important preoccupation. Paul challenges us to look to God as our first and highest loyalty. Is that easy? No, it's usually difficult. With God's loving presence and the witness of people like Florence, though, it is possible.

O God, whose love constantly seeks me and whose care never falters, show me the way to give to you my utmost loyalty and to be preoccupied only with you. In Jesus' name. Amen.

HOPE BEYOND TODAY

In today's reading from Mark's Gospel, John has been arrested. His ministry has concluded, and Jesus has entered the stage of announcing that the time that John had been preparing people for had arrived—in him. Jesus preaches that believing and trusting God's good news leads to changed hearts and to lives lived in hope.

This change may seem easier said than done, though. How do we change our hearts and lives when that may make us appear weak to others, as if we can't make up our minds? How can we prepare to live in God's kingdom when living in this world is often so difficult? Why should we trust God when we see so much hatred, violence, and anxiety daily? How can we be expected to believe in good news when we're barraged daily with bad news?

Jesus doesn't answer those questions. What he does do, though, is offer us the hope of faith. Though we live amid trouble and anxiety and need, those things are not the last words. God's steadfast love is. Believing that to be true can give us hope and confidence that, despite the troubles we see and experience daily, God is still in charge. This hope can transform us because it reminds us that God can see beyond today, even though we can't. Thanks be to God who sees today as well as tomorrow, whose power is leading to the final victory of love and good, and who calls us to live each day in that confident hope!

God of today and tomorrow, give me faith for today, hope for tomorrow, and a love that allows others to see you through me. In the hope-filled name of Jesus. Amen.

COME, FOLLOW ME

In this reading, Jesus calls four ordinary people out of their ordinary lives. "Come, follow me," he says (NIV). There was no introduction, no description of what they were being called to do, no map of where they were going, no explanation of why they were being called. Just, "Come, follow me." And they did! Would we have followed?

Several things can be noted. Jesus' call requires our giving up the desire for answers and certainty because Jesus' call usually results in more questions than answers. There is no certainty of what happens next. God knows more than we do, though, and can be trusted to guide us and care for us along the way. Jesus' call is often costly and difficult. It can result in going places we would rather not go, speaking words we would rather not speak, and confronting people and situations we would rather not confront. We can trust that God will strengthen and defend us on even the most perilous journey. Jesus' call is into an unknown tomorrow. We don't know what the results of following the call will be. But we are called to say "yes" and to follow anyway.

Trust is the key. Simon, Andrew, James, and John knew that. They followed without hesitation into an uncertain future. They didn't second-guess the one doing the calling. They didn't allow anxiety over the unknown to overwhelm them. They trusted. That trust made all the difference. When Jesus calls, trust in God's love and care. Allow trust to propel you to say, "Yes, Lord, I'll follow."

God of the journey, help me to trust you to guide, protect, and love me along the way—wherever you may lead. In Jesus' loving name. Amen.

A Refuge to Trust

When I was a church-camp counselor, one of our activities was to take our campers for a "trust walk" in the woods. We would divide the campers into pairs. The pairs then walked—one of each pair with eyes open leading the way and the other with eyes closed being led. What a test of trust! If you were the one with your eyes closed, you needed confidence in your partner to take care of you.

Faith is a lot like that. It is fundamentally an act of trust in a loving God to guide us and protect us with mercy, wisdom, and compassion. When God calls us, we are like those campers with their eyes shut. We often don't know where we're being led until we get there. Along the way, we are simply called to trust God.

In today's reading, the psalmist praises this reliable God. "All you people: Trust in him at all times! Pour out your hearts before him! God is our refuge!" (CEB). We don't always see where God is leading us. We often want more information from God, much as those campers might have wanted to keep one eye open as they were being led. That is why confidence in God as our refuge, our safe place, is so important. We can be assured that even when the road to which we are called leads us into dangerous times and places, God will protect us and guide us. We can always trust in God's love for us. That faith can motivate and strengthen us to say "yes" when God's voice calls to us.

Trustworthy God, thank you for being my refuge. I know that your love will never let me go. Give me confidence to follow you even when the road is long and difficult. In Jesus' name. Amen.

A Reason to Trust

People love superheroes and heroines—Wonder Woman, Iron Man, Captain Marvel, Black Panther to name a few. Why are these characters so popular? We like them because of their strength and goodness. They have the power to right wrongs, to restore good from evil, and to protect the vulnerable. They allow us, at least briefly, to feel that evil is defeated, good wins, and all is right with the world.

What if we could feel that way all the time? What if we could always be confident that evil is defeated, good wins, love prevails, and we are always protected? We can! God calls us to be followers and witnesses in the world. God also assures us that we can take the bold, uncertain step into discipleship because God's love, power, and protection will accompany us. In today's reading, the psalmist reassures us of the firm foundation upon which we can build lives that daily hear God's call. Standing on that foundation allows us to walk confidently into unknown tomorrows, following where God leads.

The psalmist reminds us that so much in which we place our hopes, especially humans and human power, are temporary and will disappear. But God's love and care for us are eternal. The psalmist writes: "God has spoken one thing—make it two things—that I myself have heard: that strength belongs to God, and faithful love comes from you, my Lord—and that you will repay everyone according to their deeds" (CEB). God loves you. God's strength will care for and protect you. With that firm foundation of faith, when God calls you by name, answer, "Here I am. I will go where you lead."

God of love and strength, thank you for your daily protection and care. Send me into a dangerous and hurting world to be your hands, feet, and voice. In Jesus' name. Amen.

Power and Authority

JANUARY 25–31, 2021 • ASHLEY HALES

SCRIPTURE OVERVIEW: This week's readings center on God's authority. In Deuteronomy God promises to raise up a prophet to guide the people, and God warns the people not to listen to voices that do not speak for God. The psalmist overflows with praise for God's great works. God is powerful and awesome, yet also gracious and merciful. Paul instructs the Corinthians to place the rights of others before their own rights. A person's conscience may allow one to exercise freedom in Christ; however, with this freedom comes responsibility. We must surrender our own rights, if necessary, for the good of others. In Mark's Gospel, Jesus shows his power over the forces of darkness: Even the unclean spirits recognize and obey him.

QUESTIONS AND SUGGESTIONS FOR REFLECTION

- Read Deuteronomy 18:15-20. To whom or to what setting do you turn when you yearn to hear God's voice?
- Read Psalm 111. For what are you praising God today? How have you experienced God's steadfast love recently?
- Read 1 Corinthians 8:1-13. What do you think of Paul's statement, "Knowledge puffs up, but love builds up"? Can you think of examples of this in your everyday life?
- Read Mark 1:21-28. How do you react to the concept of authority? How does the authority of Jesus differ from the authority we may encounter in the world?

Author, speaker, podcaster, and coach who lives with her husband and four kids in the southern California suburbs; author of *Finding Holy in the Suburbs: Living Faithfully in the Land of Too Much*; aahales.com.

When my oldest child entered fourth grade, he was tasked with learning to play the recorder. He would retreat to his room, squeaking out something that sounded like notes, while the rest of us tried to drown out the noise. Steadily, his playing improved, and by the end of the year he was adept at "Hot Cross Buns" and other songs. He had begun to learn to play an instrument—his fingers and breath knowing what to do, his ability to read the notes and translate them to action sharpening.

In this second giving of the law in Deuteronomy, we discover how people are to be instruments of God, supple and obedient to their God-given vocation and message. Prophets are to be communicators of God's word to God's people, sounding clear notes of truth. At Mount Horeb, God had given the law to Moses. The mountains smoked and shook. Fire and thunder accompanied the holy God of heaven and earth. God's people were awestruck, and afraid; they wanted a person—someone like them, like Moses—to tell them God's word.

In kindness, God gives them Moses and a whole line of prophets to speak God's word in extraordinary ways to God's people. Ultimately, God comes to humanity through the person of Jesus, the Word made flesh, the savior of the world and a prophet like Moses. In Jesus, the authority and love of God are intertwined. In Jesus, we have the Son of God, full of power and authority, and the Son of Man, a person who understands our humanity. In Jesus, power and authority become accessible. Because Jesus has borne our sin, we shall not die; instead we are welcomed into a fuller life.

Thank you, God, for sending Jesus as the prophet who would communicate your truth, goodness, and love. Help me to recognize your authority as you welcome us into true life. Amen.

When we are caught up in the beauty and perfection of something, we can't help but praise it. From a friend or spouse, to a sunset or an artistic work, we are moved to praise that which we love.

In Psalm 111, the psalmist exudes praise for the steadfast love of God who shows love by feeding the people, by remembering the covenant, by providing redemption, and by acting on behalf of the people. Praise flows from the psalmist for God's majesty and splendor, God's power and trustworthy works. Following an acrostic format, the psalm highlights for the people the character of the God they worship.

The awe and perfection of our Creator can either distance us from God through fear or draw us toward God in love. The fear spoken of in Psalm 111:10 is not the fear that limits the fullness of our lives. Instead, "fear of the Lord" is a reverence and awe for God's authority and power, which leads us to worship.

Yet God has come near. The Lord has made a covenant with Israel and has sustained the covenant with redemptive works of provision and sustenance. God has given God's people a place and a trustworthy foundation for all knowledge, understanding, and wisdom. Through God's goodness, the Creator has drawn the people to worship.

How we ultimately view God will affect whether or not we are drawn toward intimate worship. Helpfully, the psalm also identifies where this reverent worship takes place: in the congregation. As we stay tethered to a community of believers in the church, we hear the good covenantal deeds of our God week by week. There we come to rehearse, sing, and praise our good God.

Help me, God, to name your good deeds in my life. May your splendor lead me to worship. Remove anything that hinders my praise. Amen.

As the songbook for God's people, the Psalms tell us an emotional and spiritual history of God's big story of redemption for God's people. Psalm 111 shows us the mighty deeds of God that make our Creator worthy of praise.

When people marry, they make promises to love, honor, and cherish each other until death parts them. They vow that no matter their circumstance—rich or poor, sick or well—they will remain faithful. Marriage is a covenant—a binding agreement of faithfulness, not a contract that can be easily renegotiated when the terms change.

Just as daily acts of kindness and forgiveness build a faithful marriage, God's deeds of redemption show us that God is faithful to God's promises. These deeds show us the character of God. God's love is proven by God's action. God is bound to the people, even if they find other lovers.

Psalm 111 speaks about God commanding and remembering God's covenant. Our first parents broke the covenant with God in the Garden, but throughout the Bible God institutes a covenant of grace. God does not relate to us as a taskmaster requiring perfection but in a context of grace. God remains faithful even when we fail. Ultimately, God commands and remembers God's covenant through the life, death, and resurrection of Jesus.

God is our faithful lover who never waivers, breaks, or ignores the covenant. God provides for us and is worthy of praise.

When we are so apt to trust our circumstances to satisfy us, or we tend to rely on a friend, child, or spouse to meet our deepest longings, may we instead run to the God who we know keeps and commands the covenant. God is the faithful One.

God, thank you for relating to us not with a contract but in a covenant, a binding agreement of faithfulness. We praise you for your faithfulness and for your work of redemption for us, ultimately in the person of Christ. Amen.

The Corinthian church was a know-it-all, the sort of kid at school who raises a hand for every question, corrects other students, and shows a bit of disdain for those who aren't as gifted. Paul writes to the Corinthians to bring them back to the main things: to the gospel instead of partisanship, to sacrifice instead of infighting, to caring for others in a culture where worship of foreign gods was part of the infrastructure of the region.

So when Paul writes that "knowledge puffs up," he addresses not only the questions of a church about food offered to idols but the heart issue—that because of their arrogance what they know has not shaped how they live. Though today we may not worship idols of stone, we are all too familiar with using our knowledge to stay in our heads alone. We know the truths of the gospel; we know the goodness of God and God's faithfulness to the covenant. We know that we are saved by grace, but often we live in ways that fail to reflect our knowledge of these essential facts. Instead our lives look as busy, frantic, and self-sufficient as the surrounding culture.

The solution for the Corinthian church—and for us—is to recall in word and deed that "love builds up." Paul shows us that as we come to know God, we also realize how deeply we are known by God. True knowledge proceeds from our primary identity as being known and loved by God, and such knowledge leads to transformation. When we know how much we are loved by God, all the questions of what we know or one-upmanship fall away. It is not that morality is unimportant or that there aren't looming questions about theology and practice. Rather, we learn that these fall into their appropriate place when we are in proper relationship with God.

God, I want to know you and be known by you. I want to be wrapped in your love and have that as my primary identity. Help me to put aside pride and to love others. Amen.

We can often tell the story of the Bible by telling a story of food—from taking the fruit in the Garden of Eden to selling a birthright for a pot of soup, from God's people being fed manna in the wilderness to birds bringing bread for Elijah, and finally to Jesus' miraculously feeding thousands, instituting the Lord's Supper, and the great party to which we're all headed. We can trace redemption through food as one way God provides for God's people.

So when Paul writes to the Corinthian church about food offered to idols, it's not some throwaway statement. Because only some of the meat would be used for sacrifice to false gods, a temple could serve as a banquet hall or butcher shop, or the meat could be later sold in the marketplace. How were these Christians supposed to respond?

Paul shows us that love is the binding feature of Christian action. While eating in the temple of a foreign god makes one a participant in idolatry, there are blurry lines too. Wisdom is required. Though one might have the liberty to eat meat, it may cause someone weaker to stumble. Like Paul, we must be willing to abstain from something if the gospel prohibits it or if it causes a newer Christian's conscience to be wounded.

While we aren't likely debating whether we should eat meat that has been sacrificed to an idol, we do face countless decisions about how we walk in the world as Christians. Are we willing to let our preferences and even our liberties go for the good of another believer? Will we care about our neighbor and sibling in Christ enough to change our behavior? And if not, how deeply has God's good grace and provision sunk in?

God, help us to fully experience grace so that we are willing to be inconvenienced for the growth of your kingdom. Spirit, examine our hearts and show us how to love you and others. Amen.

It's a classic movie cliche—the teacher is gone for the day, and in walks a substitute. The substitute doesn't have the authority or relationship with the students, so the students feel free to subvert the sub's borrowed authority with pranks and general hilarity. Authority matters. While a substitute teacher has authority in name, he or she doesn't have the same authority as a teacher who has earned it through relationship.

In Mark's Gospel, we see the authority of Jesus. Mark describes Jesus' entering the synagogue and teaching the people. He is recognized by his hearers as one with authority, not like local scribes. The type of authority Jesus has is divine. He is fully God and fully human, and his listeners recognize this authority right away.

Jesus illustrates his authority as a teacher through his actions. When a man with an unclean spirit comes to him, he names Jesus as the Holy One of God. Jesus rebukes the spirit, and it comes out of him. And again, his hearers are amazed at a "new teaching with authority." Jesus' healing ministry not only corroborates his authority but also validates his ministry of teaching.

When faced with the authority of Jesus, what will we do? Will we be amazed, will we fight against it, or will we worship? Will we recognize the authority of Jesus?

The idea of "authority" in western, individualistic cultures can feel stifling. We often want to fight against the limits and boundary lines of God's good order so we can make our own way in the world. Recognizing your desire to be in control of your own life, spend some time thinking about the goodness of God's authority. God uses authority to enlighten, to heal, to be known, and to tell us what the kingdom of God is like.

Lord God, all of creation bends to your will. Show me the places where I resist your authority and the ways I can praise you for the authority you have over your world and my heart. Amen.

The crowds flock to Jesus. He heals lepers, casts out demons, feeds the people, and teaches with authority.

After Jesus teaches in the synagogue and casts out a demon, Mark reports that his fame spread throughout Galilee. Like those crowds, we too want to be close to fame. Fame feels powerful, and those who are famous seem to be living an idealized life. We want what they have. It seems fame will somehow inoculate them from the cares of the world.

Fame seems like a golden ticket to a comfortable life. We imagine that fame or money or status or a lucky break will be the thing that gives our lives meaning. Yet often fame seems to simply exacerbate the already-existing character of the famous one. Fame often multiplies problems rather than solving them.

Jesus grows increasingly famous. Crowds gather to hear him teach, so much so that he has to regularly escape to be alone with his Father or with his disciples to pray. Yet Jesus' fame doesn't lead him to growing more distant from the pain of humanity. Instead, it draws him deeper into the pain. He illustrates the power and authority of God—not just in what he is able to do (miracles, healing, teaching)—but in how he does it.

He performs miracles to show the power of God, always in submission to the will of the Father. He is moved with compassion; he weeps over death and sorrow; he rebukes hypocrisy. Jesus' fame ultimately will lead him to the Garden of Gethsemane where he will be alone and abandoned by even his closest followers.

Jesus' fame leads to death and from death to resurrection. Through it all, fame (and its loss) show the character of Jesus: one willing to go through the heart of pain to save his people.

God, help me to see your hand in my circumstances. May you shape my character, and may I rejoice in the character of Jesus. Amen.

The Call to Pay Attention

FEBRUARY 1–7, 2021 • LYN PACE

SCRIPTURE OVERVIEW: What is the ultimate source of our strength? All the authors for this week come to the same conclusion: True strength comes from the Lord. Isaiah asks: "Who is like God?" God never grows weary and provides unfailing strength to those who wait for God. The psalmist praises God as the one who lifts up those who are beaten down. It is not those with human strength who are truly mighty but those empowered by God. In First Corinthians, Paul states that he has laid down any form of his own strength so that the gospel may advance. In Mark, Jesus heals many as a demonstration of his power over the physical world. Thus, God's power is not just a metaphor but a reality.

QUESTIONS AND SUGGESTIONS FOR REFLECTION

- Read Isaiah 40:21-31. In what ways do you call on God's unfailing strength? How is that strength sustaining you?
- Read Psalm 147:1-11, 20. How do you experience God's provision in your life? What is your response to God?
- Read 1 Corinthians 9:16-23. How are you living out God's call to you? How has your call evolved over time?
- Read Mark 1:29-39. Where is your "deserted place" where you spend time alone with God? What helps you maintain a discipline of spending time alone with God each day?

College chaplain at Oxford College of Emory University, elder in the South Carolina Annual Conference of The United Methodist Church; lives with his spouse, Ami Hernandez, and their seven-year-old, Sam, in Oxford, Georgia.

In Mark's Gospel, events happen at a rapid-fire pace. There is no time for drawn-out stories. In today's reading, Jesus is at work healing Simon's mother-in-law. Before this, he was busy calling his disciples and casting out demons. Simply reading these first verses in Mark's Gospel can overwhelm us with the busyness of Jesus' ministry.

No wonder Jesus rises early, "well before sunrise" (CEB), to find a deserted place to be alone in prayer!

Whenever I feel a twinge of guilt for taking time to do yoga, to sit in silence, or to spend time in prayer during my day, I think about the example of Jesus in this text. This is not the only scripture passage where Jesus retreats to be alone. Strangely, I find that I rarely think of these texts when I am asked to identify biblical passages that inspire me. I suspect that has something to do with our society's need to glorify busyness and use it as a measure of worth.

I am a college chaplain, which means I see so much of this busyness firsthand in the lives of young adults. Entering students come with a resume full of activities from their competitive race to get into the college of their choice. At our college, like most others, we boast that we have more than eighty clubs, which keep students well occupied beyond their course loads. Many of our students are already looking ahead to the next stop in their career journey and rarely slow down to revel in the present moment.

Jesus offers us a glimpse of what it means to slow down. Even after the crowd tracks him down, in an effort to get more down time with his small group of followers, Jesus asks them to move in the opposite direction.

What would it mean for us to slow down? What new insight could we gain about the direction of our lives?

When I was going through the ordination process, it felt like I told my "call story" a hundred times. In ministerial circles, a "call story" is the story of the way one came to be a minister. Call stories, of course, are varied. Some are dramatic, with "lightning bolt" or Damascus Road experiences. Others of us have more nuanced stories that have unfolded over time.

For me, the beauty of having told my story repeatedly is that I have discovered themes or patterns that highlighted important moments and people in my life. For one thing, I learned how central mentors, especially clergy mentors, were in my story. Both local church pastors and college chaplains shaped my journey in deeply formative ways. It is no surprise to me (or to others) that I am a college chaplain today.

In today's reading, Paul is clearly giving us a glimpse of the way he interprets his own call story. "If I preach the gospel, I have no reason to brag, since I'm obligated to do it" (CEB). "I did not choose the ministry; it chose me," he seems to be saying. For Paul, it is the message of the gospel and what it means that draws him into ministry. Everything he does is for the sake of the gospel. He provides this information without any expectation of reward.

Discerning our call story is an important part of our journey. We make meaning out of our lives as we reflect on questions such as who it is who calls us and what it is that we are called to do. We are also wise to pay attention to the strengths and gifts we bring with us.

What is your call story? What gives you a sense of meaning and purpose in life and moves you and your community toward flourishing? How is that inspired by the gospel of Jesus Christ?

Holy one, accompany us as we discern our calling. Give us courage to proclaim your gospel. Amen.

The prophet Isaiah is writing in the time of the sixth century (BCE), a time when destruction and exile have left the community fractured and in chaos. The prophet seems to recognize something about the state of their lives. The people have forgotten or have doubts about who it is that created them. Isaiah reminds them (and us), "God makes dignitaries useless and the earth's judges into nothing" (CEB). In other words, no one is God but God.

I recently attended our Martin Luther King Jr. celebration at Oxford College where I work. The keynote speaker was an alumna of the school. A strengths coach herself, she told the students how crucial it is to understand our strengths. At the conclusion of her address, she offered us snippets from a letter she had written to the current Student Government Association president. The letter contained advice that the speaker felt would have been helpful to her during her SGA presidency, including this: "Perfection is actually a liability." Isaiah might tell us that no one is God but God.

It is not helpful to compare our lives with Isaiah's community or any other in history, even when a story resonates with us. But we can allow previous experiences to inform what we may be going through now. These experiences can help us to shape new and creative responses as we live faithfully in our homes, places of worship, workplaces, schools, and communities. As we do this, we would be wise to heed the prophet's words:

> *Look up at the sky and consider: Who created these?*
> *The one who brings out their attendants one by one,*
> *summoning each of them by name. Because of God's*
> *great strength and mighty power, not one is missing* (CEB).

God, the Holy One who sits above the circle of the earth and to whom no one can be compared, help us to look up and pay attention. Help us to remember that there is room for everyone in your good creation. May it be so. Amen.

In the second half of the text from Isaiah, again we hear these words on the prophet's lips, "Don't you know? Haven't you heard?" This time, however, Isaiah gets straight to the point for this weary and worn community. "The Lord is the everlasting God, the creator of the ends of the earth. He doesn't grow tired or weary" (CEB).

Thank goodness, God does not grow weary with the world, with the church, or with us! I could easily talk at length about all of the happenings in the world right now that make me weary and sometimes angry. Poverty surrounds us in our cities, as well as our rural communities. The earth is groaning under the weight of our destructive actions. The quest for more stuff and busier lives leaves us isolated and creates frenzied chaos among us. I could go on, and I'm sure you could as well. And yet, "Don't you know? Haven't you heard?" God does not grow tired or weary.

Even when we have given up or we feel ourselves coming close to that point, the prophet reminds us that God is with us. God's understanding is far greater than our capacity to fathom it. God gives power to the tired and revives the exhausted, according to the prophet. Just as it was for the community in exile in Isaiah's time, this is good news for us today. We may be tired and weary, but our faith draws us into communion with God where we will inevitably encounter others who will also give us strength.

O God, when we are tired and discouraged, help us to remember that you don't grow weary. Remind us once again that you are with us, offering us rest and the strength to go on. Amen.

Like others in the last section of the psalter, Psalm 147 is a praise psalm. While it clearly calls us to a posture of praise, it also names a range of emotions.

Every night, my spouse and I climb into our son's bed for stories and snuggles. After the stories have ended, we share in a ritual of prayer where each person has the opportunity to recall something from the day that was a high, a low, a grateful, and a beautiful. (We just recently added that last category.)

A ritual like this can be deeply formative, for both children and adults. It is an exercise in memory, remembering moments in our day to help each day have meaning. The ritual also allows us to capture the breadth of emotions that we experience in our day-to-day lives.

The psalmist says that it is a pleasure to sing and make beautiful praise to the Lord. Yet in the next breath, we hear about Israel's exiles, those who are brokenhearted, wounds that need bandaging, the mystery of God, the poor, and that evil is a reality in the world.

This is what I love about reading the Psalms. If we spend any amount of time with them, the Psalms will reach into our lives and reflect back to us our deepest emotions. They keep life's realities directly in front of us. They will call us to praise, yes; but they will also call us to deep lament. We will hear about anger, and we will hear about those who call to God from the depths of despair. The Psalms are a gift, especially if we commit to reading all of them.

Read today's psalm silently, then aloud. Next, write the psalm in a notebook or journal. What words stand out? Pull those words together in a short phrase, and pray them throughout the day.

appearance or manifestation of a deity.

We are in the liturgical season that follows the Epiphany. In this season, we recognize the ways in which Jesus revealed himself to those he encountered in his ministry. The Magi bring their gifts to him, and in that moment they begin to understand who Jesus really is. In the readings throughout this season, Jesus' ministry with others reveals the true character of God's coming kin-dom. In this time in between the birth of Jesus and the weeks of Lent that lead up to his death, we pause for a moment. We rest in God's Spirit.

Contemplation has been one of the themes of our week. It is at the center of our Christian life, as we come to know Jesus but also the concerns of our world.

In today's reading, the psalmist reminds us of the role of God as creator of all things. God covers the skies with clouds, makes rain for the earth, and gives food to the animals. God is the one who makes mountains and the grass sprout green. God also treasures the people who honor God and wait for God's faithful love.

There is much to contemplate in these beautiful words. In order to sing this song of praise, we would be wise to ponder the One to whom we offer praise, the One who creates. In our reflection on the Creator, there is also an invitation to think more carefully about creation and our relationship with it, to "contemplate the intersection between the life of Jesus and our own,"* to consider how God is manifest in Jesus but also in the world around us.

---

*Joan Chittister, *The Liturgical Year: The Spiraling Adventure of the Spiritual Life* (Nashville, TN: Thomas Nelson, 2009), 97.

Creating God, let us be careful creation keepers who live with deep intention and purpose. Amen.

One important part of my work as a college chaplain is to begin faculty and staff meetings with an opening reflection to calm our minds and center our being. The poet Mary Oliver has been my best friend when it comes to finding appropriate material for these reflections.

When Oliver died in 2019, my Facebook feed was full of articles about her and poems by her as many people grieved her death. For me, the beauty of that moment was in seeing how people of different political points of view and various religious and spiritual traditions (and some with no faith tradition at all) unified around their love for this gifted poet and her words.

Oliver's poem "Messenger" is one of my favorites. In it, she clearly calls us back to what matters most when it comes to our vocation or calling. She writes that loving the world is her work. She goes on to talk about her love for sunflowers and humming-birds and blue plums, as she reminds us of how good creation is—we need only look up and see it.

In today's reading, Jesus does not use the same words as Mary Oliver; but it is clear that he loves the world. It is also apparent in Mark's Gospel that many people are beginning to recognize his love. His love makes such an impression that they go searching for Jesus, even while he prays. Jesus not only lives out his love for the world; he also models what it means to pay attention.

Mary Oliver says, "Let me keep my mind on what matters, which is my work, which is mostly standing still and learning to be astonished."* Jesus teaches us that learning to be astonished is a form of prayer and part of our work, the work of loving the world.

*Mary Oliver, *Thirst: Poems by Mary Oliver* (Boston: Beacon Press, 2006), 1.

Source of Life, help us remember that paying attention is an important part of the life of faith together. Amen.

The Thin Places of Transformation

FEBRUARY 8–14, 2021 • BETH A. RICHARDSON

SCRIPTURE OVERVIEW: In the week leading to Transfiguration Sunday, the texts all deal with holy, transforming light; but they also speak to the awkwardness of waiting for and finally experiencing that light. Elisha's is a stop-and-go pilgrimage before he sees the chariots of fire. The psalmist proclaims the march of the sun across the sky while also waiting for the eschatological arrival of God's justice for God's people. Paul empathizes with the believers in Corinth who are having to wait and work to "give the light of the knowledge of the glory of God." Jesus leads Peter, James, and John up a mountain where they wait and are terrified by the cloud of glory that overshadows them.

QUESTIONS AND SUGGESTIONS FOR REFLECTION

- Read 2 Kings 2:1-12. Think of a time when you waited for a blessing from God. How did the waiting feel? How did you experience the blessing when it came?
- Read Psalm 50:1-6. What helps you to be aware of God's presence with you from "the rising of the sun to its setting" each day?
- Read 2 Corinthians 4:3-6. What are the areas of your life where God is shining a light? Are there any areas where you may be blind to the light?
- Read Mark 9:2-9. Identify a spiritual "mountaintop experience" you have had. What was the lasting impact of that experience on your life as a follower of Christ?

Director of prayer and worship life and dean of The Upper Room Chapel; ordained clergy in The United Methodist Church and a member of the Mountain Sky Conference; author of several books including *Walking in the Wilderness* and *Christ Beside Me, Christ Within Me: Celtic Blessings* (Upper Room Books).

Only a few weeks ago we celebrated the coming of Light into the world in the form of a tiny baby. Epiphany was a moment of revelation—an "Aha!" Here at the close of this season of revelation, we arrive at the story of Jesus' Transfiguration.

In each scripture reading this week we find light. The star of Epiphany has strengthened and blazes forth in the vision of Elijah's fiery horses and chariot charging into the heavens. In our psalm, God the judge arrives with a devouring fire. In Second Corinthians, our hearts are illuminated with the glory of God. And in Mark's Gospel, Jesus appears in the dazzling light of the Transfiguration.

We are here in the transition between God's revelation in Christ and the road leading to Jerusalem. We have left our nets to follow Jesus, and we have no idea where we will end up. We are following our teacher into the thin places—those mysterious spaces in which heaven and earth are close. Where are the thin places you find yourself?

In recent months, I have journeyed into the thin places of three human beings facing their final hours. I don't know why it was me who ended up in these holy spaces. This is not a regular part of my job. I'm not the pastor of a congregation, a chaplain in a hospital or hospice. I seemed to be there in a ministry of presence, to hold space, to pray, sing, and witness to the presence of the Holy One.

Each of these experiences was powerful and profound. Each contained moments of revelation of the power of God's love that knits us together in our mothers' wombs, that meets us at the doorway to death, that offers comfort to loved ones and a gentle, "Welcome, faithful one. Let me walk you home."

God of light, walk with us into the thin places of transformation. Amen.

I serve on the leadership team of the Alabama Two-Year Academy for Spiritual Formation, a program of The Upper Room. As the worship leader, I plan and lead the fourteen services during each week of our quarterly retreats.

The Academy takes its inspiration from this story in Second Kings. The logo for the Academy illustrates verses 13-14 when Elisha receives Elijah's mantle, illustrating the way in which the Academy experience is transformative. At the end of the two years together—just as Elisha took on the mantle of Elijah—we take on Christ's mantle and are sent forth to bear witness to the work of God in the world.

The pattern of our weeks together transforms us from disparate individuals into a community of grace. The format (based on Benedictine monasticism) brings us together for morning prayer, afternoon Eucharist, and night prayer. We move through the day following a rhythm of learning from teachers and silence for listening and reflection. At the close of night prayer, we walk out into the great silence which is broken at the start of morning prayer the following morning. This participation in a common rhythm is the "container" that forms and binds the community together as we hunger, learn, and struggle with what it means to be followers of Christ in this broken world.

Early in the Academy experience, we carry assumptions, fears, hurts, and suspicions. Everything is unfamiliar—the schedule, the services, the people. When we come back the second time, we begin to settle in to the rhythm of the week. By the third gathering, we have begun to long for the community in the days before our journey. We sink right in to the rhythm, rejoicing in one another, singing the songs with open hearts, even sitting in the same place for prayers. We are transformed from a group of separate individuals into a community, woven together in love.

Where are the places or communities that feed your soul? Say a prayer of thanks for them.

The Thin Places of Transformation

Last spring our Academy group traveled from our retreat center into the heart of Birmingham, AL, for a civil rights pilgrimage. We walked through the Civil Rights Institute, witnessing the stories of the saints and martyrs who were lights shining in the darkness of racism in the 1950s and 60s. We walked through Kelly Ingram Park, where children and high school students were met by police dogs and fire hoses.

We gathered in the sanctuary of 16th Street Baptist Church to hold our service of Eucharist. In 1963 a bomb exploded under the steps of this church, killing four girls and injuring twenty-two other people. In this holy place, we sang together, heard the scriptures read and proclaimed. We broke bread and poured the cup. We remembered the brokenness of Christ, of our history, of today. We affirmed our hope in the One who came to bring peace, scatter love, bind up wounds, and whisper comfort.

At the end of the day, we arrived back at the retreat center tired, grateful, and troubled. We prayed the familiar words from the night liturgy: "We have wounded your love. O God, heal us. We stumble in the darkness. Light of the world, transfigure us. We forget that we are your home. Spirit of God, dwell in us."*

The liturgy, the community, our common love and struggle—all these are the "container" that allows us to see God's light illuminating our own privilege and racism. May each person find communities of love, trust, and liturgy where we can be nurtured, challenged, and loved.

---

*From "Prayer of Confession" (Night Prayer), *A New Zealand Prayer Book*: He Karakia Mihinare o Aotearoa (New Zealand: William Collins Publishers Ltd., 1989), 168.

God of transformation, may your light shine into the shadows of our world, illuminating the way to justice, mercy, and love. Amen.

The opening verses of this psalm paint a picture of God calling to us "from the rising of the sun to its setting." This transforming God yearns for us to notice that God walks before us, behind us, beside us.

A few years ago I began to learn more about my Celtic heritage and its spirituality. I learned that my Celtic ancestors lived close to the earth and its rhythms. The old ones invoked blessings of the Holy One from the dawning of the day to its close. No activity was too small or mundane to be blessed by the Creator. God's blessing was asked for the kindling of the fire in the morning and the smooring of the coals at night. There were blessings for the workers, the children, and the livestock; blessings for the beginning of a journey and the safe arrival of travelers. The tools of life were brought before God in gratitude: the loom and the boat, the seeds for planting and the scythe for reaping. All these things were transformed by prayer into connections with the One who created us and gave us life.

As I studied and reclaimed my own Celtic heritage, I began to notice more things around me.

Through these prayers, my heart of fear, obsession, or boredom is transformed into a heart of gratitude.

I have added a blessing practice to my day in the form of a "bless to me" prayer. I encourage you to try this practice today. First, think of something or someone you are grateful for. Then remind yourself of how this person or object brings you joy or gratitude. Finally, write about these things using the form, "Bless to me . . . "

Bless to me this quiet time, the meeting of hearts and minds in book today. Bless to me all those who read these words. Happy or sad, troubled or joyful, may they know God's peace. Bless to me this quiet time. Amen.

There are troubling words in Psalm 50: "Before [God] is a devouring fire." For months in 2020, we watched as Australia burned. The Australian wildfires covered an area twice the size of the state of Maryland. My mind could not comprehend the destruction on this scale. The news of this and other natural disasters overwhelmed me. I found myself turning away, averting my gaze from the overwhelming challenges that we face.

We are bound together on this earth as one people created by the Holy One. Our psalm names us as "faithful ones, who made a covenant with me." We are the creatures fashioned in the image of God, set as caretakers over the birds of the air and the fish of the sea. (See Genesis 1:26-31.)

And yet it seems that we have not upheld our part of this contract. We have used the earth and its resources in ways that threaten the future of life on this planet. Growing climate change is producing catastrophe—droughts and fires, rain and flooding, the melting of the polar caps and rising oceans. Often these days, I find myself paralyzed by fear for our future.

In Psalm 50, we find God arriving as a judge, ready to hold court with the heavens and earth as witnesses. I imagine this statement from the Creator, "Human ones, I gave you dominion over the earth and all its creatures. You have taken all that you wanted and left brokenness. I made covenant with you and you have broken my trust."

What is our reply to these charges? How will we respond in this time of crisis? May our hearts and lives be transformed by God in these days of challenge.

God of creation, we have failed to be stewards of this earth. Guide us in this time of chaos. Show us the individual actions we can take to help heal the world. Amen.

Jesus takes Peter, James, and John and leads them up a mountain. There they witness a dazzling light and the ancestors, Moses and Elijah, talking with Jesus. What do we make of this mysterious story? Peter, with his typical practicality, suggests that they make three dwellings; one each for Jesus, Moses, and Elijah.

Six weeks ago, we followed the star to find God in the form of a baby. We have seen his baptism, his journey into the wilderness, and his early ministry. In a few days, we will receive the ashes that mark the beginning of Lent and our journey with Jesus toward his death and resurrection.

This moment of transfiguration, this mountain top experience, is a call to transformation. In the Transfiguration, the glory of Jesus was revealed to the most ordinary of people: Peter, James, and John. We too are invited to see Jesus in a new way.

Our hearts are transformed when we watch for Christ in the people and experiences we encounter each day. At a recent session of The Academy for Spiritual Formation, I found myself deeply touched during the worship services. As I listened to the chanting of a psalm during morning prayer, I felt myself overflowing in gratitude for the gift of music, for the voice of the cantor, for Christian communities through the ages who have praised and worshiped God early in the morning. As I offered the cup of blessing during the Eucharist service, my heart was transformed in love for each person: "The cup of salvation, poured out for you."

I wonder, *How is God transforming me today, in this transition from Epiphany to Lent?* May we watch for Christ's presence in the experiences and the people we meet today.

Reflect on the people and places where you have seen Christ in the last few days. How have these interactions been sources of transformation for you? Say a prayer of thanks for these experiences.

The Thin Places of Transformation   63

TRANSFIGURATION

Earlier this week we reflected on Elisha receiving the mantle of Elijah and our formation in Christian community. Jesus shaped the lives of his disciples as they followed him along dusty roads and then onto the mountain where they witness the Transfiguration. Peter, James, and John hear the words of God spoken from a cloud, "This is my Son, the Beloved; listen to him." Leaving the mountain, the disciples carry those words with them into the difficult times ahead of them.

When we are on the mountaintop, experiencing the heady excitement of a "thin place," it is easy to believe that we will always feel this way. But when the dazzling light fades and we step back into reality, we face the challenge: Can we remember God's invitation?

Returning home from a week at The Academy for Spiritual Formation, I often have difficulty with reentry. As I leave the retreat center, I am flying high with love, with a sense of belonging, with the certainty that God was in that place and Christ was present in those people. Once I am back home, faced with the mundane tasks of doing laundry and going back to the office, I feel lonely and empty. I want to be back on the mountaintop.

What I am finding is that, over time, I am being transformed by my experience. While I cannot live on the mountaintop, I can find Christ all around me if I keep my ears and eyes and heart open. I can listen to the Beloved, sensing the presence of the Holy One in the ordinary and challenging world in which I live.

God's presence walks with us as we follow Jesus along dusty roads; as we sit, transformed, on a mountain; and as we follow Jesus towards Jerusalem.

God of transformation, journey with us through the broken-ness of this world. Open our ears, our eyes, our hearts to your presence around us. We are yours. Amen.

The Fast We Choose

FEBRUARY 15–21, 2021 • MARTHA SPONG

SCRIPTURE OVERVIEW: The season of Lent is now upon us, a time of inward examination that begins on Ash Wednesday. We search ourselves and ask God to search us, so that we can follow God more completely. This examination, however, can become a cause for despair if we do not approach it with God's everlasting mercy and faithfulness in mind. Although the Flood was a result of judgment, God also saved the faithful and established a covenant with them. The psalmist seeks to learn God's ways, all the while realizing that he has fallen short and must rely on God's grace. For Christians, baptism functions as a symbol of salvation and a reminder of God's covenant faithfulness—not because the water is holy but because God is holy and merciful.

QUESTIONS AND SUGGESTIONS FOR REFLECTION

- Read Genesis 9:8-17. When have you, after a season of loss, experienced new life? What was the sign of that new life?
- Read Psalm 25:1-10. How are you experiencing God's steadfast love and faithfulness in your life? How do you offer thanks?
- Read 1 Peter 3:18-22. When have you sacrificed something for the sake of someone else?
- Read Mark 1:9-15. Recall a "wilderness" experience in your own life. What helped you to move through that experience? What were the spiritual gifts of that experience?

United Church of Christ pastor, author, and clergy leadership coach; editor of *The Words of Her Mouth: Psalms for the Struggle*; lives in South Central Pennsylvania with her spouse, a Presbyterian pastor.

With Lent just days away, we have a decision to make. Will we give up chocolate or yarn-buying, or take a sabbatical from social media? We might take on a practice instead, reading a particular book or writing our own Lenten reflections, or cleaning out closets to make donations of clothes we no longer wear, or take on an exercise challenge. Any of these might show we intend to be more disciplined about our care of body, mind, and spirit.

Reading the second letter to the church in Corinth, however, we find a different kind of commitment to God by Paul and Timothy, a daunting list explaining how "as servants of God we have commended ourselves in every way." Their disciplines were the survival of afflictions, abuse, imprisonments, and hunger. They claimed fruits of the Spirit as powers for good. They survived, too, the opinions of others, overturning the claims made against them.

Paul and Timothy offer their example as a case for discipleship. They beg us "on behalf of Christ" to reunite with God. This is not a message to new believers. It is a plea to those who have let their relationship lapse.

In choosing a Lenten practice, we might consider how we keep God at a distance, whether through our actions or our inactions. We may have chosen things that make life easier with other people. We may be grieving the life we expected that did not come to be. We may have placed the life of faith low on our list of priorities. Reconnecting with God begins with confessing that we are apart and deciding to make God our primary focus, for we are God's.

Holy One, you do not promise a smooth path or a happy ending, but you do promise to be in relationship with us no matter what. May we promise the same to you. Amen.

Psalm 51 asks for God's assistance in heart renewal. This psalm is ascribed to King David and associated with the aftermath of his affair with Bathsheba and his plot against her husband, Uriah the Hittite. David smashed through most, if not all, of the Ten Commandments with his decision to take another man's wife. Nathan the prophet had to convince him of his guilt. Here David repents, hoping to heal his relationship with God.

We do not know if David actually wrote the psalms attributed to him; they may have been written later, long after David's time. But there is a strong association between David and this particular psalm, as if even the most scholarly among us cannot quite bear to part the two. This iconic figure is tender and tough, faithful and flagrant, loving and libidinous, warlike and woeful. He struggles to live up to his call. When he fails, he comes back to God and asks for help.

It can take a lot of courage to own up to the things we have done wrong, to admit that the choices we somehow justified to ourselves harmed others' lives, sometimes beyond our power to repair them. When we own up to the destruction we have caused, or even to our misdemeanors, it may seem like nothing will ever be the same. Maybe things won't be, but the psalmist knows what is possible with God and reminds us of David, getting honest with himself about the responsibility he needed to take for his actions. A clean heart requires a fresh appraisal of our lives. It is not a new heart but a renewed heart, born through the effort of being honest with ourselves and trusting God to know it all yet still love us.

Renew my heart, O God. Give me a new, faithful spirit; root it deep inside me. I own what I did wrong. Please, Holy One, let me stay with you. Amen.

ASH WEDNESDAY

A group of seminarians, mostly commuter students glad to catch up with one another, chatted on their way into worship on a Wednesday morning in February. The sun shone on their earnest faces, and once they settled into seats in the high-ceilinged chapel, they beamed happily at being together in worship on a particularly holy day. That mood remained as they received the cross of ashes and the reminder that life is short.

A professor ascended the steps to the pulpit and began to preach. "You look so pleased to be here, smiling at yourselves." His tone was heated. "Don't you know this is a day to repent?"

Ouch. Faces fell. There is a line, apparently, between appearing repentant and actually repenting. True repentance is not so radiant. True repentance is a determined turning toward God, with full clarity about how and what we need to change. That reality is spare and deep and uncomfortably introspective for most of us.

Isaiah 58 points to and challenges the same exterior piety that the seminary professor condemned. In these verses, God speaks clearly about the hypocritical choice to be publicly faithful while oppressing the marginalized around us. God does not value our fasting if we continue to commit acts and participate in systems that harm other people.

Ash Wednesday is complicated. We might appreciate the reminder of our mortality or grieve it. We might know going in what we need to rectify or find ourselves—like the seminarians—called out, either from the outside or in our own selves. This is a good day to do it, to clarify our status with the person we see in the mirror, then confess it all to God.

O Lord, I know, and I know you know, the things that need to change. Help me to be the person you expect for the rest of the life you have given me. Amen.

After the flood, Noah and his family heard from God. After shock and grief and struggle, after being quartered—quarantined—with their closest relatives and all the animals they could gather on a boat of their own making, and with nowhere to dock for weeks and weeks, they heard from God.

Wherever we are in our stories, whether we are laying in whatever we need to be prepared, wondering if we can survive the storm, waiting for word that things have changed, or catching a breath for what seems like the first time in forever, we are somewhere on the same journey Noah's family took. If we are standing on the shore, grateful to be on dry land and relieved that the world is steady beneath us, we know how it felt for them on the day when the waters had finally receded. The world as they knew it had ended.

Be it epidemic, natural disaster, or even the comparatively ordinary losses we know logically must come in life, there is a moment in the cycle of horrified recognition when we wonder why God has let this terrible thing happen. In Noah's case, the parameters are clear. The people, God's own people, have fallen into such sin that even God cannot imagine redemption and instead reboots the human experiment.

Our lives may be in such a moment; the world as we know it changed beyond recognition. For today, let's stand with Noah and his wife and children on the dry land. We will not forget what has been lost or the things that changed us. Our hope is grounded in this new covenant, this bow in the clouds. After the flood, Noah and his family heard from God, and God promised it would never happen again.

Loving God, in this world of sorrows and struggles, we give thanks for your promises and we place our hope in you. Amen.

Here at the beginning of Lent, we begin to ponder the commitment we have made to follow Jesus Christ, most of us seeking some deeper learning or choosing some stricter discipline. In the early centuries of the church, baptism came at the end of a period of formal preparation, often as part of the Easter Vigil. The candidates for baptism, who were adults, had met the criteria of the community for becoming Christians; but they did not know everything. Some early church communities kept up a spirit of mystery about the event itself. Imagine walking into the water, eager but not fully informed, trusting God.

It's understandable that we associate baptism with the washing away of sins because of the practice of full immersion and the historic connection to other rituals—like the Jewish *mikve*h, a bath used for rituals of purification. But First Peter asks us to consider the act of going into the water in less literal terms. God saved the family of Noah, who survived the waters of the flood; the epistle describes them as "saved through water." In that interpretation, the waters of the flood are less the destroyer of the rest of the world and more the conveyance to separate Noah and his people from sin. Baptism is "an appeal to God for a good conscience." It's a commitment to something we do not fully understand, a pledge to try and get things right.

When we baptize children, parents and sponsors make that pledge on the little ones' behalf, promising to offer instruction and encouragement along life's way. It's a good reminder that baptism is not an initiation, not a graduation, and that we all have more to learn from the One who saves us.

Mighty God, help us to remember our baptism, a death to the old ways and rebirth into a new life, through Jesus Christ. Amen.

Taking Lent seriously feels daunting. If we haven't figured out by Ash Wednesday how we want to approach the season, we may "all or nothing" it; or we might set the first Sunday as the next deadline for our decision. If we're in that category, today may feel like the most pressure-filled of all.

But fear not! There is still time. One path to a decision might lie in the Psalms, those ancient songs we turn to even today when we need to work through things. They are constructed to express feelings—anger, fear, grief, and joy, for starters—and to bring the person praying to some sense of resolution with and confidence in God.

If we sit with Psalm 25, we find an anxious psalmist pondering all the ways he or she might be in trouble. There is a particular concern that the opinions of other people (very bad people!) might hurt the psalmist's standing with God. But there is also a hopeful request that misdeeds committed in the dim past might be forgotten. Again and again the psalmist calls on God's steadfast love and mercy, putting a positive portrait of God in this prayer.

What are we afraid God will find fault with in our lives? Our youthful indiscretions? The half-measures or inadequate faithfulness we fear others might notice? Or simply that we haven't gotten ourselves organized to take on or let go of something for Lent? The work of the psalm moves us to reassurance: If we are willing and open participants in a relationship with God, we can rely on God's steadfast love and faithfulness to guide us along the way.

Loving God, you are steadfast even when we are changeable. Help us to embrace the practices that bring us closer to you in the coming weeks. Teach us to center our hearts and minds on you, with humble confidence in your mercy. Amen.

FIRST SUNDAY IN LENT

On the first Sunday of Lent, Pastor Lewis reached out for something she expected to find on her bedside table, but it wasn't there. Waking more fully, she reminded herself that her family had made a commitment for the season together. All their phones were plugged in to a charging station in the kitchen, the key to a mutual promise to hold off on checking email, responding to messages, or getting sucked down the rabbit hole of YouTube videos in the hour or two between arising and leaving for work, school, or in this case, church. This was the fourth day of their practice, and despite forgetting overnight she could already measure the ways they were making space and time holy together.

Mark's Gospel devotes three verses to Jesus' baptism and a mere two for the story of Jesus' forty-day sojourn in the wilderness, in which Satan, wild animals, and angels get equal time. Blink, or check Facebook, and you might miss the whole story. By verse 15 of the Gospel, Jesus' work has begun: "Now is the time! Here comes God's kingdom! Change your hearts and lives, and trust this good news!" (CEB).

Jesus is talking about himself. He is God, and God's kingdom is walking into our midst in his person.

"Change your hearts and lives" has to mean more than a fast we can manage for up to forty days, minus Sundays; but it is a start. What is getting in the way of your relationship with God? Is it something from which you can choose to fast, beginning today? Small, measurable steps will support a changed heart and a changed life.

Holy One, when we are tempted to think that following you is only two verses' or forty days' worth of commitment, help us to hear your voice in a new way, to change our hearts and lives, and to trust this good news. Amen.

A Royal Order

FEBRUARY 22–28, 2021 • CHRISTIANNE SQUIRES

SCRIPTURE OVERVIEW: We cannot earn God's love. Going back to the time of Abraham, God's blessing has been based on faith. God chose Abraham for a covenant not because Abraham was perfect but because he believed God. The psalmist reminds his audience of their ancient relationship with God and expresses the hope that it will continue through future generations. In Romans, Paul reinforces the centrality of faith. Following the law was not bad, but no one should believe that following the law could earn God's favor. Some of Jesus' disciples share with him an experience that mystifies them. Trusting God means surrendering everything in faith.

QUESTIONS AND SUGGESTIONS FOR REFLECTION

- Read Genesis 17:1-7, 15-16. What is the basis of your relationship with God? How comfortable do you feel in it?
- Read Psalm 22:23-31. Where do you find hope in troubling times?
- Read Romans 4:13-25. How easily do you live in God's grace? In what areas do you find yourself "reckoning" your righteousness?
- Read Mark 9:2-9. Do you ever find it difficult to believe in things you may not fully understand? What helps you to trust in God?

Spiritual director and member of All Saints Episcopal Church in Winter Park, FL.

It's a familiar refrain, isn't it, the promise that God will make Abraham the father of many nations? It's one of those tenets of our faith that slides off the tongue like water off a duck's back—slick, smooth, clear, and acknowledged in a blink.

But the English Standard Version puts it this way: "I will make you into nations, and kings shall come from you." The passage says of Sarah that "she shall become nations; kings of peoples shall come from her."

To be made into nations—what does that even mean? And to be told that kings will come from you—what would it feel like to hear that?

These are two people past childbearing age, the barrenness of Sarah her ongoing shame for years. Now they are told they will not just become parents but be made into nations—and not just made into nations but that kings will flow forth from them.

How are they to hold such news? How would you hold it if it were you? And how does such a thing happen?

Perhaps being made into nations happens through the royal order this promise carried with it. We're told this lineage of nations and kings was no definite outcome. God told Abraham, "Walk before me, and be blameless" (ESV). Could this be how a person is made into nations—through blamelessness and walking one's life before God?

The condition of Abraham's life and heart determined what would happen beyond him and through him. If Abraham honored the royal order of how nations and royals are made, God would bring it about. A life that's blameless, that walks steadily before God each day—are these conditions you would agree to meet if it meant the same outcome for you?

Help me, God, to follow the blameless path you desire me to walk. Bring your nations and kings from my faithfulness. Amen.

For nations and kings to flow forth from Abraham and Sarah, they need not just to walk before God and be blameless. They need not merely to concern themselves with the outward actions of the lives they live upon the soil of this earth. They needed also to acknowledge a royal order to all existence.

God says to Abraham, "Behold, my covenant is with you" (ESV). God says to Abraham, too, "I will . . . be God to you" (ESV). The covenant itself originates with God. God is the author of it; and the intention is for God to be God to Abraham and his many descendants, for God to be the one who reigns over all else in their lives.

There is a royal order at play here. God is at the top; and Abraham and Sarah and their expected rich lineage of nations and kings are to flow forth from that pinnacle of truth, subservient to God and under God's authority. This is how things were set up to be.

Would Abraham and Sarah and their generations of descendants let God be God to them? Would they trust the One who made the covenant, who authored it, who was the reason it existed in the first place—even the reason they existed? Will you?

Walking before God and being blameless—these were Abraham's instructions to secure the promise God gave that Abraham would father kings and nations. But the action of walking before God and the state of being blameless—these were lived out and sought because of a preexisting belief that God is God and the source of all promises made and fulfilled.

Dear God, I honor your authority in my life. I acknowledge you as God and ask you to be God to me in all things. Help me honor the royal order you have designed for all of life. Amen.

Sometimes the only hope we can find in the rampant chaos that thrives in our world is what today's reading reminds us—that "kingship belongs to the LORD, and he rules over the nations" and that "all the families of the nations shall worship before [God]" (ESV).

What hope do we have when nations fight nations, competing for strength and sovereignty? What hope do we have when evil people wield power for their own depraved ends? What hope do we have when the enforced laws of so many countries serve the privileged but diminish the least among us and damage our earth? What hope do we have when godlessness abounds?

We exult in this truth: In the end, on the very last day, all will worship God and acknowledge God's sovereignty. Yes, the earth has its nations and rulers. Yes, God makes nations and kings through those who are called to bring them forth. But above all that earthly authority stands the One who created all authority and holds that authority in full.

We need not despair. We need not succumb to what we see, believing it to be the only true depiction of reality. Something bigger prevails. A royal order still holds forth and will not fail. All will bow in worship of the one true God.

My God, when my heart grows heavy with grief and restless for justice, remind me of your sovereignty and the hope that never fades. Bring your righteousness forth, I pray. Amen.

We need not wait until the culmination of all things to experience the joy of God's justice. The end of days is not the only time we will witness a restoration of the rightness of God's truth and peace. No, in the royal order of God's design, God's gifts and promises are available now to those who heed and follow God's ways.

It began with the "offspring of Jacob" and "offspring of Israel" (ESV), the literal descendants of that father of nations, Abraham. But it extends forth to us, too—"those who fear him" and "those who seek him" (ESV). We are promised that we'll be seen. That our afflictions will not bypass the sight of our God. That we'll be heard when we cry. That we'll be fed and satisfied in body and soul. That God's face will not be hidden from us.

What wonderful news this is! Our God is one who sees, who hears, who feeds, who cares, and who is even seen by us. All the many needs we have, physical and emotional, are known and tended by the One who gave us the lives we live.

Our hope is not a hope that waits, unfulfilled until the very end. God's gifts can come to us now. When we fear God, when we put our lives in service of the royal order God has decreed—God above all and all else flowing from there—we receive the gifts and care of God's presence with us, God's eye upon us, and God's provision for us. Blessed be the name of the Lord!

O God, remind me of your presence always, but especially when I most need it. All the gifts you make available to me I open myself to receive. Amen.

How many times do we put expectations and restrictions on ourselves or others about what it means to be accepted by God and God's people? We have to attend church this frequently. We can't wear those kinds of clothes. We can't get that kind of mark on our bodies. We can't hang out with those kinds of people. We have to volunteer so many times a year. We have to read our Bible and pray just this way every day. We have to believe in our holiness. We need evidence of it to make it so.

It's exhausting—and completely beside the point!

Paul knew this well. He was one for following the letter of the law completely, and he was chief Pharisee among all Pharisees before that fateful day on the road to Damascus when he heard the voice of Christ speaking directly to him. Once converted to faith in Jesus, he found that same legalism greeting him among the new Christians. His letter to the Romans was a response to such soul-stripping rules and ways of exercising one's belief.

Without faith, Paul wants us to know, it all means nothing. Faith is what ushers us into the family of Abraham's long line of descendants, born not just of flesh but of that same faith that saved him that very first day he heard God's promise for the future. We become part of that royal order of nations and kings and descendants and generations that God foretold from the beginning, and it's our faith—not the letter of the law—that gets us there. That is truly the best news of all!

Dear God, thank you for the grace that saves me in my simple assent of faith. It is enough, and it is everything. Amen.

It seemed like such a good idea at the time. Who else had been granted access to such a sight in all of history? Moses and Elijah were here, and the Rabbi Jesus too, now radiant in resplendent glory. Surely the right response was to stay put, to build a shelter to honor them, to just camp out in this place.

It seemed like a good idea, but actually the disciples who had accompanied Jesus to the mountain were terrified. So maybe it wasn't a good idea, after all. Maybe it was just the best they could imagine in their sputtering, adrenaline-charged fear. Maybe it was all they could do in that moment.

And how often are we in such a place? We do the best we can under the circumstances. We feel overwhelmed, overwrought, completely flummoxed, and just plain scared. Or we feel honored, favored, privileged, and chosen above all others, our egos stroked. We're glad to be the chosen ones. We're glad it's us and not them.

But our best ideas when we're afraid tend to fall flat. Our brilliant brainstorms when we're getting puffed up with our own good press tend to take us out of order with God.

In fact, there is a royal order, a decree of all decrees: "This is my beloved Son; listen to him" (ESV). Not "listen to yourself." Not "listen to each other." Not "listen to what the world would have you do with this opportunity." But rather, listen to Jesus. What would that look like for you today?

Spend five minutes stilling your body and quieting your mind. If it helps, focus on the flame of a candle. Make the intention of this time to simply listen for the voice of Jesus speaking to you. What do you hear?

SECOND SUNDAY IN LENT

In this passage, we learn that on the way down the mountain, Jesus spoke to the disciples of the fact that he would rise from the dead. But we also know from biblical context that the disciples did not understand all that Jesus foretold about his death and resurrection in the days leading up to his crucifixion.

We know this because when it actually happened, they wandered on roads at night in great disorientation and distress, and they locked themselves away for fear of the repercussions of having followed Jesus. They grieved the loss of Jesus, and they were utterly amazed when he appeared again among them.

And so we are challenged to ask ourselves: Will we believe in a God who says things we don't understand? Will we trust that the royal order of reality puts God's knowledge far above our own, that God can proclaim as true things we cannot fathom at all and those things can still be true anyway?

Jesus told the disciples he would rise from the dead. God told Abraham, a man one hundred years old, that he would be made into nations and that kings would come from him. The psalmist wrote that every person in all existence will one day worship God, even as history and the news of our times would have us believe otherwise.

What will we choose to believe, a royal order designed and set in motion by a God whose knowledge and capacity is beyond our reckoning, or our own human sight and understanding? The invitation is clear. We're invited to follow it today.

Dear God, I know that your ways are not my ways, but I often forget it. Help me to trust in your knowledge above my own. Help me to hear the truths you are speaking to me. Amen.

Acting Out of Faith

MARCH 1–7, 2021 • NICK BAIRD-CHRISOHON

SCRIPTURE OVERVIEW: As we continue in the season of Lent, we remember another important chapter in salvation history. Just as God established covenants with Noah and Abraham and their descendants, so did God renew the relationship with the Israelites by giving them the law. Obedience to the law was not the means of earning God's love, but a response of love by the people to the love God had already shown them. The psalmist understands that God's law creates a cause for rejoicing, for it is more valuable than gold. Both Paul and John address situations in which some had distorted the worship of God. Either they considered themselves too good for the gospel (1 Corinthians), or they had violated the covenant by altering proper worship for the sake of profit (John).

QUESTIONS AND SUGGESTIONS FOR REFLECTION

- Read Exodus 20:1-17. How do you keep God as the central focus of your life? What draws you away from that focus?
- Read Psalm 19. In what ways do you experience God's laws as "sweeter . . . than honey"? When do you find yourself trying to resist God's laws?
- Read 1 Corinthians 1:18-25. What does it mean to you that "God's foolishness is wiser than human wisdom"?
- Read John 2:13-22. How do you respond to Jesus' anger and actions in this reading? Do his actions fit with the way you generally picture Jesus?

Ecumenical by way of potlucks, strong supporter of youth ministry; loves food and garage rock; elder in the Tennessee Conference of The United Methodist Church.

What a powerful example of poetic praise for God's glory! In the opening lines of this hymn, the psalmist uses a lot of big, hyperbolic language to declare and describe God's glory.

In the Common English Bible translation of this text, verse two reads, "One day gushes news to the next." The day gushes. Gushes! When one thinks of typical Lenten practices, gushing rarely comes to mind. One might think of hunger pangs, solemn prayers, and lots of silence. These things do not gush. Instead, they encourage more silence: the silence of the journey to the cross, the silence of darkness and despair that veils the news of the morning. That is the point! While we may be in constant reflection, the glory of God's righteousness expressed by heaven's proclamation is a cacophony of expression. This gushing, however, is only perceivable for those who are listening.

Verse three continues, " . . . their voices can't be heard, but their sound extends throughout the world." Again, this is big language. Sound extends throughout the world, reaching to the ends of the earth. Even though no one can recognize the words, the chorus ranges across the entire globe. Finally, in verse five, we read, "The sun . . . thrills at running its course." That big, exploding ball of fire and gas receives a personality that "thrills" as it carries out its purpose.

For what purpose does news gush, sound extend throughout the world, and the sun thrill to rise and fall? For the glory of proclaiming each day as a blessing for those in God's creation, of course! So as we silence our hearts and breathe solemn prayers, may our spirits proclaim God's glory in big language!

Abundant God, we pray that our words and actions speak to the greatness and boldly proclaim how wonderful you are. Amen.

Paul, in this letter to the church in Corinth, understands the believers' confusion about Jesus' death and what it means for his followers. To some, the proclamation of a crucified messiah is at best a mistake and at worst blasphemy. For others, a god simply could not be killed by mere mortals. It would be offensive to think otherwise.

"Nothing about this makes sense," my friend said as he ordered the peanut butter-bacon burger at a local diner. "Peanut butter belongs with bananas or jelly, not ketchup," he continued before inexplicably ordering it anyway. The burger arrived steaming hot, an opaque brown glaze coating the burger patty. My friend took a bite, and his eyes transmitted a single message: It was good.

The ingredients were all present for Jesus to fit a particular understanding of messiah or god. He was a great teacher and leader. He performed miracles. He inspired the masses. The only thing standing in the way was the thick, sticky coating of a cross that made no sense in the rest of the recipe.

That is the difficulty of believing the gospel. Everything about it sounds good if we think only of the parts we like; however, there is so much more than what we like. Paul knew his audiences would be tempted either to take only what they wanted or to throw everything out; and yet, the most crucial part of the gospel is the part we do not readily understand.

Sometimes none of this makes sense, and that is okay. Just trust that the truth is in there.

God of wisdom, help us to make sense of your Word, even when it is challenging. Grant us the courage to seek truth and answers, especially when we do not understand. Grant us patience to be graceful when we meet others who interpret scripture differently than we do, and may all your people together find your truth. Amen.

The wandering Israelites have reached the Sinai—a large peninsula connecting the lands of Egypt to the west and Canaan (modern-day Israel) to the north and east. When the people are three days into their break from traveling in this wilderness, God speaks the Ten Commandments into being from the top of a mountain.

One wonders what it would be like to be there listening to God proclaim these commandments. Which commandments would have been easy to hear? Which commandments made the audience grimace? Why were punishments for not following them omitted? We know these were the standards to which the people of God would be held for generations, so why would God not feel a need to elaborate on their purpose or meaning?

Rules are identity-makers. Between the "shall" and "shall not" language of our laws, we send a message of who we are and what we believe is important. We believe people are important, and we believe what they have that makes up their homes, families, and lives is also important. God thinks it is best we honor that which is important by not harming others or taking what they have.

As you think of what you give up for Lent, consider it as a signpost to what you hold dear. To what principles do your own personal rules point? Are they ultimately signposts to God?

Holy God, help us with discipline. May our actions and our inactions point to a desire to do your will in this world. May we be resolved in our decisions for a pure and holy life so that all who know us will see your love in all that we are and do. Amen.

When I was in seminary, one of the most referenced stories of Jesus was the cleansing of the Temple. In the Synoptic Gospels, this scene occurs as Jesus enters Jerusalem for the last time. In John, it occurs early in Jesus' ministry, after the first miracle at the wedding in Cana. This event at the Temple is a prophetic action of who Jesus is to become.

This passage gives anyone who fights for reformation a tinge of excitement. "If you can't reform 'em, whip 'em!" But that is a very different image of Jesus than what most people think of when they think of the meek and mild Savior. These people in the courts were not gambling on the altar nor were they harming anyone. They were performing services that were necessary for Temple life by offering sacrificial animals for those who had none and exchanging Roman money for the Temple tax's required shekels. Their presence was not ideal; but, in the eyes of the everyday person, it was not egregious either. Jesus' behavior would have seemed violent to many.

One of the common pitfalls of faith is seeing Jesus through simple interpretations that fit our own understandings. Was he a humble pacifist or a passionate reformer? The answer is, "Both." What makes faithfulness to God so counter-cultural is that it evokes some unpopular behaviors. Sometimes God calls us to be humble servants in the face of injustice, spending our time and efforts helping the poor rather than directly fighting the power. At other times we hold to bold standards of faithfulness, even if those standards push against current culture.

Righteous God, help us to know how and when to act in your name. Give us righteous resolve to be your people, even when it is unpopular; and help us to know how to do so gracefully and with the care that people who love you would show. Amen.

We all want change, but we want it on our terms. The leaders of the Temple do not condemn Jesus outright for pushing the salespeople and money changers out from the courts. Instead, they ask, "Who gave you the authority to do this?" (AP). That is one of the most frustrating things about living in a group. Whether as a religious community or in a family, we often want some things to change; but we allow the things we dislike to go on for years and years without taking the initiative to make changes because we fear the responsibility.

These teachers of the law had grown complacent, letting their own house of worship become a market. They failed to recognize that these sellers and money changers were probably taking advantage of the people they were supposed to assist. Is that acceptable in a worship space? Jesus comes to reclaim that space and says he does so out of a passion for God's house. If he were to perform a miraculous sign to prove his authority, they think, no one could blame them for his actions. It may seem brave for them to be so bold in asking for such a big request from Jesus, but they asked it out of fear for their own sakes.

We fear change because we fear who may be upset by those changes. We ask for signs and messages from God even when the answer is right in front of us. How can we be braver people of God, especially in our places of worship? What do we fear in living more fully as God's people, and how can we avoid waiting around for God to prove to us what needs to be done?

Merciful God, forgive us when we make excuses to avoid change. Help us to know your still, small voice so that we do not get caught up waiting for a sign. Amen.

Psalm 19 is, according to many biblical scholars, two psalms edited together. While the two are divergent in their subject matter, with verses 1-6 speaking of God's nature and 7-14 God's moral law, both proclaim the awe-inspiring qualities of God. Whereas the first part of this psalm evokes rich imagery, this second part of the psalm is more contemplative. It begs the reader to calm the spirit and make honest work of the reflection of Gods law.

God's glory enchants us, and consequently it inspires us to be attentive to God's law. This entanglement of the heavenly and the mundane speaks volumes about how transcendent God is in our reality. Because God is perfect, we follow God's perfect law. Because God's law is perfect, we recognize how grand God truly is. Both the heavens and the law point to God's glory.

The writer uses a repetitive structure by first reciting one of the synonymous names for the law (for example, statutes, precepts, commandments), then its beneficial result. After that, a prayer-like passage reinforces the goodness of God and protection for the follower, a means of grace. The final line, "Let the words of my mouth, and the meditation of my heart, be acceptable in your sight," is common among preachers as they begin a sermon. Words and proclamations are grand and inspiring in scope. Yet they start in the quiet, mundane disciplines of regular study and prayer.

Lord, I look to you for guidance. Help me to find you in small, mundane tasks and in grand adventures of faith. May all that I do speak to how transcendent you are. Amen.

THIRD SUNDAY IN LENT

When we speak of the Decalogue (a fancy name for the Ten Commandments), we speak both of the literal stone tablets brought down by Moses from Mt. Sinai and also the theological cornerstone of the faith of the Jewish people. What is relevant to note, as we finish up this week's readings of acting on our faith, is how they are listed. The first three commandments set boundaries for our interactions with God. God is the one who rescued God's people from Egypt, so it makes sense that they should honor God's wishes first. These are excellent in establishing a relationship between God and God's people. These rules remove the possibility for the people to forget who God is to them.

The fourth commandment, the call for sabbath, acts as a bridge between God and God's people. Sabbath is our opportunity to connect deeply with God. Sabbath also protects us from overworking and setting other priorities as higher than God.

Finally, commandments five through ten are about our interactions with other people. What we immediately see here is how personal these commandments are and how valuable they are in setting a central foundation of how to live as moral human beings. We may not live in a literal wilderness like Moses and his people, but we do live in a variety of metaphorical wildernesses that can cause us trouble. If we listen deeply to God's message of loving God, loving ourselves, and loving others, acting according to faith becomes a little less confusing.

God, who calls us to abundant life, even when we are prone to forget to follow you, kindly direct us through the witness of scripture and the gentle guidance of your love. With you and for you, we live and move and breathe. Amen.

Deeper into the Wilderness

MARCH 8–14, 2021 • DANIEL LYVERS

SCRIPTURE OVERVIEW: Sometimes we get ourselves into trouble by our words and actions. It's okay to admit it. It happens to all of us. The Israelites experienced this when their constant grumbling provoked God's wrath in Numbers 21. Yet even in this story, God provides the means of salvation. The psalmist echoes the refrain that when we put ourselves in bad positions, we may cry out to the Lord for deliverance. We read in Ephesians that all of us were living in disobedience to God, but God has done all the work of reconciliation by grace given through Christ Jesus. John ties all this together, gesturing to the story in Numbers 21 to teach us that Christ is the means of restoration and salvation for all who believe in him.

QUESTIONS AND SUGGESTIONS FOR REFLECTION

- Read Numbers 21:4-9. When do you complain to God? Does your complaining ever interfere with your sense of God's presence with you?
- Read Psalm 107:1-3, 17-22. What practice helps you to thank God each day for God's steadfast love?
- Read Ephesians 2:1-10. How does your sense of God's salvation and grace move you to do good works?
- Read John 3:14-21. How do you act as a creature of light in the world? What are your "deeds that have been done in God"?

Ordained minister in the Christian Church (Disciples of Christ); pastor of Heart of the Rockies Christian Church in Fort Collins, CO, where he loves hiking with his dog; graduate of Vanderbilt Divinity School where he was a Disciples Divinity House Scholar and recipient of the J. D. Owen Prize for Excellence in New Testament Studies.

We are three weeks into the season of Lent, three weeks deeper into following Jesus into the wilderness. The deeper we get into the wilderness and the closer we get to the Cross, the harder the journey becomes. Impatience, fear, and exhaustion are temptations that are calling on us. The joy of Easter feels close, but it is not here yet.

The Israelites in today's passage know a little something about trekking through the wilderness, and they know something about complaining about it. At this point in the story, this is the fifth and final of the complaining stories in the book of Numbers. The Israelites are impatient, tired, hungry, and maybe losing it a little bit. They complain about having no food and water, and in the same breath they complain how terrible the food is. Huh?

Being lost in the wilderness has that effect.

The Israelites have lost their trust in God and are expressing a fear of moving forward. It always seems easier to go back to the way things used to be. Like the Israelites, we may have times in our journey when we complain about the change God calls us to, and then we have to ask ourselves, "What is holding me back?"

As they did for the Israelites, our complaints sometimes burst out of us without enough thought to even make sense of them. Sometimes we say out loud to God, "I'm tired, I'm hungry, and I'm lost." Yet maybe naming those complaints aloud will help us to sort out our fear and start to let go. In order to begin to embrace all that will sustain us the rest of the way through the wilderness, we need to acknowledge all that is preventing us from moving forward.

God, hear my complaints and help me to let them go so that I can open my heart to all that will sustain me in the wilderness. Amen.

The Israelites in their lack of faithfulness and their distrust of God spoke out against God, and God got tired of it. There are consequences to any action. In the case of the Israelites, their unfaithfulness prompts God to send venomous snakes that attack and kill many of them.

This is a difficult story to grasp. It is not a comfortable image of God, and yet we can learn a lot from the actions of the Israelites. They turn away from God, and the consequences are painful. However, they also turn back to God, confess their wrongdoing, and ask for forgiveness. God is faithful and responds with a reminder of the life-giving hope that roots our faith.

We are not unlike these ancient Israelites, and often our behavior is like a serpent that harms our world. Our challenge is to learn how to claim our responsibility and work to repair it. Repentance is an aspect of the season of Lent, and this passage invites us to ask what that looks like in our own lives.

In the wilderness we are tempted, but we have an opportunity to turn back to God. This is often a painful process. Recognizing how our actions have harmed others and asking for forgiveness requires humility. However, to live in the world as God intends requires accountability and personal responsibility.

The path to redemption is a hard one, but God does not leave us in the wilderness alone. Healing is possible. Yet we can't see that possibility unless we are able to turn toward God and lift up our eyes to see the hope of reconciliation and salvation that God offers. When fear threatens us, we look toward the reminders of God's love that give us life and sustain us in the wilderness.

God, help me to turn toward you and to lift up my eyes to see the reminders of your life-sustaining love. Amen.

My current congregation's mission statement is simple: *Loving God. Serving Others. Changing Lives.* This statement is written on the wall above the doors so that we can't help but see those words as we walk out of the sanctuary each Sunday morning. It is a nice reminder that the world of the church goes beyond what we do on Sundays and that the real work occurs out in the world.

However, every Sunday when I read those words, I cannot help but ask myself: *When we speak of changing lives, whose life is actually being changed when we love God and serve others?*

The season of Lent reminds us of the realities of being human, and this passage in Ephesians makes us look at that directly. As humans, we mess up a lot. We tend to place our trust in misguided leaders; and, as Paul says, all of us have placed our passions before our faith. In one sense, this passage is a tough pill to swallow. It's hard to look at my own shortcomings and complicities in my participation in a broken world.

Thankfully, Paul's point isn't to admonish us but to remind us that we claim faith in a God who is rich in mercy and loves us anyway. This should encourage us to keep walking in the wilderness and encountering God in the uncomfortable places of the world. Oftentimes the Christian message is as simple as loving God and serving others. The harder thing to grasp is that when we live into that, when we experience God's grace and mercy, it is our life that is changed. As you encounter the wilderness in this Lenten season—if you are open to the experience—you will be challenged and changed because that is what God's mercy does.

God, we are thankful that you are rich in mercy. As we encounter the wilderness, we pray that we are open to the ways that living into our faith and experiencing the fullness of your grace can change us. Amen.

One of my all-time favorite camp songs is "They'll Know We Are Christians by Our Love." When I think about what faith means to me, I think of those lyrics. Working side by side, walking hand in hand, it is through our actions that God's love is made known in the world.

This is why I am often uncomfortable when I am reminded that salvation is not something that we work for. Rather, as Ephesians tells us, salvation is a gift from God. Paul tells us that this is a gift, freely given. No matter how hard we work or how undeserving we feel, God loves us.

For me, the realization of this unconditional love is overwhelming; and, as with any gift I have ever received, I want to express to the gift-giver my gratitude. Paul could have stopped at saying that salvation is a gift from God that has been given to us, but he doesn't stop there. He reminds us that we are created in Christ Jesus for good works. Paul reminds us that faith doesn't invite us into a life of complacency. When we know how loved we are, it is impossible to not want to respond to that love. God's salvation is a gift freely given, and here we rediscover that we are asked to share that gift with one another. We are still asked to journey with and partner with God.

When we are able to claim God's abundant love for ourselves, we are moved. God's salvific act, God's love, is something that we respond to. Encountering the wilderness is a movement that we don't do alone. Today, take a moment to walk a little farther in this spiritual journey and consider how "they'll know we are Christians by our love."

God, it is an overwhelming gift to know how much you love us. May we express our gratitude by sharing that love with your world. Amen.

Derik fled his home country of Honduras because of violence. He was kidnapped as he traveled through the desert, and he escaped only to find himself lost and alone for ten days on limited food and water. Can you imagine being in his situation—alone, lost, disoriented, afraid, and knowing that death is a real possibility? Derik encountered the wilderness in a very real way, and yet he would tell you that he never lost hope. Why? "God never leaves God's children alone."

Psalm 107 is a psalm of thanksgiving that sings out in gratitude to God for delivering God's people from trouble. The Israelites have encountered the wilderness; they have experienced exile; they have been lost and separated. However, the Israelites have also experienced God's saving them from their trouble. It is from personal experience that the psalmist reminds us of key truths about God's love—it endures and it gathers us in.

I can hear the words of the psalmist echoing in Derik's story. To say that God never leaves us alone in the wilderness is another way of saying that God's love endures. The Psalms tell us about God through the lens of how others have experienced God at work. Both the psalmist and Derik speak to the experience that God's love endures. And if we think about it, we realize that we too have experienced God's enduring love.

We all encounter the wilderness in different ways and at different times. When our path is difficult and hope seems lost, we find courage in a faith that assures us that God's love endures, sustains us, and gathers us in. As we go through our own wilderness journey, our experiences of God's steadfast love are our source of strength.

God, we give you thanks for your steadfast love which endures forever. Help us to experience and proclaim this in our own lives as we encounter the wilderness before us. Amen.

Ionce took a group of fourth- and fifth-graders to an observatory to look at stars and learn about constellations. We talked about how there is so much we can learn about God by sitting in the dark that we cannot learn in the light of day. We looked up through a telescope at a dying star, and one of the kids asked what happens after a star dies. The observatory guide who was helping us explained in a simple way that the light goes out, turns to dust, and a lot of the material is the foundation for new stars to be formed.

In the darkness there is light and death; and there is resurrection.

John's Gospel is defined by the themes of light and darkness. In chapter 1, John tells us of the light that has come into the world that no darkness can overcome. Now, in chapter 3, John tells us how people who do evil hate the light and those who do what is true come to the light. Is it as simple as that?

So often, we are quick to put light and dark at odds with one another when, in reality, light and darkness coexist. They complement each other and tell us things about ourselves and about God that we could not know without leaving space for both.

As I think about our trip to the observatory, I still ask the question, *What can we learn in the dark that we cannot learn in the light of day?* As we continue to encounter the wilderness season, we are challenged to ask ourselves why we are spending so much time in the dark or why we are so quick to run to the light. Encountering the wilderness is hard and requires us to sit in the tension. Maybe take a walk in the dark tonight and see what comes up for you. Then remember that in darkness, there is light and death; and there is resurrection.

God, you created light and dark. May we hold space for both in our lives so that we rediscover ourselves and reconnect to you. Amen.

FOURTH SUNDAY IN LENT

John 3:16 was the first Bible verse that I ever memorized. I remember as a child in Sunday school reciting those words over and over, "For God so loved the world . . . " I don't know if it was through the power of repetition or not, but I am certain that one of the first things that I ever really knew about God was that God loved the world.

There's more to this passage in John's Gospel than verse 16. John begins by taking us back to the book of Numbers where Moses lifted the serpent in the wilderness, which was a symbol of God's saving action. By recalling this story, John reiterates for his readers something we already know to be true—God loves the world, has loved the world, and continues to love the world.

God loves the world. How much?

John doesn't pause long enough for us to even ask that question. God loves the world so much that God sent Jesus, in flesh and blood, to be in the world with us—not to condemn the world but to save it.

The world is messy, broken, and overwhelming. I often wonder why God doesn't condemn us for the disconnection our actions create. Then I remember this truth: God loves this world. And instead of giving up on us, God chooses to be in solidarity with us.

Jesus comes into the world, in all of its messiness, and meets us right smack in the middle of the wilderness. As we close out another week of Lent, we step farther into the wilderness and closer to the Cross. What a gift to remember that God loves you, me, us, the world so much that God sent Jesus to be in the world so that God could be in even closer communion with us!

God, help us to remember that we are loved so much that you meet us right where we are in our wilderness. Amen.

Brokenness and Belonging

MARCH 15–21, 2021 • ELLIE ROSCHER

SCRIPTURE OVERVIEW: We can maintain outward appearances for only so long. At some point what is in our hearts will come to the surface. God understands this, of course, which is the reason for the promise in Jeremiah. God promises a day when God's law will no longer be an external standard that we are trying to follow but will be written on our hearts. In the aftermath of his sin with Bathsheba, David cries out in Psalm 51 for God's forgiveness and a new heart. The New Testament readings begin to focus our minds toward the end of Jesus' life. God's transformative work comes at a cost to God through the death of his Son, who suffered in obedience but through his death was glorified.

QUESTIONS AND SUGGESTIONS FOR REFLECTION

- Read Jeremiah 31:31-34. What are the covenant relationships in your life? How do you fulfill your part of the covenant with God?
- Read Psalm 51:1-12. What are the things that clutter your heart, limiting your availability to fully love?
- Read Hebrews 5:5-10. When have you offered your prayers "with loud cries and tears" as Jesus did? How does knowing Jesus' vulnerability impact your life of faith?
- Read John 12:20-33. How does this example of the grain of wheat help you to understand Jesus' crucifixion and death?

Writer and teacher around bodies, gender, parenting, and simplicity; author of *12 Tiny Things, Play Like a Girl,* and *How Coffee Saved My Life*; host of the *Unlikely Conversations* podcast; works at Bethlehem Lutheran Church Twin Cities and The Loft Literary Center.

God is God, and we are not. God makes promises, and we break them. We do things that break God's trust. Yet God keeps coming back to us. God sees us in all our human frailty and offers us abundant love. In this passage, Jeremiah invites us to remember the long, unfolding love story of God and God's people. The Israelites, our ancestors, were slaves until the Lord led them to freedom. God gently took them by the hand, assuming the posture of husband. Think about wedding vows. It's not just "I love you" or "I am in love with you" but "I promise to love you. No matter what."

Yet the Israelites fell short. Freedom from slavery was not enough. Being taken by the hand was not enough. Being loved like a spouse was not enough. The Israelites broke the covenant. They worshiped other gods. They complained and got greedy. They forgot their history and their savior. It sounds too familiar doesn't it? We fall short. What have we been complaining about? What have we been worshiping? What part of our history have we forgotten?

Broken promises hurt, creating distance between two parties, and requiring time to build up trust again. God could give up on us; yet God chooses healing, reconciliation, restoration, and love. When God makes covenants with us, it creates limitations on God's power that allow for an authentic, loving relationship where we have agency. We are free to break God's heart. God comes to us today, in all of our brokenness, and offers us promise. We belong. God is our God. We are God's people. We can leave our complaining and greed at God's feet and live into the joy of freedom. God is available to us to know and love.

God of unending love, thank you for your steadfast presence. Thank you for offering us freedom again and again. Help us to live into that freedom and to dwell in your love. Amen.

Twice in seven verses the psalmist's plea to God is, "Wash me." Isn't this, indeed, what forgiveness feels like? I think about a long, warm shower after a run in the bitter winter cold. I remember splashing with delighted kids in wading pools on hot summer days, or scrubbing dirt off my skin after physical labor. Washing brings refreshment and renewal.

I usually wash myself. Letting someone wash you requires deep vulnerability. I remember playful baths as a young child, my dad scrubbing behind my ears. When I was a teenager, after a horrible elbow injury, my mom helped me bathe. When I was pregnant and bloated, my spouse washed my swollen feet, and I cried. It felt like mercy. Jesus washed the feet of his disciples in an intimate moment of blessing. *Wash me.* We take on a passive posture. We must be still and welcome God's tender and nurturing attention. We must be willing to let God see us naked, to find dirt stuck in our creases and under our nails. Yet if we are willing, God is sure to offer mercy. We will find rest in God's soothing touch. We will rise anew and clean, filled with the joy of resurrection.

Lent is a time of spiritual check-in. It is a season to slow down and reflect, to get quiet enough to see our toxic patterns and hear God whispering to us. Through transformational practices like prayer, fasting, meditation, and confession we can experience renewal. God washes us clean. Glowing with newness and illuminated with grace, we go out in the world as living examples of good news. Death does not have the last word.

God of mercy, I stand before you, naked in all my imperfection. You know my smallness and the ways I hide and hurt. Wash me clean. Gently offer me the relief, renewal, and new life that comes with your forgiveness and love. Amen.

In Lent, there is an opportunity to dust off the soul, declutter the spirit. There is dignity in doing the spring cleaning of our very being. We live in a society that values independence. We often do our core work behind closed doors, alone, but it need not be so. The psalmist highly acknowledges that we desperately need God. If are still and open and willing, God can cleanse our hearts and offer us renewal. The pleading of the psalm is intimate. To create a clean heart, God gets a good look at the dirt piling up in the corners.

Being human is humbling. We make mistakes. We hurt one another. We hurt God. The spiritual practice of praying the Psalms reminds us that there is newness every day. We can take a deep breath and inhale new life, new opportunity, a fresh start, little resurrections. Some days it will feel like we are wallowing in the pain of our crushed bones. Other days we will smile, remembering that crushed bones can still rejoice. If we try on the willing spirit of the psalmist, joy is ours for the taking.

Pleading "Do not cast me from your presence" and "Do not take your holy spirit from me" names the fact that God is here. We are filled with the Spirit. We belong. These truths, profound in their simplicity, are often muted and obscured by our fast and full lives. We forget and think we're alone. We put our heads down and go through the motions of our lives. Dwelling consciously in God's presence—awake to the wonder of this moment, with an open spirit—is what allows God the space to fill us, enliven us, and restore us.

God of renewal, take a feather duster to my being today. I have a willing spirit, and I long for newness. Declutter my soul so that I may bask in your presence and hear the joy and gladness of all that is holy. Amen.

We are in the days of our flesh. We are alive, in bodies, experiencing the world. How awesome to contemplate the glory of God having days of flesh as well! Jesus experienced the world as a person with a body. He prayed to God as we do. He offered up prayers to a God that was separate from him yet was him. Jesus cried loudly and shed real tears. He suffered.

We worship a God who, in his days of flesh, did not become a high priest, did not live a life of worldly power and glory. Jesus was a son. He was a beloved child. He belonged to God. Whether it is our birth parents or found family, we all crave that parental love, that primal belonging. We often strive for earthly glory, to be recognized as successful; but at the end of the day we want to belong. We want arms to wrap us up, contain us, comfort us, and remind us of who we are and whose we are. Jesus extends this gift to us. He suffered and died so that when we are suffering, when we are dying, we can cry out to our God and trust that God calls us beloved children.

God saw Jesus' suffering, heard his cries, and called his body on the cross divine. God invites us to come down from our pedestals and curl up into our identities as children of God.

God saw Jesus' life, death, and resurrection as reverent submission, as divine obedience. When we live into our identity as beloved children of a suffering and life-giving God, being obedient and submitting can be claiming power in weakness and living as loving and loved creatures.

God, you hear our cries and see our beauty. You love us as your beloved children. Helps us to curl up in belonging and to embrace the power that comes with weakness. Be with us in our suffering and becoming. Amen.

Wheat has so much to teach us. My spouse has three strands of wheat tattooed on his forearm. For him, it captures the idea of *shalom*, God's reign of peace, where everyone has enough. He bakes bread, and his jobs work to alleviate hunger. I watch him knead the bread, tending to it throughout the day to make sure it rises. I watch him smell the finished loaf, cut it, and serve it to us warm, nourishing us with care. Baking bread keeps him in touch with the earth. It reminds him that he is a creature, part of the magnificent web and cycle of life.

A single grain of wheat is just that, unless it dies. What are the grains of wheat you are clinging to? What in you needs to die? How can you tend to the soil so that your life bears fruit?

My sister is a nurse in the neuro/cardio ICU unit of a hospital. We lived together as young adults. At times, I would notice her walking through her days with a heaviness. It usually meant she had a patient with a tragic story. One night she said to me, "Death is not the worst thing that can happen to you."

We are taught to fight death as the enemy, but we forget the paradox of faith. Death can bring freedom. Death can create space for something new to be born. Jesus tells the Greeks that those who want to serve him must follow him and go where he goes. This is a challenge for us. Where is Jesus? What does it mean to follow Jesus today? If we wander toward the margins, where folks are broken and dying, that is where we belong, where we will see the face of the risen Christ.

> *God of new life, help me to dwell among the fallen wheat. Give me the courage to die daily, trusting in your everlasting life. Draw me toward the margins, where I can commune with Christ. Amen.*

Here we have one of those moments in the Gospels where we get a partial glimpse of the Trinity at work. Jesus and God are separate but connected. There is clear distinction but a divine connection. Jesus is a human, having a fully human experience. His soul is troubled. He does not want to die. Yet he understands how the power of God is glorified in weakness, in death. Jesus stands opposed to worldly power and offers an alternative. It is all a little too much for us to handle.

Of course we are confused. Is it thunder? An angel? We are still fighting over who God is and what God's voice is saying. We disagree. We limit God with our earthly metaphors. We project our human-made systems of power onto the divine. We can't imagine a glory that transcends the earth. We give answers to a question that is altogether misguided.

"And when I am lifted up out of the earth . . . " Jesus models obedience. He does not try to save himself. That does not mean he sits on the couch eating chips. No, he teaches and heals and restores. He also knows when to let go. God is doing the lifting. God is giving the glory. What would it look like for us to be dependent on God? To allow God to do the lifting? To be still enough to hear the thunder and the angels?

Jesus addresses our petty disagreements with an image of his rising and embracing us. What will it feel like to be drawn to Jesus? That belonging, that sense of peace and comfort is extended to all people. The last word is a love that covers all. We will be embraced. We will be home.

God of thunder and loving embraces, draw us to yourself. Shower us with a sense of belonging. May the sense of home bring with it the courage to let go of worldly power and turn to you again and again. Amen.

Fifth Sunday in Lent

God's new covenant is endlessly exciting. It is dripping with good news. It has consequences for our bodies and beings. And it's a promise we cannot reciprocate. As we keep score and hold grudges, God remembers our sins no more. As we create a social hierarchy, God extends God's love to all people. As we create limiting binaries of right and wrong, in and out, good and bad, God is accessible and available equally.

"I will be their God, and they shall be my people." Repeat this throughout your day. It is all we need. There is no longer least or greatest. We are forgiven. We shall know God. Broken, we belong. Broken, we are beloved. All of us, without exception. In the joy of belonging to a loving God who is available to all people, we can shift our energy from binaries to radical inclusion. We can work toward wholeness in ourselves and our communities.

It is easy to forget that God lays the law on our hearts. God's handwriting is in each of our bodies. There are physical markings of this spiritual gift, lest we stray and forget. Jeremiah's words remind to look at our own hearts. Read the handwriting so beautiful and distinct that it can only be our Creator's. Our God is the God of the Israelites, the God who takes us by the hand and leads us to freedom. Our God is a God who forgives, who comes back, who gives us second chances to live in the light of God's promise. Our God is a God whose love extends to all people, whose love washes over all of us abundantly until we know through and through who we are and whose we are.

God of promise, may I be open to your grace today. Illuminate the law that you have written on my heart. Inspire me to live the new covenant and strive to know you more fully. Amen.

The Plot

MARCH 22–28, 2021 • GEORGE HOVANESS DONIGIAN

SCRIPTURE OVERVIEW: This week's readings prepare us for Palm Sunday, a joyous event. Jesus rides into Jerusalem on a donkey, a symbol of kingship in ancient Israel. The people greet him with loud acclamations. He is coming in the name of the Lord! Standing along the road leading into Jerusalem, how could anyone imagine what would happen that following week? Wasn't Jesus finally going to manifest the fullness of God's power, take his place on the throne of David, and overthrow the Romans? No, because that was not his mission. He came not to build an earthly kingdom but to lay aside his rights. He came to be glorified by being humiliated . . . for us. He came to suffer and die . . . for us.

QUESTIONS AND SUGGESTIONS FOR REFLECTION

- Read Isaiah 50:4-9a. How does your faith community reflect the servant in this reading?
- Read Psalm 118:1-2, 19-29. How are you rejoicing in this day that the Lord has made? How are you blessing "the one who comes in the name of the Lord"?
- Read Philippians 2:5-11. How does this hymn of the early Christian community speak to you as you prepare for Holy Week?
- Read Mark 11:1-11, 15-18. Spend some time imagining the scene of Jesus entering Jerusalem as described in the reading. Where are you in the scene? What do you see? What do you hear around you? What do you feel as you watch this event?

Ordained United Methodist clergy living in South Carolina; author of several books, including *Three Prayers You'll Want to Pray* and *A World Worth Saving*; enjoys playing jazz saxophone and piano.

The chief priests and the scribes were looking for a way to arrest Jesus by stealth and kill him." Later in this chapter we read that Judas Iscariot went to these same priests to betray Jesus. We see a labyrinth of intrigue as the religious establishment looks for a way to be rid of the problem of Jesus. Winding his way to the anti-Jesus establishment is Judas, disciple of Jesus. What a strange place to begin a week's devotions! The plot by the religious establishment to rid themselves of Jesus presents us with several dilemmas.

1. Was the plot of the religious establishment an instrument of God or an effort to cleanse the culture of a disruptive influence, or was it an act of evil that was turned upside-down by God?

2. Were the plotters loyal to their understanding of holy traditions more than their understanding of God's love?

I tend to agree with those who recognize that the plotting against Jesus was done by those who wanted to cleanse the culture of a disruptive influence and that God turned those circumstances upside-down.

Those who plotted against Jesus offer a lesson to all who attempt to defend God by cleansing culture of what they perceive to be evil. Whether we think of Jean Calvin's iconoclasm in Geneva or the efforts of more recent preachers and politicians to redefine a nation as a religious state, these efforts call into question our understanding of culture and faith.

We also see the beginning of the divine plot in Jesus' words concerning the woman who poured ointment on his head: "She has anointed my body . . . for its burial." The statement offers a foretaste and a reminder that goodness is stronger than evil and that the seeds of resurrection are planted somewhat discreetly in our midst.

Holy God, help us to be with Jesus this week. Remind us that you transform the evil we meet into goodness. Amen.

The rejected stone is now the cornerstone. Let us rejoice! Imagine a group of pilgrims standing before the walled old city of Jerusalem singing, "Open to me the gates of righteousness, that I may enter through them and give thanks to the Lord." They have traveled on the annual pilgrimage and have prayed and reflected on the compassion of God and on their history as a nation. Imagine their joy as they enter the city and go to the Temple.

One sin of our age is the lack of time for reflection or sabbath rest. Busyness distracts and diverts our focus on spirituality, ministry, and mission. Let Psalm 118 recall you to that purpose.

Psalm 118 is the last of the psalm sequence known as the Egyptian Hallel because they celebrate the liberation from slavery in Egypt. These psalms continue to be chanted or sung during the great pilgrim festivals: Shavuot, Sukkot, and Passover. The sequence begins with a prayer of praise that remembers that the Lord "raises the poor from the dust, and lifts the needy . . . to make them sit with princes" (Ps. 113:7-8). The Hallel sequence ends with a psalm that celebrates Israel's deliverance from battle or war. Today we rightly prepare for Palm/Passion Sunday by reading Psalm 118 and remembering God's deliverance of Israel.

As we move closer to the intricate plot, verses 22-23 may jump out and shimmer. The Messianic intent of the words may be familiar, and yet each reading brings a freshness. We marvel that God uses the one rejected by those in authority to build the new kingdom. But that is the essence of God's master plot: to turn upside-down the expectations of those in power and to lift up the needy and the oppressed. In turn we join the pilgrim song, "Blessed is the one who comes in the name of the Lord."

God, in the marvelous ways of your love, you transform our lives as you transformed the life of the Rejected One. Lift the lives of all who are needy and oppressed, and make your pathways plain for all. Amen.

The Lord helps the servant despite the effort by others to humiliate the servant.

Christians see Jesus in the four Servant Songs. The third Servant Song begins by describing the servant as having the tongue of a teacher, which points us to the parables and other teachings of Jesus the rabbi.

We also understand the Servant Songs as descriptive of a community and of the nation of Israel. How does the community teach? What does the nation chosen by God offer the world? The quest for justice, an understanding of God's loving mercy, and God's salvation are three of the many gifts God's chosen people taught and teach the world.

How do these words about the Servant connect with the church as community and what it may teach the world? As I write, the global church is divided politically, culturally, and in a host of other ways. Some observers would say that the church is not teaching the way of Christ as much as it demonstrates the values of a secular perspective. Others argue that the separation of the secular from religious tradition is not possible and that Christianity always reflects the culture in which it is grounded.

If Christianity reflects the culture, then let it reflect the cultural understanding of the servant community of Israel and the community of Christ in the New Testament. Let it reflect love and justice, mercy and salvation. Let it reflect the Servant who listened "morning by morning" to the Lord. Let Christianity reflect the way of the servant and the way of Christ who affirmed God's providence. Moving further into Isaiah 50, verses 10-11 tell us that the Servant walks through darkness by trusting in God.

Our times seem perplexing and full of conflict. Even so, God continues to plot the Resurrection, and we wait to see the fullness of that revelation.

God, may my life reflect the love and grace of your Servant Jesus Christ. Amen.

I trust in you, O LORD . . . My times are in your hand."

Psalm 31 is a psalm of lament, and we see the depth of that lamentation in verses 9-16. While the psalmist cries out about wasting away in grief and sorrow, there is also a basic affirmation: "I trust in you, O LORD . . . My times are in your hand; deliver me from the hand of my enemies and persecutors. Let your face shine upon your servant . . ." In the lament of Psalm 31, we see a foreshadowing of Jesus in his last week.

We tend to shy away from the notion of lament, possibly because this depth of grief seems too intimate for our time. We reserve lament for times of grief, especially death.

I come from the Armenian Orthodox tradition. The Armenian Gregory of Narek (Grigor Narekatsi) wrote a book of ninety-five prayers in the year 1001 that has been actively circulated since then. Armenians know his work as The Lamentations of Narek. (Thomas Samuelian's translation is the best version in English, titled *Speaking with God from the Depths of the Heart.*) In many of these prayers, Gregory writes of his sense of brokenness and how he feels that he does not measure up to his calling as a disciple of Christ. For example, here he laments and pleads: "Accept with sweetness, almighty Lord, my bitter prayers. Look with pity upon my mournful face. Dispel, all-bestowing God, my shameful sadness" (Prayer 12, C). Yet always in the prayers of Narekatsi is the appeal to the mercy of God, leading to his title as "The Doctor of Mercy," bestowed by Pope Francis who declared Gregory a Doctor of the Church.

An honest assessment of our lives may well point us to a renewed acquaintance with lament—not to live with a deep sense of sorrow but to live with an awareness of our brokenness and our need for mercy.

God, we are grateful that your love includes patience, gentleness, salvation, and glory for all people and for all time. Amen.

The Plot

Christ emptied himself, taking the form of a slave," (AP).

I often express dismay that the Bible does not include musical notation for its many hymns and songs. My imagination wants to hear the early church sing the kenosis hymn of Philippians 2. In 1870 Caroline Neal based the hymn known as "At the Name of Jesus" (UMH, no. 168) on this text. Today would our musical version of the Philippians text feel more up-tempo, or would it offer opportunity for gentle reflection? Would it feel more like a dirge or a march? The answer probably depends on which portion of the hymn we would emphasize. Do we stress the emptying that we meet in Christ or the sense of future triumph?

We know today's text as the hymn of kenosis, based on the use of the verb form translated as "emptied" in verse 7. Paul invites his audience to become like Christ who did not clutch equality with God but emptied himself to become a servant and a slave. Here we see the development of the upside-down plot as it moves closer toward its surprise ending.

How do we let the same mind that was in Christ be in us? Just as Paul and the Gospel writers knew the end of the story that they wrote and preached, so we have a sense of the end of our story. We are moving toward Christ. A Statement of Faith of the United Church of Canada reminds us: "In life, in death, in life beyond death, God is with us" (UMH, no. 883). We also try to shed the protective nature of ego, remembering the vastness of the creation and the intimate nature of God's love for each one within the creation. We remember that our mission is large but we are small. We sit in silence and open ourselves to God.

What do you need to empty from your life? What gets in your way when you seek to serve? How will you let it go?

To Jesus Christ, all power and love, majesty and glory in exaltation forever. Amen.

The plot to kill Jesus, the Last Supper, travel to Gethsemane, betrayal, trial, denial, Pilate, crucifixion, death, burial.

Reading these chapters of Mark may take more time than the usual reading of scripture connected with *The Upper Room Disciplines*. Read them unhurriedly. A slow reading of this text yields spiritual treasures that do not come from speed-reading or a quick summary. Take time to ingest the text, letting it become a larger part of your life. Which portion seems to attract the most attention? Which portion seems to shine and invite deeper reflection?

The plot to eliminate the public nuisance of Jesus comes to a head here. The plot, like all evil deeds, is planned in secret and with caution lest the people riot. A few verses later, we see the negotiation of Judas Iscariot and the chief priests to betray Jesus.

Jesus, however, continues to go about his ministry and mission. He prepares for the Passover, remembering God's act of liberation for the Hebrew people in Egypt and then offering his disciples a new meal of holy remembrance. Then Jesus and the disciples sing a Hallel psalm before going to the Mount of Olives. There we see the betrayal of Jesus by Judas and the eventual desertion of Jesus by the disciples. Then, in rapid order, we see the events that lead to Jesus' crucifixion and burial.

Throughout these chapters, we see the plot to get rid of Jesus. We gain slight hints of the divine counterplot when Jesus speaks of the anointing of his body before burial and of the blood of the covenant. We know, with the turn of a page or so that we will read of the empty tomb and the Resurrection. But now we wait and watch. Our task is like that of the disciples at Gethsemane. We stay awake and alert to the nudges of the Holy Spirit.

God, open our hearts and minds to the ever-expanding ways your love enters the world. Amen.

The Plot 111

PALM/PASSION SUNDAY

Jesus enters Jerusalem in a triumphant procession and then cleans the Temple of those who have perverted it.

Now it begins. Now we are at the beginning of the eight monumental days that end with the Day of Resurrection. Now we see crowds rallying around Jesus. They bring their understanding and expectation of the Messiah as he enters Jerusalem. Many may have expected the Messiah to liberate Israel from Roman occupation. They sing and shout words from Psalm 118, one of the Hallel Psalms, to welcome Jesus and to prepare the way for the "coming kingdom of our ancestor David." With such expectations on this day, it is no surprise that these same people would later express bitterness and unrealized hopes when the authorities arrest Jesus. Instead of receiving the reality Jesus presented, they projected their agendas on him.

We may also project our own agendas on others and on Jesus, though perhaps not to the level of those who welcomed Jesus into Jerusalem. Lines from the long form of the Serenity Prayer offer this corrective:

Taking, as Jesus did, this sinful world as it is,
Not as I would have it.

Seeing and taking the world as it is rather than as what we project remains a challenge. Our egos want to create safety by projecting a world based on images from the past or on future fantasies. We see this at work in those who welcomed Jesus as they hoped for a return to the Davidic kingdom or for an end of the Roman occupation. When we allow ego to make such projections, we fail to see present reality.

Jesus stayed firmly grounded in the present. Thus he entered Jerusalem and demonstrated love for all he met on this day and in all the days that would come.

God, help me to see the reality of our world as Jesus did. Amen.

Stretched Out

MARCH 29–APRIL 4, 2021 • RACHEL G. HACKENBERG

SCRIPTURE OVERVIEW: This week's readings take us through the depths but then into the eternal light. We walk each step with Jesus, who suffers betrayal, abandonment, and death. But it is more than that. In his suffering, Jesus also enters into the brokenness of our human condition and feels our pain, such that on the Cross he even feels abandonment by God. He walks through the valley of the shadow of death because of God's amazing, reckless love for us. This is the power of Holy Week. But that is not the end of the story. Jesus' steps do not end at the Cross, for he walks out of the tomb! Now we can follow in his steps and participate in his new life. He is risen indeed!

QUESTIONS AND SUGGESTIONS FOR REFLECTION

- Read Isaiah 42:1-9. How is God calling you to be a light? How does God empower you to follow God's call to you?
- Read Psalm 70. What is prompting you to reach out for God's help today? In what ways do you ask for that help?
- Read John 13:1-17, 31b-35. What acts of service does Jesus' example in this reading move you to perform? Choose one act you will do today in remembrance of Jesus' humility.
- Read John 20:1-18. When have you, in the light of God's love, let go of the way you thought your life would be in order to live a different reality that God intended for you?

United Church of Christ minister; author of *Writing to God* and co-author of *Denial Is My Spiritual Practice (and Other Failures of Faith)*.

Death is coming. We notice it in the signs and stories of Lent. We feel it in the pleas of the psalms. We brace ourselves for it in the building drama of Holy Week. Death is coming.

But death takes its definition from life. Without an experience of life, death loses its relevance. Without a vision for the life that was and the life that could be, the tragedies of life "as is" lack urgency. If we do not remember the summer and hope for the spring, we might make peace with the frozen grave of winter.

In the wake of the death and devastation of the Babylonian exile, Isaiah reminds the exiled people of interminable life. The promise of life after exile is made by the same God who first gave the people life and breath. The temporary death of their freedom cannot overcome the life already given and still to come. The hope of a leader who will cultivate justice is extended by the same God who unfurled the earth so it could bear fruit. The promise of a beacon to relieve despair is made by the same God who stretched stars across the heavens. Death and darkness cannot extinguish them. Death's poison cannot taint life's growth.

Yes, there has been death, sings the prophet, but remember the breadth and beauty of life. Remember the holy wildness from which life sprouted. Remember freedom that beckons even from a dimly burning lamp. Remember the promise that God holds us and keeps us.

Yes, death is coming this Holy Week, but remember that God's love is already stretched out to the heavens. God's faithfulness is already whispered between the clouds. Like perfume poured out extravagantly over dusty feet, God has poured the fullness of life across our dusty selves with the promise that more life is still to come.

For these reasons, O God, we praise you even when death approaches. For these reasons, we celebrate the abundance of life already given and look forward to the beauty that awaits us. Amen.

Life is not for the faint of heart. The stresses, insults, and injuries of the world splay our spirits and batter our flesh. We quickly pray the prayer that Jesus rejected: "Please save me from this hour!" We fall to the couch and despair with the prophet: "Our labors and energies have been spent in vain" (AP).

In moments of caffeination and pride, we might leap into life boasting that we can do all things, be all things, and change all things just as God has called us to do; but quickly we tire once again. We curl ourselves into God's refuge and ask to be replenished with youthful audacity, too wizened by the world's cynicism to find God's glory in our weakness.

The servant leader of Isaiah 49:1-7 recalls such a moment of faintness, when the work of restoring the people to their freedom and their faith seemed too great a task. Being called by God to the work, being equipped by God for the work seemed insufficient. God needed to also be the strength for the work.

Barely does this confession cross the servant leader's lips when God responds: "Restoring the people to their freedom and their faith is too small a task. I envision more than the nurture of one community; I envision the healing of the world! I will stretch you out like light, far beyond your limits. I will be reflected throughout the nations, and my faithfulness will shame their strength" (AP).

In my own faintness of heart, God's increased charge to the servant leader makes me weary just to read it. Who is strong enough to reach all nations? Who is energetic enough to go to the ends of the earth? Who is wise enough to impact global change?

Then I notice: God doesn't call the servant leader to be strong or industrious or wise. God calls the servant leader to be light.

The world stretches us thin, O God, but you stretch us out like light that refracts and reflects without dimming. Keep our faith light, make us children of light, and give us as light to your glory. Amen.

Stretched Out   115

The posture of pain and betrayal is defensive: back turned, shoulders hunched, head bowed, knees tucked in, arms crossed. We curl our skeleton around our soft core for its protection. The fetal position is not only defensive but also comforting, a reminder of the wombs that held us and the arms that cradled us. Interestingly, we adopt a similar posture around our smart phones—shoulders high, chins bent, arms up—whether in defense or for comfort may be an unconscious reaction.

By contrast, the tone of Psalm 70 invokes an image of an open posture, a body reaching out and up. The psalmist stretches out with a plea for help, heart extended to grasp deliverance. The seekers fill their lungs to sing and shout with praise. Meanwhile, those who sought to shame the psalmist are themselves turned and bent with shame. Those who wanted the psalmist to slouch and cringe instead have dishonor heaped upon their heads.

The grace and help of God cause a reversal of the body's posture from defensive to celebratory. The psalmist's need becomes a reason to lift the head, roll back the shoulders, and open the mouth to sing. When enemies come, the body has no reason to hide. When insults are spit out, they do not weigh down the righteous. When trouble stirs, God can still be glorified.

Even with a troubled spirit, Jesus stretches out to share bread across the table with Judas.

We consider Jesus. We consider the psalmist. And instead of recoiling from the fear that wearies us, we stretch out with a courageous heart. We open our ears to the lessons of each morning. We stand, unburdened, alongside the cloud of witnesses. We do not tire of breaking bread with our enemies. We take the vulnerable, daring posture of deliverance.

Lord God, will you help us when we are defensive? Will you deliver us when we are troubled? Will you comfort our hearts so that we might find the courage and perseverance to lift our heads and sing your praises? Amen.

MAUNDY THURSDAY

The signs are as plain as blood on a doorpost. The hints of betrayal are as obvious as a kiss from Judas. On Maundy Thursday, however, the more subtle indications of upheaval and reversal begin to be stretched out by the Gospel writer. The teacher puts on a servant's towel. The leader breaks open with love. The Light of God gets his hands dirty by washing feet.

If the disciples have had illusions of greatness, the sight of a stripped-down Jesus quells such aspirations. If the power of miraculous healing has gone to their heads, the power of love at their feet teaches them a different lesson. The one they have followed across land and sea, through crowds and up mountains— this one washes their feet as the journey comes toward its end.

Why not also wash their hands and heads? For that matter, why not also wash people of illnesses? Why not wash the world of its greed? Why not build a basin with an eternal fountain so that all people might be washed? How often I have wished for the power of faith to be a solve-everything power, making all things clean in such a way that they cannot get messy again!

Instead, Jesus pours just enough water into a basin to wash one pair of feet, and then another pair of feet, and then another. He commands the disciples—he commands us—to do no more and no less than this. Wash one pair of feet at a time. Love the person in front of you, every time they are in front of you. Then love the next person in front of you. Break bread with the person to your left. Break bread with the person to your right.

"Love one another," Jesus says. He doesn't say, "Fix one another." He doesn't say, "Wash the world from head to toe."

Jesus, your power stretches out in love, but so often we stretch ourselves out for the love of power. We want you to fix all things from the beginning, but you call us to love until the very end. Fill our basins, and we will do as you have shown us. Amen.

GOOD FRIDAY

A familiar story stretches out before us today. The inevitability of the events might cause us to skim the passage. But the belabored details call us to pay attention to the agony of each moment, to notice the standstill of time in each conversation, to watch Peter's impulsive actions as if they are in slow motion, to feel the disciples holding their breath through it all.

Notice how the flickering light of torches distorts the beauty of the garden. Consider why Peter attacks the man enslaved to the high priest—and how futile it is for Peter, overwhelmed and helpless, to injure Malchus, who is equally disempowered.

Feel time stretch out across the three trials of Jesus: the religious trial, the civic trial, and then the public trial. Recall your own experience of an insult or injustice that repeated itself as though it were unashamed to so blatantly cause you pain.

Pay attention to the complications of each relationship. One of the disciples knows the high priest and is waved through to his courtyard. Peter, by contrast, is stopped until the other disciple vouches for him; once inside, the two mingle in different crowds, with Peter warming himself alongside slaves and police.

Each scene yawns like the mouth of a roaring lion. Each breath catches with fresh rejection. Each wound seems to be its own timeless horror. Each expression of love becomes an anchor against the tidal wave of pain and death.

The Gospel writer doesn't attempt to give meaning to the terrible events. Meaning is usually hard to find (and inappropriate to assign) in the midst of overwhelming pain. The writer only asserts parenthetically: "This is true" (AP).

My God, my God, we are stretched out in pain, weary from groaning. Discouraged, our hearts melt. Ensnared, our words escape us. You who know these heartaches acutely, do not abandon us to our agony, we pray. Amen.

Holy Saturday

Into the grief and silence of death, the prophet whispers: "Drink plenty of water. Get something to eat. Remember that the rain will still come, and the seed will still grow; there will be grains to harvest and fresh dough to knead" (AP).

The prophet gathers the exiles in Babylon, the land that feels like it has dealt a fatal blow to the Israelites' faith and culture. Daily living in Babylon is a spiritual wasteland, an empty table, a failed promise. Yet the prophet imagines a day when the people will again be a testament of God's covenant. Until that time, they must not give in to death and despair. "Seek God, even in this foreign land, and take pleasure in the food on your tables."

Significant moments are best accompanied by food shared in community. At a table of fellowship, we find strength for what lies behind and for what may come ahead. A bit of bread keeps our spirits grounded when we might faint with anguish. A cup of water refreshes when our minds might rage against sensory inundation. A shared camaraderie draws us beyond ourselves when we might be tempted to withdraw into spiritual cocoons.

Eat. Drink. Be together. And remember, the prophet says, the work of God is stretched out across time and creation. The word of God is always unfolding, always planting and nourishing, always dying and renewing, always carving a new path like water through a rock, like the Hebrew people across the Red Sea.

When the sea flees from its usual bed, stay nourished and watch for life. When the mountains skip and the rocks melt, drink deeply and be at peace. When death overshadows and menaces, stay together and wait for God.

Your goodness stretches to the heavens, O God, even when clouds distort our view. Your promises water the earth, even when seeds are slow to grow. Keep us nourished and keep us together while we wait. Amen.

EASTER

This is the day. You have awoken in it. Your breath is still in your lungs—stretch your ribcage outward with a deep inhale and press it inward with a long exhale.

This is the day. You are part of love. Your past is a piece of love's history, and the moments ahead of you are elements of love's continuation. Without you, love is not the same.

This is the day. Perhaps yesterday feels as though it has predetermined today with lingering tasks or regrets. Perhaps tomorrow's uncertainty has interjected itself into today, blurring this day's wonder. But the grace of this day, by itself, is not in vain.

Today two of Jesus' disciples rush in and out of the tomb to witness the absence of a body; they are harried by yesterday and worried for tomorrow. But Mary Magdalene lingers, allowing herself time to pay attention to the empty tomb and to her emotions. It's as though Jesus has been taken from her all over again.

This is the day when grief and glory collide, stretching our spirits to understand hope. This is the day when mystery and intimacy interweave, stretching our perspective on life. This is the day when miracles and fear comingle, until we stretch the legs of faith and run with joy.

This is the day when an impossible stone is rolled out of place, when the lost is found, when the story continues beyond death. Like the angels who keep Mary company as she weeps, life and love keep us company through death and grief. Love calls our name. Life reminds us not to cling too tightly.

We are strained and stretched, distended and revived by the drama of Easter—by the drama of life. But this day, and each day, invites our joyful confession: "I have seen the Lord."

You are marvelous in all the world, O God most holy. You are joy to our spirits, O Christ most lovely. You are peace to our living, O Spirit most gracious. Alleluia! Amen.

Resurrection in Body and Spirit

APRIL 5–11, 2021 • BRIAN R. BODT

SCRIPTURE OVERVIEW: Easter promises us the possibility of new life in Christ, but what should that life look like? Scripture makes clear that one sign of union with God is unity with each other. How wonderful it is, the psalmist says, when there is peace among brothers and sisters. Unity and peace do not mean simply the lack of conflict but proactive care for one another. The Christians in Acts lived out this care in a practical way by giving of their material means to help one another. John in his epistle tells us that this fellowship is ultimately modeled on the fellowship we share with God and Christ, while in his Gospel, John teaches that belief in Jesus the Messiah is what binds us all together in this new life.

QUESTIONS AND SUGGESTIONS FOR REFLECTION

- Read Acts 4:32-35. In what ways does your Christian community extend generosity to those within and those beyond the community?
- Read Psalm 133. How do you experience God's extravagant love for you? What is your response to this love?
- Read 1 John 1:1–2:2. What experience of Christ have you "heard . . . seen . . . looked at . . . touched"? How do you share your experience of the risen Christ with others?
- Read John 20:19-31. How do you relate to Thomas's desire for tangible proof of the Resurrection?

United Methodist pastor who retired after forty years in the New York Annual Conference; madly in love with his wife, Carol Galloway; father of four sons; grandfather; enjoys running half marathons, skiing, tennis, and working on model trains; currently serving Hamden Plains UMC in Hamden, CT.

Y ou have to manipulate the scar." Nearly three decades ago I had cervical neck surgery requiring a horizontal incision on my neck above the collarbone. Post-surgical treatment required physical therapy. The incision, the entry point for the surgeon's skill, had healed but left a stiff, uncomfortable scar. When I told the physical therapist about this discomfort, she asked, "Have you touched your scar?" I said, "No, I am repulsed by it." I have never forgotten her reply, "You have to manipulate the scar."

Thomas has no such hesitation about scars as he encounters the news about Christ's resurrection. "Unless I see the mark of the nails in his hands, and put my finger in the mark of the nails and my hand in his side, I will not believe," he says. Thomas is "all in" with this Resurrection news—as long as he can manipulate the scar.

One problem with Christian faith is our tendency to over-spiritualize. We speak of divine things and holy things and things of heaven, but too often we disconnect them from things of earth. Jesus taught in parables to make the infinite finite. When Jesus taught his disciples to pray, he taught them to ask, "Thy kingdom come *on earth* as it is in heaven" (emphasis mine). Jesus *breathed* on the disciples. Breath is what you have when you're alive and what you don't when you're not. Christianity that promises only "pie in the sky when you die by and by" robs resurrection of its power in the world in which we live. Like manipulating a scar, earthy faith isn't always pretty. Yet it is the connection between the spiritual promise of eternal life and our daily life in the physical world.

Repulsed by your scars? Try a little of Thomas's boldness.

Lord of life, fill us with gratitude for physical life as a portal to appreciate the joys of life eternal, that we may glorify the One whose resurrection secures it forever, even Jesus Christ our Lord. Amen.

Sight and Sound Theatres in Lancaster, PA, and Branson, MO, offer live presentations of stories of the Bible. Folks from my part of the country travel, literally by the busloads, to Pennsylvania Dutch country to be entertained and inspired by the sensory experience of these dramatic interpretations of the biblical narrative.

"We declare to you what was from the beginning, what we have heard, what we have seen with our eyes, what we have looked at and touched with our hands, concerning the word of life" declares the author of First John. The writer has had a wildly sensory experience of Jesus Christ and wants to share it. The purpose is so that the writer's (or the reader's) "joy may be complete."

Yet so much of our sensory experience is sensory overload. Rapid visual images, a cacophony of sounds, touch intended to be more titillating than tender—these underwhelm in their inability to deliver complete joy. But what if instead of withdrawing from our God-given senses or bemoaning the forces that overload them, we invite our senses to be channels of the holy? What if we fill our sensory experience with "the word of life"? What if we seek, just for today, to be "self-consciously sensory" for the sake of a passionate sharing of "what was from the beginning"; that is, the good news of Jesus Christ?

If we try that, we may find the way of our spiritual walk illumined by the assurance that "God is light and in [God] is no darkness at all."

Lord of our senses, open our eyes and ears, our nostrils, our taste buds, and the tips of our fingers as channels of your gift of love, that they may excite in us anticipation of the promise of eternal life, to the glory of your name, through Christ our Lord. Amen.

O God," prays the Christian in an old joke, "it's been a good day. I've been a good person today. I haven't said an ill word to anyone, or had an unkind thought, or even a selfish impulse. It's been a good day. But in a minute, I'm going to get out of bed . . . "

Confession and absolution are faith essentials leading to tangible grace in the bread and cup of Holy Communion. In the Communion liturgy of my youth, 1 John 1:9 and 2 John 2:2 were among several scriptures the celebrant spoke with the introduction, "Hear what comfortable words the scriptures say to all that truly turn to the Lord."

Bread. Cup. Sensory gifts Jesus provided on the night before his death when his closest followers would betray, deny, and abandon him. He washed their feet—another tactile sign of holy love—and offered them Eucharist, thanksgiving for a foretaste of the eternal banquet promised in his victory over death.

These gifts help us to see more clearly. Walking in the light as Christ is in the light, our steps illumined by divine radiance, gives us courage to believe that "if we confess our sins, he who is faithful and just will forgive our sins and cleanse us from all unrighteousness."

One more thing: Sometimes our senses are compromised. My late mother became blind due to macular degeneration. When she was introduced to my future wife, she said, "Come close" and held my beloved's face in her hands. With what peripheral vision remained, she declared, "You are beautiful." So says God, even to sinful us, when we confess.

> *Lord of forgiveness, strengthen us to know and tell the truth about ourselves, that we may be cleansed by your love and fed by bread and wine, a foretaste of your resurrection banquet. Through him who died and rose again, Christ our Lord. Amen.*

Sometimes I wonder how I've gone from the kid who loved to bring the hose into the sandbox and make mud pies to the adult who reads this passage and says, "Yuck!"

It's not the family unity that turns me off; it's the "precious oil on the head, running down upon the beard, on the beard of Aaron, running down on the collar of his robes." For crying out loud, get me a towel!

Yet this description is intended to deepen spiritual appreciation of the truth of "How very good and pleasant it is when kindred live together in unity." This psalm, one of fifteen "Psalms of Ascent" (120-134), was likely sung by religious pilgrims as they made their way up to Zion, Jerusalem, the holy city. The faithful recall the priesthood established (See Exodus 28 and 29.) and the ordination ritual of sacred oil poured on the consecrated priest: a moment of great solemnity and great joy. The oil is fragrant and soothing as the unity of kindred can be.

And the oil is precious as unity is precious—as in, "not found as often as we'd like." This is especially true of the kindred unity the psalm praises. I recently saw a meme that read: "The business advertised they'd treat me like family. I didn't shop there." The phrase *church family* is one I avoid for just that reason; the word *family* is weighted with meaning, not all of it "good and pleasant."

Nonetheless, the psalmist's words are aspirational, and we should not give up on the vision or the metaphor. My aversion to an oil-soaked collar is tempered by the thought that oil sticks to you. Hmmm . . . isn't that just what God wants—unity that sticks?

Forget the towel! Give me that oil, kindred unity, and the Lord's blessing of "life forevermore."

Lord of refreshment, bathe us in the fragrant oil of your reconciling love, that our unity may draw the world to Christ by the power of the Holy Spirit; One God, forever and ever. Amen.

The kindred unity of yesterday's aspirational psalm appears to be realized in this early experiment in Christian communal living: "Now the whole group of those who believed were of one heart and soul."

I wonder what that was like. We know the experiment didn't last, and it appears that the Jerusalem Church was in economic trouble in less than a generation. (See 2 Corinthians 8.)

Still, communal living has a long, honorable history in Christianity. From the early monastic communities to the Taizé community (formed in 1940 amid Nazi-occupied France) to the Koinonia Farm (formed in 1942 amid the racism and poverty of the southern U.S.), communal living subordinates the "I" to the "we" in human relationships. Perhaps such a lifestyle was part of what enabled the apostles to give "with great power . . . their testimony to the resurrection of the Lord Jesus."

Many such communities produce foods to feed the larger community and to fund their communal way of life. Bread, cheese, and wine are staples of what moderns call "social entrepreneurship" but which ancients practiced centuries before. Years ago my family visited Saint Benoit-du-Lac Abbey in the Eastern Townships of Quebec. It was my idea to go to hear Gregorian and Latin chant, but we left with maple syrup, cider, and cheese! If, as the old adage claims, the way to one's heart is through one's stomach then—though it grieves me to suggest it—perhaps we need more potlucks and less liturgy!

Psalm 34:8 invites us, "Taste and see that the LORD is good." As you eat your meals today, pray not only God's blessing on them but also that they may strengthen you to give, in words and life, a powerful testimony to Christ.

Lord of manna, bread, and all of life's sustenance, feed us in body and soul so that we may share with others the power of Christ's resurrection, to the glory of your holy name. Amen.

There was not a needy person among them" is an arresting thought. In my part of the country, especially in the warmer weather and at intersections and the end of highway exit ramps, there are needy people. Many hold signs asking for help.

When and how (although not whether) to care for others have been conundrums since the earliest days of the Christian faith. My study Bible on this passage notes that Christians took care of the needy among them. But early on, controversy arose over equity in the treatment of widows. (See Acts 6.)

This need of those I see asking for help on the roads contrasts sharply with my possession-filled life, notably railroad artifacts that delight my inner child. The scale models, lanterns, and hats are tactile delights but unquestionably unneeded possessions.

Did Joseph, whom the apostles named Barnabas, "need" the field he sold? Was it, in that agrarian culture, a luxury he did not need; or was the money laid at the disciples' feet an extravagance from his liquidated old-age nest egg? Was it a field he had farmed or romped on, like the "Ball Field" we sold as we liquidated my late father's property? We'll never know.

What we do know is that this "son of encouragement" gave and that we are to give. As the hymn reminds us:

To give and give, and give again, what God hath given thee;
To spend thyself nor count the cost, To serve right gloriously
The God who gave all worlds that are, And all that are to be.*

---

*"Awake, Awake to Love and Work," Geoffrey Anketel Studert Kennedy, hymnary.org

Lord of encouragement, teach us to give as a tangible expression of your love that the needy among us being served, we may give glory to your name. Through him whose giving has secured for us everlasting life, even Jesus Christ our Lord. Amen.

It has always troubled me that in some circles, this Sunday after Easter is called "low Sunday." Don't misunderstand. I know that the Easter throngs have mostly disappeared, the flowers have been taken home or to the homebound, and the special musicians may not be heard again until Christmas.

The absence of high celebration is not what makes it "low Sunday." It's we as Christian leaders and disciples who decide there's something lacking in those who do not return and the diminished spirit in those who do. Are we so quick to judge, to see the speck in our neighbor's eye and not the log in our own? (See Matthew 7:3.) It's we who call him "Doubting Thomas."

Maybe there are people who have never had a doubt. Introduce me, please, because I've yet to meet one. Coming to authentic faith means wrestling with honest doubt. One of my college professors counseled, "Answers divide, questions unite." That wisdom has served me well.

We do not know why Thomas demanded tactile and tangible proof of the resurrected Christ before he would believe. Perhaps it was simply that he was not in the room when Jesus first appeared to the other disciples. Or perhaps he knew the other disciples too well and questioned their reliability.

What we do know is that this same Thomas proffered courageous loyalty at Lazarus's death (See John 11:16.) and, encountering the resurrected Christ, declared, "My Lord and my God!" Tradition holds that Thomas evangelized India and died for his faith. Let's be like Thomas and demand to manipulate the scar. What God then does with us today will be anything but "low"!

Lord of resurrection glory, fill us with boldness in tepid times and in the face of tepid faith so that, living as resurrected people, our lives will witness to your victory over death and despair and to your promise of eternal life. To the glory of your holy name. Amen.

Encountering God: A Child Shall Lead

APRIL 12–18, 2021 • LEANNE HADLEY

SCRIPTURE OVERVIEW: A repeating theme in scripture is our failure to recognize God's work among us. In Acts, Peter declares that the death of Jesus happened because his fellow Israelites acted in ignorance. The psalmist decries the fact that so many people follow lies, yet God's blessings for the faithful continue unhindered. John tells his audience to expect that the world will not recognize them as God's children because the world did not recognize God to begin with. In Luke, Jesus appears to his doubting disciples. He proves the reality of his resurrection by allowing them to touch his body and by eating food in their presence. Only then do they feel certain that they recognize him. In what places in our lives do we not recognize God's work?

QUESTIONS AND SUGGESTIONS FOR REFLECTION

- Read Acts 3:12-19. Recall a moment when you felt the presence of Christ in your life in an unexpected way. How does that moment stay with you in the times when you feel overwhelmed?
- Read Psalm 4. Do you feel free to cry out to God when you are in distress? If not, what inhibits you?
- Read 1 John 3:1-7. How does your identity as a child of God empower you to deeds of love in your daily life?
- Read Luke 24:36b-48. What story of the risen Christ do you have to share with others? How will you share your story?

Ordained Elder in The United Methodist Church; specializes in ministry to children and families; Minister to Children and Families at Christ Church UMC, Louisville, KY; speaks, trains, and consults with churches through her ministry, A Time for Children; leanne-hadley.com.

When we were babies, we had no shame about crying for help. We can't remember it, but when we were hungry, we cried out. When we had wet our diapers and felt uncomfortable, we cried out for help. When we were hurting or wanted to be lifted up out of our crib after our nap, we cried out. Then, as we grew, we became self-conscious. Somewhere we learned that crying out when we are hurt or in need is embarrassing, wrong, and weak. Somewhere between the time when we were babies and today we learned to suppress our feelings and pretend that everything is fine. Even when it comes to prayer, we hold back our true feelings, afraid that we are not worthy to share our truth with God.

The writer of Psalm 4, David, the shepherd boy who later became king, is not afraid to cry out! He trusts in a God who he knows loves him as a parent loves a baby. He begins this psalm boldly by saying, "Answer me when I call to you, my righteous God. Give me relief from my distress" (NIV). David feels no shame. He does not apologize for his feelings or hold them in. Instead, like a baby crying out for a parent to come and bring comfort, he cries out. And as he continues to cry out, he indeed finds the comfort he was seeking. By the end of the psalm he is filled with joy and peace and is ready to lie down and sleep. Like a troubled child soothed by its parent, the psalmist moves from distress to comfort.

O God, in my times of pain and distress, remind me that you love me as parents love their baby. Give me the courage to cry out to you, trusting in your love so that I may find the joy, rest, and peace only you can give to me. In Christ's name. Amen.

When my grandson was five years old, he had already figured out how to use my phone better than I could! His favorite part of my phone was voice command. He could ask the woman on the phone if it was going to rain, to play his favorite song, or to help his granny find directions to the closest ice cream store. One night, he was learning to write and asked the phone to spell the words, letter by letter while he wrote th   I didn't even know the phone could do that!

One night I asked my grandson a question. "Griffin, who are you talking to when you ask the phone a question?" He looked at me, and I could see his mind trying to find an answer to my question. His face was confused and puzzled as he tried to figure out who the woman on the voice command was. Finally he said, "I guess she is my . . . my friend?"

He had no idea that his "friend" on the voice command was not a person. He knew that the voice came from the phone, and he knew the voice didn't belong to anyone he knew; but he was confused. My grandson is not the only one confused about reality in a world that is changing faster than we can keep up with. It is increasingly difficult to know what is real, who is telling the truth, and what or who is leading us where we do not want to go. It is time to be discerning and careful or we will find ourselves filled with the "delusions" and enamored with the "false gods" that Psalm 4 warns us about.

God, set me apart as you did David and keep me far from the delusions and false gods that tempt me. Help me, in your wisdom, to discern what is right and best for me and for those I love. In Christ's name. Amen.

One Lenten season, during children's church, we began practicing contemplative prayer. We would sit still for one minute and just "be" in the presence of God. At first, it was difficult; but as the weeks went on, the children and adult leaders began to slow their minds and relax into this time of prayer. Then I asked if they had experienced God during the silence. Many children felt love, warmth, or peace. One four-year-old said, "You know when the light of God rushes through your whole body and you just know he is alive? That is what I felt!" This little girl had experienced the living Jesus, the same one who rushed through the body of the lame man whom Peter healed in this passage from Acts. Just like the people who watched the the healing of the man and who "wondered and stared" at Peter, the adults who heard the words of this little girl stared in wonder.

We know that Christ is risen. But at times his resurrection can feel like a one-time story from long ago. And then there are those moments when we feel the living presence of Christ and we are struck with the wonder of it all! A friend calls just when we need them, and we are suddenly aware that there is a living Christ who knows our needs before we even ask. We do not have enough money to pay our bills, and an unexpected check arrives in the mail. We have almost given up hope, and suddenly we feel a calming presence of the living Christ and find peace and comfort.

The people stood in wonder after witnessing the healing of a lame man, and Peter reminded them that they were witnessing the power of the risen Christ.

O God, as the risen Christ, you show up in my life time and time again, and I am filled with wonder! Thank you! In the name of Christ. Amen.

I was recently looking at Facebook, and a beautiful picture of one of my childhood friends popped up in my feed. She looked great and had hardly changed a bit. As I stared at the picture, I realized that this was not my friend; it was my friend's daughter! She looked so much like my friend, I could hardly tell the difference. It is amazing how much a child can resemble a parent. Sometimes I look into the mirror and see my mother's reflection and realize how much I look like her.

In the scripture for today, John reminds us that we are the beloved children of God. He writes, "The reason the world does not know us is that it did not know him" (1 John 3:1). These words are still true for us today. Many people do not know God or have turned away.

John reminds us that as children of God we are created to "be like our dad." We are called to be the hands, feet, and heart of God in the world. We are called to be like the One who lavishes great love on us. For the only way the world will see our Father now is through us.

Wouldn't it be wonderful if a person looked at you or me and could hardly tell the difference between us and our Father, just as I could hardly tell the difference between my friend and her daughter on Facebook? Wouldn't it be wonderful if we could love as God loves, forgive as God forgives, and have the patience God has? Wouldn't it be wonderful if someone met us and because we resembled our Father so perfectly, that person came to believe in God?

O God, I am so proud and happy to know that I am your beloved child. Help me to share your love with all those I meet today, for they are your children too. In Christ's name. Amen.

I have always marveled at what a great father my dad was, especially considering that he had such a difficult childhood. His parents were neglectful and drank way too much. At an early age, he chose to leave his home and went to live with his grandmother. Because of his early childhood, my father always asked us to stay away from alcohol; and I did. I obeyed my father not because I was holy or a "good girl" but because it would hurt him if I drank.

When I was in seventh grade, visiting my friend, she talked me into tasting whiskey. I only took one taste, and it was terrible! But then I was wracked with regret and went home and told my dad what I had done. His reaction was not the anger I had imagined but rather a deep sadness. I will never forget the look on his face. He did not need to punish me or tell me once again why he did not want me to drink. I loved him, and I had hurt him. That was all the punishment I needed. Instead, I needed his forgiveness. As he hugged me and told me that he forgave me, I made a vow that I would not hurt him again. I was never again going to risk damaging our relationship!

Today's scripture reminds me of this story from my childhood. John's words reflect the lesson I learned from my father. Once we truly understand how much love God has for us, we will not sin. We obey God not because we might get into trouble but because we do not want to do anything to damage the loving relationship between ourselves and the God who loves us so completely!

O God, keep me far from temptation and sin. I desire nothing more than the loving relationship I have with you. May I be discerning, and may my actions show my love for you. In Christ's name, Amen.

Irecently spent time babysitting a darling two-year-old and was amazed at how many things she put into her mouth. It started with her toys. It was as if she had a ritual.

She began by noticing a new toy, looking at it first out of the corner of her eyes. Then she would focus on it with both of her eyes. Next she would touch it, then pick it up, and then stick it into her mouth. I watched as she did her little ritual with ten different toys. After she finished with the toys, she moved on to the corner of a table, then a book I had laid on the coffee table, and then she grabbed my cup. She would look, touch, and taste! Then she started her ritual with a small piece of dust she had found on the floor. Luckily, I knew the ritual by then and stopped her. Toddlers put everything in their mouths. That is how they learn about the world around them. They see, touch, and taste.

After Jesus' resurrection, the disciples were like babies in a new world. They had never before seen a person risen from the dead. They had no concept of a "risen Christ," much less how to relate to him. Jesus understood their confusion and knew that his disciples, like toddlers exploring their new world, would need time to understand this new reality. Jesus says, "Touch me and see." In today's story, Jesus does not judge their inability to understand; he gives himself completely to them.

Understanding the risen Christ and absorbing Christ's love for us is a process. Like a toddler exploring the world, we must take time to explore, question, touch, and see.

O God, give me the desire to read, pray, and share with others as ways to touch you, see you, and discover how present you are in my life. In Christ's name. Amen.

I recently found a journal that I had kept daily for the first five years of my son Julian's life. During that period of time, his younger brother Britton was born, my marriage fell apart, and I was caring for my mother who had been diagnosed with a terminal illness, Lou Gehrig's disease. Needless to say, every entry in my journal began with the words, "I am tired today." Those were some of the most difficult days of my life. The agony of divorce, the pain of watching my mother slowly die, and the physical and emotional needs of my babies were almost too much to bear.

My journal reminded me of the pain and hardship of those years, but my memories are mostly of a God who held me tight and loved me through my deepest, darkest days. I know there is a God who sustains us through difficult, hopeless times because I witnessed God's love and power in my own life.

In today's scripture, the disciples have just been through the worst experience of their lives. The One they have followed, learned from, and loved dearly, has been arrested, beaten, and killed on a cross. It was traumatic. But now he has risen! And because of all they have experienced, it is time for them to bear witness and share their story with others. Like those disciples—because I witnessed the power of God through the dark times of my life—I have a story to share. I am a witness to the risen Christ too. Think of the times in your own life where you have been a witness to the power of God. This is your story to share!

O God, I have seen your glory and experienced your presence in my life. I hear your call to share my story with others because, like the first disciples, I am a witness of all these things. In the name of Christ. Amen.

The Good and Faithful Shepherd

APRIL 19–25, 2021 • BRADLEY BUNN

SCRIPTURE OVERVIEW: This week's readings open with a confrontation in Acts between Peter and John and some of the religious leaders. Peter speaks in harsh terms to the leaders, stating that they had killed Jesus; yet by the power of Jesus' name, a man who could not walk has been healed. By that same name spiritual healing happens as well. The other three passages employ the metaphor of the Good Shepherd. "The Lord is my shepherd," the psalmist declares, and the shepherd cares for all our needs. In John's Gospel, Jesus declares that he is the Good Shepherd who lays down his life for his sheep. First John repeats this imagery. Jesus proved his love when he lay down his life for us. If we truly love one another, we also ought to sacrifice in tangible ways.

QUESTIONS AND SUGGESTIONS FOR REFLECTION

- Read Acts 4:5-12. When have you gotten into difficulty for exercising your Christian faith and values? If never, why not?
- Read Psalm 23. What is your first memory of hearing or reading this psalm? Has it had a significant role in your life of faith? If so, what has its role been?
- Read 1 John 3:16-24. How do your actions reflect your love for God and for your fellow children of God?
- Read John 10:11-18. What "wolves" have you faced in your life? How have you experienced the presence of the Good Shepherd with you as you faced these threats?

United Methodist pastor in the Michigan Conference; blogger and visual artist who enjoys combining the arts in ministry with the written and spoken word.

Jesus the Good Shepherd is a shepherd of second chances, as evidenced in today's scripture reading. The setting in which Peter and John find themselves is reminiscent of Jesus' earlier inquest by the Sanhedrin. (See Matthew 26:57-67.) The high priest and others are questioning the authority and power by which the crippled beggar was healed. It may have been the Sanhedrin's hubris that initiates the questioning in the first place. After all, it was Caiaphas who suggested to the Jews "that it would be good if one man died for the people" (John 18:14, NIV). They may very well have thought they had snuffed out this whole Jesus movement.

However, Peter, with the Holy Spirit's strength, recognizes his *déjà vu* scenario and is emboldened to proclaim the gospel message this time around. (See Matthew 26:69-75.) The memory of a rooster's crow may have drowned out the line of questioning as he mustered the strength to speak the name of Jesus as the one and only authority by which the crippled man was healed. He recognized his second chance to proclaim the source of his power, Jesus the Christ.

It's never a good feeling when we recognize missed opportunities to show Christ's love and compassion to others. We often pile on guilt and remorse until we ultimately can't pray or even read the scriptures without feeling inadequate and isolated. Jesus understands our frailty and our insecurities, and that's why he continually seeks us out among the terrain of missed opportunities. As a good and faithful shepherd, he desires to bring us back into the fold. When we acknowledge his love and are empowered to do his will on earth, second chances emerge. Ask yourself this week: *What second chances are awaiting me? What will I do to proclaim, with the Holy Spirit's help, the Author and Source of my being?*

> **Come, Holy Spirit, empower me this week to seek your truth and guidance within life's second chances. Amen.**

Can we boldly proclaim as Peter does, "Salvation is found in no one else, for there is no other name under heaven given to men by which we must be saved" (NIV)? This preferential claim automatically sets us at odds with believers of other religions and even those who are nonbelieving. For the dutiful Christian, who is attempting to build bridges instead of burn them, this statement of belief causes internal tension. But if we take a closer look at Peter's statement and its context, we begin to understand his argument for Jesus as the new covenant.

Peter is reiterating what he previously preached to the Israelite people, "Moses said, 'The Lord your God will raise up for you a prophet like me from among your own people; you must listen to everything he tells you. Anyone who does not listen to him will be completely cut off from his people'" (Acts 3:22-23, NIV). Peter is proclaiming Jesus as this emerging prophet and messianic figure. Thus, Peter's claim that salvation is found only in the name of Jesus rings true for him and the other apostles based upon the Mosaic prophecy. Today, most Christians know that the name of Jesus equates to salvation, based on the good shepherd's promise to receive those who are willing to listen to his voice for guidance and direction. (See John 10:16.)

We can be confident that the good shepherd is calling out to our neighbors and the strangers among us. We can also remain confident in our heart of hearts that Jesus is using us, his sheep, as obedient witnesses of our good shepherd. Knowing that salvation is found in no one else, we can be free to share with others how Christ has transformed our lives. Maybe someone in the crowd is listening for the good shepherd's voice.

Jesus, salvation is found in you. May I be worthy of this claim. Amen.

Psalm 23 is familiar to most churchgoers. Read aloud on some of the most somber of occasions, it reflects the believer's spiritual journey here on earth as well as one's future residence in heaven. The psalm provides us with words of assurance, comfort, compassion, and love within a relationship with the good and faithful shepherd. It mirrors this divine relationship in rich and grand ways—for example, the strength and support found when one relies on God for direction and guidance; the reconciliation offered during table fellowship with those we disagree with; and an anointing of God's blessings for our personal and communal restoration.

To say that God is the good shepherd is implied in the psalm. For those who would question whether God is benevolent, the psalmist and the Christian can say with utmost biblical authority, "Yes, God is!" The psalmist most likely understood that his readers would know that sheep needed lush grass to forage in—a challenge, to say the least, for a shepherd to find among erratic, winter rains in parts of Palestine. But God, the good shepherd, knows where to find green pastures and leads the sheep to such a place of nourishment. We too find rest and nourishment for our souls as we "lie down in green pastures." Thus, the preacher on Sunday morning can exclaim, "God is good!" and hear the resounding response from the congregation, "All the time!"

Our passage today reminds us that God is present indeed! It's easy to get lost amid the ambient noises in our lives—a backdrop of distractions and busyness. However, we aren't alone as we experience the "valleys" in our lives. During those arid seasons of faith, we traverse the desert landscape as the good shepherd leads us toward a heavenly oasis filled with vegetation, water, and rest for our souls.

God, good and faithful shepherd, carry me toward lush pastures so I can find rest for my soul. Amen.

John, the disciple whom Jesus loved, gives us an account of how Christians are to love one another—a lesson taught by Jesus himself through his sacrifice for humanity. It's as if John understands our contemporary notion that "talk is cheap." And yet words do have their place. What we say to one another impacts our relationships. However, words pale in comparison to the action or deeds they represent. The love of Christ (an *agape* love) seeks not self-fulfillment or self-satisfaction; instead this type of love is made complete in the sacrificial giving for the other. This could take the form of caring for another person when it's not convenient to do so, or even the response to a missionary call in a developing country without the securities or familiar accommodations in place. *Agape* love challenges us and the church to act when needed—an action reminiscent of the caring shepherd tending the flock.

If we are to love as Christ loves us then we must be willing and ready to listen for his voice. John reminds the early Christian church that the sheep know the voice of the shepherd, and only then will they follow. If the voice calling is a stranger's voice, the sheep resist and run away. In other words, Christian love is not merely our efforts to do good. Instead, Christian love is the very presence of the living Christ actively transforming us as we attempt to offer Christ's transforming *agape* love to others.

For most of us, loving a brother or sister in Christian love seems straightforward. But as we take a closer look not only at the passage but also at our heart's intentions, we may notice a blemish or two. Regardless, we have opportunities to emulate the good shepherd every day. Who in your life's circle especially needs Christ's love?

Jesus, open my heart to the opportunities to practice Christian love. Amen.

What does it mean to believe? Recently I asked that question at a Bible study. At first there was an awkward silence and trepidation among the group, but eventually someone chimed in, "Belief has to do with the things I hold dear to my heart." I appreciated her answer, and it struck a chord with me as I reflected on the things (people, ideas, and places) that mattered most to me.

When I read John's words, "If our hearts do not condemn us, we have confidence before God and receive from him anything we ask, because we obey his commands and do what pleases him" (NIV), I think of parishioners who have shared their stories of unanswered prayers with me. I sympathized with them as they recounted their bewilderment. From all accounts, those faithful persons loved Jesus and loved others yet their prayers went unanswered. So how could they continue to have confidence in praying to God? How could they continue to believe?

John "believes" that if we obey Jesus' commands, we will have his assurance and presence living in us. God, through Jesus Christ, does not turn away from the predicament of being human with all its limitations and its dreams and desires. God knows the pitfalls and stumbling blocks we encounter. If belief is entrusting what matters most to us in this life, shouldn't we be able to let go of our fears and uncertainties, trusting that the things that matter most to us also matter to God? Holding on to things tends to bring forth anxiety and bondage. The shepherd, who adores each one of the sheep, wants us to experience freedom from that bondage. We can always trust God to guide us through the challenging terrain of our heart's desires.

God, the shepherd of my heart, help me to rely on your promises of love, acceptance, and hope. Amen.

Johhn reminds us that Jesus is not only the good shepherd because he's willing to die for his sheep but also because, in contrast to the hired hand, he's invested in the sheep's overall well-being. Jesus will not abandon the sheep when danger lurks.

If we reflect on the fact that this cosmic God, this manifestation of an invisible God, this compassionate, dutiful shepherd is invested in our lives and all that matters to us . . . well, isn't that mind-blowing?

I would imagine we have all had jobs (paid or volunteer) that were tedious and laborious to the point that we couldn't wait until our shift was over. Our only investment involved a paycheck or mere obligation. We've all played the part of the hired hand in some form or fashion in our lifetime. The part of the wolf, within the context of Jesus and his disciples, may have very well been the religious critics and his own people who had neither "ears to hear or eyes to see." Because of their misunderstanding of Jesus' mission, they attacked the sheep through words and deeds, causing them to scatter and lose hope. I'm sure we could list the wolves in our own lives and how they've attempted to strip us of hope, love, and faith. And yet we get a picture of what Jesus is not (a hireling) in order to assure us that his goodness comes from his desire to know us fully—to see us and accept us for who we are.

There is tremendous power in being known, especially in being known by the good shepherd: "I know my sheep and my sheep know me" (NIV). If the good shepherd is willing to lay down his life for us, then who could ever rob us of God's gift of grace and peace?

God, protector and sustainer, thank you for investing in my life. Thank you for knowing me. Amen.

Jesus' prophetic statement of bringing other sheep into the fold can be viewed as John's commissioning for the early church—a command to welcome and receive others into the life and ministry of the Christian church. Jesus understands there are others outside of the current sheep pen who know his voice despite their ethnicity, class, or faith traditions. We get a sense from this passage that his ministry would not be fulfilled until those other sheep rally to his voice. He alone has the authority, through his Father, to lay down his life for all his sheep and to take it up again when needed. His authority and power come from his foresight about his resurrection promise.

For Jesus, those other sheep may very well have represented the Gentiles throughout his itinerant ministry, but today Christian churches are challenged to ask where the other sheep are outside their walls. I would imagine most congregations take their evangelism and outreach efforts seriously. But are we hoping for more of the same—people with similar vocations, backgrounds, economic status, and so on? Or are we welcoming differences and seeking the stranger? Will our sheep pens be places of inclusion (celebrating diversity) or places of division (reinforcing homogeneity)?

As we discern how to welcome others into the Christian fold, let us be cognizant of the times we were left out of the group due to circumstances out of our control. Maybe we were the new kid at school, the transplanted coworker, or the new family in the neighborhood. Whatever the situation, we were outside looking in, at least in the beginning. Most likely it took the initiative from someone in the group to welcome us in a new place that we would eventually call home.

Loving God, challenge me to welcome the stranger in my midst, so that no one will be left behind or left out. Amen.

Moments of Grace

APRIL 26–MAY 2, 2021 • ANDREW GARLAND BREEDEN

SCRIPTURE OVERVIEW: Two primary themes emerge from our readings for this week. In Psalm 22, we find the promise that faraway nations will turn and worship the Lord. The book of Acts provides partial fulfillment of this promise. Through the action of the Spirit, a court official from Ethiopia hears the gospel and can take it home to his native land. The Johannine readings focus on abiding in God. "God is love," the epistle states, so all who claim to abide in God manifest love to the world. The author pushes the point: If we maintain animosity toward others, we cannot claim to remain in the love of God. In John, Jesus states that we must remain in him if we want to bear good fruit for God.

QUESTIONS AND SUGGESTIONS FOR REFLECTION:

- Read Acts 8:26-40. When has an unexpected encounter led you to a deeper understanding of God?
- Read Psalm 22:25-31. Recalling that Psalm 22 begins with the cry, "My God, my God, why have you forsaken me?" do these verses of praise seem surprising? When have you seen this kind of movement in your spiritual journey?
- Read 1 John 4:7-21. How does your assurance of God's love for you move you to love others?
- Read John 15:1-8. How secure do you feel about being attached to the vine? What has God done in your life to make it more productive?

Acquisitions editor of *The Upper Room* daily devotional guide; graduate of Lipscomb University and Vanderbilt University Divinity School; lives in Charlotte, TN.

During my freshman year in college, one of my teachers made a note in the margin of an essay I had written that said, "You write well." I don't think he could have imagined how those three words would carry me along a particular path, one that I would return to time and time again. He recognized something in me and first put words to a desire and call that I was aware of vaguely at best.

We never know when the moment of grace might occur, what form it will take, or who will help usher it into our lives. It may be someone we have known for a very long time, a teacher we have known only since the beginning of the semester, or someone we have never set eyes on before today. This is how Philip encounters the Ethiopian eunuch.

On his way to Gaza, Philip meets the eunuch, who is reading Isaiah. Philip asks him, "Do you understand what you are reading?" to which the eunuch responds, "How can I . . . unless someone explains to me?" (NIV). The story continues, "So he invited Philip to come up and sit with him." I wonder whether the eunuch had any idea how much this seemingly minor and ordinary encounter would change his life, that he would never be the same, that he would go "on his way rejoicing" (v. 39).

For me, grace has often taken the form of unexpected encounters, small and seemingly insignificant twists and turns that have ultimately had a great influence on my life's direction. Whatever shape it takes—whether an encounter on the road to Gaza or a note in the margin of an essay—a moment of grace leaves us in an entirely different condition than it found us.

O God, keep our eyes open for moments of grace that can alter our paths in unexpected ways. Amen.

When I enrolled in a graduate degree program to study theology, I went because a friend had suggested that I go and because I didn't have any other concrete life plans at the time. My years as a graduate student were often difficult and not always enjoyable. I questioned whether I was where I was supposed to be and doing what I was supposed to do. I often wondered whether I had made a mistake. But the years since have softened my thoughts on the experience; and with distance I am better able to see the value in my questions, doubts, and fumbling around. Now it looks less like a mistake and more like a season that prepared me for who I am today, where I am today, and what I am doing today. Now it looks a little more like grace.

Sometimes I am guilty of thinking about grace as sweet and gentle and something that rewards us instantly and without much of our own effort. But reflecting on it, my experience of grace—more often than not—has been anything but sweet and gentle. In my experience, it has often been painful, scary, confusing, and even risky.

I wish we knew more about what became of the eunuch after Philip baptized him. All we know is that he "went on his way rejoicing" (NIV). I have a little bit of holy envy for the eunuch that his life seems to change so dramatically and instantaneously. For me, rarely—if ever—has it been that dramatic or instant. I am learning more and more, however, that it's not really about the speed at which grace works because it is always there—whether we notice it now or ten years from now—working in us and shaping our lives into who God wants us to be.

God, help me to embrace new challenges as opportunities to experience your grace in my life. Amen.

Like most people, I want a smooth journey from points A to B; but that's not always what I get. When I'm out hiking—one of my favorite activities—sometimes the path is unobstructed for the duration of my trek. Other times, I have to cross streams with knee-deep water, circumnavigate fallen trees, or figure out a way forward after coming to a washed-out bridge. Reading Psalm 22 reminds me of my backcountry pastime. The psalmist, in a few lines of poetry, reminds us of the shape that our experiences along life's journey sometimes take.

By the time we arrive at the last seven verses of Psalm 22, it's easy to forget what we went through to get to this point. Earlier the psalmist writes, "My God, my God, why have you forsaken me? Why are you so far from saving me, so far from my cries of anguish?" (v. 1, NIV). But what started as despair ends in praise. The psalmist concludes with a series of exclamations about the Lord's greatness.

Though not always quite as linear, it seems that many times my life has followed a similar pattern—despair to praise, trepidation to trust, skepticism to faith, angst to rest, questioning God's presence to exclaiming God's faithfulness. Things might get off to a rough start, they might look like they are about to fall apart halfway through; but look at where they end up: "The poor will eat and be satisfied; those who seek the Lord will praise him!" (NIV). This psalm is my reminder that there will be deep water to cross and obstacles to find a way around. And though any one journey might have its moments of anguish, it is likely to end in praise.

God of hope, when I feel overwhelmed by my circumstances, remind me of your presence so that I may turn my lament into songs of praise. Amen.

Not long ago I drove past the building that was at one time the location of the public library in my hometown. Seeing the old building reminded me of the many summer afternoons I had spent there with my grandmother. One of our favorite activities was to go to the public library.

The building evoked in my memory the love my grandmother has shown me all my life. She was always patient, gentle, and fun. Her love took the form of attentiveness and her more than generous gift of time to my sister and me.

Perhaps this is why to me one of the best ways we can show our love for others is to give them our time. For many of us, time is in short supply; to give it to another person is no small sacrifice. It means that we put someone else's needs, desires, and concerns above our own. It means that we might give up part of our weekend to help a neighbor who is sick or pause for a few moments on our way out the door at the office to listen to what's on a colleague's mind.

My grandmother's love for me is my example of how to love others. It is difficult for me to understand the depths of God's love—a sacrificial love beyond anything that I can imagine. But the love my grandmother showed me—especially the time she gave me—is among the simplest, clearest, most concrete example I have of what God's love looks like for me and for us all.

Loving God, thank you for the people who demonstrate your love to us in lasting and meaningful ways. Help us to follow their example as we seek to love others. Amen.

Growing up, I heard many sermons that focused on specific behaviors: what I should and shouldn't do, with a heavy bent toward the "shouldn't." Each Sunday the preacher delivered his dire warning of the consequences of my stepping out of line. I had a picture of God watching me carefully from the sky, keeping tally of my sins—when my mind wandered during the sermon or I embellished a story for dramatic effect or I didn't do my homework. I was convinced that God kept detailed records of these transgressions to use against me one day.

Today's reading says, "There is no fear in love. But perfect love drives out fear, because fear has to do with punishment" (NIV). If you are anything like me, maybe it comes as a surprise that fear plays a part in a discussion on love. Its role, however, becomes much clearer in the phrase, "Fear has to do with punishment."

The news related in First John 4:18 doesn't get much better for any of us who, like me, grew up thinking that God was mostly vengeful, just waiting for us to slip up so as to cut us down to size. It has taken me the better part of my adult life to see God more as a God of love and less a God of fear and punishment. Sometimes I fall back into the notion of God as divine punisher, but scripture is full of arguments to the contrary. I have to look no further than my own life—from the people God has placed in it to the challenges, setbacks, and obstacles that God has seen me through. If I look carefully, I see a love so deep and so wide that there is no room for fear. God is love, and God wants each of us to live in the joy that comes with knowing that we are loved more than we can imagine.

O God, immerse me in your love so that there is no room left in me for fear. Amen.

Acharacter in one of my favorite western novels, *Lonesome Dove*, is so fond of a Latin dictum that he emblazons it, albeit somewhat incorrectly, on a sign. The phrase seems to mean something along the lines of, "A grape changes color when it sees another grape." The idea, as the novel goes on to suggest, is that we cannot help but be changed by the people in our lives. We absorb who and what we are around, even if we are not entirely conscious of it.

I find much in my life that is owed to the people around me. If I am in any way headed in the direction of intellectual and spiritual maturity, it is due in no small part to these people. Their lives continually influence and transform my own—and I hope that maybe even the opposite is true.

It seems to me that in one sense this is what Jesus is talking about when he says, "Remain in me . . . No branch can bear fruit by itself . . . If you remain in me and I in you, you will bear much fruit" (NIV). The idea here is proximity, connectedness—surrounding ourselves and staying close to whom and to what we want to be most like. Each time I read about Jesus' miracles in the Gospels or the faith of the early Christians in Acts, I cannot help but be changed by what I read. When I am part of a community that shows Christlike love and compassion to others, the odds of my doing the same are good. Jesus' invitation to remain in him is an invitation to relationship, a relationship that is life-giving and bound to change us more than any other.

Thank you, God, for the people who accompany us along our journey through life. Amen.

Driving to work one morning, I listened to a song by a musician I like. A friend had recommended him to me, and I thought about how I might not have discovered his music otherwise. What an ordinary but wonderful reminder of all the ways that the people in my life have shaped who I am. People have been and continue to be the most concrete and earthly expressions of grace I know. My life is so much richer because of the people in it, even in ways as simple as the music I enjoy, my taste in literature and visual art, and the recreational activities that I devote my time to.

Even an introvert like me recognizes the need for and value of community and all the people who at different times have been part of mine. I am reminded how much Jesus' life can teach us about relationships, and John 15:1-8 is a good example. Jesus wants so much to be in relationship with us that he uses the metaphor of a vine and its branches to describe the bond. If we cut ourselves off from relationship with him, we will not experience growth. But if we stay in relationship with Jesus, our lives can "bear much fruit" (NIV).

From Jesus to eunuchs to grandmothers and good friends, I am convinced that among the most important manifestations of God's grace is the people we encounter—the people who make our lives richer, fuller, and, in the more challenging times, bearable. They show us how to love, how to do good to others, guide us past our obstacles, and, even unwittingly, help us find our way along life's path.

God, thank you for the gift of community that shapes and supports me. Help me to be a faithful companion to the people in my life. Amen.

To the Ends of the Earth

MAY 3–9, 2021 • CHUCK KRALIK

SCRIPTURE OVERVIEW: The Acts passage continues to tell the story of the advance of the gospel. The Holy Spirit falls on a group of Gentiles. They believe and are baptized, thus showing God's inclusion of all peoples in the plan of salvation. Psalm 98 is a simple declaration of praise. All creation will sing to and rejoice in the Lord. The two passages from John are linked by their emphasis on the relationship between love and obedience. We do not follow God's commandments in order to make God love us. On the contrary, because God has first loved us and we love God in return, we follow God's teachings. Jesus provides the model for us, being obedient to his Father out of love.

QUESTIONS AND SUGGESTIONS FOR REFLECTION

- Read Acts 10:44-48. When has the Spirit of God brought you to a new understanding?
- Read Psalm 98. Where have you encountered "a joyful noise" in creation? How do you make a joyful noise in praise of God?
- Read 1 John 5:1-6. When have you considered God's commands as burdensome? When have you found them freeing?
- Read John 15:9-17. Are you accustomed to thinking of your relationship with Jesus as a mutual friendship? If so, what does it mean to you to be Jesus' friend?

Pastor and Christian author whose most recent publication is a children's book called *Finished,* which tells a fictional story of Jesus' childhood; chuck-kralikauthor.com.

"Sing to the LORD . . . Shout for joy to the LORD . . . Make music to the LORD . . . " (NIV). The psalmist implores us to celebrate the wonderful works of God, for the Lord has brought salvation to the world and has revealed it to the nations. This loving and faithful God is worthy of our praise!

It would be neither appropriate nor possible to contain such praise as we worship the One who has made and redeemed us. Yet even if we were to remain silent, the rest of creation would still worship the Creator. The sea and all that is in it would "resound." The rivers would "clap" their proverbial hands. The mountains would join together in song. Silent indifference is never an option.

Many years following the writing of the Psalms, Jesus would ride into the city of Jerusalem seated on a lowly donkey. The crowds, mistaking him for a conquering king who had come to save them from their Roman oppressors, failed to understand that Jesus had come to do much more. A humble servant-Savior, Jesus would conquer death and Hell and save the people from their sins. Jesus' followers announced his triumphal entry into Jerusalem shouting, "Blessed is the king who comes in the name of the Lord!" (Luke 19:38, NIV). The Pharisees commanded Jesus to chastise his disciples for their shouts of praise. It is in this context that Jesus states, "If they keep quiet, the stones will cry out" (Luke 19:40, NIV).

What an incredible statement! Only the Creator can elicit such praise from the creation. May we join with all of creation in crying out in worship to the One who is worthy!

Creator and Redeemer God, may I never cease to worship you.
You are worthy of all my praise. Amen.

It was an unusual visit, albeit a divinely orchestrated one. The Jewish apostle Peter had been invited to the home of a Gentile soldier named Cornelius. Certainly Peter has his reservations. After all, Jews did not associate with Gentiles. The Jews were God's chosen people, and they considered the Gentiles unclean and unwelcome in the family of God. Still, a strange vision provides Peter the assurance he needs concerning the importance of this God-ordained task.

As Peter visits Cornelius, he shares the good news of the gospel of Jesus Christ; and the Gentiles who are present receive the Holy Spirit. Validated by the Gentiles' sudden ability to speak in tongues, the Jewish believers who are present witness a miracle and receive an unmistakable message: These Gentiles are neither unclean nor unwelcome to God. Peter insists that Cornelius and the other Gentiles be baptized and welcomed into the family of God.

Like the Jewish believers in this story, we too may make judgments about who should be included in God's plan of salvation—and who definitely should not. It's important for us to remember that God's love is for all people and that Jesus' sacrifice on the cross secured for all of humankind the forgiveness of sins. Jesus said, "God so loved the world that he gave his one and only Son, that whoever believes in him shall not perish but have eternal life" (John 3:16, NIV). This statement is not limited to only a few individuals or a certain group. It is inclusive of all people.

May we too welcome others into the family of God, just as God first welcomed us. God's grace is wide and accepting, and God is always worthy of our praise!

All-inclusive God, thank you for your grace demonstrated in Jesus Christ. Thank you for welcoming each of us into your family. Amen.

The Greek word for the kind of love Jesus is speaking of here, *agape,* means "unconditional love." It is the type of love that puts the needs of others ahead of one's own needs. *Agape* love is sacrificial in nature and best demonstrated for us in Jesus' self-sacrificing death.

In this Gospel reading, Jesus makes an interesting statement. He says, "As the Father has loved me, so have I loved you" (NIV). Understand the magnitude of this statement! Jesus is saying that the love that God the Father has for Jesus is the same type of love that Jesus has for each of us!

There are additional implications to Jesus' claim of unconditional love, and it's here that things get a bit difficult. Although God loved Jesus greatly, Jesus suffered an agonizing death for our sins. Jesus faced betrayal and abandonment by his closest friends. He was mocked and beaten by Roman soldiers. He spent six painful hours on a cross. His eyes closed in death as he breathed his last breath.

Jesus asks us to "take up [our] cross daily and follow" him (Luke 9:23, NIV). While this act may look different for each of us, the idea is that we too must demonstrate *agape* love. Perhaps this love will be shown in how we give of our time or finances. Maybe it will be demonstrated in the way we serve those in need within our community. It might even be the actual laying down of our life for a friend.

Agape love is amazing, but it does not come without a price. God gave us his son, Jesus, who gave his life for us. We too are called to bear our cross as we serve those around us.

Dearest Jesus, thank you for the love you have shown us. May we take up our cross in love for others. Amen.

Borrowing the language of social media, one might say that God has "friended" us. Jesus said it this way: "I no longer call you servants . . . Instead, I have called you friends" (NIV). Think about that for a moment! The God of the universe, the One who speckled the nighttime sky with stars, who set boundaries for the oceans, who sent the planets spinning through space, is the same God who calls each of us "friend."

Jesus has every reason to call us the opposite of "friend." Perhaps "enemy" would be a better name for us, as we constantly break God's commands and God's heart. In the best-case scenario, Jesus might call us "servant," forever indebted to our Master in Heaven. But Jesus calls each of us his friend.

Not only does Jesus call us his friends but he was willing to pay the ultimate price for us—death on a cross. By dying for us, Jesus destroyed the labels of "enemy" and "servant" forever. Through his sacrifice, Jesus made certain that he had established a friendship that would not only last a lifetime but would endure for all eternity.

As friends of Jesus, we are called to offer sacrificial friendship to others, even if it means laying down our life for a friend. At the very least, as followers of Jesus we are commanded to lay down our life for him, to take up our own cross and follow him, whatever that might look like.

I am thankful that Jesus calls us his friends. I give thanks that this friendship with Jesus is unconditional and will last forever.

Dear Jesus, thank you for being my friend even though I've done nothing to deserve it. I praise you for your kindness to me. Amen.

In today's Bible passage, we read Jesus' words to his disciples: "You did not choose me, but I chose you" (NIV). These words provide us an important lesson with deep spiritual implications, that God takes the initiative in relating to people.

In some theological circles this is referred to as "prevenient grace," the grace that God extends to us even before we are aware that we need it. The apostle Paul writes that, "While we were still sinners, Christ died for us" (Rom. 5:8, NIV). In other words, God doesn't wait for us to get our spiritual lives in order before offering us grace. Rather, God makes grace available to us, bought by the blood of Jesus on the cross, to be received by faith. Moreover, even this faith by which we reach for God's grace is a gift of God's Spirit, who is persistently stirring our hearts toward repentance.

Paul further writes in his letter to the church at Ephesus that God "chose us in him before the creation of the world to be holy and blameless in his sight" (Eph. 1:4, NIV). Even before God created night and day, divided land from water, and brought plants and animals to life, we were at the forefront of the Creator's thoughts. God chose us, not only to be invited to be followers of Jesus but to be saved by Jesus.

I am grateful that God chose me and you. God loves each of us, and we are our Creator's treasured possession. To God be the glory forever!

Holy God, thank you for choosing to love and save us. We are holy and blameless not because of what we do or have done but by your grace. In Jesus' name we pray. Amen.

In my younger years, I viewed the commands of God as burdensome. I thought of God's law as an exhaustive list of spiritual "dos" and "don'ts," of "shall nots" and "should nots" to which I could never measure up. I failed to love God with my whole heart, as I viewed God primarily as a divine rule-giver and judge. Moreover, I fell short in loving my neighbor as myself and always possessed a bit of a "what's-in-it-for-me?" mentality. In both regards, my love was always tainted with selfishness and undermined by fear, intolerance, and indifference.

As I grew in faith, my perspective concerning God's law changed. As I came to understand God's unconditional mercy, I began to see God's commands as liberating. Far from being burdensome, I discovered—as today's reading says—that loving God means loving God's commands. I learned that God is not against me and that even when I fail to obey God, there is abundant grace available to me.

Psalm 1 speaks of the person "whose delight is in the law of the LORD, who meditates on his law day and night" (v. 2, NIV). This psalm says that the person who delights in God's law is "like a tree planted by streams of water, which yields its fruit in season and whose leaf does not wither . . . whatever they do prospers" (v. 3, NIV).

I want to be like that water-fed tree. I want the fruit of good deeds to grow in abundance in my life. I want the good things I do to prosper. And so I meditate on God's rules for right living. I study God's ways and seek to obey God's commands. I am far from perfect in my obedience, but I am beginning to delight in God's law. I have learned that it is not burdensome, and that God's grace is amazing!

God, thank you for giving us rules to live by and for forgiving us when we fail. May we learn to truly delight in your law. In Jesus' name. Amen.

Today's text teaches us that as followers of Jesus, we are overcomers. This is pretty amazing since in this world there is so much difficulty to overcome. We face daily a bombardment of news of catastrophic events around the world and in our communities. We are faced with the constant demands and pressures of work, society, and family. Depression, anxiety, temptation, addictions, illness, and fatigue only complicate matters, often making it seem impossible to overcome much of anything. Still, today's reading reassures us that as followers of Christ, we are overcomers.

I suppose ultimately we are overcomers because Jesus, the one whom we follow, was an overcomer. Jesus chose to take on human flesh and live within the confines of our fallen world. In doing so, he faced the harsh realities of life. Jesus experienced hunger and thirst. He felt loneliness, rejection, and betrayal. As the author of Hebrews so aptly puts it, Jesus was "tempted in every way, just as we are—yet he did not sin" (Heb. 4:15, NIV). Jesus was an overcomer. He overcame even the horrors of death! Make no mistake, Jesus was dead on a Friday. Yet on Sunday morning, Jesus appeared before his followers, alive and well!

Jesus once told his disciples, "In this world you will have trouble. But take heart! I have overcome the world" (John 16:33, NIV). Jesus shares the same encouragement with us. Through faith in Jesus, we too will overcome whatever this life and this world may throw at us. We overcome it all because Jesus overcame it all for us. What great news we have to share!

Jesus, thank you for being an overcomer. By your power and example, may I overcome the difficulties of life. Amen.

Jesus: Present in His Absence

MAY 10–16, 2021 • DENISE W. MACK

SCRIPTURE OVERVIEW: Scripture tells us that in our lives, especially in our spiritual lives, we need to distinguish what is true from what is false. The psalmist admonishes us to follow the truth of God and flee wicked ideas. This week we read about Judas, who did not follow that advice—with disastrous results. In Acts, the apostles seek to replace Judas with a witness to Jesus who has not been led astray. In John's Gospel, Jesus bemoans the loss of Judas and prays that his followers will cling to his words. First John reminds us that God's words are trustworthy above all. They bear witness to the life that comes through Christ, whose legitimacy was confirmed by his ascension into heaven.

QUESTIONS AND SUGGESTIONS FOR REFLECTION

- Read Acts 1:1-11. How do you experience the power of the Holy Spirit in your life? How does the Spirit guide you?
- Read Psalm 1. Who are the people around you who exhibit the strength and fruitfulness of those described in this psalm?
- Read 1 John 5:9-13. How have you come to know the testimony of God in your heart? How do you live differently as a result?
- Read John 17:6-19. What helps you to sense God's presence and protection in your life?

Pastoral associate, Church of the Assumption Roman Catholic, Rochester, New York area.

Our local multi-racial, interfaith, anti-poverty group trudged along trying to get the work done. Some of our task forces functioned well, but for months our board meetings were unproductive. Our chairperson told us he might resign. We prayed; we kept showing up; we talked with and listened to the Lord. And God opened our eyes and our hearts to someone who had been with us for a while, was about to retire from a big job, and was eager to lead us. We engaged in a process known as a Restorative Circle which allowed us to connect with purpose.

God showed us our new leader's strengths as she listened to board members and community leaders. We saw her ability to empower us to do better work. She equips the saints for ministry. (See Ephesians 4:11-16.) Despite her aching back, her presence as we gathered to pray for families at our border showed solidarity with those in need of humanitarian aid. We stood shoulder-to-shoulder at city council meetings where we decried brutality against young people of color. We were with her in press conferences featuring our local clergy and the parents of unarmed youth who had been shot. And she supported our education task force as they surveyed parents of students in our under-performing city schools.

After Jesus' ascension, when his followers gathered to pray with one accord, they elected Matthias as an apostle. Acts 1:14 tells us "certain women" were among the 120 persons praying together. Mary of Magdala, to whom Jesus first appeared after his resurrection and who was sent by Jesus to bring the best news of all times to his followers, was likely among them. Jesus still sends us bearers of good news. (See John 20:1-19.) Jesus helps us discern community leaders today.

God, help us to recognize those whom you call to leadership. May we cooperate with grace and help to call forth their gifts. Amen.

Our reading describes the strength and fruitfulness of those whose "delight is in the law of the LORD." I think of a group who visited my church in 2019 to share their experiences of volunteering at the U.S.-Mexico border in El Paso, TX. The group included a lawyer who assessed asylum claims and three nuns. One sister is a nurse; another served in Chile for many years. Another had spent time in Guatemala with families who had experienced the gang murder of one of their children.

Our visitors did not describe grim detention centers; they spoke of faith-based oases of care and hope called Annunciation Houses. These centers are staffed by volunteers who are also "like trees planted by streams of water, which yield their fruit in its season." Support from El Paso's religious congregations blessed the Annunciation Houses with food, music, and clothes. As parents hoping for asylum washed clothes and filled out paperwork, children drew colorful murals of their villages back home. The families stayed only a short time before connecting with relatives in the U.S.

Several years ago, Pope Francis called for each faith community to sponsor a refugee family to help solve the worst refugee crisis since World War II, and people of all faiths have been responding to the needs of migrant families. But the number of people fleeing violence is overwhelming. The United States is just one of many nations whose resources are being stretched in response. The demand is much greater in some other nations. This crisis can feel overwhelming; but when we are tempted to turn away from the suffering of those fleeing violence and persecution, we can remember the God who promises that as we are rooted in God's law we will yield fruit in its season.

Gracious God, help us to hear and to respond to the cries of those in need. Remind us when we feel overwhelmed that you are our strength. Amen.

We live in a time when it is often difficult to know what to believe. We all know people who have had a hard time accepting human testimony. An eighty-year-old woman whose husband and she have never agreed on politics was named the best social studies teacher of the year twice. She led the Model UN and International Friendship Council and took high school students to what was then the Soviet Union eight times. Her husband left his law practice to work for the State Department in Cairo and Botswana. When others his age retired, he worked at a multinational base. This couple serves the common good, and they raised their children to do the same. And they still disagree on whose testimony to believe.

They do agree on church attendance and on listening and adhering to biblical imperatives. For this couple, "the testimony of God is greater." Take for instance the testimony Jesus gave as he separated the sheep from the goats and tried mightily to convince us all to feed Jesus by feeding the hungry, to clothe Jesus by clothing the naked, to give Jesus something to drink by giving drink to the thirsty, to visit Jesus by visiting the prisoner, and to welcome Jesus by welcoming the stranger. (See Matthew 25:31-46.) Jesus even proclaimed that if we do not feed, clothe, visit, and welcome him in this way, we will not be saved.

Eternal life is given in Christ. First John urges us to believe the testimony God has given about his Son. If we say that we believe that testimony, we must ask ourselves whether our lives reflect that belief. Do we live in a way that shows Christ in us?

Good and gracious God, I do believe; help me live into that belief. May your will be done on earth as it is in heaven. Help us all to discern your will in our lives. Amen.

ASCENSION DAY

Jesus speaks with authority. His followers fumble as they try to grasp his meaning. In that way, we are like Jesus' first followers. Do our priorities indicate our ignorance?

Jesus' mission, while clear as crystal to some, is as opaque as split pea soup to others. His first disciples thought that Jesus came to rescue Israel from the Romans. Some members in our congregations may have learned the error of that expectation. But we may have other expectations of our gracious God—such as the notion that if we pray enough God will eradicate cancer or reduce global warming or make peace with or without our investing ourselves in the effort. Could disappointment when such expectations are not met lead some to give up on God? Indeed, suffering, loss, disillusionment, and lesser reasons have lured many away from church.

Jesus instructs the disciples to wait for the Father's promise. We sense in that instruction a powerful call to discernment. We are to ask God's direction and listen and watch for it. We step up our praying with sacred scripture; we choose to be quiet in God's presence so that we can better listen to the still, small voice of the Spirit. Those first disciples may have stood there with their mouths gaping open as they watched Jesus ascend, but we know Jesus is anything but gone from this world. Our gracious God keeps sending the Holy Spirit pulsing through our communities.

God, may the Ascension remind us that Jesus is in communion with you. May we deepen our intention to be part of the body of Christ. Help us be in communion as Father, Son, and Holy Spirit are in communion. May Jesus' Ascension help us to prayerfully wait for and attentively discern your will, gracious God. Thank you for your gift of the Holy Spirit, assuring us we are not alone to tend to our sorely troubled world. Amen.

Jesus' hosts in Emmaus realized their hearts had burned within them as they listened to Jesus open the scriptures to them. And Jesus opens the minds of his followers to understand the scriptures in preparation for his parting from them to ascend to heaven. He says that repentance in his name will be preached to all the nations.

I don't hear much preaching on repentance these days. What's more, I rarely preach about it myself. While I personally repent, admitting to God and others how sorry I am, I preach repentance only during Lent or when an assigned scripture calls for it. I do not bring it up on my own. Am I not following the Holy Spirit's promptings?

When I hear a person in power violate a value I hold dear, I sign a petition or send an email calling their attention to the problematic words or actions. Yet I had never called for the person to repent. Could this be the time? I wondered whether a politician or his or her staff member would even read my plea for repentance. Would they care that I had made it?

Even as I entertained these questions, I realized they were distractions from the real isssue because I sensed that I *should* call for repentance. Immediately I began to rationalize: *Doesn't that indicate I am judging their behavior? Who am I to judge?* Still, there were vulgarities, bad judgment, misuse of resources, and blindness to what is true, good, and needed for the common good being blocked from any but the very richest. There were lies, inhumane treatment and policies, and callous disregard for the dignity of the human person. So yes, I have written to political figures about these issues. And I have asked for their change of heart—because that is what the Spirit prompts me to do.

Dear God, help me trust you to open my eyes, heart, and mind to repent and to call for repentance when that is your will. Show me the repentance you want preached. Amen.

Since the sixteenth century, many scholars have called John 17:1-26 "the high priestly prayer." Jesus prays to the Father for his disciples. The pathos in his plea is comforting as Jesus tells the Father what he knows the Father already knows—that he is going to the Father. Jesus' concern for his followers is palpable. He wants us to be one as Jesus and the Father are one, and he wants us to be protected from evil. Since we both want and need Jesus to protect us from evil, we listen keenly to those who look out for the common good.

As I immerse myself in John's narrative of Jesus' heartfelt prayer for our protection from evil, I weep for all of us, for the whole human race. And I ask myself whether Jacinda Ardern, Prime Minister of New Zealand who influenced sensible gun legislation after a massacre, might be a contemporary prophet. I think of Greta Thunberg's protests, seeking to protect God's creation from destruction and of her saying that she was inspired by the outspoken students of Parkland High School who advocate for sensible gun control after a mass shooting at their school. I call those surviving students who inspired Greta "our Parkland prophets," as they carry a godly message in their efforts to prevent the evil of murder. Similarly, I consider Greta a prophet as she tries to protect us from the evil of climate catastrophe, which is upon some parts of our planet already.

Who are the prophets you hear in our world today? Who are those trying to protect us from evil? How is God calling us to respond as those for whom Jesus prayed to be "sanctified in the truth"?

Thank you, gracious God, for protecting us from evil. Help us to work to curtail violence, and help us to listen to the prophets among us. Heal us and give us the courage and the will to do your work in the world. Amen.

We are commissioned to be Jesus' witnesses to the ends of the earth. That's a tall order! Are we each to bring the gospel to far-off lands? More likely we are commissioned to be Jesus' witnesses in our families, neighborhoods, churches, schools, and workplaces. We each have a contribution to make toward transforming injustices in Jesus' name. We each have a unique gift, an insight, a challenge, a comfort. We each have a question that probes thoughtfully and prayerfully, prompting collaborative research into the causes of oppression, racism, militarism, sexism, consumerism, terrorism, and more. The Holy Spirit pulses within us as we do our part in caring for God's creation, finding best practices, planning practical approaches, and ministering to the common good—all because we are Jesus' witnesses. Jesus empowers us with the Holy Spirit, who helps us learn how and when to act and what actions are needed.

Does being Jesus' witnesses require us to focus on other people's individual salvation, or can we be more effective witnesses by focusing on trying to be the most compassionate person we can be with the help of the Holy Spirit? After all, we are called and gifted to love one another as we cope with the joys, struggles, and sorrows of life. I think of our refugee resettlement team. They witness by finding safe apartments and helping our newest neighbors apply for work, master bus routes, and learn how to live in our community.

Remembering Jesus' ways and words will cushion our falls, inform our conscience, and build our integrity. Spending time with scripture and with our community in prayer and service are foundational to congruent faith witness. Recall Jesus' words: "You will receive power when the Holy Spirit has come upon you; and you will be my witnesses."

Dear Jesus, help us to know your words and ways so well that we grow in the ability to become credible witnesses of your love. Amen.

Come, Holy Spirit

MAY 17–23, 2021 • SUSAN MUTO

SCRIPTURE OVERVIEW: This week's readings remind us of the powerful role of God's Spirit. For many Christians, the Holy Spirit is the person of the Trinity we understand the least. In the book of Acts, the Spirit empowers the apostles on Pentecost to speak in other languages and, in so doing, initiates the establishment and missional reach of the church to the wider world. The psalmist uses a wordplay on *ruach*, the Hebrew word for breath or spirit, to teach us that God's Spirit was present at Creation and is necessary for the ongoing survival of all life. Paul writes that God's Spirit confirms that we are children of God and can approach God with confidence, not fear. Even the disciples feel uncertain about what will happen when Jesus leaves, so John provides Jesus' assurance that God will remain with them and with us through the presence of the Holy Spirit.

QUESTIONS AND SUGGESTIONS FOR REFLECTION

- Read Acts 2:1-21. How often do you take solace in praying in private? Or are you more inclined to move to take action in the public square without praying first? Which site is the more comfortable for you?
- Read Psalm 104:24-34, 35b. Where have you seen evidence of nature's resources being spent? How can you help?
- Read Romans 8:22-27. How consequential is it to you to acknowledge that God prays for us and the world? Why?
- Read John 15:26-27; 16:4b-15. What instructions do you wish Jesus had left for you?

Dean and Executive Director of the Academy of Formative Spirituality and the Epiphany Association; speaker, teacher, and author of more than thirty books on formation and spirituality.

The day that will mark the birthday of the church has come, but no one knows what to expect. It will not begin with a gentle breeze but with a violent wind. What happens next will transform the lives of the apostles and send them where they would not have chosen to go. Tongues of fire settle on their heads and redirect their powers of speech so that all who hear them understand. The crowd responds not with belief but with bewilderment. How can these Galileans address people from many lands and be understood? Their words of power can change lives. Should the people bow in awe or sneer?

Let us imagine ourselves in that crowd of people torn between devotion and disbelief. What would it be like to hear for the first time of Jesus Christ, who died, is risen, and will come again? Would we accept this awesome revelation or demand logical answers to our incredulous questions? Would our response to the coming of the Holy Spirit be doubtful or full of delight?

This event reminds us of how great the leap of faith really is. The revelation we are inclined to take for granted ought to evoke both fear and trembling. Faith is a gift that defied understanding on the part of these first Christians and that still takes us beyond what our eyes can see or our ears hear. The message conveyed at Pentecost penetrated the barriers erected by doubt, and from that moment that message changed the world.

Come, Holy Spirit, illumine our minds with the light of faith. Draw us past perplexity so that we are led to ponder our personal calling and be enkindled by your love. Amen.

Peter, the betrayer of Jesus, who became the rock on which Jesus would build his church, speaks with authority. Flanked by the apostles, he addresses the crowd's concern. No one among them is drunk. They have never been more sober. He reports that at nine o'clock that morning the Spirit hovered over them with tongues of fire, reformed them from within, and made them messengers of the Most High. Not with his own words but with those of the prophet Joel, Peter explains what happened. Let us listen to this prophecy as if for the first time, personalizing its declarations, each according to our own gifts.

We may be young or old, male or female, slave or free, Gentile or Jew and yet be designated by the Divine as prophets who refuse to be satisfied with the status quo. Life as we know it takes another turn. Nature itself records the end of one era and the beginning of another. This transformation will take us with Jesus from the agony in the garden, through the scandal of the Cross, to the glory of Easter morning. Blood, sweat, fire, smoke, and mist—these and other symbols of turmoil point to the change that earth and its inhabitants are about to undergo. With the coming of the Spirit, our salvation is at hand.

As the apostles were given a new start by the Holy Spirit, so too must we become Pentecost people, shunning all projects of self-salvation and letting God be God in our lives. Our posture becomes one of abject humility, for only when we bow down before the Most High and call upon God's name can we detach ourselves from all forms of idolatry and make a radical commitment to charity.

Come, Holy Spirit, pour upon bare heads and bruised hands the balm of salvation. Anoint us with the oil of gladness that we may have the courage to proclaim that Jesus Christ is Lord. Amen.

Come, Holy Spirit   171

This psalm ebbs and flows between observations of nature, God's first revelations, and our response to them with childlike wonder. From the most minute grain of sand to the magnificence of the stars, God's handiwork defies description. No human mind can fathom the beauty and order found in the universe. Only the wisdom of God could have calibrated the mysterious movements of the heavens and the earth, their violent upheavals and subsequent restorations.

Stand at the edge of the ocean and try to imagine the creatures inhabiting it and every crevice of creation. Look at the sand crabs crawling swiftly to safety as seagulls swoop to have their fill. From killer whales weighing tons to bait fish light as a feather—all that God has made, great and small, gives praise to the Almighty and looks on high for sustenance and protection.

So generous is the Divine, so loving and reliable, that it hurts us when God seems to turn away. This apparent absence, though usually a sign of God's deeper presence, leaves us feeling as if this bout of aridity will never end. Our hands and hearts are empty. When will the Holy fill them?

We respond to this divine-human game of hide-and-seek with heartfelt prayer. We beseech God to renew the face of the earth; to let us plant seeds of faith, hope, and love in family life, church, and society; to gather us around the Communion table to share the bread and wine that nourishes us in body and soul. With every breath we pray that God will send the Spirit to grace us anew. Only then can we integrate sanctity and service, worship and work, presence and participation in fidelity to our calling in Christ.

Come, Holy Spirit, and form us into the people of God we were meant to be. Discard our old, unfruitful selves. Let us not die and return to dust before we have been transformed by you. Amen.

This part of Psalm 104 contains three petitions, all signifying the meaning of mature faith. The first is at once simple and profound. With the psalmist we acknowledge our deepest intentionality: that the glory of the Lord will endure not for a while but forever; that the grace of God will not be here today and gone tomorrow like a reed blowing in the wind but that it will last from the beginning to the end of time. Praise the Lord!

In the second petition, we ask God, despite our sinfulness, not to forsake the works of God's hands that span the vastness of creation. Flawed though our vision may be, we cannot help but behold their beauty. Even in the face of natural wonderings ranging from volcanic eruptions and violent storms to lush rain forests and flowing streams, we acknowledge with joy that God's providence prevails. Our main duty is not to lament our losses but to adore and praise God.

We ask thirdly that this meditation on the wonders of creation, complemented by the admission of our own smallness, be found pleasing to God. We can choose to grumble about life's limits, but a better choice would be to rejoice in the Lord and trust that God's ways are not our own. Our place is to pray that the good may prevail and the evil perish while knowing full well that final judgment is God's alone to give. Our duty is not to label anyone as deserving of ultimate condemnation, for only God can read the secrets of a person's heart. Our role is to defer to Divine Wisdom and say, "Bless the LORD, O my soul."

Come, Holy Spirit, and teach us how to adopt the mind of God. Convert our hearts that we may turn from what is false and follow the path of truth. Put on our lips the words the psalmist uttered: "Praise the Lord!" Amen.

The readings so far have been pointers to the apostle Paul's declaration that the whole of creation—wind and rain, seas and mountains, fields ripe for picking and deserts plagued by drought—all that has been made and held in being by God, especially all of humankind, has groaned for the Day of the Lord. The groan that arises, at times against our will, signifies that there is another transformation we must undergo—from the alienation of sin to the adoption of grace.

For Paul and for us the hope of salvation is what has kept us from despair. Fortified by this virtue, we wait for the coming of the Lord with patience and unshakeable trust. Seeing our sincerity, God mercifully sent us an Advocate who assures us that though we are weak in power, we are strong in faith. When no words of prayer rise to our lips, we can proclaim the truth that we are not alone. When we do not know how to pray, the Paraclete, the Holy Spirit, intervenes and prays in us "with sighs too deep for words."

All too often our minds become clouded with endless questions and confusing responses. Our attempts to reach self-perfection come to naught. Now is the time to descend from the distractions of a busy mind to the longings of a faithful heart. Here we ponder the unique communal call God intended for us from the beginning. Here the Spirit draws us to conform to Christ in obedience to the will of the Father. We make this intercession in abandonment to God's providential plan for our lives. Though we may not understand how it will unfold, knowing that the Spirit prays in us is enough to assure us that a Divine Light will be our guide.

Come, Holy Spirit, and remove whatever obstacles prevent us from hearing and heeding your call to be holy. Teach us to say with Jesus, "Yes, Father, your will, not mine, be done." Amen.

In these unforgettable words from the Farewell Discourse, Jesus announces that he will go to the Father. Sensing fear in his friends, Jesus assures them that he will not leave them to fend on their own. The Spirit will be with them wherever they are and whatever they do.

What they cannot know at this tender moment of having to say goodbye to Jesus is that on Pentecost the promise of the coming Advocate will be fulfilled. Then bickering among them will have to cease. They may suffer due to their commitment to discipleship, but many converts in and beyond the house of Israel will be baptized by them. Instead of being overwhelmed by the demands made on them by conformity to the Cross, the disciples will embrace them. They will come to know the Father, the Son, and the Holy Spirit in the intimacy of the Trinity.

In these final declarations, Jesus proclaims the distinctive doctrine of Christianity—the revelation of one God in three persons. No other faith (neither polytheistic nor monotheistic) teaches this truth. Having been with Jesus from the beginning of his public life, his followers know the meaning of faith not merely from an informational but from a formational perspective. Because their faith was weak, Jesus performed miracles that amazed their minds and moved their hearts. They marveled at his explanations of the teachings of the prophets. They witnessed the futility of the attempts initiated by treacherous foes to trap him. Though his departure has been foretold, Jesus comforts them as he has always done. Because they are his friends, they have no need to worry. The Spirit will inspire the words and witness they need to draw their listeners to a new way of life, pleasing to God.

Come, Holy Spirit, and lead us where Jesus Christ asks us to go.
We ask for courage to testify to the saving power of his word.
Amen.

PENTECOST

At the end of his earthly life, Jesus unveils the truth that all shall be one in him. This underlying unity is the fruit of our intimacy with the Trinity. The love between the Son and the Father manifests itself in the Spirit whose presence Jesus communicates to us as his lasting legacy.

The Spirit, who will glorify Jesus, will give us the strength to illumine minds, uplift hearts, and transform lives—all thanks to the grace of God. Diverse as this burgeoning faith community of ours may be, what we, its members, have in common is our belief in Jesus Christ as our Savior. No alien power will prevail against the church Christ came to establish. Our love for one another will be its citadel of strength and its witness to unity in diversity.

The knowledge of redemption entrusted to us will be passed on from age to age by all who have ears to hear and eyes to see. As believers blessed by the Spirit of truth and encouraged to share with others all that Jesus teaches us, we will continue to grow in faith through the power of his word.

Then and now it is the commission assigned to every Christian to glorify God and to declare in word and song, in silent witness and bold proclamation, the revelation for which Jesus gave his life for the saving of the world. We are to humble ourselves as he did and practice the art and discipline of self-emptying love. Only then can we hear the call to follow the Master despite the cost of discipleship. To be an epiphany of God's presence wherever we are is not a duty but a privilege.

Come, Holy Spirit, and radiate through our finitude the infinite goodness and mercy of God. Teach us to see in every obstacle a formation opportunity. Lead us to eternal peace and joy in oneness with the Trinity. Amen.

Insignificance and Significance

MAY 24–30, 2021 • MARY KAY TOTTY

SCRIPTURE OVERVIEW: This Sunday we will celebrate the Trinity, the Christian belief that God is one being and exists in three persons: Father, Son, and Holy Spirit. Christian theologians point out that there are many references to this doctrine in the Bible. In Isaiah, the voice of the Lord asks, "Who will go for us?" not, "Who will go for me?" In Romans, Paul speaks of all three persons of the Trinity: We pray to the Father through the Spirit because of the work of the Son. Jesus also speaks to Nicodemus about the role of all three persons of the Trinity. This may not be the simplest of Christian doctrines, but it is foundational because it explains the nature of God and God's work throughout human history.

QUESTIONS AND SUGGESTIONS FOR REFLECTION

- Read Isaiah 6:1-8. Can you recall a time when you said to God, "Here I am; send me"? What prompted you? What helped you feel empowered to serve?
- Read Psalm 29. As you read about the power of the Lord's voice, do you find yourself frightened or drawn in? How approachable is God to you?
- Read Romans 8:12-17. When has fear controlled you? How does being led by God's Spirit free you from fear?
- Read John 3:1-17. How has your life been reshaped by the Spirit? How did sins and failings manifest in the new creation?

Elder in the Baltimore-Washington Annual Conference of The United Methodist Church; pastor of Seward UMC in the Great Plains Conference; co-chair of the Program Council for the Methodist Federation for Social Action; artist and maker.

In this psalm, the writer meditates on the power and strength of God, declaring how God is able to shake up the world with merely God's voice. God's voice has the ability to "shake the wilderness" and "causes the oaks to whirl." Folks living in California or Oklahoma may know first hand what it feels like when an earthquake hits. I've only endured one unexpected earthquake that rumbled through Virginia and the District of Columbia in 2011. It was discombobulating. Previously, my experience had led me to trust that the ground beneath my feet was a steady surface upon which I could depend.

Most days, the ground is steady. But sometimes the earth shakes, and I remember that there are far more powerful forces at work in the universe than my daily concerns. The natural world around us is brimful of the evidence of God's majesty and power, from the steady spin of the earth on its axis day and night in constant, unending cycle to the stunning array of colors of leaves, flowers, and sky that no artist, paint, or camera can ever quite duplicate. Sometimes we need to be reminded of God's majesty in order to regain perspective on our own lives.

How often do we become obsessed with trivial, insignificant matters, allowing them to take up more room and energy than they deserve? When do we become bogged down in the minutia and miss the significant? How do we learn to discern between the insignificant and the significant? This psalm ends by asking God to bless humanity with peace. Maybe it is the peace of God which enables us to recognize clearly what is significant in our lives.

God of creation, continue to surprise us with awe and wonder. Keep us mindful of your presence. Teach us to align our priorities with your will. Amen.

Insignificance and Significance

Isaiah 6 begins with a recounting of Isaiah's vision. It was clearly an overwhelming experience for Isaiah. He sees God in a vision of splendor and wonder. He sees seraphs flying around and singing. The vision is so overwhelming that Isaiah immediately recognizes his own insignificance and does not feel worthy of the honor of experiencing God in this way. It may be difficult for us to understand what Isaiah means. It may be a little like meeting a favorite celebrity, like the awe and delight I felt when I met Julie Andrews at a local bookstore for a signing.

Of course, Isaiah's experience of God is of a different magnitude altogether. Isaiah is not a fan seeing a hero in real life. Isaiah comes face-to-face with the overwhelming awareness of God—up close and personal. In that moment, Isaiah recognizes his own insignificance in the grand scheme of things. It is as if Isaiah fears he will shrink away to nothing with the realization that his place in the universe is not as important as he may have thought. Some folks have a similar reaction when standing on the prairie or being in the middle of the ocean—they have a sense of being overwhelmed by the vastness of the universe and feel insignificant.

And yet . . .

God's grace lifts Isaiah from insignificance to usefulness. This passage ends with God's call for someone to help and Isaiah volunteering. When standing in the middle of the flat prairie, one may feel insignificant. And yet on the prairie, anything that is upright can be seen from great distances—paradoxically both insignificant and significant. So it is with Isaiah. So may it be with us.

Holy One, we are in awe of you. Keep us humble enough to know our insignificance. Keep us confident enough to know that we may make a significant difference. Amen.

Over the years I've heard so many people say that they wish God would just reveal God's self to them in a dramatic way. Many folks long for their own burning bush experience. Most of these times, people are struggling with doubt and are longing to experience God with their five senses, in the same way they experience most of life. Though I usually bite my tongue, what I want to say is, "BE CAREFUL!!!" We tend to forget what happens to people who have dramatic, overwhelming experiences of God. Their lives get turned upside down, shaken out, and reoriented. It happened to Isaiah, who had an overwhelming experience of God. The next thing he knows, he is saying, "Yes" to God's call. Moses with the burning bush, Gideon with his fleece, Mary encountering the angel Gabriel—they all had their lives disrupted by an encounter with God.

I too had a mystical experience of God, though nothing as dramatic as Isaiah. Instead, I heard the still, small voice of God which Elijah speaks of in 1 Kings 19:12. God called me to be a minister. In that moment, my life turned upside down and went a very different direction than I had planned. So be aware of the possible ramifications that could result from longing for an overwhelming experience of the presence of God. God may ask you to do things you have not previously imagined. Sometimes God works in our lives in simple, undramatic ways—a gnawing hunger to do something more, people who see in us more than we see in ourselves, the persistent return of an idea to help someone. Whether God's call comes in dramatic or subtle fashion, saying yes to God may take us to surprising places, sometimes risky places, sometimes significant places.

God of dramatic visions and gentle nudges, grant us willing hands and steadfast hearts to say, "Here I am; send me" when you call. Amen.

Though there will be times when we recognize our own insignificance, today's words from Romans remind us that in God's eyes we are important. Paul wrote this letter to the followers of Christ in Rome at a time when Christians were scorned and often persecuted. Jesus' followers at that time may well have been marginalized social outcasts. Paul offers encouragement by reminding his readers that those who allow their lives to be shaped by God's Spirit are children of God. He goes further by saying they are also heirs of God. Inheritance customs and laws are often very prescriptive, with matters of legitimacy and illegitimacy coming into play. So to be heirs of God is to be legitimate in important and significant ways. Paul is saying to people who are outcasts that they are valuable and worthy.

I wonder if Paul's first readers felt a bit like I did when, in sixth grade during physical education, we were playing kickball and for the first and only time ever I was not the last person picked for a sports team. To this day, I remember the team captain who picked me third or fourth. I remember how accepted I felt. I remember feeling like I belonged. On the surface, this may seem a trivial example. And yet here I am more than four decades later, and I still remember. A sense of belonging is significant!

When do you experience a feeling of belonging? How can you help others experience belonging? How does a sense of belonging empower you to act with courage?

Incidentally, the game where I was not picked last was also the one and only time in my life that—through a series of fumbles and errors—I got a home run in a kickball game.

Holy One, grant that your Spirit may shape our words and deeds. Give us courage as your heirs to work for justice and peace. Amen.

In this passage, Paul reminds his readers that we are God's children, and more so we are God's heirs. This knowledge is significant and empowers us to move beyond fear. To be adopted as God's heir is to have value, worth, significance.

When we think of earthly families, we think in terms of a limited number of heirs; only a select few inherit wealth or family property. How very different it is with God! There is no limit to the number of people who will be God's children, adopted as God's heirs. While in earthly terms being an heir can be a very exclusive, privileged status, in the realm of God all who are led by God's Spirit are heirs. There is an abundance to God's love and grace. There is an abundance to the realm of God. There is room for everyone to be an heir of God. One of the challenges underlying this passage is recognizing ourselves as God's heirs. Moreover, how do we recognize and accept all people as God's heirs? How do we live open to difference and diversity? How do we move beyond our inherent biases and begin to see every person as a child of God?

One of the first lessons I learned as a child in Sunday school was that God loves all children—no matter what color their skin, every single one is precious to God. As adults, we know that in many parts of the world racism is systemic sin causing oppression and suffering. How might taking seriously that we are all God's heirs help us in the work of dismantling racism? How might seeing each one we meet as God's child help us in our individual work of acceptance and inclusion?

God of all people, you love each and every person. Help us to love as you love. Amen.

John 3:16 is one of the most familiar verses of scripture. Many people may have memorized it in childhood Sunday school challenges. It shows up on banners at sporting events. Conversely, John 3:17 may be one of the least familiar verses of scripture: "Indeed, God did not send the Son into the world to condemn the world, but in order that the world might be saved through him."

I worry that one of the reasons the church is dying is that we have forgotten John 3:17. Too many people claiming to be Christian spend too much time condemning those who believe, look, or behave differently. Too often the church's message has been, "Do this, believe that, give up those, change these, and *then* God will love you." Have we forgotten that love and non-condemnation go hand in hand?

Consider John 3:16, "For God so loved the world that God gave God's only son" (AP). God did not wait until the world was perfect to send God's gift of love. God became incarnate in Jesus of Nazareth precisely at a time when the world was a mess. In the same way, God loves all people just as we are—mess and all. God loves. God does not condemn. God saves.

Love. Do not condemn. Save. That would be a good action plan for the church. God loves us, no strings attached. Let us begin by loving others with no strings attached. Love people simply as they are. Rather than condemnation, let us foster curiosity that seeks understanding. When encountering difference, let us ask questions and listen. With love, without condemnation, we work to save folks—from evil, injustice, and oppression "in whatever forms they present themselves." (UMH, no. 34).

Divine Love, teach us to love without judgment or condemnation. Amen.

TRINITY SUNDAY

Today is Trinity Sunday, when Christians contemplate this unique understanding of God as Holy One, Holy Three. This text from John is one of the few places in scripture when God Creator, God Savior, and God Spirit are all present in the same passage. There is much about a trinitarian image of God which is life-giving and powerful. In particular, it highlights the importance of community and relationships. If God's own self is relational, then we too need to be attentive to community and getting along with others.

Yet the Trinity can be difficult to understand, and various metaphors are offered. Jeremy Begbie, in his book *Resounding Truth: Christian Wisdom in the World of Music,* suggests that most metaphors for the Trinity rely on visual imagery which makes it difficult to explain how three might occupy the same space. He suggests that music provides a helpful way to understand the Trinity and talks about a three-note chord. When considered audibly, we recognize that three distinct notes may be heard at once and be individually discerned.* This resonates for me.

In many ways, it is good that the concept of the Trinity remains a bit of a mystery. God is always greater than we can conceive. So we dance with images and metaphors. One image may be meaningful for a season; a different metaphor may speak at another time. What images and metaphors for God do you turn to most often? What new images might remind you that God is greater than our human thoughts?

---

*Jeremy Begbie, *Resounding Truth: Christian Wisdom in the World of Music,* Grand Rapids, MI: Baker Academic, 2007, p. 293, (electronic edition).

Holy One, Holy Three, beyond our understanding and closer than the air we breathe, make us aware of your abiding presence, and enable us to be ever more compassionate. Amen.

Deliverance Among Relations and Nations

MAY 31–JUNE 6, 2021 • ANTHONY PETERSON

SCRIPTURE OVERVIEW: We sometimes struggle to believe in the power of a God we cannot see. The psalmist declares that God is greater than any earthly king and will preserve us in the face of our enemies. However, in the time of Samuel, the Israelites demanded a human king to lead them into battle. God was not enough for them. Paul admonishes the Corinthians not to repeat this mistake. We should not think that what we see is the ultimate reality. What we see is temporary; what cannot be seen is eternal. Perhaps Jesus is teaching a similar idea in this somewhat troubling passage in Mark. Jesus is not against family, but he is emphasizing that human families are temporary; spiritual family is eternal.

QUESTIONS AND SUGGESTIONS FOR REFLECTION

- Read 1 Samuel 8:4-20. How are you influenced by the culture around you? What helps you try to align your priorities with God's?

- Read Psalm 138. When you "walk in the midst of trouble," how do you remember God's presence with you?

- Read 2 Corinthians 4:13–5:1. How do you find yourself being renewed today in spite of parts of your "outer nature" that may be "wasting away"?

- Read Mark 3:20-35. Who is your spiritual family? Whom do you identify as your brothers, sisters, mother, and father?

Educator, editor, and writer in Nashville, TN; holds a master's degree in Christian education and has served in United Methodist, Baptist, multidenominational, and nondenominational churches; teaches and leads in areas of diversity, equity, and inclusion.

If everyone else jumped off a cliff, would you jump also?" That might be the question Samuel wanted to ask the elders when they demanded a king "like other nations." Samuel had served his time as judge, asking God for direction while leading the people.

For years, judges had ruled, resolving disputes as they arose. Samuel had served, and he appointed sons Joel and Abijah to serve in the southern region of Judah. Like Samuel's mentor Eli, Samuel raised sons who grew to be corrupt, demanding bribes and perverting justice. According to the text, Samuel's sons did not "follow in [Samuel's] ways."

With lament over the ways of Samuel's sons, the elders approach Samuel with a request from the people. Although they mention the unfaithfulness of Samuel's sons, they focus on another reason for wanting a king: to be like other nations. They were a people set apart by Yahweh, but they wanted something else. Rather than reveling in their uniqueness, the people wanted to find rest in sameness.

The feeling is not altogether unfamiliar to us today. There is comfort in sameness. In fact, we gravitate toward those who are like us. Whether in our courageous or fearful moments, we may even seek to make others like us.

And yet each of us is loved by God in our very uniqueness. As God called a distinct people, God calls each of us in our distinctness. Even when our calling is unclear, it is ours uniquely. Each of us is chosen and loved by God, not for our conformity but for our unique image of the God of the universe.

Giving and loving God, thank you for creating us each with a unique calling. Guide us as we work to find ways for our uniqueness to be a blessing to others and bring glory to you. Amen.

Dejected and depressed, Samuel turns to the Lord with the elders' appeal. Not satisfied with governance by judges, they demand a king. Perhaps their dissatisfaction has something to do with Samuel's sons, whom he has appointed judges but who "do not walk in [Samuel's] ways." The Lord says that the people are not rejecting Samuel; they are rejecting the Lord.

The elders disclose another reason for wanting a king: to be "like other nations." But why? Maybe their envy of other nations is actually a quest for power. A king is always on the throne, always in control. But the system of judges is not about perpetual leadership. Judges step in to settle disputes as they arise. There is freedom in that, but freedom can be frightening.

Perhaps the demand for a king is a demand for assured dominance against other peoples. There is security in authoritarian leadership; but it is a precarious security, dependent on the whims of the leader. Leaders can be good or bad, as much of the books of Samuel, Kings, Chronicles, and the prophets outline.

Samuel names the potential dangers: conscription of children, confiscation of property, imposition of capricious taxes, seizure of employees, and even slavery. But the people still want a security that they believe kingship brings.

In this passage, the Lord Yahweh models a different kind of leadership by saying, "Give the people what they have asked for," even before describing for them the dangers their request can bring. The All-Powerful One demonstrates the value of leadership that is not steeped in power.

Each of us can exercise that kind of leadership in our lives. Each of us can set an example, can live purposeful lives, can live lovingly even in the midst of uncertainty.

Yahweh, remind us that we can lead in our own lives. Remind us of the model of leadership that respects everyone. Amen.

Warnings abound regarding hyper-partisanship globally. While many around the world work for peace, just when we think a new age is on the horizon, new hostilities break out somewhere. Those hostilities breed dissatisfaction and discord, government action and inaction, attacks and war. Some issues that we think should be inconsequential or easily resolved escalate, fueled by non-negotiable values.

Perhaps the hostility impulse is universal. We celebrate and denigrate athletic feats with the force of ultimate ideas. We deify our team and demonize the other, mostly with no legitimate reason for our loyalty. Maybe it's our locality or our family history or even our favorite color. Our team is right; all other teams are wrong. Our views are right; there is no other legitimate view.

At first glance, the idea of deliverance from personal enemies as expressed in today's reading may seem foreign. But sometimes we actually pray for the victory of our sports teams! And beyond that world, we may have rivals for employment or competitors in business. We might have political opponents. We might have religious views in conflict.

These differences need not breed enmity on a visceral level. And yet they often do. Each of these temporary relationships can be elevated to something from which we need deliverance.

As with the psalmist, our best focus is not on that adversity or enemy but on God's steadfast love and faithfulness. God is the source of our deliverance. And according to the psalmist, God overcomes all those hostilities with a nature that supersedes "enemies," "kings," and "gods."

The reality of this psalm is that we can turn to God for protection and peace, regardless of the nature of our hostilities.

God of peace, I call on you to deliver me from adversity, and I commit to work for peace even in the midst of adversity. Amen.

The psalmist begins with overflowing praise to the Lord. This psalm exudes relief, triumph, and gratitude. The Lord is exalted above both heavenly beings and earthly monarchs. We do not know the circumstances of the turmoil. But we do learn that the psalmist sees the steadfast love and faithfulness of the Lord demonstrated personally in his or her life. And the turmoil could be physical, emotional, spiritual, or relational; there are hints of each throughout the song.

This psalmist gives thanks to God in relation to three groups: the gods (vv. 1-3), the kings of the earth (vv. 4-6), and enemies (vv. 7-8). The expression *the gods* could mean deities worshiped by other peoples or it could mean angelic beings. In either case, the psalmist means to invoke the spiritual world. *Kings* is shorthand for any earthly government or movement leaders. And *enemies* appears to encompass difficulties on a personal level which can feel overwhelming.

The exuberance in the song flows from a natural reaction of relief, a relief that is not of the singer's own making. As essential as God's protection and deliverance are, our response to God's action is also essential. This song does not appear out of detached deliberation. It is an outburst of gratitude and relief. Sometimes we feel gratitude but fail to express it. This psalm exemplifies the value of expressing gratitude.

Expression can enhance gratitude. The initial outburst of relief or thanks or resolution can be exuberant. But expressing our gratitude before others can intensify the reaction, and that expression can become a graceful blessing to those who hear it. The psalmist says, "Look what God has done!" And the hearers of the message can find hope.

Gracious God, thank you for the times you have delivered me. I will praise you in the presence of gods and kings and enemies. Amen.

Jesus continually demonstrated that the reign of God does not correspond directly to any earthly entities. In this passage, the demonstration becomes rather pointed.

A crowd has gathered so quickly around Jesus and the twelve that they did not even have time to find food. We are reminded of another time when Jesus baffled his hearers by saying, "My food is to do the will of [God] who sent me" (John 4:34). This time it is Jesus' own family who seem baffled. They hear others suggest that Jesus is not in control of his own faculties. It is unclear if they are worried for him or perhaps embarrassed. They clearly do not fully understand him. Even Jesus' rejection of the charges—"How can Satan cast out Satan? If a kingdom is divided against itself, that kingdom cannot stand" —may be baffling to them all.

Finally someone lets Jesus know that his mother and siblings are in the crowd. And he utters those words that seem antithetical to some twenty-first century ideas of family: "Here are my mother and my brothers! Whoever does the will of God is my brother and sister and mother."

Depending on our situation, these words can be radically troubling or radically comforting. Many of us have experienced family situations that have encompassed all that is valuable in human connection. For them, Jesus' words can be disturbing.

But others have experienced the need to find family beyond biology. Many find community in like-minded people in groups like church. When we find community with shared values, such as doing the will of God, we find family and sustenance. Jesus said it this way: "Whoever does the will of God is my brother and sister and mother." "My food is to do the will of [God,] who sent me."

God, thank you for providing both family and food as I try each day to do your will. Amen.

From the beginning of life, we begin dying. This is true of all living things. We don't know if other creatures conceive of this reality. But humans do develop this knowledge, though we often suppress it. In some cultures, we fight actively against the reality of death. While children long to grow older, adults begin to idealize youth and to try to put off anything that appears to be a sign of aging.

Advertising and other messaging prey on our fears of mortality and our longing for youth. They promise we can look younger and, in some cases, actually "become younger." But the signs of our "wasting away" are everywhere. And the signs grow as we age. When Paul speaks of the "outer body" deteriorating, he is not referring only to our physical shells. We see the deterioration in our faculties and sometimes even in our relationships.

Paul is a worthy teacher in this area because he has already endured what many of us unconsciously fear. His examples are often physical, but they point to all those other ways that we are deteriorating. Our sense of mortality grows, but those signs and that sense do not have to be accompanied by fear.

In fact, Paul gives us reason for great hope. In verse 16, he repeats the line from 4:1, "We do not lose heart." If we have been dying from the beginning, we can also trust that something in us is living and renewing. For Paul, "our inner nature is being renewed." We are not subject only to the laws of biological nature. We are spiritual beings who can grow in love, compassion, wisdom, service, and companionship. We are subject to spiritual laws that supersede fear and even death. Perhaps we are all born to die; but even more deeply, we are born to live loving lives that survive our physical deaths.

Gracious God, help us not to lose heart. Amen.

When Paul wrote the letter we now call Second Corinthians, his relationship with the believers at Corinth was already well established. He had lived among them for at least eighteen months. Along with visits, he likely had written other letters besides the two we have preserved in Christian scriptures.

Paul is not writing a disinterested treatise for readers to debate. He is writing a personal appeal, born of his own life and his mutual life with his readers. And his interactions with them were not all pleasant. Later in this letter (chapters 10-13), Paul addresses the difficulties between him and some of the Corinthians. He brings to light charges of hypocrisy ("timid" when face to face but "bold" in letters). He charges some Corinthians with unwise boasting. He defends himself against charges of lack of affection. And he names some of his detractors as false prophets.

But the bulk of this letter, including today's passage, is more conciliatory. In addition, the Corinthians are aware of Paul's triumphs and his adversities. They know what he refers to as this "slight, momentary affliction." They know his afflictions have been many and that he does not lose heart.

And their knowledge of Paul's afflictions is not simply from a detached distance. They are aware of his sacrifices and the gift of the good news he has brought them. They know what his commitment to them has cost him. He is writing out of gratitude and a desire for reconciliation.

We too experience afflictions of various kinds. Our relationships are healthy and unhealthy, strong and weak, rewarding and empty. But Paul points to the possibilities. Hope endures even over our greatest obstacle, and our most difficult relationships.

God, help us in times of our "light and momentary afflictions." Give us the gifts of reconciliation and hope in our circumstances. Amen.

To See Our Lives as God Sees Them

JUNE 7–13, 2021 • KENNETH H. CARTER JR.

SCRIPTURE OVERVIEW: From a human perspective, we tend to judge people by appearances: how attractive they are, how wealthy they seem to be. God's standard, however, is not outward appearance but the attitude of the heart. David was the youngest brother in his family, but God knew his mighty heart and chose him as the next king of Israel. The psalmist declares that God gives victory to those who put their trust in God, not in the outward appearance of might. Jesus reinforces this truth with the parable of the mustard seed. Paul tells the Corinthians that we should no longer judge by what we see on the outside, for God changes what really matters—what is on the inside.

QUESTIONS AND SUGGESTIONS FOR REFLECTION

- Read 1 Samuel 15:34–16:13. When have outward appearances prevented you from seeing someone's value as a child of God?
- Read Psalm 20. How do you discern whether your "heart's desire" is in line with what God wants for your life?
- Read 2 Corinthians 5:6-17. In what ways are you "urged on" by the love of Christ? How do you behave differently because you know Christ's love?
- Read Mark 4:26-34. When have you seen God make much of a small gift that you offered?

A bishop of The United Methodist Church who from 2018-2020 served as president of the Council of Bishops.

Samuel is given the responsibility of anointing the next king of Israel, and he will make the selection from among the sons of Jesse. He begins the ritual with the assumption that he will select from among the seven older sons. In each instance, this is not the outcome; the Lord speaks to Samuel and says, "This is not the chosen one." Samuel asks if all of the sons are present. There is one, David, who is tending the sheep. The Lord speaks, "Anoint him; for this is the one." Given the circumstances and traditional privileges, the power and blessing should have been conferred upon one of the older brothers. But God's wisdom is clear: "The LORD does not see as mortals see; they look on the outward appearance; the LORD looks on the heart."

In the kingdom of God, we often discover a reversal of our values. God's strength is present in human weakness. God's power is demonstrated in human vulnerability. God's victory is won through the humiliation of a cross. Again and again in the history of Israel, in the life, death, and resurrection of Jesus, and in the witness of the apostles, God does the unexpected.

The church in western culture struggles with its alliance with power. We have known privilege and enjoyed access to status and influence. Over time, we have focused on outward appearances—our institutions, buildings, and properties. We have forgotten that, at best, these are outward and visible signs of an inward and spiritual reality. And we have often neglected the inner resources that are at the heart of God's concern. In the anointing of David, we are reminded again that God's ways are not our ways. We can never presume to know how God's story is unfolding.

O God, in your wisdom, you call us to serve you. Cleanse our hearts, remove our claims of privilege and status, and anoint us to serve you and your people. In Jesus' name. Amen.

In this psalm, a petition for God's intervention and protection in a forthcoming battle, there is a strong connection between God's will and the action of the ruler. There is something comforting about this request to God, but there is a complexity to it as well.

Our hearts' desires resonate deep within us. It may be related to a relationship, our work, the resolution of a problem, or recovery from illness. In the psalm, the heart's desire is the defeat of the enemy and the blessing of the king's military plans. In prayer we speak to God from the heart, bringing all that we have and are to the One who has the power to grant our requests.

All of this is at the heart of the spiritual life. We must also admit, however, the complexity of our petitions, even of our hearts' desires. This is rooted in our capacity for self-deception. We may connect what we want with what we believe to be God's will. Our petitions may have more to do with our human sin—greed, envy, pride—than we care to admit. A classical definition of sin is the heart curved in on itself. Our heart's desire may be destructive, to ourselves and to others. The Bible itself tells the story of kings who went to war for the wrong reasons.

It is essential that we place our petition that the Lord will grant our heart's desire in the context of the psalm. The action preceding this request is entering the sanctuary, making a sacrifice to God, and allowing God's holiness to purify us. And the affirmation following this petition in the psalm is that we place our trust and confidence in the power and providence of God.

We do ask for God to fulfill our hearts' desire, but we do so by placing those desires within the greater wisdom of God's will.

O God, may the desires of my heart reflect the intentions that you have for my life. Remove my capacity for self-deception, and lead me to rejoice in your will. Through Jesus Christ our Lord. Amen.

On first impression, a psalm describing a king preparing for battle and a petition for victory may not seem relevant to most of us. Is David giving his blessing to violence or power? We may struggle with this idea. Yet an honest engagement with the psalm can teach us about ourselves and the human condition that is consistent across these three thousand years.

As the king prepares for battle, there is a humility and dependence on God and a need for protection. Violence is a part of human nature. Many persons of faith find themselves in the presence of violence and call upon the honest words of the psalmist for answers in times of trouble, for protection in the face of harm.

As kings prepared for battle, they would first enter the sanctuary to offer sacrifices to God. In our cynicism, we may view this as asking for divine blessing of human intentions. But it may also be a lesson to us that we need to purify our intentions, set aside our egos, and place our plans in submission to God.

Psalm 20 is a prayer for victory, but it clearly acknowledges our human limitations and our need for God's help. In warfare, horses and chariots are crucial resources. The warrior can see them, measure them, and come to depend on them. But the psalmist calls us to trust not in horses or chariots—in other words, our own human power—but in God.

The reader of Psalm 20 enters into a text that is on the surface about battle and victory. But as we move more deeply into these petitions and prayers, we encounter purification, humility, trust, and dependence on a strength that is not our own. In the subtle ways we are tempted to do violence and abuse power, we can learn again and again from the Psalms.

O God, help me to trust not in external power but in your unseen strength that is always with me. Amen.

The apostle Paul writes to the church at Corinth with the weight of concerns bearing upon him—despair, criticism, opposition, fatigue, suffering, human limitations, mortality. He imagines what it might be like to be in the presence of the Lord and yet reckons with the reality of life "in the body."

Life in the body is life in service to others. Ministry is always offered in the midst of complexity. Some receive our gifts, others question them, and yet others may reject them. Paul is grounded in the inner life, his conscience and heart. Why does one continue in ministry? As a young adult I listened as a bishop preached a sermon to those being ordained. In the midst of the message, the bishop made a comment that seemed unscientific a the time: "If you do not spend time in prayer and scripture reading each day, you will not be in the ministry in five years."

I sense now the truth of that bishop's conviction. Despite the challenge of external circumstances—and Paul is honest about them—the apostle does not give up or lose heart. (See 2 Corinthians 4.) What motivates us to continue in service and ministry to those whom God places in our path each day? "The love of Christ," Paul notes, "urges us on." The crucified Jesus loved us and gave himself for us. (See Galatians 2:20.) And there is the persistence of the word *all*. Jesus died for all. And so we are compelled to serve, compelled to speak, compelled to love, compelled out of a sense of love, the greatest gift. (See 1 Corinthians 13.) In our humanity, we are weak and limited, discouraged and despairing. Yet the love of Christ urges us on. And in the midst of the weight of concerns that bears upon us, we live by faith (not sight), trust and confidence. We meditate on Jesus, crucified and risen.

In the midst of all that weighs upon me this day, O Lord, remind me that you are near and that in the Cross you love me and have given yourself for me. Amen.

Someone has noted that we see others not as they are but as we are. The apostle Paul is writing to the mature spiritual leaders of Corinth and now to us when he confesses, "From now on we regard no one from a human point of view." The churches of the first century were always tempted to define themselves by human categories—Jew or Greek, slave or free, male or female. (See Galatians 3:28.) We are not so different. And indeed we are shaped by country of origin, class, gender, race, age, politics, language. Our individual identity should not and cannot be suppressed.

Yet Paul calls us to see one another in a different way. To say that "from now on we regard no one from a human point of view" is to see the image of God in one another, to acknowledge the sacred worth of the other, to view that person not as a stranger or enemy but as a brother or sister.

Our identity is a part of this sacredness, and yet it can become the very way we are separated from one another and the very cause of our willingness to do harm to one another.

Once we regarded Christ from a human point of view, Paul notes, but no longer. The crucified Jesus has been raised from the dead; God was in Christ reconciling the world to himself (v. 19). What was separated is now united. And there is now a new creation in Christ. The old has passed away, and everything has become new. What passes away are our mindsets, our assumptions, our prejudices, our stereotypes. These realities are deeply embedded within each of us, and their death is painful. But out of death there is resurrection and a new creation. There is one new humanity in place of the two. (See Ephesians 2.) To be converted is to see all things with a transformed vision.

Lord Jesus Christ, light of the world, open our eyes to see you present in each person we encounter today. Amen.

Jesus often taught in parables, stories that drew his disciples' attention to their ordinary surroundings. The kingdom of God, he says, is like the scattering of a seed upon the ground. In this reading he likens what God is up to in the world to the common labor of a farmer, who plants in order to ensure sustenance.

In our rhythms of life, we work and rest. In the economy of God's kingdom, as we sleep, the work continues. The seed sprouts and grows, and we cannot account for this!

One of my temptations is to believe that I am self-sufficient. I want to convince myself that I have earned what I possess. I can point to particular projects or academic degrees. I have entered into fields of labor. I have grasped handfuls of seed and scattered them. I have been intentional, conscientious, and deliberate.

And yet in the rhythm of work and rest, I have at times set the labor aside. I came to the end of my capacity. And at times I have watched as something mysterious and even miraculous occurred. There was change, growth, even transformation. And, if I were honest, I could take no credit for it.

In God's kingdom, there are divine gifts within every living being. Generativity is built into the fabric and design of all of life. If we work and watch and wait, we will see order—first the stalk, then the head, then the full grain in the head.

As accomplished and invested as we might be, we cannot produce growth. Growth is always a miracle. It is always a gift. We cooperate with the Creator, but in the end we confess that we do not know why or when the harvest is to come.

We know only that God calls us to be faithful—to scatter the seed—and to give thanks for the mysterious gifts that surround and sustain us.

O God, your kingdom comes as a gift. Accept our labors, and yet make us attentive to the mystery of your grace in the midst of our work. Amen.

The kingdom of God, Jesus taught his disciples, is like the smallest of seeds. In the church we can become preoccupied with size. How many gather for worship? How large is the membership? What is the financial offering? And in many areas of the world, implicitly and explicitly, we assign God's favor to abundance. This is the prosperity gospel. If we gather in large numbers and our resources are significant, this is of God.

So Jesus' story about the smallest of seeds is a reversal of our worldly expectations. Jesus is profoundly present where two or three gather to pray in a house church amidst persecution. Members of a small, rural church choir faithfully meet each week to practice their offering of praise to God. The Holy Spirit whispers in a still, small voice.

The kingdom of God is like a mustard seed. We offer our small and seemingly insignificant gifts. When these seeds are planted, there is growth. Here we are called to exercise the gift of imagination. As Paul writes, God is able to accomplish abundantly more than we can ask or imagine. (See Ephesians 3:20.)

We often look upon our small gifts with limited or lowered expectations. And, of course, the kingdom of God is a reversal of our human perspective. From a small seed there is growth; and here the tree puts out large branches, and birds make nests in their shade.

Whenever I see a tree, I now try to imagine the person who planted the seed. In a warm climate, the tree provides shade and respite. The person who plants does not often reap the benefit of the labor. And yet in God's economy, a small gift offered in faith has an extraordinary influence. We are not called to do great things today. We are called to plant small seeds.

O God, help me to offer a small gift today. Move me to plant a small seed; prompt me to take a next faithful step, trusting every outcome to you. Amen.

Fear: It's Risky Business

JUNE 14–20, 2021 • CLAIRE KEENE

SCRIPTURE OVERVIEW: As children of God, we will face opposition; but God will ultimately give us victory. The psalmist cries out to God asking for deliverance from oppression at the hands of his enemies and concludes the psalm with the assurance that God will do so. Tradition credits this psalm to David, who as a boy had risked his life against Goliath based on that same assurance. Goliath mocked the Israelites and their God, but God gave the victory. Paul recounts his sufferings for the gospel, yet he is not overcome or in despair, for he trusts in God. Jesus calms a storm and is disappointed that the disciples show so little faith. Why do they not believe in God's deliverance? And what about us? Do we still believe in God's deliverance?

QUESTIONS AND SUGGESTIONS FOR REFLECTION

- Read 1 Samuel 17:1a, 4-11, 19-23, 32-49. What "armor" do you use to protect yourself? When have you found the courage to put aside your armor because it was holding you back?
- Read Psalm 9:9-20. When have you been provoked to cry out, "Rise up, O Lord?" On whose behalf did you cry?
- Read 2 Corinthians 6:1-13. How have you commended yourself as a servant of God?
- Read Mark 4:35-41. How do you find the quiet center when the storms of life rage around you?

Priest, preacher, poet, potter; retired in Knoxville, leading retreats and teaching in the Episcopal Diocese of East Tennessee; still singing with beloved Grandpa Mike and the St. Elizabeth's Episcopal Church choir.

Fear is quite a risky business. Sightseeing in Italy drove this point home. My friends and I were in Umbria, walking through ancient towns and churches. One bright, chilly afternoon in March we walked into a fortification on top of a hill. Built after Roman rule dissolved and every town depended on itself, this high, rectangular stone wall bore arrow-slits around its top and a turret on each corner. We strolled through a wide passageway where the city gate had stood onto a grassy interior courtyard. These days, I imagined, picnics, weddings, local celebrations happened here.

Curious, I climbed up a turret's stone steps. Unobscured by trees or tall buildings, the panorama seemed to curve with the earth, a quiet retreat above the fray. And then I realized the turreted wall was a military installation. It allowed guards to see attackers far off, to gather residents home from the fields and inside a locked gate. Then, from the turrets, the guards could handily ward off the threat.

But imagine if the marauders were able to encamp for a while, allowing no one out to work the farms; no one to bring in water, firewood, or food; no possibilities for sanitation or burial. Then this walled city would be a death trap.

Fortifications—whether built of stone or emotion or rationale—wall the enemy out, yes. But they also wall us in. A rush to self-protection can destroy us, as we trip on the very snare we've set. Thanks be to the Holy One for a different stronghold: a Presence who promises to move us past walls that separate and destroy, who remembers our need, who frees us in ways we couldn't have imagined. After all, says the psalmist, we are only human, captive to our fear and the destruction it spawns. God's grace and mercy are our real refuge, open to all.

Slow our racing hearts, Lord. Relax our defenses. Gather us in your peace. Amen.

Saul has been dosing himself with music from David's lyre. Lately that medicine has been Saul's only relief from the troubling spirit which possesses him. Today Saul's weightiest worry is the Philistines piling up like thunderclouds on the hilltop. At reveille the Philistines send out their most impressive weapon, Goliath, who strides down toward the battle line flaunting his might. "Today I defy the ranks of Israel! Give me a man, that we may fight together," Goliath bellows. King Saul—and all Israel—are "dismayed and greatly afraid."

It's not an auspicious start to the day. Those of us who suffer from even occasional depression know that just getting out of bed for another day's fray can be the hardest battle. Being roared at by a nine-foot warrior who is wearing 125 pounds of bronze armor and carrying a spear whose point weighs fifteen pounds would probably be enough to make any of us hide *under* the bed, not just in it. When my Philistines arrive—disguised as overdue bills, arguments, or painful memories—I want to turn the news off, turn the tunes up, shut the bedroom door, and hide my nose in the best fiction I own. That's my armor, my army.

Of course, that never works with Philistines, historical or existential. Somebody has to claim the authority to kick those rascally giants out of our hearts or off our calendars, to show them where our soul's buck stops if we are to claim our God-promised abundant lives. But to win that territory back from the Goliaths who defy us, we usually need to become less defended. David shows us: Armor's not worth the trouble. It immobilizes us, weighs us down, disables us from moving deftly toward our fears and beyond them. Simplicity, clarity, focus, and a daring trust may be the smooth stones already in our pocket.

Train our vision, Lord, lest we miss the mark today. Amen.

Sometimes love and circumstance push through our reticence like a swollen river finally pouring through flood gates. We release our pent-up pain, and another's heart opens to receive it. That's what Paul attempts as he bares his love to the Corinthian church and recounts his sacrifices, begging them to release their hearts' doors toward him too.

Decades ago, as I prepared to leave my parents' home at the end of our Christmas visit, they asked where things stood between me and my estranged husband. I had spent months in deep, constant wrestling—therapy, spiritual direction, reading, writing, ruminating. I hadn't talked much about my guilt or his. I'm the oldest daughter, mother of their first grandchild. And Dad was my hero—reserved, principled, tender. I liked reporting my successes, not my transgressions. But they knew.

It was time to admit that I expected to file for divorce. That wasn't the answer they wanted. My dad feared I was wishing on a star. My situation was tenuous. My son was only seven. I had an apartment and a job that didn't pay much yet.

"Can't you give him another chance?" my dad asked. I shook my head no.

"Maybe you've already given him a lot of chances," Dad said. Bingo. I couldn't go back to the man who wanted to punish me into staying but wouldn't risk himself or his money for counseling unless first I promised to stay.

Finally, my father looked me in the eye. "What you did was wrong," he said. "But I've loved you since the day you were born. I still do. I always will." Those words changed my life.

With whom do you need to pour out your passions, pains, fears, or failures? Can you open up the whole truth for love's sake, as Paul does?

Gracious One, flood our failures open with love and reveal our belonging. Amen.

What is it about storms in the evening? They are so much more frightening than storms in the middle of the day. Our creaturely vulnerability takes over at sundown, I guess. With daylight gone, we put down our strength and obey our fatigue. We reward ourselves with food and drink, wrap company and shelter around us. We just want rest, comfort, security.

Jesus certainly has that impulse in Mark's Gospel. Since his baptism in the Jordan and his temptations in the wilderness, Jesus has traveled, taught, and healed all over: in Galilee, in Capernaum, in the grain fields, in the synagogue, by the sea where crowds press in upon him, up on the mountain, back in Capernaum again, back again at the seaside teaching parable after parable to the crowds. No wonder that when evening comes he escapes by boat. No wonder he falls asleep!

But they're heading for Gentile territory. It's night after a long day, and the disciples are on duty without their master. The water becomes choppy. Wind howls, raising ever-taller waves that begin to swamp the boat. The disciples shout, "Teacher, do you not care that we are perishing?" Though they are able fishermen, their trust is instantly gone, as if Jesus has abandoned ship. They don't ask for his help; they leap to blame him for infidelity: "Don't you even care about us?"

A little fear, and they're angry. A little fear, and they act as if Jesus has betrayed them. A little fear, a little darkness, and they act as if the storm threatens them alone, not their sleeping rabbi. In a storm of fear and darkness, their love—our love—disappears.

But when Jesus commands our storm to stop, could it be that we are more terrified? Perhaps we wanted rest, comfort, security—not the Almighty beside us in the darkness, on the deep.

From fear's treachery, good Lord, deliver us. Teach us to trust that love is behind your power. Amen.

Fear: It's Risky Business

Presumption—it's hard to avoid falling into that pit. Whatever we've gotten used to thinking, we presume really *is* and should be. Psalm 9 should give us pause then because it reminds us that God may see things quite differently.

Years ago a middle school friend pointed out one of my presumptions. She had been worrying about the "bad" grade she had made on a test. "What did you make?" I asked. "*B*," she replied. "*B*? That's not a bad grade," I said, trying to encourage her. "It's not good enough for you!" she answered. Ouch! She recognized my unspoken presumptions about academic skill and privilege, based on my arrogance and fear. Arrogance because I thought I should make better grades than my friends, and fear because I didn't know who I would or could be without a string of *A*s on my report card. I shared her indignation: I had already betrayed my friend, omitting her from my imagined circle of academic equals. Had I ranked love and friendship below success? That wasn't who I wanted to be.

Is our national report card better than that of other nations? Must we be best or worthless? Loving without presumption is not easy. We will have to learn the gifts, rights, and suffering of those who first cared for our continent. We will have to unlearn our fantasies about the brave and religiously superior colonists who founded our country. We will have to unlearn slippery notions of separate-but-equal. We will have to unlearn some heroic tales about World War II, the Cold War, the space race, and the competition for nuclear and economic superiority. We will have to unlearn rhetoric that excludes, demonizes, dismisses.

All the nations are only human, Psalm 9 says. That includes us. May we trust first the One who delivers us from false judgments.

Rise up, O Lord! Save us from our delusions. Amen.

Who or what is your Goliath? Who will protect you mightily, battle for you, gather spoils into your treasury? Who stands between you and your least-desired future? What wealth or weapon lies ready in your vault?

When COVID-19 reached my hometown last spring, churches and universities ceased face-to-face gatherings. Hospitals were buying extra space for quarantine wards. The stock market plummeted. Masks, respirators, and hand sanitizer were in short supply. Sports championships were cancelled. A huge sinkhole gaped maw-like on campus. Already operatives had attacked our digital security. The Southeast had flooded; then a nighttime tornado struck Middle Tennessee, killing thirty-one.

This was a different sort of March madness. Our medical systems, transportation, economy, infrastructure, entertainment, and internet were faltering. We could no longer blissfully depend on them. Those Goliaths could not underwrite our dreams.

We breathe in; we breathe out. Ah, yes. The Spirit still brings life.

Babies will be born today. Parents will conceive today. Some kindly hands and hearts will serve up chili for the hungry. Some pilot will land the plane safely. Some firefighters will save bodies from flames. Some nurse will gently bathe a patient, some doctor save a heart. Some voices will sing hymns, chant prayers to lift our souls. A dad will do the laundry, a mom feed and bathe the little ones. A grandparent will read stories to children whose heads nod sleepily. Some scientist may discover a never-before-seen star. Some teacher will inspire a lifetime's pursuit. Some priest will bless and pardon, some sailor turn the rudder toward home. Some young shepherd will stand up to a giant and save the people. We love as God anoints us, and the Spirit—not Goliath—empowers our life.

Breathe yourself into us, O God, that we may depend on you alone and breathe you out upon each other. Amen.

Fear: It's Risky Business

SUNDAY, JUNE 20 ~ *Read 2 Corinthians 6:1-13*

Today's the day! Today God is pouring grace all over us, believe it or not. Today is the day when God's grace anoints us as a place where heaven and earth connect, like the stone near which Jacob saw angels ascending and descending.

Yes, I know: most days don't feel so revelatory or reassuring. But then, God is a surprise. Gracious love heals but doesn't always soothe us. It comes wrapped in such wild disguises!

Take parenthood, for example. When I was pregnant, then as a new mother, I read books about child development and parenting. But the child I imagined wasn't the child who developed right before me. I thought he would be quiet and thoughtful, a reader like me, enjoying school, drawing, daydreaming. I would explain everything; he would understand and comply. Instead, he was a physical, energetic boy who wore Superman underwear with an old beach towel pinned to his shoulders as he sped his big wheel off the edge of our deck, yelling, "Yahoo!" (Forget "Mr. Rogers." His favorite TV show was "The Dukes of Hazzard.") He followed our dog down an old logging road along the crest of a hill into the woods—miles of woods. It was January, snowing.

So grace in parenting has often come in sudden shocks. I asked, "What do I do now?" Sometimes grace has come slowly, when my answers proved faulty and my enforcement too uncertain. Inadequacy was the real means of grace; it stripped away my anxious self-reliance. Eventually, I learned how best to love him: to relish the humor and to take the long view, leaning back into the One who embraces without comparison, without measure, without end.

Today is always the day of salvation. Let go of what you thought you wanted. Lift your head to love's anointing.

Your grace frees us readily, Lord, but we are slow to see the offer. Open our hands. Teach us to say "yes" and "thank you." Amen.

Fear: It's Risky Business

Standin' in the Need of Prayer

JUNE 21–27, 2021 • CATHERINE WILLIAMS

SCRIPTURE OVERVIEW: David is remembered in scripture as a mighty king but also as a great poet. Many of the Psalms are ascribed to him. In Second Samuel we find a song of lament over Saul and Jonathan. Saul was violently jealous of David, yet David still honored Saul as God's anointed king. Jonathan was David's best friend. David bemoans Israel's loss of these leaders. The author of Psalm 130, although probably not David, appeals to God in David-like fashion. The Gospel shows the power of a woman's faith. In Second Corinthians, Paul deals with practical matters, appealing to the Corinthians to send promised financial help to the believers in Jerusalem.

QUESTIONS AND SUGGESTIONS FOR REFLECTION

- Read 2 Samuel 1:1, 17-27. What part does music play in your prayer life? Do you sing both songs of lament and songs of praise?
- Read Psalm 130. When have you cried out to God from the depths of your despair? What was God's response?
- Read 2 Corinthians 8:7-15. How do you maintain your eagerness to practice your faith?
- Read Mark 5:21-43. What has been your experience of God's healing?

Assistant Professor of Preaching and Worship at Lancaster Theological Seminary, Elder in the Greater New Jersey Annual Conference of The United Methodist Church, and tea enthusiast.

What is there about song and singing that resonates with us when we're grief-stricken? I think about the many moving spirituals, composed and sung by enslaved persons in the milieu of death and loss. They plumbed a depth of devastation that mere spoken words could not reach. I also think of that entire genre of popular music called the Blues, popular because heartache is never far away. There is just something about a fittingly sad tone or a minor key that vibrates on the same frequency as the burdened soul, massaging the aching psyche.

The creativity within King David rises up to do the one thing sure to express the raw emotion in the pit of his stomach. The warrior king is standing in the need of prayer; so the psalmist king steps forward to do the only thing that will express this raging torrent of complicated grief. At this moment the grief does not need to be tempered or tamed; it needs fulsome expression. Anger needs an outlet. Despair needs ventilation. Sorrow needs a conduit. Rage could use a playlist.

Certain shared social norms sometimes require that we tone down grief. But some of us cannot live with the pent-up burden of sorrow. Is there in our musical storehouse a hymn, a poem, a dirge, a lament through which we can wail, cry, groan, or moan as we attend to the trouble in our souls? A stiff upper lip may be good for appearances, but it does not heal the soul. David pours out his heart in this Song of the Bow. I invite you to pause with me as we think about our individual outlets for deep sorrow and loss.

Someone's praying, Lord. kum ba yah. Someone's crying, Lord, kum ba yah. Oh, Lord, kum ba yah! (UMH, no. 494).

Oh, the desperation in these first two verses! The psalmist seems to be shouting above the noise of the churning waters of chaos in order to be heard. The depths are places none of us signs up for when we embark on this journey of faith. None of us hopes or plans for those times when all hell breaks loose and the road plunges sharply downward without warning. None of us likes to think of ourselves in the pit of life, that place of darkness and anxiety where we struggle with situations that cover our lives with storm clouds that seem as though they could burst any minute, and then they do! I imagine it is someplace dark and desolate that the psalmist calls the "depths." Is that where Jonah was in the belly of the fish? Is that the place St. John of the Cross "called the dark night of the soul"?

I remember a time I was there. The physical space was my bathroom floor, where I lay in a sobbing heap, in emotional and financial chaos. The bathroom floor was my throne of grace and mercy at which I pleaded, *God, where are you?*

The state of desperation is not a tourist attraction, especially for anyone socialized to believe in the merits of self-sufficiency and independence. Yet this distressed mindset of the psalmist plays out against the backdrop of an ever-present God who remains the psalmist's present help in times of trouble. Oh, for such eyes of faith to see the ever-present God. Oh, for senses tuned to the realm of the spirit where God's presence is known. Oh, for grace to know that even in the depths of life's circumstances—tragedy, sickness, grief, and pain—God is...

Let me at thy throne of mercy find a sweet relief, kneeling there in deep contrition; help my unbelief. Savior, Savior, hear my humble cry; while on others thou art calling, do not pass me by (UMH, no. 351).

Who of us has never blamed ourselves for something that went wrong? If I had only . . . I should have . . . I could have . . . Iniquities are those aspects of life that remind us of our mortality and finiteness. Some of us are so prone to self-blame that it may even be our default stance when things go wrong. But the psalmist puts our humanity into divine perspective when he asks, "If you should mark iniquities, who would be left standing?" (AP).

Blame doesn't share very well; it likes to keep the burden to itself. When we think, "Why am I in this deep mess?" we generally don't share the blame around. It tends to pile up on one person, and if that person is the self, that only compounds the situation. Not only am I in trouble, but it is also all my fault!

Let's follow the psalmist's gaze as he shifts and widens perspective. It's not about the depth of my transgression. It's about the depth, the height, and the breadth of God's amazing love. "There is forgiveness with you." We are often so slow to forgive ourselves, it becomes hard to imagine the readiness of God to forgive us. Today we are invited to relax the hold on our failures. Release them; exhale as they fall into the hands of a loving God, who knows what to do with wrongdoings and shortcomings. Words of assurance are just as important as prayers of confession in our worship liturgies. Confession: *O God, our iniquities abound and overwhelm us.* Assurance: *Hear the good news, friends of God, there is no offense or mistake, no sin of omission or commission, no fault or failure that can separate us from the love of God who forgives.*

> *In the midst of faults and failures, stand by me; in the midst of faults and failures, stand by me. When I've done the best I can, and my friends misunderstand, thou who knowest all about me, stand by me (UMH, no. 512).*

We might well wonder what's going on here? A guilt trip? A stewardship moment? This passage has been lifted out of a larger appeal or petition made by the apostle on behalf of another church in need. In some cultures where kinship values prevail, it is not unheard of for a family with more children than they can care for to "give" a child to a childless couple within that extended family, to raise for the sake of the wider family. It is an informal fostering system to be sure, but one that works on much the same principle upon which the apostle makes his appeal. It's a way of redistributing the burden, sharing the load, bearing one another's burdens. Whatever the language used, there is an attempt to be fair so that "the one who had much did not have too much, and the one who had little did not have too little."

This system of just sharing is not one we warm up to in much of our North American culture. Many of us consider self-sufficiency a noble goal. We strive toward it in our educational endeavors and in our financial planning. Yet, in this passage we see another way, one that takes seriously the *koinonia* of Christian community, the socioeconomic principle upon which the early Christian church was built. As we think about how we respond to human need, what might it look like to share the load? When we pray for others in need, how prepared are we to be part of the answer to our prayer? As we pray for those standing in the need of prayer this week, how can we be open to the ways in which God might respond? How might we invite others to be part of the answer to our prayers?

For the healing of the nations, Lord, we pray with one accord (UMH, no. 428).

FRIDAY, JUNE 25 ~ *Read Mark 5:21-24*

My own prayer life has been formed under the mentorship of praying women, my mother being the primary role model. These women taught me how to "stand in the gap" as I prayed for family and friends who were standing in the need of prayer. The church called these women "prayer warriors" because of the intensity and tenacity of their prayer life. The tone of their prayers said, "God it's you or nothing, and since we won't accept nothing then we will remain before your throne of grace and mercy for as long as it takes."

It is this going to God on behalf of another, combined with a sense of desperation, that we see in Jairus. His words and behavior indicate, "Jesus, it's you or nothing!" It is not typical that we hear of men who intercede like this. We live in a world where paternal and parental abuse has devastated too many lives. This is why, whenever we find a contrast to such abuse, we need to recognize and salute fathers and parents who do what it takes for their daughters and sons to thrive and flourish. God hears their prayers and the prayers of many others who come to God on behalf of someone else who cannot.

These first verses of this story remind us we can approach God on behalf of our loved ones, on behalf of any urgent situation we care deeply about—deeply enough that we are willing to virtually throw ourselves at God's feet, making repeated petitions for God's mercy to intervene in a humanly impossible situation. This kind of prayer is not daunted by the very real possibility that the petition may not be answered in the way we expect. In the moment, it knows only deep love and desperate faith.

We share each other's woes, our mutual burdens bear; and often for each other flows the sympathizing tear. (UMH, no. 557)

All kinds of touching happen throughout this twin narrative. First there is Jairus falling at Jesus' feet, possibly grasping him in desperation, begging him to " . . . lay your hands on my daughter." Then there's the crowd—the pressing, pushing, jostling mass of people—all touching one another, many possibly trying to touch Jesus. Then there is that show-stopping touch of the nameless woman and the corresponding divine touch upon her body. Might her heart also be touched by Jesus' tender offer of kinship? Finally, there is the life-giving touch of Jesus as he moves past ritual restraint to touch a lifeless body, restoring a child to her place within the family and the community, restoring a broken relationship, if you will, between a daddy and his girl.

Touch is a powerful parental gesture—for good or for ill. Medical experts who study the phenomenon of touch tell us that this is the first language we learn as infants. If touch is a language, then we should learn it well! We should use it fluently, articulately, and eloquently to communicate God's amazing grace to people who may not get the message as clearly or as deeply otherwise! To be sure, touch is a culturally defined gesture; touch as a language communicates best when it stems from a heart of goodwill and understanding. And what of touch as prayer? As a chaplain beside the bed of non-communicative persons in the throes of sickness, I've often had to resort to the wordless prayer of a gentle touch upon a patient's hand; even a virtual touch, simply extending a hand toward the person, hoping and praying for that spark of divine energy to do what only God can do.

Prayer is the soul's sincere desire, unuttered or expressed, the motion of a hidden fire that trembles in the breast. O Thou, by whom we come to God, the Life, the Truth, the Way: the path of prayer thyself hast trod; Lord, teach us how to pray (UMH, no. 492).

This is not the only time the Gospels give us reason to hope beyond hope that our prayers for humanly impossible situations might be answered. There is Jesus' delayed response to Lazarus's illness-turned-death. There is Jesus' stopping the funeral procession so he can reunite a widow and her dead son. Whatever our understanding of these "late" divine responses, the truth is they reflect a human conundrum around God's timing. When is it okay to give up hope that a prayer will be answered?

A friend of mine prayed fervently and tenaciously for healing from cancer every day she lived with the disease. Those of us closest to her dared not hint at the thought of a different outcome, so fierce was her determination to live. When her body ultimately succumbed to the disease, the family asked me to preach her funeral sermon. Time for some deep, personal, theological reflection! My personal experience bore witness to welcome and unwelcome outcomes to prayers for healing. My sermon preparation led me to the eleventh chapter of Hebrews with its powerful examples of persons who died in faith, having not received the promises they had believed in. It comforted me to know that not receiving from God what we hope for is not a strike against our capacity to believe God for the impossible. It is a rugged faith that will travel smooth and rough terrains with the same mindset—God before me, God with me, God behind me. It is the enduring, tenacious presence of God as experienced in prayer that keeps us standing—"Standin' in the Need of Prayer."

*Robert Lowry, "My Life Flows On," The Faith We Sing, (Nashville, TN, Abingdon Press, 2000), 2212.

*What though my joys and comforts die? I know my Savior liveth. What though the darkness gather round? Songs in the night he giveth. No storm can shake my inmost calm while to that Rock I'm clinging. Since love is Lord of heaven and earth, how can I keep from singing?**

We're Marching to Zion

JUNE 28–JULY 4, 2021 • JAMES A. HARNISH

SCRIPTURE OVERVIEW: The readings from the Hebrew scriptures this week celebrate Jerusalem, the capital of the great King David, who united the ancient Israelites and built up the city. The psalmist praises Jerusalem using the image of Zion—a name used for earthly Jerusalem but also a gesture toward a future day when God's people will abide in a heavenly city. In Second Corinthians, Paul explains that even though he is an apostle, he struggles like everyone else. Speculation surrounds the "thorn" that plagued Paul; but his point is that when he is weakest, God is strongest. In Mark, we see God's power working through Jesus, who sent out others to expand God's healing work.

QUESTIONS AND SUGGESTIONS FOR REFLECTION

- Read 2 Samuel 5:1-5, 9-10. What qualities of leadership are important in this reading? How do those qualities square with your experience with those in power?
- Read Psalm 48. Bring to mind a place where you experience God's presence. What is it about that place that makes you especially aware of God's presence?
- Read 2 Corinthians 12:2-10. When have you experienced weakness becoming a source of strength and power?
- Read Mark 6:1-13. When have you discounted someone because of your assumptions about them?

Husband, father, and grandfather; retired pastor in the Florida Conference of The United Methodist Church; author of *A Disciple's Path, Extraordinary Ministry in Ordinary Time,* and *Easter Earthquake;* blogs at jimharnish.org.

Inever cease to be inspired when I arrive in Washington, D.C. and ride past the Washington Monument or walk around the Lincoln, Jefferson, and King memorials. They are architectural witnesses of the yet-to-be-fulfilled vision that gave birth to this nation. They inspire hope that we may yet accomplish the promise of "liberty and justice for all."

I've experienced similar inspiration walking around the Houses of Parliament in London, climbing the steps of Constitution Hill in Johannesburg, or standing on Corcovado Mountain beneath the statue of Christ the Redeemer stretching his arms over Rio de Janeiro. The architecture inspires the vision of what God intends for the world to be and who we may yet become.

Psalm 48 is one verse of a trio of songs (46-48) that celebrate Mount Zion as "the city belonging to our God . . . the joy of the whole world" (CEB) The psalmist moves from observing architecture to affirming theology in declaring, "God is in its fortifications" (CEB). Walking around the city inspires the psalmist to declare, "This is God, our God, forever and always" (CEB).

The psalm reverberates with joy in the hope Mount Zion represents. Jerusalem becomes the physical expression of God's intention of the whole world and the ultimate destination of our spiritual journey. In Revelation, the New Jerusalem becomes the fulfillment of the promise of a world in which God's will is done and God's kingdom comes on earth. John envisions a city where all nations are welcome and "its gates will never be shut" (Rev. 21:25, CEB). That's why faithful disciples in every generation sing, "We're Marching to Zion."

Come we that love the Lord, and let our joys be known; join in a song with sweet accord, and thus surround the throne. We're marching upward to Zion, the beautiful city of God (UMH, no. 733).

The lectionary reading leaves verses 6-8 out of this passage. It's not unlike the way we try to hide the ugly stories in our history.

Located on the border between Israel and Judah, Jerusalem was a strategic location for David to establish his capital as he united a divided people. The Jebusite residents mocked David by saying that "the blind and lame" could defeat him (CEB), thereby becoming the target of David's vengeance. The blind and lame were specifically shut out of the city.

Ugly stories of exclusion, racism, injustice, and violence are embedded in the history of every city and nation and continue to infect our lives each day. We all have reasons to repent for the ways we succumb to the worst demons in our sin-infected economic and political systems. But the Lord was with David. Through all the ugly stories in David's life, God never gave up on him. God's faithfulness to David gives hope that we may yet rise to the "better angels of our nature."

Over time, the vision of Mount Zion became more inclusive. Isaiah saw a new Jerusalem in which all people were welcome and whole. (See Isaiah 65:17-25.) Jeremiah included the "blind and the lame" in the return from exile (Jer. 31:8, CEB). Micah said the Lord would "gather those who have been driven away" including "the lame" (Mic. 4:6-7, CEB). In the Gospels, "People who were blind and lame came to Jesus . . . and he healed them" (Matt. 21:14, CEB). John envisions the New Jerusalem where all nations will find healing. (See Revelation 22:1-5.)

Our hope is that when we repent of the ugly stories in our past, God will forgive, heal, and give us a new future.

Give us, O God, the strength to build the city that hath stood too long a dream, whose laws are love, whose crown is servant-hood, and where the sun that shineth is God's grace for human good (UMH, no. 726).

While we are "marching upward to Zion," what kind of leader can we trust to show us the way?

The first reason the Israelite tribes gave for choosing David was, "We are your very own flesh and bone." They knew David was one of them and they were one with him.

When Doris Kearns Goodwin studied the leadership of Franklin D. Roosevelt, she found a direct link between his personal struggle with polio and his ability to lead the American people through the great depression and World War II. She called FDR "the living emblem of a man who had truly transformed his own pain and necessity into glorious gain."*

Living among patients at Warm Springs, GA, FDR learned humility that was "of a different order than merely accepting one's limitations. By sharing those limitations with his fellow polios, by listening and learning from them, he . . . developed a new empathy, allowing him to connect emotionally with all manner of people to whom fate had also dealt an unkind blow."*

On our journey to Mount Zion, we don't follow a leader "who can't sympathize with our weakness but . . . one who was tempted in every way that we are, except without sin." We follow Jesus Christ who "learned obedience from what he suffered . . . [and] became the source of salvation" (Heb. 4:15, 5:8-9, CEB). In the Incarnation, God became our "very own flesh and bone." We follow Jesus because we know that he is one of us, and one with us.

---

*Leadership in Turbulent Times, (New York: Simon and Schuster, 2018), pp. 170, 173.

All praise to thee, for thou, O King divine, didst yield the glory that of right was thine . . . Alleluia! (UMH, no. 166).

David was a strong leader. People remembered the way he "led Israel out to war" and took Mount Zion by force (2 Sam. 5:2, 9, CEB). In our capital cities, we erect monuments to courageous generals and powerful politicians. We are attracted to leaders who promise to solve problems by their personal power and persuasion. We are tempted to follow religious leaders who claim superior faith based on esoteric spiritual experiences.

Paul is defending himself from leaders and "super-apostles" (2 Cor. 11:5, CEB) who brag about out-of-body spiritual experiences. Paul models a different kind of leadership. He acknowledges the struggle that leads him to humble dependence on God's grace. He doesn't brag about his strengths but about the weakness in which he finds strength that only Christ can give.

In studying the development of character, author David Brooks described "the feeling of smallness and sinfulness" by which "one gets next to the awesome presence of God." He observed the humility that "comes from daily reminders of your own brokenness [and] relieves you of the awful stress of trying to be superior all the time."*

The humble strength Paul's leadership portrays grows over time as we confront our limitations and failures. It emerges as we deepen our relationship with God through the spiritual disciplines that form us into the likeness of Christ who, "though he was in the form of God, did not consider being equal with God something to exploit, but . . . humbled himself" (Phil. 2:6-8, CEB). In humility we experience grace and find strength.

---

*David Brooks, *The Road to Character*, (New York: Random House, 2015), p. 205

O Master, let me walk with thee in lowly paths of service free; tell me thy secret; help me bear the strain of toil, the fret of care. Teach me thy patience; still with thee in closer, dearer company, in work that keeps faith sweet and strong, in trust that triumphs over wrong (UMH, no. 430).

We're Marching to Zion

The journey to Mount Zion is never easy. Sooner or later, disciples who are "marching to Zion" discover the ways God's purpose challenges the way we live in a sin-damaged world.

Jesus ran into that kind of resistance in his hometown. At first, his former neighbors were impressed by what he was saying and doing. But then they began asking, "Where did he get this? Isn't he Joe's boy?" (AP). In Luke's version of this story, after Jesus announced his mission, the people were "filled with anger . . . and ran him out of town" (Luke 4:28-29, CEB).

Perhaps the memory of the questionable circumstances of Mary's pregnancy resurfaced. Perhaps they could not believe that such an ordinary boy could grow up to do such extraordinary things. Perhaps they resented the way this hometown kid was getting "too big for his boots." Or perhaps they questioned how someone so much like them could be the Son of God.

Whatever the reason for their rejection—and for ours—the Greek verb Mark used here (6:3), *skandalizo*, is the same verb he used to describe people who began to follow Jesus but stumbled along the way, turned back, or became deserters. (See Mark 4:17; 9:42-48; 14:27-29.)

In my first pastoral appointment I was deeply invested in youth ministry. Four decades later, I know the joy of seeing some of those teenagers continue to grow as faithful disciples of Christ. But I also know the pain of those who stumbled or turned back along the way.

The sad commentary on Nazareth is that Jesus was "unable to do any miracles there" (CEB). Whatever our reasons, our resistance still gets in the way of God's power being released in our lives. Then Jesus went on to another village.

Are there no foes for me to face? Must I not stem the flood? Is this vile world a friend to grace, to help me on to God? (UMH, no. 511).

Passengers arriving at the O. R. Tambo International Airport in Johannesburg, South Africa, are greeted by a large mural that declares, "If you want to go fast, go alone. If you want to go far, go together."

That African proverb could be the caption on the picture Mark paints of Jesus sending his disciples out in pairs. He tells them to travel light, which is good advice for anyone going on a long journey. In contrast to his rejection in Nazareth, Jesus tells them to go where they are welcome. He commissions them to do what he was unable to do back home. Through them, the promise of the coming of the kingdom of God in the future becomes a reality in the present.

The shocking message is that ordinary disciples are commissioned to participate in the coming of the extraordinary promise of the kingdom of God. Jesus commissions us to live now in ways that are consistent with the way this world will be in that day when the vision of Mount Zion becomes a reality among us; when the New Jerusalem comes down from heaven; when God dwells with humankind; when there will be no more injustice, violence, suffering, or death; when God makes all things new. (See Revelation 21:1-6.)

If Jesus promised a quick fix to the brokenness of this world, we could make that journey alone. But because it's a long road, we are sent out together. We cannot march to Zion alone. The good news is that we don't have to! We are sent out in mission with other disciples to do what Jesus would be doing if he were physically present among us.

Lord, give us faith and strength the road to build, to see the promise of the day fulfilled, when war shall be no more, and strife shall cease upon the highway of the Prince of Peace (UMH, no. 567).

Psalms 46-48 are a trio of psalms that lift the vision of the worshiper above a jingoistic celebration of the city of Jerusalem to the God who is "king over the nations" (Ps. 47:8, CEB). Mount Zion is "the joy of the whole world" (CEB). Perhaps John remembered Psalm 46:4 when he envisioned the river that flows through the New Jerusalem and the tree that brings healing to the nations. (See Revelation 22:1-2.)

The Washington National Cathedral stands on the highest point of land in the District of Columbia. Above the High Altar is the massive carving of "Christ in Majesty" in which the risen Christ holds the globe in his hand. On this day when citizens of the United States celebrate the ideals that gave birth to our nation, the cathedral points to the Christ who reigns above every city or nation. The whole world is held in God's grace and judgment. Any city or nation fulfills its highest purpose when it becomes part of the fulfillment of Jesus' vision of God's Kingdom, coming on earth as it is already fulfilled in heaven.

I don't know why the editors of *The United Methodist Hymnal* placed "We're Marching to Zion" as the last hymn in the book, but it seems like just the right place to me. It suggests that when we have said or sung everything we have to say or sing, there is still more out ahead of us. We are always on the way toward the fulfillment of God's purpose that is captured in the vision of Mount Zion. God always has more for us. We're always marching on "to fairer worlds on high."

When Isaac Watts published the hymn in 1707, he titled it, "Heavenly Joy on Earth." With the psalmists, we live with confident joy as we march onward to Zion.

Then let our songs abound and every tear be dry; we're marching through Emmanuel's ground, to fairer worlds on high. We're marching upward to Zion, the beautiful city of God (UMH, no. 733).

Grace Runs Down

JULY 5–11, 2021 • ROSALIND C. HUGHES

SCRIPTURE OVERVIEW: Two readings this week focus on welcoming God's presence. David does this by bringing the ark of the covenant into Jerusalem. As the ark arrives, David dances, worshiping God with reckless abandon. The author of Psalm 24 poetically calls a city to open its gates and welcome the great king. These passages invite us to consider how willingly we receive God into our lives. The reading from Ephesians speaks of God's eternal plan. While circumstances may seem chaotic, God holds an eternal perspective and has sealed us with the Holy Spirit. Mark tells the sad story of the execution of John the Baptist, yet another example of a righteous person experiencing persecution.

QUESTIONS AND SUGGESTIONS FOR REFLECTION

- Read 2 Samuel 6:1-5, 12b-19. How do you bless others in your daily life?
- Read Psalm 24. In what ways do you honor the Creator in the ways you care for God's creation?
- Read Ephesians 1:3-14. Where have you stumbled on your faith journey and found God ready and willing to help?
- Read Mark 6:14-29. When have you experienced a guilty conscience? Did you resolve the issue that was causing the feeling?

Rector of the Church of the Epiphany (Episcopal) in Euclid, Ohio; contributing editor at the Episcopal Cafe (www.episcopalcafe.com), and author of *A Family Like Mine: Biblical Stories of Love, Loss, and Longing* (Upper Room Books).

Who shall ascend the hill of the LORD?" the psalmist asks. Last time I set out to climb a small mountain, it was without supreme confidence that I would make the summit. I would have to scramble over exposed crags and sharp ridges. The breathless elevation was only occasionally relieved by shallower stretches. I was far from convinced that I had the heart, strength, and grit for it.

But the mountain makes companions out of strangers. They share footholds and caution against surprise drop-offs. Their energy encourages; and if they stumble, you cannot help but shore them up. Alone, I would not have made it.

"Who shall ascend the hill of the LORD?" the psalmist asks. Those with clean hands and pure hearts; those who tell the truth.

I try to be a good enough person. But whenever I read the more self-justifying psalms, I become uncomfortable. I am not certain my conscience can altogether bear such confidence.

But the company of those who seek the face of God includes sinners as well as saints. This week's readings are full of both. David stumbles in his commitment to bring the ark of the covenant to Jerusalem. Michal despises kings from her lofty balcony. John the Baptist succumbs to the sword, and Jesus is creating unrest in the heart of Herod. Paul assures us that God has chosen us to be holy and blameless, not on our own account but because of the overflowing richness of God's grace, which we inherit as God's adopted children—the communion of sinners and saints.

"Who shall ascend the hill of the LORD?" We are on the quest in mixed company, seeking God's face together. We rely not on our own strength and righteousness but on the companionship of fellow adventurers and the merciful vindication of the God of our salvation.

O God, the week stretches weary before me. Help me to find you in the crowded schedule, encouraging me on to glory. Amen.

Sometimes when the lectionary skips a few verses, they hold arcane detail unlikely to illuminate any but the most dedicated archaeologists of the Bible. Other times, they reveal uncomfortable information that would interfere with the simple, smooth story that we prefer to tell. In this week's passage from Second Samuel 6, the lectioneers jump from verse 5 to the end of verse 12, omitting a telling lesson from the triumphant tale of the ark's journey to Jerusalem.

On the way from Baal-judah to the city of David, the ark is jolted into the barn at Nacon for an overnight stay. Uzzah reaches out to steady it. But somewhere between the stumbling and steadying, Uzzah falls down and dies. His death is interpreted as an act of God. David is suddenly overcome with fear of his responsibility to take care of God's covenant with the people. He sends the seat of holiness to stay in the house of a foreigner, letting him bear the risk of God's favor.

When we let others take the risks of love instead of investing ourselves, we also disinvest from the interest love accrues.

After three months, David hears that Obed-edom's household has been blessed by the presence of the ark, so David resumes his rejoicing and brings the ark up to the city. He offers sacrifice every six steps, to be safe. He dances his heart out in praise. He blesses the people and shares the bounty, inviting them into and implicating them in the covenant of God.

Underneath his royal trappings, David was afraid to grasp the covenant that God offered him. But he tried, shedding the armor of fear, the costume of finery, the disguise of status, stripping down to the bare essentials, just as the boy once had before the giant Goliath, as he danced and prayed his way toward Zion.

Gracious God, fear of you is only the beginning of wisdom; perfect love dissolves fear. Help me to shed the falsehoods that fear tells me. Show me how to bare my soul to you, trusting your affection. Amen.

I despised Jane (not her real name). I disdained the blue ribbon in her hair. I sniffed at her brown shoes. I thoroughly disliked the way her mouth hung open over her workbook. Seven-year-olds are so judgmental. Most of all, I despised the casting of Jane as Mary in the school nativity play. I could hardly look at her in her blue dressing-gown costume. I did not consider her good enough. I wanted to be considered better.

Whether it is power or innocence, enthusiasm or freedom, the emotion of despisal usually says as much about our own insecurities or injuries as it does about the despised.

Michal despised David. She cringed at the sight of his body. She may have had reason to be angry at him. Probably she considered it hypocrisy, watching him dance, as though all were right between him and God, and between the world and God. Michal despised him because she was unable to dance as though all were well with the world.

There is a saying about cutting off one's nose to spite one's face. The people gathered before the tent of the ark and shared in the ritual, sacrificial food, their communion with God and with one another, a sacramental sign of God's blessing among them. Michal remained apart, imprisoned behind her window of pain.

I considered sulkily sitting out the nativity play. But my teacher saw through my bitterness. Because her own heart was tender, she was able to humble mine enough not to push Jane off the donkey, and even to find some satisfaction in singing the part of a chorus angel.

Bitterness, envy, even injury can be isolating, building up walls between our hearts and the heart of God. Dismantling our defenses of contempt or despair is best done gently. But love always finds a way.

"A broken and contrite heart, O God, you will not despise" (Ps. 51:17). Deliver me from bitterness, soothe the scars of my heart, and seal it and heal it for love. Amen.

The soft edges of the road were filled with hard rocks, sheep, and goats. Parking in the empty lot, we hiked the path that circled the flat-topped mountain. The landscape was pockmarked with caves, any one of which might have been John's final prison: dungeon cells hacked into the hillside that served as the foundation of Machaerus, the Herods' fortress. At the summit, the wind whipped across an abandoned and ruined site. It was surprisingly small. A couple of columns still stood. There was a small archway, and a deep and frightening pit in the center. For all his bravado and brash promises, what survives of Herod's inherited, elevated palace two thousand years later is mostly sand and the sighing of the wind.

The tragedy of Herod is that he fails to learn even from his own conscience. Herod is perplexed by John, yet he shields him from the violence of Herodias until the day comes when his pride outweighs his fear of God. This is Antipas, Herod of the hand-me-downs. They called his father "the Great." This Herod, forever uncertain of his place in the world, tries to assert himself before God and humans by hanging out with holy people—and killing them.

Later when he heard of Jesus, Herod wondered if John had returned to haunt him, still calling upon him for repentance. Later still, when the opportunity came again to stand on the side of righteousness, he failed to recognize the chance Jesus gave him for redemption. He handed him over to be crucified.

Unless we can confess to ourselves—much less to God—our sin, how can we experience forgiveness? Unless we are willing to receive the healing grace of God for our own hurts and injuries, we will be unlikely to share it with anybody else. What then will our legacy be?

My God, "I know my transgressions, and my sin is ever before me" (Ps. 51:3). "Lord, I am not worthy to receive you, but only say the word, and I shall be healed" (Traditional prayer).

Grace Runs Down   229

According to the notes in all of my Bible translations, the dedication of this letter to the people of Ephesus is optional. Why does that matter? It matters because Paul is offering a vision of such love and embrace that we can hardly believe it applies to us. But what if the letter *is* meant for all those whom the word of God has touched? What if it is for us, saints and sinners, and all our companions laboring to ascend the hill of the Lord?

Journeying through the ups and downs of David and Michal, Herod and John (even the Baptizer had his moments of doubt, sending word to Jesus to ask, "Are you really the Messiah?") we have found ourselves in the company of mixed motives and, at times, downright dirty dealers. In the mirror of their sin, we are tempted to judge ourselves.

But from the beginning of time, Paul says, we have been chosen to be blameless. This is not because we are better than our ancestors but because God has loved even these, anointing some, sending Jesus to speak directly to others, whispering through the dark times. God knows our secret fears and our stifled pride. God has seen our wounded doubt; and God's response has been to pour out grace, to forgive our sins. God sets us on our feet like a parent picking up a child and dusting her off, longing to gather her up in arms of love.

As children, we fall, we learn, and we try again to walk with steadiness and integrity. As God is patient with our stumbles, can we be as patient with our own family of creation and of faith? As God has forgiven our trespasses, can we forgive those who trespass against us? If we can learn to claim this grace for ourselves, can we learn to extend it to one another?

God of grace and glory, as you forgive our trespasses, help us to forgive those who trespass against us, for the healing of hearts and the glory of your reconciling Spirit. Amen.

Iknew that I was adopted before I knew what the word meant, long before I understood the other stories behind the word. I knew that I was claimed and sealed under law into a new relationship before I recognized any rift in the original.

When I heard from the lectern at my childhood church that we all had been adopted by God, I understood from my everyday experience that this had happened before I knew my own name. It happened without any need for my petition or signature. It was an embrace made ready for me to fall into before I knew I needed it. I understood this before I had ever heard the word *justification*, let alone *atonement* or *theology*.

When our parents adopted their children, they had no idea who we would become. (The same goes for any parent, I have found.) They made promises based not on prophecy but on faith, on trust. The court stamped its approval. A legacy was created.

God has a pretty good idea of our potential and our pitfalls. God knows that we are but children, trying and erring, working through growing pains and hard lessons, in constant need of encouragement. God knows that this relationship would try the patience of saints, that our rebellion would be repeated and predictable. God has faith that the measures for our redemption that God has put in place will be enough to bring us home when we wander.

Like many grown-up children, and parents, I am often wary of parental images for God. We know that families do not always turn out as we would like. But adoption almost always has an aspirational aspect: the hope of something new and redemptive for all concerned. The idea that God invests God's hope in me takes my breath away.

Hopeful God, I give you thanks for the love which you invest in me, and I pray for your help to live into it fully, faithfully, and forever. Amen.

Grace Runs Down

"Who shall ascend the hill of the LORD?" the psalmist asks. We return to the question that opened our week together. The psalm continues, greeting God the King of glory whose advent opens the gates and lifts up the doors, whose victory liberates the city at the summit.

We, as adopted children of the king of glory, ride on the royal coattails through the high gates. The doors cannot be closed against us. We do not need to deceive ourselves about the state of our souls because God, who knows us inside and out, has granted us safe passage across the borders of holiness into the nearer presence of grace. We have only to wash our faces, raise our heads, and seek the face of the God of our ancestors, whose inheritance is ours.

But if we turn aside, whom do we find walking with us? Will we notice David, and is he fearful still? Will we see Michal, looking down but reaching up? And where did we leave Herod?

On the hillsides of England and Wales, intersecting with strangers, I have received more grace than I have offered. I think I have needed more! But perhaps we all feel that way from time to time. Maybe a younger woman has, in fact, taken courage from seeing this old body heave itself over one more obstacle. Grace is impossible to imprison, after all; she spills out of any vessel that tries to contain her. Like water, she finds her way to the lowest point, to the person struggling for a foothold at the bottom of the crag; and grace revives the parched heart.

We belong to God as beloved children, God's own creation, imprinted with the divine image, which cannot be erased. Let us, as a created and redeemed family, encourage one another toward the summit of God's love.

God of our ancestors, God of our children, God of our past, God of our present, God of our wandering hearts, carry us over the threshold of your love, and hold us forever. Amen.

The Compassionate Builder

JULY 12–18, 2021 • DAVID E. RAINEY

SCRIPTURE OVERVIEW: David was God's anointed king over Israel. He believed God desired a house, a temple worthy of God. But God wanted David to understand that only God can build things that truly last. Thus, God promised to construct a dynasty from David's family. From this line will eventually come the ultimate King, the Messiah, who will rule God's people forever. The Messiah will complete God's work of uniting all people as children of God, and the author of Ephesians declares that this has happened through Christ. All God's people—Jew and Gentile—are now part of a holy, spiritual temple. In Mark, Jesus shows that part of being a great king is showing compassion. He puts aside his own desires to help those in need of guidance and healing.

QUESTIONS AND SUGGESTIONS FOR REFLECTION

- Read 2 Samuel 7:1-14a. When have you changed your opinion on something significant? What led to the change?
- Read Psalm 89:20-37. What helps you recall God's faithfulness in times when you may feel abandoned?
- Read Ephesians 2:11-22. Where have you found Christ breaking down dividing walls between groups of people? What part does your Christian community play in bringing people together?
- Read Mark 6:30-34, 53-56. When have you had an experience of illness or accident that left you isolated from community? How did that increase your awareness of others in that situation as you moved to health?

Husband, father of three, retired United Methodist pastor in Nashville, TN.

As we continue the saga of King David, we find the monarch mulling over his success and coming to an embarrassing realization. He is living in a fine palace; but the symbol of the Lord's presence, the ark of the covenant, remains in a tent. David consults with his chief advisor, the prophet Nathan, and they agree that it's time to build a proper temple for the Lord. The royal architects might have started work the very next day had it not been for the vision which Nathan had that night.

It seems that the Lord actually prefers a tent! A tent is mobile, flexible, able to respond to changing circumstances. With a tent, there are no illusions that God can be boxed in. "What do I need with a palace?" the Lord asks Nathan. "In all the years I have moved about with my people, have I ever even hinted I wanted a palace?" (AP).

Among other things, this story raises the question of what kind of house best reflects and honors the Lord God.

There is a historical marker in front of Edgehill United Methodist Church in Nashville, TN, honoring the life and ministry of Rev. Bill Barnes. Rev. Barnes was the founding pastor of this urban congregation, a church which continues to serve the city's poor and marginalized out of a remodeled home and garage. One of Bill's strongest commitments was to working for affordable housing. Appropriately, the historical marker includes this prophetic insight, attributed to Bishop Oscar Romero of El Salvador: "The temple shall remain unfinished until all are housed in dignity."

How can we build a house which will honor God? Bill Barnes believed it was by housing the most vulnerable of God's children.

Gracious God, grant us a vision of housing which honors you and your children. Then give us the heart and the will to build. Amen.

While King David is obviously at the center of today's scripture, I find I am drawn to the prophet Nathan. Nathan is introduced here as a kind of spiritual advisor to the king. We don't know whether he applied for this position or was appointed, but he is there when David begins to reflect on the need to build a house for the Lord. When David observes that it is a shame the ark of the covenant is still in a tent, Nathan quickly supports him. While it might appear that Nathan is simply being a "yes man," we have no reason to think that he doesn't actually agree with David. A temple would be a wonderful way to honor God!

By the next morning, of course, Nathan has changed his mind. Or more accurately, God has changed it for him. It is not David's job to build a holy temple but to trust God to build a holy people. This is an amazing and courageous shift. Just the day before, Nathan saw things one way. Now he sees them differently. And he is ready to say so, even to the king.

The Christian Century magazine has occasionally featured a series called "How My Mind Has Changed." In this series, various religious leaders have shared how their thinking on significant issues has shifted over time. These faithful thinkers were not being wishy-washy. They were just ready to keep listening to the voice of God and changing their minds as they had new insights and experiences.

Certainly we are called to be unwavering in our commitment to the basic tenets of our faith—loving God and neighbor. But God's Spirit may change our hearts and our minds about how we live out these foundational beliefs.

Guide us today, O God, so that we can be attentive to your Spirit and have the courage to change our minds. Amen.

This week's psalm was quite possibly written during the time of the Babylonian Exile. A few years before, the Temple in Jerusalem had been destroyed by a foreign power, and Israel's people had been left leaderless—if not deported to a strange land. It was a time of great discouragement, and many felt hopeless, even abandoned by God.

In that hard time, the psalmist recalls God's promise to King David generations before, the pledge in 2 Samuel 7 that God would sustain David and his children forever. The psalmist uses the word *covenant*, a holy promise. It is much greater than a contract. Even if David and his descendants were unfaithful and had to suffer the consequences of their sin, God would never forsake them. The covenant was a promise of God's steadfast and ultimately redeeming love.

We have our own times of discouragement, of course. Even in our homes or homeland we may feel like exiles. Whether because of our own sins or the sins of others, we may fear that God has abandoned us. In times of illness or grief, we may feel forsaken. The psalmist reminds us that others have felt such things and urges us to trust the covenant. God will stand firmly with us to the end.

A frame near my desk holds a certificate which records the day my parents presented me as an infant for the covenant of baptism. This document reminds me that even before I knew my name I was being held by the steadfast love and faithful promises of my family, my community, and most enduring of all, the love and promises of God. Even before I could make—or break—any promises, God's loving covenant was already and forever in effect.

O God of the loving covenant, help us to trust this day that you will never forsake us. Amen.

Our scripture today is full of architectural imagery. The writer of Ephesians celebrates how Christ has broken down a "dividing wall," and is building a new dwelling place for God and God's people. In this passage, the writer is particularly concerned about the wall which separated Jews and Gentiles in the first century BCE; but this letter is surely relevant to every time and place. Christ continues to break down walls of hostility and bring people together!

As a young man, I worked with a carpentry crew for several years. We repaired and remodeled older homes. Among the things I learned was the critical difference between load-bearing walls and partition walls. A load-bearing wall, as the name implies, carries weight. It supports the ceiling, the floors above, and the roof. A load-bearing wall is structurally essential. If one is torn down, the house itself may fall. Partition walls simply divide space. They carry no weight and can be removed without any damage to the integrity of the structure. In a remodeling project, to tear down a partition wall is simply to open up and rearrange things for the sake of the people who will live there.

We live in a world of many walls—physical, social, cultural, national, and religious. Often we imagine these walls to be load-bearing, essential, but many of them are just partition walls of our own creation—walls of fear, prejudice, or self-interest. The writer of Ephesians tells us that Christ the carpenter has broken down such walls. Christ remodels our lives, our church, the whole world for the sake of new life. We don't have to be afraid that the house will fall! We are simply being invited into a more open and gracious dwelling place.

O skilled and gracious Builder, you have created space for each of us and put out the welcome mat! Free us from fear so that we can all come home. Amen.

When I worked as a carpenter remodeling older homes, I was sometimes part of the demolition crew. As the name suggests, this involved tearing things down, breaking through old walls which were sometimes permeated with years of coal dust, and removing ancient two-by-fours. The work was often messy and occasionally even dangerous. Still, I must confess that swinging a sledge hammer had its appeal. It could be wonderfully satisfying to knock things down! Tearing down old walls was selective, of course. Our crew didn't want to bring the whole house down—just remodel it. It was wonderful to be involved in rebuilding as the project moved along, to trade in a sledge hammer for a finish hammer, to create new rooms in which a family could live, love, and grow.

While the scripture from Ephesians begins with the breaking down of a wall, it goes on to celebrate new construction. There is now peace and reconciliation between those who once were separated and regarded one another with hostility. The writer rejoices in the building of a new Temple, an inclusive household. Continuing to employ the imagery of architecture, Ephesians describes the apostles and prophets as the foundation of a new Temple with Christ as its cornerstone. Gentiles and Jews alike are joined together like so many building blocks, fashioned into one structure by Christ himself, the artisan as well as the cornerstone of this new dwelling place for God.

In our own time clearly there are walls of hostility which need to come down. There are other walls which need to be maintained. And there are new walls to be erected—walls which protect human dignity and give sanctuary, walls which give structure and continuity to life and love, to faith and community.

O gracious Architect, help us to discern the work you need done on any given day and our part in it! Amen.

Mark's Gospel is breathtaking, both in its pace and its content. We are still reeling from the story of John the Baptist's execution when the disciples return to Jesus with an account of their recent mission trip. No doubt it was both exciting and exhausting! No wonder Jesus was ready to lead them all to a remote place for a time of rest and recovery.

Soon they were in a boat headed for some quiet spot; but when they arrived, a crowd had gathered. It is here that Mark pauses with some of the most poignant words in his Gospel. He writes that Jesus "had compassion for them, because they were like sheep without a shepherd."

It's not a part of our reading for this week, but we know what happens next. Jesus the Shepherd feeds the crowd with his words and then involves his disciples in serving a miraculous dinner on the grounds. Everyone is fed. Everyone has enough—more than enough. Then the disciples are off again.

It's natural to identify with the disciples in this story, but perhaps the first thing for us to do is to claim our personal place in that crowd on the shore. That's where we all start, isn't it? We are like sheep without a shepherd, hungry and weary, lost and afraid, sometimes badly led. It's where we start and where we may find ourselves again from time to time. Perhaps today. The Gospel invites us to look up and meet once more the compassionate gaze of Christ!

Good Shepherd, help us to trust that you are close at hand right now, to know that you see us clearly and compassionately. Feed us, we pray, and lead us in the days to come. Amen.

The second part of this week's Gospel follows an interlude in which Jesus has again instructed his disciples to set out in their boat. Jesus himself goes off alone to pray, but then he notices that the wind has picked up on the sea and his disciples are struggling against the elements. Mark then describes Jesus as striding out on the water, as if it were the most natural thing in the world! When he sees that his friends are overwhelmed with fear and exhaustion, he joins them in their boat; and the wind becomes still.

Mark helps us to keep our focus. The disciples have their work to do, and so do we. But the good news is never about the strength of the disciples. It's about the compassion and steadfastness of Jesus.

Our reading picks up as the boat lands on the far shore. Once again there is a crowd. As Jesus is recognized, people rush to bring those who are sick, confident that he can help them. Mark is wonderfully suggestive with regard to the diversity of the people in need when he describes Jesus as going into "villages and cities and farms" (AP).

The gospel calls us to be aware of the great variety of people and places for whom Christ has compassion. The good news in Mark's busy Gospel is that none of us has been abandoned to the forces of chaos and death, no matter how those forces may present themselves. In Jesus, we see God coming to us wherever we are. He comes when we are hungry or sick. He comes when we are struggling against adverse conditions. He comes as we share together the excitement of our work. He comes as we reflect on his words in quiet solitude.

O God, we are grateful for all the ways you come to us. Heal us today as we once again reach out to touch the fringe of your cloak. Amen.

Just As I Am

JULY 19–25, 2021 • ELIZABETH MAE MAGILL

SCRIPTURE OVERVIEW: The Bible is filled with the stories of imperfect people. David is a classic case. In Second Samuel he uses his power to have sex with another man's wife, tries to cover it up, and then plots the murder of her husband. How can this be the same man who penned this week's psalm, which decries the foolishness of people who act in a godless way? Like us, David was a fallen person who needed God's extravagant mercy. In Ephesians we read of this same extravagance given through Christ, whose power can do what we cannot—namely redeem all of us who are also foolish and fallen. The Gospel author demonstrates the power of Jesus through what he describes as "signs," which Jesus performed not primarily to amaze the onlookers but rather to point them to his identity as the Son of God.

QUESTIONS AND SUGGESTIONS FOR REFLECTION

- Read 2 Samuel 11:1-15. Where in today's world do you see the selfishness of powerful people bringing tragedy for people with less power?
- Read Psalm 14. Do you number yourself among the wise who "seek after God"? Why or why not?
- Read Ephesians 3:14-21. How does "being rooted and grounded in love" manifest itself in your life?
- Read John 6:1-21. Where do you see yourself in this story?

Pastor of Ashburnham Community Church (UCC/UMC) in Massachusetts; author of *Five Loaves, Two Fish, Twelve Volunteers: Growing Relational Food Ministries* (Upper Room Books); creator of a street church for people who do not have homes and trainer for other outdoor and street churches.

Who are you in this story? The boy who is kind enough to share, even though it may not be enough? Are you one of the disciples, more anxious about spending too much money than about caring for their neighbors? Maybe you are one of the people in the crowd, distracted from listening to Jesus because you are hungry. Most of us take on varying roles in this story as the context around us changes.

I'm often worried about my own needs. When I travel to conferences, I bring little bags of dried fruit and nuts because I'm anxious that I will get hungry between meals. Over the years I've learned that this is a ridiculous worry. Most often the problem is too much food, not too little! And yet every trip I arrive with treats tucked into my knitting, right next to my notebook, extra pens, and a charger for my phone. On the trip home almost all of my snacks remain.

It is interesting that in this story, no matter which role you play, you get enough to eat. Everyone has more than enough! The image is of the kingdom of God—so much food there are twelve baskets left over. Jesus brings about the time when there is more than enough for everyone. No one asks who was a complainer, who trusted God, who shared with their neighbors. The generous boy and his family get enough to eat; but so do the disciples, the people just there to listen, the people who came to prove Jesus wrong, even the woman in the back hoarding little bags of fruit and nuts.

There is no test of who is good enough for dinner.

We are certainly called to be disciples and to do right for others, but even if we don't there is plenty in God's kingdom.

Thank you, God, for the plenty of food that is found in your kingdom. Help me to be generous with what I have and confident that you will provide. Amen.

This story is not uplifting. David, King David, an ancestor of Jesus, has sexual intercourse with a woman against her will. He sees her, he takes her, and he sends her away. Although sometimes told as a story of adultery, it is more likely rape. Bathsheba has no right and no ability to say no to David's advances. He is her husband's boss and her king. What are modern Christians to do with this?

First, believe Bathsheba. Don't downplay David's actions, don't excuse him, don't make arguments about the time period, and don't suggest it's a lesson for her to learn.

Second, accept that this is horrible. Don't jump to the end and try to find hope that Bathsheba later becomes the mother of a king. Sit with the discomfort that rape and other forms of violence do to an individual. Love survivors of violence by spending time sitting in the atrocity of it.

Third, keep the focus on Bathsheba. Pay attention to the feelings she must have had. Honor her by respecting the ways she responds to these tragedies. This account has nothing of her feelings, her frustrations, her despair, her resistance, her self-care. Yet we as readers can put them into the story. Understand Bathsheba as a real person.

This story fits in the world that we know today. Spend some time praying for yourself and for others. Pray for survivors of rape and other traumas. Believe them (believe yourself). Accept it as tragedy, and listen for the reality.

Trust that God knows all of Bathsheba's story, and ours. God was with her when the violence happened. God is angry, and God sits with her in mourning. God cares for Bathsheba, and for all of us, when humans cannot do the right thing. When hard things happen, God is there.

Holy Spirit, we need you here with us as we contemplate the violence humans create in this world. Hold us; heal us; help us. Amen.

For several years, I have taken songwriting classes. I enjoy the chance to play with words and find phrases and word patterns that describe ordinary human emotions. It is interesting to try to figure out where I have found the words I have written. Often, they are expressions, phrases, and lines I got from someone else. Sometimes my poetry tells other people's stories.

This is a psalm of David, yet you can hear Bathsheba saying these words, crying as she bathes, shamed by David's actions, alone as she discovers she is pregnant. When one person violates another, I imagine they are the fool who declares, "There is no God" or even "I am God."

After a time of violence it certainly feels like there is no wisdom among human beings. It seems right sometimes that God would declare that all humanity is perverse. When we see people suffering, millions of people suffering, it seems that humans cannot lift ourselves up to do good for others. God is proclaiming that evildoers are eating God's people as if they were bread.

Can you hear this as a rant from a person who has been violated by others? Can you hear this as a rage against the systems that allow oppression and violence to go unpunished? Read this psalm when you are angry at racism, sexism, classism, able-ism, homophobia, and other oppressions. Read this when you are so angry you cannot speak.

The message is that God is with the righteous. The world may interfere with the plans the poor and oppressed have made, but the Lord will always be a refuge. When we need to get away from the evil of humankind, God is here, waiting to sit with us in our tears. Just as we are, we are held by a righteous God.

God our refuge, hold us close in our despair. Hear our stories as we cry out to you. Restore our fortunes in impossible times. Amen.

Davidis the greatest king that ancient Israel has ever known. David is a sex offender who is planning to have Uriah murdered. These two things are true at the same time. The Bible is full of characters who fail to do the right thing. Later David will be called out, at least for his role in Uriah's death. But many characters are not. Like today, people get away with grossly inappropriate behavior.

Our best selves, our worst selves, and all our in-between selves exist together. The Bible is descriptive of the wide variety of people who answer God's call. They are not role models, prescribing how to respond to God. Rather they are examples of God's reaching out to people who are broken in many ways.

God reaches out, encouraging our best, guiding our improvement, and prompting us to repent of the harm we have caused others. Repentance is changing direction—the words "I'm sorry" are not enough. To repent is to turn away from bad behavior, make restitution, and to live in new ways.

What is amazing is that repentance is not a test we pass to earn God's love. God loves us right now—exactly as we are—before we repent and change. God is reaching for each of us, for David, for people who have committed crimes, for survivors of crimes, for rule-followers, for you, for me. God loves us right now.

Repentance is not a requirement for love but rather a response to that love. If we can feel God's love, we are better able to imagine finding a new path for our lives. A better way is possible. God comes along with us, holding us as we turn, and supporting our new direction. Nothing keeps us separated from God.

Forgive me, God, for the ways I have hurt other people. Help me to turn toward the way of love. Thank you for reaching out to me, just as I am. Amen.

All of us—perpetrators or survivors of crimes, sharers or eaters of bread and fish—all of us need time away.

There are many bits of scripture like this one, where Jesus withdraws to be by himself. In two lines here, half a sentence there, scripture shows us that Jesus needs time alone. His work requires deep compassion—caring for individuals and crowds, teaching and preaching, and arguing with religious leaders, with the disciples, with large expanses of people. In between those encounters, Jesus pulls away.

Why?

These are Jesus' sabbath moments. Time away allows space to connect to God and to remember the purpose of the work he is doing. God wants Jesus to be who he is called to be—and that is hard! So Jesus takes space to be with God just as he is.

God calls us to ministry as well, ministry to the world we live in. As the world storms around us, we must take some time away. Think of it as shelter from the waves that threaten to overwhelm us. This break from the work enables us to avoid the trap of being blown every which way by the crowd; it helps us to see through the fog, to find the direction God is sending us.

Time apart cuts down on thinking we are in charge, making the ministry about us instead of about Jesus. The crowd in this story wanted to make Jesus king. Pulling away returns him to God's image of kingdom instead of the earthly view of a king.

God loves us just the way we are. To be fed by that love we need time with God, alone—in the mountains, in the wilderness, by the sea, wherever we are able to get away and spend time with our Creator. This time allows us to feel God's affirmation, redirection, encouragement, and peace.

Holy God, push me into a silent, private space so that I may hear what you are sharing with me. Amen.

Imagine the disciples, overwhelmed by a storm, suddenly seeing Jesus right there to help them. They are terrified to see him. They are working hard to handle the water coming into the boat and the wind and water threatening their stability. They don't have much time to make sense of Jesus walking on water through the storm. Still, along with a feeling of terror, they might have been thankful for the arrival of help. Did they want to solve the problem of the dangerous seas themselves?

Are you terrified when help appears? Are you afraid to let others know the mess that is your life? When you are feeling like only a miracle can fix your situation, would you be shocked if a miracle actually happened? Are you terrified of running into Jesus?

Jesus' message to the disciples is, "It is I, do not be afraid." It is hard to say whether that means, "Don't be afraid of the storm. I'm here to help," or "Don't be afraid of the stranger walking on water." What is certain is that living with fear makes our startle reflex stronger. When we are always on guard, even the sight of a friend can make us jump.

Living unafraid requires practice. We must ask for help even when it's embarrassing; go places that seem unknown; take small, manageable risks. We develop skills in fearlessness by looking out during storms to see who is around, saying hi to people we don't know, and offering help to strangers. If you expect Jesus to walk on the rough waters around you, you will see him in the people who are holding out their hands, offering you the miracle of neighborliness.

Don't be afraid. Jesus wants to help you to the safety of the shore.

Help me, God, to live without fear. Help me to ask for the help I need and to trust the body of Christ in the community, ready to appear when I need you. Amen.

In the verses before this, Paul celebrates that he can bring God's grace to the Gentiles. Paul, who persecuted Christians and saw non-Jews as on the outs with God, now has the work of sharing good news with the very people he once condemned. He is humbly grateful for this work; and this passage opens with bowing down before God, the source of our very names.

Sharing good news in a social context that prioritizes wealth and prestige is hard work. Thus Paul prays for the people of Ephesus to be strengthened by the Spirit and rooted in love. Knowledge, which gives a person privilege, is superseded by Christ's love and the fullness of God.

It takes strength to remain confident that God loves us just as we are. Life today is filled with a flurry of pressures to do more, to be more, to want more and more. You don't need to be the wealthiest person on your street to get prestige today. You can get that with the nicest house or car, or going on the most luxurious vacation, or by being connected to the most important people. At work we compete with one another over how tired or overworked or overwhelmed we are.

Yet what we do or what we have is not our ultimate source of power. That comes from God who overwhelms us with love, which we then can share with others. Paul insists we will accomplish more by the fullness of love than by anything else.

What does it take to do this? Trust that God loves us as we are. Ask for forgiveness for what we have done to hurt others. Scream and holler about the horrors of the world, and know that God did not want those things to happen. Take time away in the wilderness and reconnect to God.

Fill me, God, with your fullness. Help me to accomplish in love the work you have set before me. Amen.

Toward Confession and Forgiveness

JULY 26–AUGUST 1, 2021 • JOE E. PENNEL JR.

SCRIPTURE OVERVIEW: David thinks he has gotten away with his sins, but God sends Nathan to tell David a story. The story angers David, but Nathan reveals that the story is really about David's own behavior. Indeed, it can be tempting to condemn others' sin, while we justify our own. Psalm 51 is David's appeal to God for forgiveness and restoration. If we want to please God in our own lives, what does this look like? Ephesians tells us that the signs of a redeemed life include humility, love, patience, and building up one another (the opposite of what David displayed). In John, Jesus has crowds following him because they want a free meal. The lasting nourishment they truly need, Jesus teaches, comes through believing that God has sent him.

QUESTIONS AND SUGGESTIONS FOR REFLECTION

- Read 2 Samuel 11:26–12:13a. When has someone else helped you see that you have sinned? How did you respond to that person?
- Read Psalm 51:1-12. When have you felt "unclean" before God? How did God restore you?
- Read Ephesians 4:1-16. What are your gifts? How do you use them to build up the body of Christ?
- Read John 6:24-35. How do you feed your soul?

Bishop of The United Methodist Church (retired).

In the Hebrew Bible, we see two portraits of David, who is now seen as one of the towering figures of the Israelite people.

In today's reading, we see a person who has messed up his life. Much of the Bible is about people who have botched things badly in their lives. David has "displeased the Lord." He has had Uriah murdered and taken Uriah's wife to be his own wife. She bears him children.

In the book of Ezekiel, David is pictured as a completely different person. Ezekiel writes about David who has become the king of Israel and a servant who has become a prince forever.

Like David, we are mixtures of good and evil, right and wrong, love and hate, truth and falsehood. We are both takers and givers.

I am now in my eightieth year, and I find myself reflecting on my life. Most of the time this happens when I am tossing and turning between 3 and 4 a.m. I relive the times when I have lived as one who displeased the Lord and times when I have lived like a loving person.

In today's texts, we get a clue as to how and why David was able to move from God's displeasure to becoming a prince of Israel. David said to Nathan, "I have sinned against the Lord." He confessed his sin to another person, and the Lord forgave him. He moved from confession to forgiveness. The same can happen for each of us.

When we displease the Lord and fail to live by what love requires, we can confess, repent, and move toward forgiveness. Just as the Lord forgave David, so the Lord will forgive us.

Give me the strength, O Lord, to practice confession so that I can feel forgiven in my mind and heart. Amen.

David has broken the moral law. He does not rationalize or blame others for his sinful ways. Nor does he try to cover up what he has done wrong. Instead, he repents and laments. He turns to God to be cleansed. He prays that God will have mercy on him and blot out his transgressions.

Sin is any thought, word, or deed that separates us from God, our neighbors, or ourselves. Therefore, we have all sinned and fallen short of God's intention for us. We do not have the natural strength to cleanse ourselves. Denial or keeping quiet will not heal our brokenness. It will not rejoin us to others, to ourselves, or to God.

We can try to justify ourselves, or we can follow the example portrayed in Psalm 51. This writing speaks about the importance of lament and repentance. I once attended a congregation that did not have a prayer of confession before inviting worshipers to the Communion table to receive the bread and wine. It is important for us to confess our personal and social sins before receiving these symbols of God's forgiveness.

The congregations that I served as pastor always had a prayer of confession. That has also been my experience since childhood. One Sunday morning a man with a frown on his face came out of the sanctuary and came charging over to me. He said, "Why do we need to have that confession of sin? I haven't done anything wrong!" He thought that he did not need to be cleansed. He had no guilt or shame about how he might have hurt others or himself.

If we desire truth in our inward being, we must truly believe that God stands ready to wash us thoroughly, as only God can. This happens when we sincerely confess and repent.

Loving God, help me to be honest with myself about my sinful ways so that I am ready to repent. Amen.

Disunity is all around us and everywhere to be seen and experienced. We see it in families, in politics, and in the church—both locally and globally. Disunity builds walls between people. It is difficult to take down those walls because disunity is so embedded. Disunity hurts. It causes us to be strangers and aliens to one another.

It is sad to say that we are eyewitnesses and "earwitnesses" to the lack of unity in the body of Christ. But today's scripture reading is unambiguous with regard to the pursuit of unity in the church. Christianity is grotesque when it turns its back on unity. When this happens, it is not Christianity but something else entirely.

According to Paul, the church needs to strive for unity in the Spirit. Organic unity is not the main thing. It is the Holy Spirit which transcends our differences and makes us one in Christ. The Holy Spirit strengthens us to bear with one another in love.

As I write this, I serve on the faculty at Vanderbilt Divinity School in Nashville, TN. We are a diverse community. Our students claim more than two dozen denominations and traditions. They come from all over the United States and from many other countries. The faculty is also a mixture of theological perspectives.

Though we have glaring differences, there is a spirit of unity as we study, worship, and fellowship together. I can feel the unity in both my heart and my head. Division among Christians must be a wound in the heart of Christ. Paul challenges us to "maintain the unity of the Spirit in the bond of peace." May it be so!

Help me, O God, to bear with others with gentleness, patience, and love, for you are above all and through all and in all. Amen.

Words have power. They can hurt, or they can heal. They can make this look like that. They can enlighten our minds and hearts, or they can cloud our understanding. They can be sincere, or they can be deceiving. They can be used to build walls between people, or they can be used to tear down walls.

In this reading, we are called upon to speak the truth in love so that we will grow in Christ. Words of love knit us to others and to God.

As a pastor since 1979, I have had many experiences of congregants speaking the "truth" to me. Some spoke from the heart of love; and some uttered words from hard, unloving hearts. Both, I am certain, tried to be true to what they believed.

The comedian Minnie Pearl was a member of the congregation I served in Brentwood, TN. She had performed at the Grand Ole Opry and many other venues. She knew how to use words to evoke laughter and applause from audiences. One of her favorite sayings was, "Laughter is the hand of God that rocks the cradle of a troubled world."

One day I went to see her because I was getting some painful feedback on my sermons. I shared some of the critical notes I had received, and I shared my pain. I asked her to give me her feedback on my sermons. She was reluctant to do so, but I insisted. Finally, she spoke the truth in love to me. She said, "Joe, just give us one take-home that we can apply to our lives. You also need to work on your punchlines." Those were the loving words I needed to hear.

God of love, help me to use words that increase love in the world. Amen.

Our humanity is challenged every day. Something is always happening that needs to be fixed or taken care of. We never seem to be able to put down a period.

Also, being fully human is often challenging. Being the person God created us to be takes great intentionality. We believe that every person is gifted in some way. We need to know how we are gifted and how to use the gifts that we have been given. The most contented and assured people are those who let their God-given gifts flow through their lives. This is one fact of being truly human.

I am a spouse, father, brother, pastor, teacher, friend, colleague, and neighbor. Our natural, God-given gifts can be helpful in all these relationships. We experience both satisfaction and failure in all these connections. In each of our relationships, we realize that being the naturally gifted person that God created us to be can be pleasant or grueling.

Moving through the maze of life can cause us to commit the sin of omission. It is not what we do; it is what we fail to do that puts our witness in jeopardy. We sin when we fail to use our gifts to increase love. We do not need to make a splash. All that is needed are small acts of charity. We need to be attentive to the use of our gifts because the world is waiting for our expressions of love.

It would take much more space than I have here for me to list all of the times I have been guilty of the sin of lack and lapse. The words of Psalm 51 bring comfort to me. God does not abandon me. God both holds me and holds me accountable.

Even though I have sinned, O God, please do not cast me away. Cleanse me. Amen.

Ican scramble a few eggs, and I can make a grilled cheese sandwich. Beyond that, I have no competence in the world of cooking. I envy a friend who has a gift for making wonderful bread. He is known for his capacity to bake many varieties, and he gets great joy from sharing his bread with others. It is one of the ways he demonstrates his love for people.

I am a bit jealous of his knowledge and ability. There have been times when I thought that I would like to learn how to make bread. However, my thoughts have never taken me to the oven. My motivation has been lacking; I have never baked even one loaf.

A few weeks ago, I made a decision to try to see every piece of bread as a symbol to remind me of Jesus who said, "I am the bread of life." When I remember to do this, I am reminded of Christ's love for me and for all people.

We meet Christ in the people we encounter each and every day. We experience Christ in the poor, in those we love, and in those we find difficult to love. We are called to be the bread of life for every person every day. It is so easy to eat bread as a symbol of Christ's presence and then to relate to others as if we had never eaten the bread. Bread can indeed be an important symbol. Symbols can point beyond themselves to the God who is far beyond us, deep within us, and all around us. Paying attention to everyday bread as a symbol can remind us to be mystically one with the Lord who is the "Bread of Life."

Loving God, help me to love others as if I have truly eaten and digested the Bread of Life. Amen.

It happened when I was attending a meeting in Chicago, an important gathering of the Council of Bishops of The United Methodist Church. The staff served us a delicious and abundant buffet meal.

One thing was missing; there was no bread at the serving station. For me, without the bread the meal seemed incomplete. I asked the server if we could have some bread. He said, "We do not serve bread with this meal."

Bread sustains us. It is extraordinarily symbolic for those of us who live in the tradition of the Hebrew Bible and the New Testament. We remember how God gave manna to the Israelites as they traveled in the desert. God took the initiative to feed the people and provided what they needed for the journey. No one cooked the bread; it was God who gave it. In the story from John 6, the crowd who went searching for Jesus finally found him. But Jesus cautioned them not to be consumed by the food they ate but to be about finding and "digesting" the spiritual food that would lead them to eternal life. This food—this bread—Jesus said, is more important than the manna they received in the desert. This is the bread that sustains us throughout our lives. It is a gift that Christ offers himself as food for the journey of life. Jesus said, "I am the bread of life. Whoever comes to me will never be hungry, and whoever believes in me will never be thirsty."

The bread that is made sacred for us at Holy Communion becomes for us the Bread of Life. As we feed on this bread, we feed on the presence of the living Christ. With confession, we are assured that we are forgiven. Every day has its challenges, but if we allow ourselves to be sustained by the Bread of Life, we are blessed all our days.

Help me, O God, to represent the Bread of Life in a brittle and hard world. Amen.

Relationship Matters

AUGUST 2–8, 2021 • KEN NASH

SCRIPTURE OVERVIEW: David's family was a mess. Among his children there was rape, murder, and a plot to overthrow him by his son Absalom. Violence followed, and Second Samuel tells the story of Absalom's death. Even though Absalom had betrayed him, David still loved his son with a parent's never-ending love—the kind of love that God demonstrates perfectly for us, as David celebrates in Psalm 34. The author of Ephesians warns against acting out of anger, wrath, and malice (the very things that tore apart David's family). We should instead forgive, as God in Christ has forgiven us. In John, Jesus restates that he is the path to God because he teaches God's truth. Jesus will give his own life, then raise up those who believe in him.

QUESTIONS AND SUGGESTIONS FOR REFLECTION

- Read 2 Samuel 18:5-9, 15, 31-33. What helps you to "deal gently" with others? What makes it challenging at times?
- Read Psalm 34:1-8. When have you been able to "taste and see" God's goodness?
- Read Ephesians 4:25–5:2. How do your words and actions reflect what you profess to believe about Christ?
- Read John 6:35, 41-51. God comes to us in unexpected ways. Is there someone you have overlooked or dismissed as a servant of God? How can you work to see people as God sees them?

Lead pastor at Watermark Wesleyan Church in Hamburg, NY.

Have you ever thought that this world would be wonderful if it weren't for people? Our reading today shines the light on the beautiful complexity of personal relationships, particularly family relationships. At best, David and Absalom had a tenuous father-son relationship. The handsome and charismatic son was filled with potential and deeply loved by David. However, Absalom lost a tremendous amount of respect for his dad when David failed to punish Amnon for the rape of his sister. As Absalom consistently failed to listen to healthy advice, he temporarily usurped his father's throne in Jerusalem. In an effort to avoid a civil war, David left the capital city under jeers and mockery. And yet we find no evidence of an embittered heart within David. Imagine the gossip in town! The scandal! The tabloids of the day would certainly be buzzing about the king falling to a more politically savvy son. David has met his match, or so it seems.

When we find ourselves in family feuds or broken friendships, the temptation is to retaliate, to punish those who have wronged us. But David was a different kind of man by this point in his life. He had received a new spiritual heart from the Lord through his previous brokenness. He was a new creation. His response could therefore reflect the kind and merciful heart of God. This is where we find grace in real life.

As it became clear that Absalom was dangerous as a leader over Israel, David knew he needed to regain the throne in Jerusalem. He had every right to tell his leaders to kill his son, the traitor, but instead he showed mercy, telling them, "Deal gently with the young man for my sake." Where can you spread similar grace with your words today?

Merciful God, give me the strength to offer the same grace to others that you have so freely offered to me this day and every day. Amen.

Respect. In this rapidly embittered world of Twitter wars, sound bites, and social media onslaughts, there is a critical need for the respect of others' perspectives. It is comforting to know that we are not the first culture to face this challenge. David gives one piece of instruction for the commander of his army, "Deal gently with my son." His advice is not to avoid justice, ignore the offense, or even let Absolom's treachery stand. Instead David urges, "Deal gently." However, Joab cannot honor his king's request. Joab hears that Absolom is vulnerable, and he takes advantage of that vulnerability. Seeing the damage Absalom has caused to the nation, Joab simply cannot accept a gentler punishment. Israel is in turmoil, set ablaze at the hands of this traitorous king. Joab feels compelled to act decisively.

Joab kills Absalom as he is caught in that jagged tree. Joab's actions are not a surprise. He is filled with rage, and his vengeance is real and premeditated. It is human and natural, but it is not beneficial. Joab lets his need for revenge cloud his judgment. What is fascinating about our reading is how quickly the rest of the men join in. They pile on and decimate the body of a man who is already dead. By doing this, they compromise their integrity and deeply wound their own king whose request they have totally disregarded. The warning to us is obvious. Our reactions impact not only our own lives; their influence reaches far beyond what we often realize. Add social media to our reactions and the reach is endless. May this lesson give us pause in our moments of anger. When we are offended, filled with a need for revenge, may we hear the Spirit whisper, "Deal gently with my child," as we honor the image of God within those with whom we find fault.

Dear Lord, you ask us to turn the other cheek in times of conflict and to pray for our enemies. Give us the strength to be respectful in the midst of tension. Amen.

S abotaged by grief. There remain few other words that so accurately describe the power of grief. Grief steals our stability and our sense of peace, crushes our hope. In our reading today, we find David in such a place. Completely shaken by loss, David makes it clear that his own death would be more bearable than the death of his son, even though we have seen the complexity of David's relationship with Absalom. Therefore, it isn't a stretch to believe that in the midst of his mourning David was also filled with regret. He had failed his son on many fronts throughout his lifetime. Even as he was awaiting news, he asked multiple times about his son's safety. Yet even the power of a king can't ensure that. What others view as victory is nothing but loss upon loss for David. Grief has a way of exposing our darker memories and thus leaving us with a feeling of hopeless emptiness. "My son Absalom, my son, my son . . . my son, my son!"

That is why it is comforting to know that David is in the very bloodline of Jesus Christ, another son who was sacrificed at the hands of the enemy. David's story helps us to witness the depth of complexity that comes in sacrificing a son for the greater good—the greatest good. In Jesus, we find our source of stability and peace. Through him, even death has lost its sting. This leads us to a core principle: If things are not good, God's not done yet. Knowing this allows believers to walk in hopeful confidence. David's story doesn't end with the death of Absalom, nor does God's story end with the death of Jesus. There is always hope because Christ is the resurrected Lord.

Thank you, loving Savior, for the hope I find in you. Even in the dark nights of the soul, your light of life comforts and restores me. Amen.

You may have heard it said that Christianity isn't a religion, it's a relationship. There is one simple truth about relationships—they can exist only when both parties participate. Today's reading illustrates this concept beautifully. After reading the Samuel passage, it is important to note that David wrote Psalm 34 as a grateful response to the rescue from his enemy King Achish, which he saw as God's provision. The beautiful part is that David doesn't have to respond this way. He could attribute his safety to his own acting skills as he feigned madness. Instead, David extols and glorifies the Lord, giving praise because the Lord answered his cries and delivered him from his fears. David understands what so many simply do not understand: God is an active participant in our world, both personally and globally.

God isn't a distant God who simply spun the world on its axis and left us to fend for ourselves. God is present in all aspects of our lives—including our emotions. David acknowledges that not only was he rescued from his enemy but also from his fears. We often think that circumstances are "just the way it is," or "I am just the way I am," pushing aside the compassion, power, and provision God possesses that compel God to understand our feelings and change our circumstances. Sometimes we don't ask, and sometimes we don't see. "Taste and see that the LORD is good." David did, and he couldn't help but praise the Lord.

Reflect today on where you have seen evidence of God in your life in the past twenty-four hours. Did you sense the Lord through a restful sleep last night? Then praise the Lord. Did you experience God's peace through a calmed spirit in the midst of a family argument? Give God glory. Did you experience a tangible answer to prayer? Celebrate our personal and relational God.

Lord, for those times I trust in my own abilities and talents, help me to see the ways you intervene and provide. You are always worthy of my praise! Amen.

Did you know that, pound for pound, the jaw is the strongest muscle in the entire body? Nevertheless, our reading makes the case that in a battle of strength—jaw versus tongue—the tongue wins every time. While the jaw is physically strong, the tongue has the ability to inflame an environment with anger and rage. Just one lie can shatter the reputation of a person with great character. A faith-filled family can be thrown into a feud based on words from that often uncontrolled body part.

The obvious question is, Who controls your tongue? The answer is plain and simple: you. That is precisely why the apostle Paul warns us not to let any unwholesome talk come from our mouths. It's no wonder that we are instructed not to "grieve the Holy Spirit" precisely in the midst of these warnings. In other words, our misguided and untamed words cause the Holy Spirit to grieve with deep sadness prompted by the damage ill-advised words cause. With words of rage, slander, unforgiveness, falsehood, bitterness, and gossip, the tear ducts of a sensitive, loving, brokenhearted God pour open with sorrow.

Yet our words also have the power to change the atmosphere in the room in the best ways possible! They can build people up, make them feel loved, be a soothing balm to their souls, and bring laughter in the midst of pain. They can bring life to dying relationships and hope to hopeless situations. It's no coincidence that we are informed in Genesis that God birthed this world through the spoken word of the divine tongue. Let's model our Creator today by speaking life to others.

Thank you, Lord, for the gift of communication, the expression of thoughts and ideas to commune with you and with others. Help us to use care as we speak life today. Amen.

Today's reading is one simple verse, our shortest of the week. So read it one more time. Did you see it this time? The word *never*. As our bread of life, Jesus said that we will never go hungry. We will never go thirsty. Do you understand the gravity of what Jesus is saying? Of course, even the newest believer could comprehend that Jesus is referring to spiritual nourishment. Regardless, *never* is a dramatic concept. What does that mean in the context of our relationships?

Relationships are complex. They ebb and flow through our care, or lack thereof, toward one another. In our brokenness, we sometimes say and do things that cause great damage. We can wound hearts and souls. Likewise, we are sensitive and easily hurt, often retreating and isolating ourselves for self-preservation. The give and take, push and pull of wins and losses in relationships gets exhausting and time-consuming. Does a particular relationship come to mind as you read these words—a relationship that is malnourished, depleted, or starving? Enter Jesus. He is our source of nourishment and strength. As we remain fixed on him, we are promised never to go hungry or be thirsty again. That means that we have the resources to be tenacious as we always hope for the best in relationships, knowing that we are always filled with the spiritual nourishment that comes from Christ. Through him, we have endurance. Sure, we may need to keep healthy boundaries, but we have the spiritual strength to try again and again and again and sometimes even again to care for the distant spouse, the misunderstood in-law, the wayward son, the estranged sibling, the long-lost friend.

Thank you, Jesus, for being our Bread of Life. Nourish us again today so that we have the sustaining power to invest in relationships. Help us never to have malnourished relationships with the people in our lives. Amen.

Are you familiar with the term *groupthink*? It's when a person foregos personal responsibility and critical thinking to join the consensus of the group. Jesus encounters this in its fullest form as he offers himself as the Bread of Life, the very spiritual nourishment his listeners were starving for. But they do not stop to pause and ponder the remarkable relationship they are invited into. One person reminds the group that Jesus is merely "the son of Joseph," making it easy to simply slip into one collective idea and, as a result, miss the miracle standing before them.

"I am life. I am a gift from heaven. I am provision, a sustainer of life. I am nutrients and necessary and fulfilling." Even when Jesus explicitly said it, it was still unbelievable to those who heard it. However, I wonder how many got it. How many grew excited, hearts racing, arms covered with goose bumps? How many felt this excitement but left anyway because the group questioned, "How can this man give us his flesh to eat?"

Scripture calls us to be in community; it is a core blessing of the church, filling our lives with meaningful relationships. However, John's story reminds us that groups aren't always filled with wisdom. Because of that, Jesus emphasizes the personal nature of a relationship with him when he says that anyone may live forever as they partake of his body. Intimate moments with him are critical aspects of our spiritual journey. Enjoy the time building your own personal discernment. Soak it up. Learn. Then engage with the group.

Take some time today to reflect on what the Spirit is revealing to you. Are there areas of Groupthink that are slowly creeping in? Gossip you've joined with? Group grumpiness that changed your demeanor? Bigoted behavior you've engaged in? Hurtful jokes you've laughed at?

Jesus, thank you for community and personal moments with you. They are a gift from heaven, allowing us to walk in that great intimacy with you. Amen.

Finding Faithfulness

AUGUST 9–15, 2021 • BRENNA LAKESON

SCRIPTURE OVERVIEW: If you could ask God for one thing, what would it be? God offered this chance to Solomon, and the king asked for wisdom to rule God's people well. God honored this request by giving Solomon many other gifts too, as long as the king followed God's ways. (Later on, unfortunately, Solomon lost his way.) The psalmist tells us that wisdom begins with understanding who we are and who God is. Ephesians addresses practical implications of wise living: follow the will of the Lord, be filled with the Spirit, encourage one another, and be grateful to God. The Gospel passage continues Jesus' metaphorical description of himself as the Bread of Heaven. Here Jesus anticipates the sacrament of Communion, in which we partake of his body and blood by faith.

QUESTIONS AND SUGGESTIONS FOR REFLECTION

- Read 1 Kings 2:10-12; 3:3-14. Do you hesitate to ask God to show you your call? Why?
- Read Psalm 111. Where have you seen God's faithful and just actions in your life? In the world?
- Read Ephesians 5:15-20. How do you live wisely and make the most of the time?
- Read John 6:51-58. What is the significance of Holy Communion in your life of faith? How has your understanding of this sacrament changed over time?

Queer feminist pastor and social activist in Atlanta, GA; holds an MDiv from Candler School of Theology; provisionally commissioned as a United Methodist pastor by the Western North Carolina Conference; works at Central Outreach and Advocacy Center, serving people experiencing homelessness.

As Solomon takes over reigning in place of his father, David, it's understandable that he feels inadequate and overwhelmed. David has been honored by God and revered by God's people as a wonderful king. David has also reigned for a long time, so Israel is used to having David as a leader and might resist this change of leadership. However, in this passage, Solomon shows great potential because of his self-awareness. As he confesses to God in his dream in 1 Kings 3:7, Solomon knows that he is young and inexperienced. For all these reasons, Solomon marks the beginning of his reign by going to Gibeon to make a sacrifice to God. There, he asks God for wisdom.

Is there a place in your life where you feel unworthy or ill-equipped? Maybe you're facing a challenge at work, feeling overwhelmed as a parent, or transitioning into a new phase of life. We face new challenges all the time, and they can be especially hard when we have big shoes to fill, as Solomon did. However, from this story we know that God is present in these times of transition and insecurity. God reveals wisdom to us through prayer, scripture, and others around us.

The last piece of God's promise to Solomon, though, depends on Solomon's continued faithfulness. God rewards the faithfulness that Solomon has already displayed with the first part of the promise—wisdom, fame, and wealth. God ensures Solomon will continue to be faithful with the second part of the promise—a long life. If Solomon continues to be faithful, God will allow him ample time to produce heirs and form a legacy.

How can you continue to display faithfulness to God, even when you're facing a challenge?

Promise-maker, you honor our faithfulness. You provide when we are overwhelmed. You meet us in our sacrifice. Guide our dreams, supplement our weakness, fulfill our longings, so that we may be righteous leaders for your people, bringing the completeness of your kingdom to earth. Amen.

One of Solomon's first actions on the throne is to travel to Gibeon to make sacrifices and burnt offerings to God. This is one of the most sacred acts of faithfulness, laid out by the early law codes of the Israelites. The concept of the early Israelite temple is built around the concept of offering sacrifices to God as an expression of gratitude, worship, and repentance.

What's more, Solomon travels to Gibeon to offer these sacrifices. The history of Gibeon is a tumultuous one. In the book of Joshua, the Israelites take over other territories in order to grow their kingdom. The people of Gibeon hear about this and fear they will meet the same violent fate as the other societies the Israelites have defeated. So instead of enduring battle, they trick Joshua and his people. The Gibeonites dress in rags and go to the Israelites claiming to be poor foreigners and asking to enter into a covenant with the Israelites so they will be protected. Joshua obliges but later discovers their deception. However, because he has already entered into a covenant with Gibeon, he does not kill them or take their land. Later, he goes to battle on behalf of the Gibeonites, further honoring their covenant.

The story of Gibeon is one of layers of faithfulness: the Israelites' faithfulness to God, God's faithfulness to the Israelites, and the Israelites' faithfulness to the Gibeonites. Therefore, it is symbolic that Gibeon is the location of Solomon's sacrifices to God. Solomon longs to be a faithful king like David, worthy of leading God's people. So his journey to Gibeon and sacrifices to God display his ability and his desire to be a faithful king.

Victory-bringer, you are the covenant-keeper of Joshua. You are the protector of Gibeon. You are the giver to Solomon. Lead us through conflict. Repair our disagreement. Soothe our apprehension so that we may be faithful in dispelling violence, fear, and pain in the world. Amen.

This psalm of praise and thanksgiving begins with an invocation: "Praise the Lord!" The psalmist then spends several stanzas reflecting on God's deeds and promises, evidence of why God is praiseworthy. The work of God is described as great, full of honor, majestic, and wonderful. God is known by all people because of these deeds, which are kind and forgiving.

In verses 5-6, God is acknowledged as a provider. First, God provides food, a resource crucial to survival. But God's people do not have to worry about provision because God keeps the divine promises to provide. God's people will not perish due to lack of resources. The psalmist recalls God's history with the Israelites, how in the wilderness and in the desert God provided food, water, and a path to safety.

Lastly, the psalmist addresses the reader. After absorbing such magnificent attributes of a God who keeps covenant, gives sustenance, offers mercy and grace, and provides order in chaos, we might wonder how to go about receiving such blessings. The psalmist tells us that to gain this wisdom we need to practice respect for God and follow God's law, which will lead to understanding. What are ways in which you have seen God provide? Consider times of healing, strength, and abundance. How has God shown up for you, just as God did for the psalmist? Find a way to participate in praise today.

Holy Provider, you offer us mercy; you provide for the faithful; you praise your creation. We lift up our praise. We glorify your righteous acts. We receive your wisdom, so that all creation might participate in your covenant, worshiping you in thanksgiving. Amen.

In verse 6 of this psalm, one way God has shown faithfulness is by giving the Israelites the "heritage of the nations." Initially, this seems like a strange gift. The word translated in the New Revised Standard Version as "heritage" is the Hebrew word *nachalah*. It's translated in *Strong's Concordance* as "possession, property, inheritance, or heritage." This word is used in scripture primarily in Numbers, Deuteronomy, and Joshua in reference to instances when the Israelites overtook other nations. God brought them victory so the *nachalah* of other nations became theirs.

Early in the Old Testament, law codes were laid out for the Israelites. They were to follow the laws as a sign of obedience to God; in turn, God would provide what they needed. Sometimes this meant manna in the desert, and sometimes it meant a military victory. The fact that God, throughout the history of the Israelites, provided for them was a sign that God was upholding God's portion of the law codes. It meant that the Israelites were being faithful and were therefore deserving of God's promises.

In the tradition of wisdom literature (books such as Psalms, Proverbs, Ecclesiastes, and Job), this is how one can make meaning out of difficult circumstances. Wisdom literature can be easily criticized as black and white thinking, but it can also be a comforting way to find meaning in hardship by recalling other times when God was faithful. The psalmist reminds readers that God's commandments are firmly established, unchangeable, and reliable. If God's followers hold up their end of the covenant, then God will be faithful and provide. God's name should be held in awe and reverence because God's promises are fulfilled.

Conqueror of Lands, you provide; you prevail; you prosecute. Uphold your covenant; fulfill your promises. Reward our faithfulness so that we may proclaim your goodness and offer your redemption throughout the land. In the name of the God of Joshua, David, and Solomon. Amen.

Ephesians was written to an audience of Gentiles. The Ephesians weren't familiar with Jewish law codes, so this letter introduces them to the concepts of faithfulness and obedience. This particular passage contrasts being a wise and thankful person with being a foolish and riotous person. A key aspect of being a faithful Christian is to act in the ways of wisdom: being kind, grounded, diplomatic, and worshipful. Verse 16 states that our time on earth is short, so we need to make the most of the time we have by acting in ways that carry out God's desire for our lives.

The author plays up the contrast of wisdom and foolishness, a common theme throughout scripture, by pointing to the example of drunkenness. Modern readers often get stuck on this aspect of the passage, either using it to insist on sobriety or by becoming angry that scripture would try to control their behavior. However, what's important in this passage is not necessarily the drunkenness itself. The takeaway, instead, is a contrast between the drunk people rioting about and the faithful people singing songs of praise. Verse 17 is telling the reader not to be absorbed into the behaviors of their culture but to live in a way that is visibly different. Instead of participating in debauchery and lacking self-awareness, followers of Christ should use their energy to offer thanksgiving to God through song. Instead of focusing their hearts on fleeting desires—such as wealth or momentary pleasures—the Ephesians should focus on opening their hearts toward God and the gifts God gave them through the life of Christ.

Revealer of Wisdom, your will is pure, and your truth is abundant. Guide us in our obedience. Forgive us in our foolishness. Fill us with songs to sing out of gratitude so that we may serve as models of your will obeyed, bringing your comfort and order to places of pain and chaos. Amen.

The language of Holy Communion is familiar to most Christians today. But in this passage, the disciples are understandably confused. Leading up to this moment, the disciples are pestering Jesus to give them proof that he is who he claims to be. In John 6:31, they specifically point to God's gift of manna to the Israelites as an example of the kind of proof they are seeking. Jesus responds by repeatedly discussing the bread of life as a metaphor for the wholeness that his salvation offers. But the disciples remain confused and continue to question. Either they're missing the point, or the answers Jesus is giving are not the answers they want. The disciples want to know what to do to be faithful followers. But because Jesus is offering something brand new, there's no text that has these answers. The answers Jesus offers are cryptic at best. Faithfulness is not as straightforward as the disciples want it to be. Sometimes being faithful means interpreting difficult situations or living into answers that don't yet make sense.

Faithfulness involves real and difficult sacrifice. In verse 53, Jesus says that without eating the flesh and drinking the blood of the Son of Man, his disciples will have no life in them. They will be dead, either metaphorically or literally, unless they participate fully in the new life Jesus offers. In contrast, those who do eat and drink and become a full part of Jesus will receive eternal life. Making sacrifices of faithfulness involves a life beyond what can be imagined while living in doubt and fear. Jesus makes it clear that the path he demands of his followers will not be an easy one, but it will be one with great rewards.

Bread of Life, you nourish our bones; you feed our famine; you quench our thirst. Answer our questioning; offer understanding. Raise us up so that we may eat and drink in remembrance of you, participating in the eternal life that you graciously offer. Amen.

In this passage, Jesus draws heavily on the story from Exodus of manna in the desert. As the disciples press Jesus to give them concrete evidence of his identity, they point to God's gift of manna to the Israelites as an example. Jesus counters this with an unexpected answer. He has more than bread to offer them; he has salvation in the form of his own body. However, the disciples have yet to witness the Crucifixion and Resurrection, so Jesus' words don't make much sense to them. They want Jesus to offer them something to save them in the wilderness. That is exactly what he's doing—and more—but they can't yet see it.

In the same way the manna in Exodus appeared to rain down from above, Jesus descended to the earth as a human. He is the bread that has come down to offer sustenance for starving people. While manna offered salvation in the form of food, Jesus offers salvation to those who feel helpless and hopeless.

In verse 58, Jesus points out that while the manna saved the Israelites from famine, they still lived as finite humans who died of old age. Jesus states that the bread he offers is even greater than the bread offered in Exodus. Not only will it fulfill needs on earth; it will offer a life not yet imagined—a life where hunger is not a concern. The manna of the Israelites is a landmark of God's faithfulness, so for Jesus to assert that he can offer the same gifts of the manna and more is revolutionary. Jesus offers not only life but life everlasting to those who are faithful.

Manna from Heaven, you rescued the Israelites from famine. You offer eternal life to your followers. You save your believers from death. Satisfy us, enliven us, fortify us so that we may bring your holy vision to earth, offering sustenance to those who need it most. In the name of the Living Bread. Amen.

Abiding in God

AUGUST 16–22, 2021 • JAMES Z. LABALA

SCRIPTURE OVERVIEW: God had prevented David from building a temple in Jerusalem but then permitted David's son Solomon to build it. In First Kings, Solomon places the ark of the covenant in the holiest place, and God's presence descends. The psalmist rejoices in the Temple and would rather be in its courts than anywhere else because that is where God dwells. The New Testament readings remind us that the people of God have always met with resistance. The author of Ephesians compares living the Christian life to going into battle, so we must be prepared. Jesus also meets with resistance in John. His teachings are too hard for many to accept, so they abandon him. When we face resistance, therefore, we should not be surprised; but we are also not alone.

QUESTIONS AND SUGGESTIONS FOR REFLECTION

- Read 1 Kings 8:1, 6, 10-11, 22-30, 41-43. How does your faith inform the hospitality you show to friends? To strangers?
- Read Psalm 84. How do you find joy in the Lord? Recall a recent time when you felt a deep sense of this joy.
- Read Ephesians 6:10-20. How do truth, righteousness, peace, faith, salvation, and God's word help you live boldly as an ambassador of the gospel of Jesus Christ?
- Read John 6:56-69. How do you respond to Jesus' question: "Does this offend you?" This teaching was hard for his disciples. Where do you struggle with it?

Conference secretary of the Liberia Annual Conference of The United Methodist Church.

IN THE PRESENCE OF GOD

King Solomon has followed through on fulfilling the direc-
tive of the Lord to build the temple that his father, David,
had designed but could not build because God didn't allow it. In
the preceding chapter, we are told that all of the final finishing
work of the Temple has been completed. The final step is the
installation of the ark of the covenant. As a sacred object which
symbolizes the presence of the Lord with God's chosen people,
the ark contains the two stone tablets of the Ten Commandments.

King Solomon gathers the leaders and elders of the kingdom
to convey the ark to the Temple in a great, elaborate procession.
At the climax of the procession, the ark is carefully and precisely
seated in its designated place. The placement of the ark indicates
that the Temple is now ready for the dwelling of the Lord.

The apostle Paul refers to our bodies as temples of the Lord.
(See 1 Corinthians 6:19-20.) But God does not "move in" to
dwell in our lives until our lives are properly "furnished" with
open and repentant hearts. I have learned from my own Christian experience and from this text that in order for the Lord to
come into our lives, we must prepare ourselves by repenting and
opening our hearts to God. Our life was constructed by God as a
dwelling place for the Holy Spirit. When we prepare our hearts
and make them ready, as Solomon prepared the Temple, God's
Spirit will come in and take residence.

*Dear Lord, please give me the grace to prepare my heart for you
to come in and make it your dwelling place. Amen.*

GOD COVERS US

In today's reading (and preceding verses), King Solomon, the leaders and elders of the people, the priests and Levites have brought the ark of the covenant from the city of David, Zion, to the northern part of Jerusalem where the new Temple has been built. The Temple—now equipped with the ark of the covenant, the symbol of the presence of the Lord—has become the proper dwelling place of the Lord. Thus a cloud fills the Temple.

In the story of the Exodus we read that as Israel journeys in the wilderness, they experience the cloud as the presence of the Lord. (See Exodus 13:21.) When the people see the cloud, they know that the Lord is present in their midst. Then the Lord instructs Moses to construct the ark of the covenant. It was the point where the Lord will "meet with you" (Exod. 25:22). Therefore, the ark symbolized the physical presence of the Lord among the community as they journeyed to the Promised Land for permanent residency. The ark is carried by the priests, and its location is critical in the religious life of the people.

And now that Israel has settled down, it is necessary to have a permanent dwelling place for the Lord among the people. The ark is installed in the holy place inside the Temple. After the priests complete the installation of the ark, a cloud fills the Temple, indicating God's approval of the Temple as God's dwelling place in the midst of the people.

Today, those who believe in Jesus as their Lord and Savior become, through faith, the living temple of God as we invite God's Spirit into our lives with repentant and open hearts.

Gracious Lord, move me to open my heart to you so that you may fill me with your presence and power in the name of Jesus Christ our Lord. Amen.

TRUST GOD'S FAITHFULNESS

Faithfulness is something that many people struggle with. From the beginning of my spiritual journey, I have tried to be faithful. Because of this, I automatically assume that others have the same desire to be faithful. The problem is that we make promises that we do not keep. But the God of the Christian faith is always faithful. Our text for today shows how reliable and constant the faithfulness of God is.

In this reading, King Solomon is in the Temple with the gathered community of Israel. Solomon and the whole community have just experienced the presence and glory of God manifested in the symbol of a cloud. The king stands in front of the gathered community to make petitions for them. God has kept the promise to David that his descendants would always be on the throne of Israel, as long as they were faithful and obedient to the word of God. What is clear here is that since God has been faithful to Solomon's father, David, God will also be faithful to Solomon as long as Solomon remains obedient to God. Solomon has already taken the first step in obedience by building and dedicating the Temple to God. He prays now that God will dwell in the Temple and enable the fulfillment of its purpose as a place where the people will come to praise and worship their God.

As God's people in this age and time, we are called to boldly approach God's altar with our petitions. As we abide in God's word, we see God's constant faithfulness to us. Our trust in our Creator need never waiver. Our God will never disappoint us!

Dear Lord, give me the grace to always trust in your faithfulness and to be obedient to your will for my life. Amen.

EMBRACING STRANGERS

In our text today, Solomon intercedes for the foreigner who has come to be in Israel because of the reputation of the Lord. The reputation of the God of Israel is the story of the power of God demonstrated when God set Israel free from slavery in Egypt. It is the story of how God defeated Israel's powerful enemies with an outstretched hand.

Solomon sees that these saving actions of God will induce reverential fear in the people of other lands and attract them to Israel. As a visionary leader, Solomon is preparing the ground for immigrants who will come to his kingdom in the future. With a discerning spirit and deep care and concern for those under his leadership, Solomon prays for those who are yet to be a part of the community he leads. This prayer is not about the one who is praying but about the God to whom the petition is being made. God will answer the prayers of the immigrants in this Temple because the Temple bears God's name.

We live in a time when immigration issues are regularly in the headlines. The rate of migration from less developed countries to developed and affluent nations is rising rapidly. It seems that the more this rate rises, the more the care and treatment of migrants deteriorates. In today's reading we see the kind of leader we need in our own time—on national and international levels, as well as local and personal levels. The God we serve loves and cares for the strangers among us.

Lord, help me to love the strangers as you love them, to care for them as you care for them, and to treat them justly. Amen.

LONGING FOR GOD

The fact that all humans were created by God suggests that we all have an emptiness within us that can only be filled by God. Some of us, like the psalmist, have recognized our need for God. Though we live in our earthly home, we are convinced that it is in God that we have our home in this life and the next.

The psalmist expresses a deep longing and yearning for God, to be in the home of God, where God dwells. The writer proclaims that those who have their home in God are blessed and acknowledges God as almighty and king. The psalmist affirms entirely loyalty to God. Psalm 84 expresses both the psalmist's longing for communion with God and the well-being that results from encountering God. It proclaims the good news that our destination, daily and eternally, lies in God. This good news contains the transforming power through which we find strength, value, and life itself.

The psalmist acknowledges that the pilgrims' strength is in God. Even as they travel through harsh realities, the presence of God takes them from strength to strength. Like those early pilgrims, we too are on a lifelong journey, seeking to be at home with God. We must desire to live daily and eternally in the presence of God. Though our Christian journey can sometimes be difficult and full of tears, we can be assured that we are at home with God, who promises to be with us always. Though we encounter trials and temptations, we can trust that God's strength is sufficient for us and that God's grace makes us perfect. So, like the psalmist, we can rest assured that in God is our surest and safest place to be.

Give me a daily desire for you, O my God. Amen.

Jesus Is Life

Though we are alive, separation from God means that we are dead and lost. We are in need of life. We can only receive this life through Jesus Christ, who is life and gives life.

In the text for today, Jesus tells the crowd that whoever eats his flesh and drinks his blood will have life. Some in the crowd say that Jesus' teaching is hard. He claims that he is the true bread that comes from heaven. He tells them this is not like the bread that their ancestors ate and died. Those who eat this bread will live forever.

At the beginning of John 6, the crowd followed Jesus. He multiplied bread and fish and gave it to them to eat. The next day they went to look for Jesus again. He told them that they were not looking for him because they understood his miracles but because he had given them bread to eat. Jesus told them to work for the food that lasts for eternal life. And they asked Jesus to give them this bread always. But he tells them that he is the Bread of Life.

We must seek Jesus daily so that he can live in us and we in him. If we follow Jesus hoping to gain material possessions, we miss the mark. When we eat Jesus' flesh and blood, we enter into an intimate relationship with him. This intimate relationship means allowing Jesus to direct our lives. Seeking Jesus daily means feeding on the word of the One who provides light for our journeys, the One who gives us strength through the trials and temptations we face. In John 10:10 Jesus says, "The thief comes only to steal and kill and destroy. I came that they may have life, and have it abundantly." We all need life in abundance!

O Lord, I want to abide in you and for you to abide in me so that I may live abundantly, as you intend for all your people. Amen.

STANDING IN GOD'S POWER

In our reading for today, the apostle Paul uses the imagery of a soldier to urge his readers to build up their strength in the Lord's mighty power. As Christians, we have no power of our own. The source of our strength is in God through Jesus Christ in the power of the Holy Spirit. Paul writes that Christians must put on the full armor of God to enable them to stand against the devil's evil tricks. This armor we are to put on is spiritual because the battle is spiritual. As a soldier is dressed with a complete uniform, the Christian must be fully dressed with the spiritual armor to engage the enemy.

Paul says that the armor of God includes the following: The belt of truth, which is the knowledge of the truth of Jesus Christ, the gospel; the breastplate of righteousness, which is the righteousness that Christ gives, which helps our integrity and our character remain intact; the sandals of the gospel of peace, which are the shoes we wear to make us ready to take the gospel anywhere God sends us; the shield of a firm faith in Christ, which enables us to block spiritual assaults against us; the helmet of salvation, which protects us and gives us hope of deliverance from this body of sin; and finally, the sword of the Spirit, the word of God, which is the only offensive weapon the believer carries. This eternal word—the truth and strength of God—has more than enough power to defeat the enemy.

Lord Jesus, help me to stand firm in your power. Amen.

Tending the Soil of Your Heart for the Fruit of Your Life

AUGUST 23-29, 2021 • ENUMA OKORO

SCRIPTURE OVERVIEW: The poetry of Song of Solomon is thick with romantic imagery, and most scholars agree that these lines mean what they say on the surface; they are written from the author to the beloved. Psalm 45 echoes the refrain of admiration and desire. Such desire is not wrong if it is awakened at the proper time, as the author of Song of Solomon says elsewhere. James argues that ethical living is done not in word but in deed. True religion is not putting on a show but displaying mercy and controlling the tongue. In Mark's Gospel, Jesus rebukes some of the religious leaders on this very account because they talk of obedience to God but do not live it out. What we say and what we do should match.

QUESTIONS AND SUGGESTIONS FOR REFLECTION

- Read Song of Solomon 2:8-13. The narrative poetry of Song of Solomon invites us into scripture in a different way than other texts. How does God speak to you through this poetry?
- Read Psalm 45:1-2, 6-9. How do your relationships honor the gift of love?
- Read James 1:17-27. When do you find yourself as merely a "hearer" of the word and not a "doer"? What motivates you to act on God's word?
- Read Mark 7:1-8, 14-15, 21-23. What human traditions or rituals do you tend to make too important?

Writer, speaker, and teacher; certified and practicing spiritual director in the Ignatian tradition; holds an MDiv from Duke Divinity School and is a member of the Roman Catholic Church.

As the most romantic book of scripture, Song of Solomon explicitly explores the intimacy of relationship, describing the growing love between a man and a woman. Although the book is attributed to King Solomon in the early stages of his kingship, some scholars and religious leaders also choose to see in the book a metaphor for Jesus Christ's love relationship with his bride, the church. However you choose to read this beautiful book, one can't deny the rich descriptive images of adoration, deep love, and commitment.

In the second chapter of Song of Solomon, the maiden and her beloved banter back and forth about their appreciation of each other. But at the heart of this mutual flattery is the awareness that it is the appropriate season for new life and for love. Verses 11-13 speak of the winter ending and of the new signs of life in the flowers, the turtledoves, the fig tree, and the blossoming vines. In the right season there will be signs of life that affirm the goodness of whatever is developing.

This is a beautiful message to those of us who seek to discern the fittingness of a relationship, romantic or otherwise. How can we know the relationships we are to continue to nurture? From chapter two we might surmise that relationships worth pursuing are those whose words of love come from a genuine recognition of our value as children of God, with our own unique attributes. The words of the lovers stem from the condition of their hearts toward each other, and it's played out further in their actions. The pericope of 2:8-13 is bordered by verses that describe the beloved's awareness of the maiden's uniqueness and the maiden's declaration of commitment. The words and actions of this couple are nurtured in the soil of their heart.

Lord, help me to pay attention to the soil of my heart, that I would feed it with the nutrients of your Word so that my own words and actions would grow from that foundation. Amen.

Psalm 45 is a wedding song that ultimately celebrates a king and his bride. Like Song of Solomon, the king in question could be King Solomon, here preparing to marry the princess of Egypt. But again, the power of the psalm can be found in the focus of the king's character. Who the king is on the inside is what shows on the outside. These early verses of Psalm 45 are about a type of physical beauty mediated through a beautiful heart that is concerned with the things of God: righteousness, truth, equity. Have you ever met a person who just seems to radiate with the spirit of God? There is something about them that naturally draws you toward them, and regardless of your normal standards of judging beauty you find them lovely to behold. That is usually someone with a genuine heart for God.

In verses 1-2 we see that because of the way the king's heart turns toward God, not only are his words pleasing to God, but his physical appearance is affected by his focus on a "goodly theme." The king is considered the "most handsome of men" because the "grace [of God] is poured upon your lips." It's important to note that both God and the king are working here. The king chooses to focus his heart toward God. It is an act of will. And from that focus, the king can offer words that lead to life. When he describes his tongue like a pen of a ready writer, we should remember that a ready and skillful writer selects words after much consideration, choosing what is fitting and appropriate to the desired result. For a person with a heart fixed on God, the desired result is to foster life and love, truth and joy, righteousness and equity. God delights in our efforts, regardless of our imperfections. When we truly set our hearts on the things of God, there's a visible testimony of beauty in our lives.

God, make my tongue like a ready writer. May I be thoughtful with my words, choosing to speak life and love into the world. Amen.

The book of James is often attributed to James, the brother of Jesus, who was writing to an audience of Jewish Christians probably living outside Palestine and undergoing persecution. There are a few overarching themes of the book that scholars might argue do not always have a single message running through them. But James is concerned that Christians both put their faith into action and also realize that words have power to lead to life or to death. But from the onset, James wants to remind his audience that God's actions toward us are the starting point. In James 1:17–18, the writer notes that God is the giver of all good things, the first of which is giving us life by the Word, which is Christ, but also by the words of God's mouth, the gospel. We are made in the image of God; and because God gives, we can give. Because God speaks life with words, we can speak life with our words. We do because God has already done. God, who is unchanging, is the giver of all good things.

But to do as God does requires active faith and intentional actions. Our job is to refuse that which is not of God and to make ourselves hospitable and available to what is of God. When we are quick to listen and slow to speak, our words—like those of the psalmist from Psalm 45—are considered and considerate. When we are slow to anger—when we, as James instructs in verse 21, "accept the implanted word"—we are acknowledging that if we want to speak life, the condition of our hearts matters. And at the center of that condition of our hearts is God's righteousness and grace. We acknowledge that to do as God does requires both divine grace and our intentional human choices.

Lord, make me quick to listen today, to you and to the people I encounter throughout the day. Sharpen my ears to hear your words, and grant me an obedient and humble heart to let your words do their work in me. Amen.

A reasonable question we might have for James is, "What does it look like to accept the word, especially if it's already in us?" Well, it starts with a dose of truth serum. James dives right in to warn us about self-deception. He knows full well how easy it is for us to know what to do but to choose not to do it, especially if it's uncomfortable for us. He likens listening to the word and not doing it to looking in the mirror, seeing our face, and walking away to forget what we look like. This would actually require some effort on our part to forget what we look like! It suggests more of a glancing in the mirror rather than looking. When we glance, we don't have enough time to really see, to assess what we see, and to act accordingly. I don't know about you, but I tend to only glance at things I consider unimportant or that I want to avoid. Few of us likely consider the look of our faces unimportant, but we may want to avoid seeing what will require effort and discipline and consideration on our part. It's a great analogy because looking intently at scripture will require very different actions from us than will merely glancing.

When we take the time to study the Word, it calls us to both belief and action. If we say we believe and listen to the Word but we don't do anything with what we hear, it's no better than a cursory glance that effects no change in how we live. We haven't invested ourselves in seeing. We haven't chosen the freedom of submission to God. And according to James, this is the same as blocking our own blessings. Why would we choose not to do the very thing that will bless us? Likely this is because our cursory glancing deceives us into thinking that God's law is limiting. The truth is that God's law frees us to use not only our words to bless and to be blessed but also to use our hands and our very lives to serve those in need.

Lord, grant me the courage to look long enough into your Word to be convicted in love toward acting justly in the world. Amen.

What has the final word in how you live your life? Is it the things you've learned from the authority figures and traditions of your church and community, or is it the word of God? At the heart of this passage from Mark is the reality that we can so easily get lost in human-made rules and rituals that we lose sight of following God from a faithful heart steeped in the word of God. The Pharisees came to question the validity of Jesus' ministry. To do so was natural; there were many false prophets going about at the time, claiming to be sent by God. But in this instance, the leaders had already decided to find fault with Jesus' teachings, so they came looking to pick a fight.

They confront Jesus about how his disciples eat without first performing the ceremonial washings, a part of oral law that began as an interpretation of the written law of the Hebrew Bible. Over time, this practice took precedence over the written law in the worship life of certain Jews. Jesus points out that by focusing so much on these traditions, these leaders are more invested in their rules than in abiding by the word of God. They are more concerned about the appearance of faith than about the condition of a believer's heart. They have become like those who glance in the mirror and forget what they look like. They have forgotten who they are—children of God.

When we forget who and whose we are, the only natural progression is to live our lives based on false guidelines. You can't follow the words of your parent when you no longer remember whose child you are. Choosing human teachings over the word of God is like forgetting who your parents are. We may claim we know God, but the condition of our hearts is what steers us either toward or away from the things of God. If you want to know who or what people most identify with, watch their actions.

Lord, help me remember whose I am. Yours. Amen.

Jesus wants to emphasize a point. It's not just about people following tradition, rather than God's word. It's about knowing the human heart as the source for both good and evil. It can be tempting to read these passages and point a finger at church leaders or "certain types" of believers. But if we do that, we are missing the message Christ has for us. In Mark 7:14, Jesus says, "Listen to me, all of you, and understand." He's basically saying, "If you thought this lesson didn't apply to you, think again!"

Jesus was not just condemning the Pharisees, nor was he necessarily trying to fully negate the Jewish dietary customs found in Mosaic Law. He was more broadly trying to show that we should be more concerned about the conditions of our hearts than about what we eat or how we eat. We so readily like to imagine that evil, sin—whatever your term for separation from God—comes from outside of us or is more readily found in certain types of people. But Jesus says that if we don't pay attention to our heart, we are just as likely as anyone else to be the source of sin and evil and all that separates us from God. Our words can bring life or death to ourselves and into the world depending on the condition of our hearts. Our actions, regardless of whether they appear righteous or justified in our minds, can have varying intentions and results depending on the condition of our hearts.

Reading this passage brings to mind all the psalms that speak of giving our hearts to God, searching our hearts, asking God to cleanse our hearts, heal our hearts, teach us so that the meditations of our hearts are pleasing to God. The psalmist knew the depth to which the human heart can both rise and fall. Jesus is trying to teach us to know the same thing and to constantly seek to choose Life.

Holy Spirit, teach me how to search my heart with honesty before you. Help me learn how to cultivate a heart from which true life flows in my words and actions. Amen.

If we have been afraid to look in the mirror, Jesus holds it up for us regardless. The litany of sins in Mark 7:21-22 should make us shudder—not because they are so bad but because they are so normal in our world and, sadly, within ourselves. We may start off reading them and feel fine. After all, we're not murderers or thieves or adulterers—at least, most of us reading this are not. But as the list goes on, we start to squirm a bit. Jesus won't let us just take a glance and forget who we are. It's vital that we see ourselves for who we might be and what is truly possible within us. Greed, malice, deceit, lewdness, envy, slander, arrogance, and folly—each of us could pick at least one thing from this list and give an example of when this has manifested in our lives. It's not pretty, and it doesn't feel good to acknowledge. And yet, though it is not Jesus' aim to shame or condemn us, it does seem important that we understand the power inherent in our hearts to breed such harm against others and ultimately ourselves.

The saying "knowledge is power" applies here. Once we know and accept what we are capable of, we can begin to dwell on what else is possible. The heart can also breed love and kindness, joy, gentleness, peace, goodness, faithfulness, forbearance, and self-control. We have a say in what comes out of our hearts. But it requires knowing the word of God, dwelling on it, letting it take root in our hearts, feasting on it, nourishing it with our own words and actions. It is no good to simply read this list of sins and feel shame or contrition. The next step is to seek to cultivate the fruit of the Spirit. And God has shown us how to do so—by submitting to God and bearing one another's burdens, by encouraging one another in faith and with kindness and love, and by encouraging one another to good works and good living.

Holy Spirit, as I find the courage to see myself more fully, lead me to repentance; help me make daily choices that foster life. Amen.

The Maker of All

AUGUST 30–SEPTEMBER 5, 2021 • WILLIAM DOCKERY

SCRIPTURE OVERVIEW: It is sometimes an uncomfortable subject for many, but God does have ethical standards. The author of Proverbs declares that those who act unjustly, particularly if they oppress the poor, will provoke God's judgment. The psalmist repeats the refrain that God blesses the righteous but is not pleased with those who choose a consistent lifestyle of rebellion against God. James challenges us practically on this point. Do we judge people by their wealth or status? This is not from God. True faith shows no partiality and prompts action. Jesus models this in Mark when he heals two Gentiles. Jews and Gentiles generally remained separate (an ancient form of racism), but Jesus did not discriminate based on their ethnicity. He cared only about their hearts.

QUESTIONS AND SUGGESTIONS FOR REFLECTION

- Read Proverbs 22:1-2, 8-9, 22-23. How has God shown you that there is no difference between persons who are rich and persons who are poor? How does this affect your actions?
- Read Psalm 125. When have you seen righteousness in someone the community (or the church) has labeled "wicked"?
- Read James 2:1-17. How do your works support your faith? How does your faith in God move you to action on behalf of others?
- Read Mark 7:24-37. God calls us to love all our neighbors. How can you be a good neighbor to those your community has excluded?

Retired journalist and research writer; Unitarian Universalist who attends Central United Methodist Church in Knoxville, TN; state-trained advocate for people with disabilities; East Tennessee native who marched with Dolly Parton in their high school band.

We met the young man when he was caught rifling through men's lockers at the local gym. My wife, Emalie, was visiting the Y when employees brought him to the front desk. A retired inner-city teacher who never met a troubled youth she didn't embrace, Emalie rescued him and drove him to the shelter where he and his mother and younger brother were staying.

We didn't know much about him—we couldn't even drive him to the door of the shelter because the family's whereabouts were secret. We learned that he and his mother had substance abuse issues.

In the next few weeks, the young man became a regular at our house. He was short on education but, with guidance from Emalie, soon showed us real-world fix-it skills and an enthusiasm for hard work. We paid him for his work, and he helped us with tasks needing to be done.

Unexpectedly, he showed us one way his life differed from ours when Emalie stopped to fill the car with gas. After she had swiped her credit card and put the pump on automatic, she got back in the van. The young man watched the pump and began to stir when the dial neared $5.

"You want me to stop it?" he asked, preparing to get out of the vehicle.

"No, it's okay."

"Now?" At $10 he opened his door.

"No, I'm going to fill up."

He sat in silence until the tank was full and the pump clicked off. Only then did Emalie realize that he was not used to riding with someone who could afford a full tank of gas.

"The rich and the poor have this in common: The LORD is the maker of them all." Sometimes what we take for granted hides others from us.

O Creator, peel back our prejudices so that we see the divine in everyone. Amen.

I administer a small neighborhood page on Facebook and keep up with another neighborhood email list. I've found that in the pseudo-privacy of the internet, many people openly express their deep prejudices against others, especially those have few material possessions.

One discussion sprang up after someone posted a photo of a man and his dog. The man stood at the bottom of an exit ramp holding a will-work-for-food sign printed on a cardboard box top. His dog lay at his feet. People admired the dog, wondered if the man had stolen it, speculated about its health, and proposed to rescue it. Not one person suggested that they might help the man in his need.

In another discussion, people posted comments about a church parking lot that had become a gathering place for people experiencing homelessness. The talk was that the people were vagrants and drug users, and some called for the church to contact police. No one talked about going to the group, inquiring about their needs, and maybe even inviting them to church services.

On my Facebook page, a group began to fight the location of a dollar store on the edge of my neighborhood, where the store could serve a nearby community that lacked access to a food store. The arguments ranged from the quality of the groceries to the need for a quaint coffee shop. Finally, one commenter got to the real fear: A store for a poorer clientele would drive down property values.

The scriptures have a plain answer for this: "Those who are generous are blessed, for they share their bread with the poor. Do not rob the poor because they are poor, . . . for the Lord pleads their cause."

O Source of all worth, lead us to act with the same compassion we receive from you. Amen.

We don't believe in demons these days—they are so first-century. Nor do we place much stake in contemporary miracles. Modern science and engineering have explained away ancient puzzles and given us even more wonders that serve, amaze, and sometimes confound us.

That contemporary viewpoint complicates our reading of the seventh chapter of Mark, which bring us the story of Jesus exorcising a demon from a young girl.

Jesus is approached by a Gentile woman whose daughter is possessed by "an unclean spirit." The woman begs Jesus to heal her child, and Jesus responds with a curious saying: "Let the children be fed first, for it is not fair to take the children's food and throw it to the dogs." Jesus' words seem nonresponsive, but the woman answers in kind: "Even the dogs under the table eat the children's crumbs." Jesus then tells her to go to her daughter, who is no longer possessed of the demon.

Scholars tell us that the story is part of a first-century dialogue between Jewish followers of Jesus and the Gentiles ("dogs under the table") who were being attracted to Christianity. According to Mark's narrative, Jesus first tells the woman that he has brought his message primarily for the "children," the Jewish people. When she responds that even the Gentiles ("dogs") can benefit from his message, he relents and casts out the demon.

Today we long for the simplicity of demons and the convenience of miracles. We want to live in a magical world with a deity who can utter a few mysterious words or deliver a healing touch and make problems disappear. But do we really want divine intervention that fades our cares and fixes our fears? Do we expect God to make magic for us? More importantly, what does God expect of us?

O Thou Most Able, have patience with our wants. Amen.

The church I attend has a massive presence in the quiet residential neighborhood that surrounds it. Built in 1927, the brown brick building with the bulky Gothic Revival tower occupies almost an entire city block. It houses a soaring sanctuary that seats 1,600 people and was the largest auditorium space in the city for decades in the mid-20th century.

These days about 160 parishioners attend services. The congregation is still vital, but demographic changes have left plenty of empty pew space. I love to slip into the sanctuary midweek for quiet reflection. Glowing amber windows, discreet burgundy carpet, dark pews, pale walls—the space fairly reeks of sacred.

The demons are downstairs, in the fellowship hall. These are not the "unclean spirits" that Jesus vanquished. They are modern devils—habits and diseases and addictions that bring together people seeking to escape the destructive forces that are preying on them and to wrest back control of their lives.

People in 12-step recovery programs pay about a thousand visits a week to the church. The people downstairs rarely come to services on Sundays (though they are welcome), but they create their own worship each time they gather. They forge the bonds with one another that allow them to get in touch with their own healing reality. They are not the only people who use our building. We host a food pantry, a winter farmers market, election polling, large community meetings, and most recently a prom for LGBTQ+ high schoolers. I am in awe of how people moved by their steadfast faith in Jesus more than ninety years ago built this building so that later generations could find healing and spiritual health. The words of the psalmist come to mind: "Those who trust in the LORD are like Mount Zion, which cannot be moved, but abides forever."

Show your goodness, O Lord, to those who are good and to those who are true in heart. Amen.

As coronavirus deepens inequality, inequality worsens its spread," read the article by Max Fisher and Emma Bubola on the *New York Times* website on March 16, 2020.

James offers a clear-eyed view of class and income inequality among first-century followers of Jesus when he writes, "My brothers and sisters, do you with your acts of favoritism really believe in our glorious Lord Jesus Christ?" He speaks out against those in early Christian assemblies who are quick to favor the rich but leave the poor to sit on the floor or stand in the back.

James reminds his readers of Jesus' commandment, "You shall love your neighbor as yourself." James goes on to add, "But if you show partiality, you commit sin."

Do we actually believe that we should love our neighbor as ourselves? Then we too must seek a clear-eyed view of the distinctions that class (and race, income, ability, and gender) make in the way we treat our sibling children of God.

In the early days of the 2020 COVID-19 pandemic when my family was sheltering in place, I drove to a fast-food restaurant. As I paid for our burgers, I looked in at a handful of low-wage workers who were definitely not sheltering in place. They were busily preparing food for those of us who were.

As the pandemic got under way in the U.S. last year, the *New York Times* reported that people in lower income groups were more likely to catch and die from the disease. And "they are likelier to suffer loss of income or health care, . . . potentially on a sweeping scale."

James's warning should challenge all disciples of Jesus who seek to live a life—and build a society—that doesn't make distinctions.

O Creator of all, help us as we struggle to love all. Amen.

In the earliest days of the 2020 coronavirus pandemic, many churches closed to protect their members and slow the spread of the disease. It was a time of danger and anxiety. Health authorities discouraged public gatherings of even a handful of people, and individuals and families were told to shelter at home. The danger of the highly contagious virus required separation and isolation, even as we sought ways to connect during this vulnerable time.

The church I attend set up a call list of older members and ones in fragile circumstances who might benefit from a check-in. Many were lifelong members who had played a vital role in shaping the congregation's ministries. It soon became clear that one of their biggest problems was being separated from activities they were part of through and for the church. Without the ability to be of service they were cut loose from their moorings. Their "works" were a crucial expression of their faith, embodying what it means to follow Jesus. Often, those we called to check on volunteered to become callers themselves.

"What good is it . . . if you say you have faith but do not have works?" James writes. "If a brother or sister is naked and lacks daily food, and one of you says to them, 'Go in peace, keep warm and eat your fill,' and yet you do not supply their bodily needs, what is the good of that?"

In one of the most controversial verses in the New Testament, he concludes, "Faith, by itself, if it has no works, is dead."

The fight over whether salvation comes through faith or works has raged for centuries, but it usually misses the kernel of truth in James's observation: "Works"—day-to-day caring for and about other people—is an outgrowth of deep discipleship. When our church building was closed, we found how central "works" are to faith.

O God, may our faith be evident in all we do. Amen.

There is one fact that is easy to miss in this week's readings: Nothing is required from those who are in need.

Judaism has an epochal history of advocating for the have-nots, those on the fringes of society who are poor or strangers from other lands or widows and orphans. The verses from Proverbs reiterate that: God takes the side of the poor and afflicted because, just like the rich, God is their maker. And James reminds us that God has chosen the poor to be heirs to the kingdom. From the biblical point of view, people in need are simply those who lack a necessity, whether it is food or shelter—or respect.

And no one who has—wealth, social standing, material resources—is absolved of the need to share those things with the people who don't have them. The scriptural record addresses those of us whose need for "three-squares and a cot" are more than met, who are self-assured about our standing in the community.

James makes clear that we are all peers before God, and respect for one another is a central requirement of the gospel. We are not to move the wealthy to the front of the line or the reserved seating.

Nowhere does the gospel obligate those who receive our care to do or be or become anything other than what they are. They don't have to sign a pledge card or bring a covered dish or walk the aisle or even say thank you. They don't have to be what we want them to be. Our call is to love them in the way that we love God, the way that we love ourselves, and the way that God loves us and them—as God's beloved children.

O God, we are all poor and needy. Keep us rich in your love. Amen.

How Then Shall We Live?

SEPTEMBER 6–12, 2021 • BETH TAULMAN MILLER

SCRIPTURE OVERVIEW: Through the scriptures and the guidance of the Holy Spirit, God shows the paths of righteousness and warns against the ways of destruction. The writer of Proverbs describes this as the voice of Wisdom crying out, yet some refuse to listen—to their peril. The psalmist rejoices in the law of the Lord, for God's decrees teach us how to live well. Living a godly life includes paying attention to our speech. How can we, James asks, praise God with our lips and then curse others with those same lips? Peter is tripped up by his words in Mark. He declares Jesus to be the Messiah, yet in the next scene he recklessly rebukes Jesus for speaking of his death. Our words matter, and God desires purity and consistency.

QUESTIONS AND SUGGESTIONS FOR REFLECTIONS

- Read Proverbs 1:20-33. How clearly do you hear Wisdom's call? What prevents you from answering that call?
- Read Psalm 19. Where in creation do you hear God speaking to you?
- Read James 3:1-12. How do you use your words in wise ways? When do you struggle with your words?
- Read Mark 8:27-38. Who do you say that Jesus is?

Pastoral counselor in Chicago; founder with her husband, Greg, of Thrive Resources, an organization that helps people in their journey of emotional and spiritual health; graduate of Bethel Seminary and North Park Theological Seminary; mom of two adult sons, Jacob and Caleb, and a rescue dog, Lucy.

The best storytellers know that to really get a reader's attention, it's smart to create a twist or come from an unexpected angle. Some of the most fun discussions I've had in a book club center around how we experienced a writer's use of various literary tools like flashback, multiple narrators, or subtle foreshadowing to tell their story. In the beginning of Proverbs, Solomon's writing is straightforward, almost textbook-like, explaining that the goal of the book is "for attaining wisdom and discipline." Then about halfway through chapter 1, Solomon makes a turn into more poetic writing by personifying wisdom into Wisdom, a wise, discerning woman who is desperately trying to get the attention of the "mockers" and "fools" who aren't listening to her. Her voice is urgent and pleading. The streets are noisy, and yet she seeks to be heard over the chaos. What follows is lyrical in its rhythm and flow—and surprisingly, unexpectedly harsh. It's challenging to read Wisdom's predictions of "calamity" and "distress" for those who have ignored her. Frankly, passages like this can be troubling and ones we'd rather rush through. Yet isn't that exactly what the voice of Wisdom is pleading with us not to do? While the poetic language is severe, just maybe it's designed to get our attention.

Wise adults are willing to slow down and listen to the sage voice of our Wonderful Counselor. Maybe we don't believe that we are so bold as to "hate knowledge," but our refusal to center down and attune to God and God's wisdom can be just as dangerous. Actually it may be even more dangerous because we've fooled ourselves into believing that we are listening and are without consequences. May we notice how God is seeking to get our attention and call us to wise living.

God of Wisdom, draw us to center down and be attentive to your guidance for our lives. Amen.

Solomon personifies God's wisdom as the discerning (and fired-up) female voice of Wisdom. She's expressing her righteous anger that "fools" haven't been listening. At first glance, the text is full of energetic rebuke, and it seems as if calamity is inevitable. But what first appears as harsh judgment may actually have another layer to it. Elsewhere in Proverbs, Wisdom is speaking again and explains that "whoever finds me, finds life and obtains favor from the Lord" (Prov. 8:35). She isn't just arbitrarily angry; she's passionate. She knows that healthy, abundant life is not possible without wisdom. Driven by the love of a concerned parent, Wisdom knows that our unwise actions, words, and choices have painful consequences. Her anger has the ring of a lament—and one of the beautiful truths of lament is that often a declaration of hope is found at the end. This is no different: "But those who listen to me will be secure and will live at ease without dread of disaster." The passage lands softly, in an encouraging invitation.

Where we may have ignored the call for wise living, we are now once again being invited to take notice. Whether it be, for example, in a particular relationship, with our finances, how we treat our body, how we navigate our sexuality, or how we traverse anger—we are bidden to make wise choices that create safety (for us and those around us). And if we don't quite know how to do that—wise people learn to ask for help. One of the most discerning things we can say is: "I don't know how to do that."

What area of your life isn't healthy, marked by some unwise choices? Consider listening to what God desires for you in that arena, and find ways you can reach out for support if you need it.

Psalm 19 is a beloved psalm for many. For C. S. Lewis, it was the "greatest poem in the psalter."* Structured into three parts, the lyrical psalm focuses on knowing God through creation, knowing God through the goodness of God's Word, and David's prayerful response to both.

The leader at a retreat I attended invited us to watch the sun rise over the ocean for our morning prayer. No words were spoken other than "Dear God" at the beginning and "Amen" as we closed. For ten minutes in between, we communed with God by soaking in the beauty of the skies and the sounds of the ocean. It was almost completely wordless, yet so much was said. The first section of Psalm 19 is a poetic description of creation where "there is no speech" yet so much is spoken as the heavens tell of God's glory and the firmament proclaims God's handiwork.

Stop for a moment and recall experiences in which you noticed creation speaking to you in wordless volumes: A day in the mountains, a fresh snowfall, a sunset that stopped you in your tracks, a field of sunflowers that took your breath away. When we attune to the splendor of nature, it evokes a response. During a hike in the Rocky Mountains, I was surprised by how the beauty along the trail awakened my grief for my beloved father who had died the year before. Without words, the majesty of God's creation invited me to be present with the sadness I didn't realize was just under the surface. Surely part of knowing God through creation is the way creation invites us to know ourselves; and in worshipful response, we can offer our presence.

---

*C. S. Lewis, **Reflections on the Psalms** (New York: Harper One, 1958), 73-74.

Find time today to be present with how creation is declaring God's glory, and engage it as prayer with "Dear God" at the beginning and "Amen" when you finish. Attune to what it evokes in you.

In the first half of this poetic psalm, David calls forth the revelation of God through nature. In the second half, he moves into exalting God's revelation through scripture. The language is again lyrical as David describes God's word as another dimension of creation. Notice the call-and-response flow of the passage: The law of the Lord is perfect/reviving the soul; the decrees of the Lord are sure/making wise the simple; Moreover by them is your servant warned/in keeping them there is great reward. God's creation, whether in the beauty of the world or the goodness of God's precepts, calls to us—and asks for a response.

David's response to the "call" of the created world and the law of God is this: "Let the words of my mouth and the meditations of my heart be acceptable unto you, O LORD my rock and my redeemer." Even the description David uses for God mirrors nature (God is our rock) and the scriptures (God is our redeemer). As God calls to us through taking in the beauty of nature or soaking in the precepts of God, it begs the question: How then shall we respond? Thankfully, the text communicates that it isn't about our willing ourselves to change. Rather, it's God's living word that revives, enlightens, and makes us wise, stirring within us the movement to make different choices.

Lectio divina *is an ancient and sacred way to engage scripture, inviting us to listen to the same passage four times with silence in between. Read Psalm 9:14 and allow the words to wash over you. Sit quietly and listen. Read the passage again, listening for a word or phrase that stands out to you. Remain still and listen. After reading the verse a third time, listen for an invitation God may have for you in these words. After the fourth and final reading, consider if you have a response for God as you sit in silence.*

Reminiscent at times of Proverbs, James is a collection of practical admonitions that encourage wise living while using literary techniques along the way for emphasis. Here James focuses specifically on the lack of wisdom often reflected in our communication with one another. Using hyperbole, the author suggests that "anyone who makes no mistakes in speaking is perfect," meaning none of us is free from this struggle. Talk about practical!

James has an urgent, prophet-like tone to his writing, speaking about our speech in metaphors like bits in horses' mouths, rudders on ships, and forest fires started by sparks. Designed to underscore the seriousness of the issue, James's harsh language is at times jarring, referring to the tongue as an evil, deadly poison that is "set on fire by hell." In truth, as jolting as those words may be, all of us can attest to how upsetting it is when wounding things are said to us or words aren't spoken when they need to be. Either is a misuse of our gift of speech. And likewise, we all know that there are times when we have deeply hurt others by painful things we've communicated or by a deafening silence we perpetuated when something needed to be said and we chose to remain silent.

The culmination of James's admonitions leads to the troubling inconsistency of using our tongue to bless God while cursing our fellow human beings who are made in God's image. It's not just that one seems to contradict the other; speaking ill of others, who are made in God's image, is comparable to cursing God. At times we live our lives compartmentally, praising God one moment while degrading others the next. It comes full circle. To do one is likened to the other.

Help us, God, to recognize how blessing one another through our words is a way to love and praise you—and loving you, and being loved by you, leads to our capacity to love others well. It comes full circle. Amen.

The Gospel of Mark begins with the announcement of "Good News," but it's a bumpy ride at times. As Jesus is becoming more widely known, he explores with his disciples who others say he is (Elijah, John the Baptist, a prophet). Then Jesus asks them directly: "Who do you believe I am?" At first glance, it seems Peter is starting to understand: "You are the Messiah." When Jesus explains the suffering and descent his journey will reflect, we see Peter's perception of "Messiah" is more in line with a political messianic ruler. Peter can't yet envision that Jesus has something very different in mind from what Peter expects. We are often no different. If we're honest, we often long to be rescued from our pain and heartache by a "messiah" or other type of inaccurate image we have of God rather than being led through our struggle on a journey of descent and formation.

When Peter starts to rebuke Jesus, Jesus' response is forceful: "Get behind me, Satan." Mark's treatment of Jesus' experience in the desert is brief—only two verses (Mark 1:12-13)—and many scholars wonder if this experience with Peter is the one Mark chose to more greatly emphasize in reflecting the temptation Jesus experienced. It makes sense that in his humanity Jesus wouldn't naturally be drawn to the path of descent—and a friend tempting him to embrace power and ascent wouldn't help. That perspective makes you wonder if Jesus' strong words were less about admonishing Peter and more about the intensity he felt to stay the course and the challenge in doing so. It stirs a compassion for the humanity of Jesus and the magnitude of the task he was embracing.

"You are setting your mind not on divine things but human things," Jesus tells Peter. Consider if there is a place in your life in which God is inviting you to surrender into a different vision than what you had imagined.

It's easy for us to read the question posed to the disciples and offer the right answer: You are Jesus, the Messiah. The more important question for us to wrestle with, though, is how might we (like Peter) misinterpret what it means to follow one with this title. For the first time in his ministry, Jesus is more direct in what he's asking his followers to do. "Denying" ourselves is strong language and could be misunderstood as an over-simplified practice of ignoring ourselves while putting others' needs ahead of ours or not learning to listen deeply to ourselves and our God-given intuition. Years ago, I heard suggested through the acronym *JOY* that right living is found in putting the following in a hierarchical order: Jesus, Others, You. If the call to deny ourselves isn't realized with more nuance, it may result in our practicing self-forgetting instead of self-denial. We need to square this command with Jesus' other instructions on what it means to follow him when he teaches us to love our neighbor as ourselves.

Could it be that rather than self-forgetting, Jesus is calling us to shed our false selves—or our ego as some refer to it—and ground our identity in Christ? Out of that awareness, we "deny" the parts of us that hustle for security, affection, and control—not by saying they don't exist but by humbly acknowledging them and not feeding their growth. "Take up your cross" is an invitation to many things as we seek to follow Christ, one of which is to engage a journey of growing into emotionally and spiritually mature adults who are able to love God, others, and ourselves well. In the upside-down kingdom of God, we "lose" our old way of living. In so doing, we gain our true selves in Christ.

Wonderful Counselor, grant us wisdom and discernment as we seek to shed our false selves rather than forget or ignore who God created us to be. Amen.

Walking in Spiritual Wisdom

SEPTEMBER 13–19, 2021 • ANGELA SCHAFFNER

SCRIPTURE OVERVIEW: Proverbs describes the noble wife and sets a standard that can seem impossible. This woman is capable and respected but also generous and wise. She serves but is not weak. Is she a "superwoman," and do all women need to be "superwomen"? No, she is noble because she follows the counsel of the psalmist and is deeply rooted in the teachings of God. Therefore, she represents a standard for everyone to emulate, not just women. James, another teacher of wisdom, encourages believers to show these same characteristics by following the wisdom given by God. In Mark's Gospel, the disciples display a lack of wisdom by arguing over who is the greatest. Jesus reminds them that greatness in God's eyes comes through service, not through seeking recognition.

QUESTIONS AND SUGGESTIONS FOR REFLECTION

- Read Proverbs 31:10-31. How have societal expectations shaped your life? How do you allow them to shape the ways you interact with others?
- Read Psalm 1. What fruit are you yielding in this season?
- Read James 3:13–4:3, 7-8a. In what ways does your life reflect "gentleness born of wisdom"? How are you gentle with yourself and with others?
- Read Mark 9:30-37. How do you seek to serve others in your daily life?

Counseling psychologist in private practice in Atlanta, GA; author of *Revealed: What the Bible Can Teach You About Yourself* and *Gather Us In: Leading Transformational Small Groups*; loves spending time with her family (Dusty, Carlson, Caleb, and Zach) and practicing Taekwondo.

The psalmists' expressions can represent our own experiences. In Psalm 1, the happy meditators of God's law are delighted as they prosper. They are trees planted beside a stream, enduring and yielding fruit. In contrast, the wicked are unable to stand and are easily blown aside by the wind.

We want to identify with the righteous, the strong trees yielding fresh spiritual fruit of love, joy, peace, and patience. We want to claim the identity of one who has self-control, one who is kind, good, and gentle with other people. But in many of our encounters, we feel more like the chaff, blown in all directions, unable to stand. We sin and scoff. In this passage we find the dichotomy of being human. We are struggling and evolving but also beautiful. We are flying through the air like chaff in the wind, but we are also rooted in Christ, our nourishing source of living water. When we seek paths of fulfillment outside of God, we lose our sense of being spiritually grounded; we suffer in the chaos and uncertainty of the windblown chaff. Instead of labeling ourselves as wicked and retreating into guilt that distances us from God's grace-filled love, we can embrace the image of the tree next to the stream and return to the source of our nourishment. When we return to God, our spiritual thirst is satisfied.

In this passage, we find an opportunity to embrace the truth: our lives do not reflect a claim to live in one of these two realities but a challenge to embrace the tension of living a life that vacillates between chaff and tree. When we feel blown in all directions, we can look for the next season of fruit-bearing prosperity. When we make our least wise choices and sit with the chaffy parts of ourselves, we can once again return to God's ways of meditative sustenance and stand in the way of the righteous.

God, you love us in moments when we lose our footing and in moments when we stand strong. When we feel caught up in chaos, revive us with your grounding love. Amen.

Proverbs 31:25 outlines some admirable qualities: "Strength and dignity are her clothing, and she laughs at the time to come." As a psychologist and eating-disorders specialist, I encounter many people who experience passivity rather than strength, shame rather than dignity, and intense anxiety rather than carefree laughter. A woman comes to believe she is undeserving of food and cannot see her value, and she struggles to voice her needs and preferences. A young man feels shame about his sexual experiences and tearfully shares his feelings with his therapist while trying to overcome binge eating and compulsive exercise behaviors. A teenager battles bulimia as she finds herself caught in the tension of striving to meet her needs while feeling she must compensate for having any needs to begin with.

God's wisdom calls us to heal from our experiences of suffering, though the path may be rocky. We may need to visit vulnerable, painfully honest places within ourselves in order to experience strength, dignity, and carefree joy. When a person or system preaches the gospel of passivity, we can respond in strength, asserting our voices. When a person or system preaches the gospel of shame, we can rise in dignity, shamelessly claiming our uniqueness and identity. When a person or system preaches the gospel of anxiety and fear, we can embrace the love of God with a carefree laughter that does not minimize our pain but releases us from rigidity born of fear. Asserting our voices, claiming our full identity, and embracing a carefree spirit are easier said than done. But as we move toward wisdom and healing, we become more confident in our ability to embody empowerment, uniqueness, and spontaneity. Complex and chaotic as our next obstacles may appear, God can supply strength, dignity, and laughter—exactly when and for as long as we need it.

God, supply me today with the strength, dignity, and carefree laughter I need in order to face what is happening and what is yet to come. Amen.

For most of my life, I read Proverbs 31 as an individual challenge. I felt, and was taught, that it was a yardstick for measuring my success as a Christian woman. My perspective fed into a destructive perfectionism that alienated me from God.

In recent years, I've come to embrace this passage in a different way, approaching it as a collective challenge rather than an individual one. I breathed a sigh of relief as I realized that I did not need to rise early and stay up late, buy fields and manage the household, all while rocking toned arms, in order to be a good Christian. We each have our calling and our place within the body of Christ, and God calls us to be a collective success. I can celebrate that my neighbor is more tuned in to the details of what's happening in the neighborhood and that my colleague has a different specialty than I do. My friends can teach Sunday school, cook church dinners, plan events, and prepare sermons, while I write books and volunteer with the refugee ministry. When we come together in community, we transcend what any of us could do individually and move together as a whole body in a rhythmic flow that serves God's purposes. An emphasis on individual achievement tends to feed perfectionistic thinking and encourages comparisons. A collective focus joins us more intimately with the purpose of loving God and one another well.

As you reflect on Proverbs 31, consider what your one part in the collective calling could be and how you could take one step today to live that out. Release yourself from the unrealistic expectation of being every part of this calling at once. Instead of using it as a perfectionistic yardstick for your worth as a Christian, let it be an invitation to find your place in a community of believers, bigger and more effective than what you can do alone.

God, show me one part of the collective calling that you have just for me, and help me take a step today to live into it. Amen.

The disciples have been arguing about who among them is the greatest. When Jesus inquires about their conversation, they have nothing but an awkward silence to offer in response.

We are so scared to let Jesus know how important it is to us to be great. But Jesus already knows. The disciples did not have to recount their conversation for Jesus to know what they had been talking about. Jesus knows, sits with their awkward silence, and lovingly responds. He challenges them to become "servant of all." Then, as an unforgettable visual aid, he brings a child among them and embraces the child. He urges them to welcome children as he does. Jesus only asks them to do what he is willing to do.

The disciples' preoccupation with greatness is born of misunderstanding and fear. We too can get sidetracked by pursuing false standards of greatness. Our problem is not in wanting to be great but in how we define greatness. Jesus reminds us that being great is about living humbly. It is about welcoming those who have great need and cannot care for themselves.

Where in your life are you serving all? Do you strive to be great through humble service, or through seeking recognition and achievement? Do you need a particular seat at church, a prestigious title, or the acceptance and approval of certain people? Jesus tells the disciples that they do not need such recognition. Instead, they are to serve all. We can embrace this challenge too. Jesus calls us to adopt an attitude of humility among all people—not just those who look and live like us, not just those with well-balanced lives, and not just those in our familiar corners of the community. Jesus provides both the instruction and the example. If we want to be great, we will humble ourselves among all, as he did.

Jesus, help me remain mindful today of what it really means to be great. Help me to welcome those with great need and adopt an attitude of humility. Amen.

What do we believe makes us great? We answer that question through the decisions and pursuits of our lives. Some value education and achievement. Others value status, wealth, and power. Others value social connections and service, parenting and work. Some place relationships or ministry at the forefront. Others value thinness or fitness or eating according to a specific plan. We are all participating in an ongoing discussion about greatness, spoken or unspoken. In this discussion, our lives speak for us.

Jesus did not reprimand the disciples for wanting to be great. He just wanted to make sure they were pursuing the greatness that would reflect their love for God. The competitive relational sparring among them turned to silence when they encountered Jesus. We would be wise to let our fruitless competitions and comparisons fall silent as we encounter Jesus' presence. Let's listen to his call to greatness: Strive to be great but do so by welcoming and serving those in need.

What does "serving all" mean in our lives today? We are stewards of our stories, our resources, our experiences, and our knowledge of God. Every gift from God provides an opportunity to serve. So how do we offer our gifts without entering into a type of pathological giving that is itself a need-based, misguided competition that feeds our ego? We can look at Jesus' example. I cannot think of any story where Jesus tried to one-up someone, interrupt, prove himself worthy, or win an argument. Instead, he gently offered wisdom, responded with truths that astounded his listeners, and remained unwavering in his faith. He was the non-violent, loving, human reality of God.

What does your life say about what it means to you to be great? What would it look like for you to be a "servant of all"?

Jesus, servant of all, may our fruitless comparisons fall silent in your presence. Make us faithful examples of true greatness. Amen.

SATURDAY, SEPTEMBER 18 ～ *Read James 3:13-4:3, 7-8a*

Iwork daily with people who face difficult decisions about how to cope with family conflicts, depression and anxiety, eating concerns, and career obstacles. When we look for God's guidance, we may ask, "How do I know if a decision or plan represents God's wisdom?" James offers insight that serves as our filter for spiritual wisdom. It is God's wisdom when it meets a few key criteria: It is pure, peaceable, gentle, willing to yield, full of mercy and good fruits, and without partiality or hypocrisy.

There are daily messages in our world that communicate and encourage entitlement, unyielding agendas, hypocrisy, and judgment of those who do not meet the standard set by influential people and systems. This kind of spiritual foolishness is so powerful and present that at times we mistake it for spiritual wisdom. For instance, our culture tells us that we will be fulfilled by restricting food in unhealthy ways, attaining wealth through dishonest practices, compromising our values, or using excessive amounts of alcohol and drugs to numb ourselves. But these strategies leave us feeling worse. The outcome is often self-judgment, regret, and emptiness rather than good fruit.

If you feel God is leading you to enact a harsh, unyielding judgment toward yourself or others, step back and reassess. Remember the filter for spiritual wisdom that James offers. When you feel drawn to thinking that excludes others, remember the love and radical inclusion that Jesus extends. Relationships suffer, churches split, and businesses fail when two opposing perspectives lack a willingness to yield, do not allow room for substantial mercy, and lack the good fruit of love.

When you recognize yourself turning toward harsh words, rigidity, or efforts to be fulfilled apart from God, return to the peaceable and pure spiritual wisdom from God.

God, help us to see clearly so we can discern your wisdom from among the many messages that surround us. Help us to seek, recognize, and embrace spiritual wisdom. Amen.

James argues that when we experience envy and self-centeredness in our hearts, we should not be boastful by lying to ourselves about it. James seems to assume that there will be times when we envy others and seek our own well-being at the expense of other people. It's part of the human experience. Our call is not to be shocked when we see these qualities in ourselves or even to eliminate these states altogether but to avoid an arrogant mentality that refuses to acknowledge and take ownership of those parts of ourselves that are tough to face. I've seen many clients experience relief as they find words to name the parts of themselves that they fear will be rejected and unloved. I feel honored by their vulnerability and connected to them in a common understanding of what it means to be human. As we realize that our feelings are normal and common, they lose the power to isolate and separate us from the love of God and those around us.

We benefit from being as honest with our Christian friends as we are with a therapist or spiritual director. We are wise to share with trusted companions that which comes up in our private journaling and vulnerable prayers, in our deepest and most honest selves. We will experience envy and selfish ambition, and it is best acknowledged. Left unattended, these harmful spiritual states lead to disorder and chaos in our lives. The antidote is first to be honest with ourselves and others and then to be open to the radical intervention of the Holy Spirit, who guides us into wisdom that is pure, peace-loving, gentle, and willing to yield. When we make space for all of our selves to enter God's healing light, God brings peace.

Holy Spirit, show me the parts of myself that tend toward envy and self-centeredness. Help me to experience relief that comes with honestly naming these qualities, connecting with others in our common struggle, knowing I am loved, and making space for your peace and wisdom. Amen.

Jesus Is an Experience

SEPTEMBER 20–26, 2021 • VONA WILSON

SCRIPTURE OVERVIEW: The Jewish people have faced possible destruction numerous times. The story begins not with the Holocaust in Europe but far back in history during the time of Esther. The wicked Haman plots to wipe out God's people, but God saves the people through Esther's courage. The psalmist praises God for this kind of salvation from seemingly impossible circumstances. Although we may not face genocide, we have our own struggles. James encourages us to pray with faith, believing that God can and will answer. Our prayers are powerful, James assures us. Jesus teaches us the importance of letting nothing stand between God and us. Using vivid hyperbole, he admonishes us to put the pursuit of God above everything else and to support others in that same pursuit.

QUESTIONS AND SUGGESTIONS FOR REFLECTION

- Read Esther 7:1-6, 9-10; 9:20-22. When have you chosen to speak out in a way that made you vulnerable in order to help someone else?
- Read Psalm 124. Recall a time when you had a strong sense of God's being on your side. What was the situation? How did that assurance come?
- Read James 5:13-20. How do the members of your faith community pray with and for one another?
- Read Mark 9:38-50. Whoever is not against you is for you. How can you share God's love with those outside your inner circle?

Senior associate pastor at Franklin United Methodist Church in Franklin, TN; began her career as a paramedic and later served as an organizational development professional; former YMCA chaplain and community volunteer who loves investing in a community of people in the context of faith.

There may be no moment that requires as much humility and vulnerability as the moments we realize the choice we have to make may cost us more than we would ever really want to give. Our choices impact many people.

Esther is a young Jewish girl who ends up in the favor and presence of the king. She has a position many would want. She is in contact with her family, though not living under their roof. And in just a few days' time, Esther's place, position, and power are on the line.

She is confronted with the choice to risk her own life by telling the king something about her own heritage—that she is Jewish—in order to possibly save the Jewish people from being destroyed in a horrible act of genocide. There is no guarantee of the outcome. Esther may lose her own life, and her people may still be killed. But in this moment, she has to make a choice. Whatever she decides will affect the lives of many others.

Risky moments come along often in our lives as disciples. We are called on to make hard decisions. Sometimes those decisions mean we will be set aside or removed. And sometimes those decisions will release an oppression or situation that is crying out for the redemption, grace, and freedom that only come when God is involved. Where are you being nudged to make a decision that opens the door to abundant and new life for someone else? What is the choice that leads to life?

God of mercy, help us to be willing to take risks when we find ourselves in situations like Esther's. When our choices will impact others' lives, give us the wisdom and courage to be faithful. We need you in such moments we may face today. Thank you for always being present with us. Amen.

Iam encouraged when people share their everyday experiences of God. I think of these as glory sightings—the simple and powerful ways people have seen or experienced God at work in their ordinary days.

Our church serves as an emergency shelter for people in our community who are homeless. One of our regular guests, Abby*, is a smart and articulate woman. She once held a stable job with a salary that could support her. But things happened in Abby's life, and ultimately she found herself living in her car and parking in the Walmart parking lot each night. Occasionally she found short-term work that gave her enough money for food.

When the emergency shelter was open, Abby always came; but she was not open to our attempts to find transitional housing for her. Then the day came when Abby's car wouldn't start. It was winter but not cold enough for the shelter to be open. She didn't know what to do, so she asked a police officer to call the church. With the help of the community, we were able to get her car repaired and to talk through with Abby what it might be like if she moved into transitional housing. She was ready. This scenario changed the priorities of our church staff that week. Abby's car breaking down opened her to new possibilities. God led all of us through this path of compassion and care.

We often begin our church staff meetings with the devotional practice of asking each person to respond to the question, "Where have you seen God?" Many of our stories are of those who show up as guests at the emergency shelter. These friends show us the face of Jesus again and again. From despair to hope, God is always turning our suffering into blessing.

*Name changed to protect the guest's privacy

> **Start a meeting or conversation with this devotional questioning: "Where have you seen God this week?"**

Do you ever find yourself desperately praying for help? Do you ever feel like you need God to be on your side or you simply won't survive? David served as the king of Israel, God's chosen leader. He wrote Psalm 124 expressing how faithful God is in times of great challenge. It's important to name God's faithfulness to us in seasons of difficulty.

Our enemies are not always soldiers at war. We have silent enemies too. Fear, addiction, and isolation are enemies that war within us while we cry out for release. Although grief is a normal and healthy response to loss, it can also be overwhelming as waves of it overshadow our days. And even in the face of these situations, God is present and working with us. God is walking through the valleys and dangers and fear with us. God never gives us up to the enemies that seek to destroy. In our baptismal vows we say that we "accept the freedom and power God gives [us] to resist evil, injustice, and oppression in whatever forms they present themselves" (UMH, no. 34). That vow reminds us that God is ever present. And in the depths of our battles, the Lord will not let us go. In Christ, we have power to resist.

The song "Rescue" by Lauren Daigle expresses the depths and heights to which God will go to bring us out of destructive circumstances or to find us when we have walked down paths that do not lead us home. My favorite line in the song is:

I will send out an army to find you
in the middle of the darkest night.

God never abandons us, never stops searching for us. That is why we can say with confidence, "Our help is in the name of the LORD who made heaven and earth."

Whenever you are feeling engulfed or overwhelmed by a difficult circumstance, try praying through Psalm 124 and naming the specific situations and difficulties when God has been at your side, guiding you through overwhelming challenges.

Something beautiful happens when people come together to pray. In moments of gratitude and joy, it is easy to sing praises. And in moments of seeking or sorrow or struggle, our prayers become like incense rising in the presence of God.

Sometimes when people come to the altar for prayer at the church where I serve, we anoint them with holy oil. Blessing the oil and placing it on their forehead, making the sign of the cross, we remember the advice of James to "call for the elders of the church and have them pray over them." Often the presence of God moves us to tears. We lay hands on people as they kneel or stand at the altar, speaking words of intercession and care. Being before God in sorrow or praise is both vulnerable and powerful because the Spirit of God comes into those moments with much grace.

When we pray for healing, we trust the Lord to know how, when, and where that healing will come. We place our belief in a God who heals and restores us, a God who beckons us to bring our hearts and bodies and minds to the altar of prayer.

As a pastor who has prayed over many people at the altar, I have experienced the overwhelming presence and compassion of God for each of us. Sometimes we feel that presence and compassion in the simple and brave act of getting on our knees or lying face-down before the Lord and saying, "God, this is the cry of my heart today. Please hear me and come near."

Merciful God, heal the brokenness in our hearts and minds. Take our fragile bodies and strengthen them for today. Allow us to walk in the healing steps of your love. God of mercy, inspire us to come to your altar and pray. Amen.

My grandmother Lester was a woman of prayer. She included a saying in her prayers that family members have continued throughout the years: "This is what we're praying for, and now we're waiting to see." Often when we share concerns within our family, we end with her wise words which serve as a faith builder for us.

Prayer is an integral part of who we are as children of God. Imagine a child who never talks with their parents or a parent who never hears the cries and joys of their child. How difficult it would be to deepen such a relationship! How easy it would be to begin to think that love, care, and concern did not exist in the relationship! God beckons us to pray and to trust that our prayers are heard and met completely with God's gracious and steadfast love.

When Elijah prayed for the rain to stop, he did so to show God's power and faithfulness. (See 1 Kings 17:1.) Elijah had a close relationship with God. His praying was constant. He brought his anger, confusion, doubt, hopes, dreams, and sorrows straight to the God of heaven. His prayers were effective. They changed him, and they changed the lives of people around him.

My grandmother Lester had nine children, twenty-eight grandchildren, and many great-grands after that. Her prayers for us were constant. We often reflect on the blessings of love that are present in our family. Did we create that love? Or is it the answer to the faithful prayers my grandmother prayed for us each day as she prayed with the trust of a daughter, a child of God: "Lord, this is what we're praying for, and now we're waiting to see"?

Lord, forgive us when we fail to bring all things to you in prayer. Thank you for reminding us that you are with us in prayer. You are faithful to respond, and our prayers are moving mountains that we will one day see. Thank you for your faithfulness. Amen.

One of the great joys I experienced during the three years I served as a chaplain with the YMCA was the opportunity to work alongside spiritual leaders from many denominations and faith traditions. At first, I could sense my hesitation when I encountered spiritual expressions that were different than my own tradition. But with every encounter I grew in grace. Over time, I came to deeply appreciate the faith of others. Occasionally I would get a call reporting that someone from a different tradition was in the chapel praying and asking if that was OK. The answer: Yes! What could be better than all of us praying in the same space?

A great strength of Jesus' followers is faithfulness. We want to be faithful, and we also want to be "right." Wanting to honor God in everything we do is wonderful. Yet sometimes our desire to be "right" causes us to question the motives or actions of others—and even to take responsibility to stop them if they are not conforming to our particular traditions or expressions. It can be hard to let that go.

But Jesus does let it go. What if we simply focus on discovering what or where the most powerful force of love and humility is in a particular situation and center our words and actions there? That kind of response might be like a cup of cold water in the heat of a desert—something a servant would offer.

Holy God, we can look at your creation and see your love for diversity in every living thing. We also know you call us to deep faithfulness—faithfulness to you. Help us to let go of wanting to control what others do and to embrace the many ways you give us to express your love in the world. We love you, and we trust that you are transforming us all, one moment at a time. Amen.

Jesus loves us fiercely. God hears the cries of the broken-hearted and of those whose voices have been silenced. God feels the pain of those who are being rejected and forgotten. It is humbling to think that sometimes our actions put stumbling blocks in the paths of others.

When Jesus shares these strong words about removing body parts if they cause us to stumble, it sounds pretty gory! Really? Is it that important? I hear in this teaching the fierce love of a God who will do anything to help us avoid the destruction of our souls. I hear the strength and compassion of Christ, who urges us to understand that nothing is worth missing the love and grace of God. Nothing.

Life can get pretty messy sometimes. It may not be a hand that causes us to stumble. It may be a friendship that is destructive or an addiction that is taking captive our days and relationships. It may be a way we are eating that is hurting our bodies or a habit that is eroding our self-confidence. Jesus is saying, "Stop! It's not worth it!"

We hear this echoed in Hebrews 12:12-13: "Therefore lift your drooping hands and strengthen your weak knees, and make straight paths for your feet, so that what is lame may not be put out of joint, but rather be healed."

We continue to face the challenges life presents. But when we remove the sources that cause us to stumble, we are able to walk in our healing rather than in our affliction. And as we are healed, those around us are blessed by God.

Lord, we stumble so often on the journey. And sometimes we cause others to stumble by putting blocks in their way. Forgive this destructive behavior, and transform our minds to follow the path of wholeness and grace that you offer us each day. Thank you for your faithfulness. Amen.

It's time to order

The Upper Room Disciplines 2022

Regular edition: 978-0-8358-1957-2

Enlarged-print edition: 978-0-8358-1958-9

Kindle: 978-0-8358-1959-6

EPUB: 978-0-8358-1960-2

Bookstore.UpperRoom.org

or

800.972.0433

Disciplines App Now Available
Read *The Upper Room Disciplines* on the go with your mobile device. Download the app through your smartphone app store.

Did you know that you can enjoy
The Upper Room Disciplines
in multiple formats? Digital or print?

The Upper Room Disciplines is available in both regular and enlarged print, but are you aware that it is also available in digital formats? Read a copy on your phone, computer, or e-reader. Whatever your preference, we have it for you today.

The Upper Room Disciplines is available in a variety of formats:
- Print (regular print and enlarged print versions)
- E-Book (Mobi and EPUB)
- Digital subscriptions (website and app)

For more information, visit Bookstore.UpperRoom.org or call 800.972.0433.

What is a standing order option?

This option allows you to automatically receive your copy of *The Upper Room Disciplines* each year as soon as it is available. Take the worry out of remembering to place your order.

Need to make changes to your account?

Call Customer Service at 800.972.0433 or email us at CustomerAssistance@UpperRoom.org.
Our staff is available to help you with any updates.

God Is Present Even in Suffering

SEPTEMBER 27–OCTOBER 3, 2021 • KERRI HEFNER

SCRIPTURE OVERVIEW: This week we read about Job, an upright man who faces severe trials but never loses his faith. Job's story brings us face-to-face with the fact that living a godly life does not make us immune to suffering. Like Job, the psalmist wonders why he suffers, even though he lives according to God's standards. Hebrews presents Jesus as the ultimate example of unwarranted suffering, yet because of his perseverance he is ultimately glorified. In Mark, some Pharisees test Jesus on the interpretation of the law concerning divorce. Jesus makes strong statements about marriage, but his larger concern is that their hearts have become hard. He contrasts them with little children, who model faith by receiving God with an open heart.

QUESTIONS AND SUGGESTIONS FOR REFLECTION

- Read Job 1:1; 2:1-10. What helps you to live with integrity?
- Read Psalm 26. Do you feel free in your prayer life to honestly share with God all that you are feeling?
- Read Hebrews 1:1-4; 2:5-12. In what ways does God speak to us in our day?
- Read Mark 10:2-16. What qualities found in children do you try to cultivate in your spiritual life?

Pastor of New Hope Presbyterian Church in Chapel Hill, NC; enjoys time with her family, hiking with her Labrador retriever, and ACC basketball.

A college student once told me that he had undergone a certain rite of passage. "Now that I'm old enough, my mom is sharing all the family secrets with me," he said with a chuckle.

Biblical texts about violence or extreme suffering are usually omitted from children's Bibles and Sunday school lessons—and for good reason. Yet I often find that adults, who are old enough to discover all the "secrets" of the Bible, do not want to read difficult texts such as Job. Perhaps the book strikes too close to home. Perhaps we who have already experienced suffering, don't want to hear any more about it.

This week, think of Job in a different way. The book tackles tough questions that you will face at some point in your life, if you haven't already. Why not engage the questions that you are already asking, such as: Is there any purpose in suffering? Is God actually present in the midst of my toughest challenges? Who is in charge around here?

Take on this week's readings with the perspective of the young college student. Pretend you are waking up to the realities of adult life: the overwhelming joys, the deep sorrows, the bitter disappointments. In many of this week's readings, you may not encounter the type of inspiring verse that you would see posted on the wall in a Sunday school class or illustrated in a children's Bible. But you will come face-to-face with a God who will not leave you, even in the starkest examples of human suffering. You will come face-to-face with a God who desires a covenant relationship with you and hopes that you desire that covenant too.

Faithful God, I know that you will be with me this week. Be with me in my reading, in my prayer, and in my relationships with others. Be with me especially when I feel far from you. Amen.

What was the last straw for Job's wife? When we meet her in chapter 2, she and her husband have already sustained unimaginable losses. Their children have been killed, meaning no future legacy for the couple. All of Job's assets are gone, meaning no livelihood for the couple. Job grieves after these two tragedies, but his wife is mysteriously absent. We hear from her only after Job has resorted to sitting in the ash heap, scraping the gruesome sores that have overtaken his skin.

We might view the wife as a disagreeable character. Yet take a closer look at Satan's challenge in verse 5: "Stretch out your hand now and touch his bone and his flesh, and he will curse you to your face." In the Hebrew scriptures, the expression "bone and flesh" refers to close familial relationships. Job's wife, his only surviving "bone and flesh," was previously silenced by immense grief. Yet now she has been touched, just as Job's skin was touched. Job's wounds are visible on his skin; her wounds are audible in her pessimistic words.

Grief is a complicated process. Many people attempt to be tough through terrible losses: death, serious illness, loss of livelihood. Yet one small thing can set off a torrent of emotions and break through our supposedly thick skin. Job's wife sees her formerly strong and successful husband sitting in the ash heap, and she descends into bitterness and anger.

Job gives his wife a sharp retort, after which they go their separate ways for a while. As harsh as his words may be, they are a gift to him and to her. By not giving up, Job gives himself a chance to face his God—and time to face bare truths about himself.

God, watch over me when I am at my wit's end. Strengthen me against bitterness. Forgive my gloomy outlook, and open my eyes so that I can see my situation differently. Thank you for being with me even when I don't want to be with you. Amen.

God Is Present Even in Suffering

Agood number of the psalms, such as the psalms of lament, deal with the personal trials and tribulations of the psalmist. They are the prayers of an anguished heart.

Psalm 26 may seem like an odd prayer. What is the psalmist's intent? Is he justifying himself to God? Is he asking for special treatment?

The psalmist pours out human emotion before God, holding nothing back. The feelings reflected in Psalm 26 are very real and relatable. We've all experienced these feelings, as the psalmist fears being judged unfairly and having his good character go unnoticed.

This week's theme is "God is present even in our suffering." One way God is present in our suffering is that God does not judge our heartfelt prayers. God may not answer our prayers in the way we expect or hope, but a sincere prayer is always acceptable to God.

If all our prayers are sincere, it follows that some of our prayers will not sound pretty. But that doesn't matter! Private prayer is different from the prayers pastors offer during worship. When no one else is listening, we do not need to worry about good grammar or flowery language. We just need to pour our hearts out to God.

Lord, help me to approach you sincerely and honestly, holding nothing back. You know the yearnings of my inmost heart, so I give them all to you. Amen.

Learned people challenged Jesus on all sorts of topics: healing, observance of the sabbath, taxes, marriage, and more. They hoped to trip him up with hair-splitting questions on technicalities of living the faith. Each time, Jesus responded with a challenge to deeper discipleship. In this passage, Jesus first challenges the learned people to honor the scriptural description of marriage as "one flesh," and he privately admonishes his disciples to avoid divorce.

Human relationships are never guaranteed to work out. Sometimes things beyond our control put our relationships to the test. Sometimes we don't bring our best selves to our relationships. Sometimes we have to make painful choices in order to go on living.

I have puzzled over the difference between Jesus' words for the larger audience and his strict teaching for the smaller group of disciples. Does he intend for the "no divorce" teaching to apply to everyone or only to his closest companions?

I don't know if I can answer this question, but I can say that Jesus calls each of us to treat human relationships as gifts from God. Jesus challenges us to accept each person we meet as a child of God, made in God's image. He treats the woman at the well, who has been married multiple times, as the child of God she is, worthy of love. (See John 4:1-30.) He instructs the lawyer to show mercy and be a good neighbor. (See Luke 10:25-37.) Jesus challenges his listeners to forego rights and privileges in favor of the more vulnerable in society.

We are called to see the image of God in each person and to treat others accordingly. When our relationships suffer, we are called to lean on the One who made us in the divine image.

Lord, help me to see others with your loving eyes. Keep me from insisting on my own privileges, and help me see things from the perspective of those more in need than I. Amen.

Jesus paid particular attention to those who were most vulnerable in his society. Children were among those vulnerable people. Jesus healed a number of sick children during his ministry in Galilee.

As Jesus ministers to the children in this passage from Mark, it seems to me he is leading a service of worship. Jesus takes the children in his arms, the way a minister would hold an infant or toddler during baptism. Jesus lays hands on the children; today Christians still practice the laying on of hands. Jesus blesses the little ones as they end their time together, much as a worship leader blesses the congregation at the end of the worship service.

Jesus' interaction with those children leads me to a question: If Jesus worshiped with those who came to him as vulnerable children, what does that say about how we should come to worship? So often we enter worship with outsized expectations of the sermon or the music or the attendance. When we come to worship with those expectations, we may miss the simple benefit of just being in God's presence. Instead, we may want to try entering worship as a child—expecting foremost to be held in God's arms, prayed for, and blessed.

I hope that in each of our churches and homes, children will be valued, prayed for, and blessed. I hope that children and vulnerable adults will be protected. I hope that in our schools and communities, children's safety and health will be of utmost importance. As we recall our responsibilities toward children, we can pray to remember this teaching of Jesus and approach our worship of God with a childlike spirit of openness and trust.

Lord God, I thank you for the way you hold me, and indeed the whole world, in your hands. Lord Jesus, I thank you for welcoming me with open arms. Lord Holy Spirit, I thank you for praying for me and with me. Amen.

Hebrews addresses believers who have been on their journey of faith a long time. They have read scripture, worshiped together, endured trials and tribulations, and have kept going for the long haul. The book encourages the readers to keep up the good work, not allowing the flame which has been burning for so many years to die out. The first few verses are a fitting introduction to such a book.

To me, the first four verses of chapter 1 sound like an affirmation of faith, such as the Apostles' Creed or Nicene Creed, that worshipers might recite during a service. In those few verses, the author describes: God's work long ago, God's recent work, Jesus' nature, and Jesus' work. This affirmation sets the framework for encouraging believers in their practice of faith.

During my two decades of ministry, I have often wondered what new thing I could say to the oldest members of the congregations I served, those who had attended week after week and listened to sermon after sermon. Now I realize that in all the challenges we experience over a lifetime, we need to hear the words of faith afresh. I am encouraged by a member of my congregation who is almost one hundred years old. She reads her devotional every day. She listens to our recorded worship services when she cannot attend in person. I can see God's Word and work sustaining her in her daily life.

A phrase from verse 3 is especially meaningful to me: "[Christ] sustains all things by his powerful word." In difficult times, I know my Lord sustains me and everything around me. When I pray for others or for myself, I may not know exactly what to ask of God, but I know that God will sustain us with love.

Lord, sustain me day to day with your powerful Word. This day, reveal to me your imprint and your glory in Jesus, your Word made flesh. Amen.

Near my house is a museum with a space exhibit. The exhibit features everything from early astronauts' suits to a full-size prototype of the Apollo 15 Lunar Lander. Each time I visit, I get a clammy feeling looking at the moon landing equipment. The thought of being so far from home, totally dependent on a vehicle less than half the size of a cement truck, is both wondrous and frightening to me.

Those early space explorers knew the danger of their pioneering work. In fact, astronauts left a memorial on the moon to those killed in the pursuit of space exploration. Other pioneers, in work ranging from medicine to civil rights, have also been familiar with danger in their work.

Jesus became well acquainted with risk, danger, and even death in his pioneering work of salvation. Some may like to think of Jesus as a brave or intrepid leader, one who leapt into worlds beyond without suffering so much as a scratch. The truth is that he did feel afraid, and he did experience pain.

I am grateful to follow a pioneer of faith who suffered. For me, it would be difficult to follow a Savior who had never experienced pain or grief or fear. Following such a person would create unrealistic expectations on my part. I would be unable to keep up.

However, frail as I am, Jesus is not ashamed to be my Savior. He is not ashamed of anyone he has saved. He calls his followers brothers and sisters. I do not have to worry, because whatever fear or suffering I encounter, I find that Jesus has encountered it too. I do not have to compare my progress to anyone else's because Jesus has already laid the path for us all.

Jesus, pioneer of my salvation, keep me faithful on this journey. Help me to trust in the work you have already done. Amen.

Lament and Grace

OCTOBER 4–10, 2021 • J. R. DANIEL KIRK

SCRIPTURE OVERVIEW: Faithful people still have questions for God. Job wishes he could sit down with God and plead his case because he wants God to justify what has happened to him. The psalmist also feels abandoned by God and wonders why God is not coming to his aid. God can handle our questions. Job wanted an advocate, and Hebrews says that Jesus now fills that role for us. He is our great high priest and understands our sufferings, so we may boldly approach him for help. In Mark, Jesus deals with the challenge of money. It is a powerful force and can come between us and God if we cling to our resources instead of holding them loosely with thanksgiving for God's provision.

QUESTIONS AND SUGGESTIONS FOR REFLECTION

- Read Job 23:1-9, 16-17. When have you, like Eliphaz, attributed your own suffering or that of others to wickedness on your part or on theirs? How often do you find yourself blaming others for the situations in which they find themselves?
- Read Psalm 22:1-15. How could your prayer life be more honest and transparent? What feelings do you hold back?
- Read Hebrews 4:12-16. When God shines the spotlight on your soul, what does God see?
- Read Mark 10:17-31. How do you square your "wealthy" life with Jesus' call to discipleship?

New Testament scholar whose work explores the intersection of history, biblical interpretation, and real life; author of several books, including *A Man Attested by God: The Human Jesus of the Synoptic Gospels.*

Job is a faithful companion for us through life's valleys because Job knows that life with God does not give us easy answers. Job knows that God is powerful over all things, and so he can complain to God about what he thinks God has allowed to happen. Job also knows that he has been faithful to God and that God will vindicate him if given the chance.

But God is nowhere to be found. The darkness that causes us to call out, "Why, God?" is often made deeper by God's silence.

Job prods us to keep crying out in the darkness. When we have the boldness to say that God is just but our world is not, when we have the boldness to cry out to God and demand that God heed the voices of those who demand that God's righteousness be made known, we play the part of the faithful righteous.

In the pursuit of humility, we must ensure that we do not give up on the idea that goodness exists on the earth and God should honor it. We too easily give up on the idea that the suffering we see or experience is unjust. Or we too easily give up on the idea that our God wants to act to make all things right. Job stirs us to remember that the very means by which God has chosen to make God's presence known in the world is divine response to the cries of God's people.

In the end, the injustice that Job experiences as "God's heavy hand" and Job's "I cannot perceive him" are one and the same. The injustice of the world tries to hide from God, but divine glory is displayed in justice, grace, and mercy.

Almighty God, display your justice so that all may see you and know you. Amen.

What does it mean to be forsaken by God? As Christians we sometimes take a few quick leaps that go something like this: Jesus cried out, "My God, why have you forsaken me?" This, then, is when God the Father turned God's back on the Son while the Son was bearing our sins. And so, being forsaken by God is an experience of spiritual abandonment, when we no longer experience the presence of God with us.

Spiritual abandonment, or a "dark night of the soul," is a real and significant spiritual experience for many. Yesterday we saw how the hiddenness of God worsened Job's experience of rejection. But it begins with the realities of embodied life.

This is the psalm for people who can boldly and rightly cry out to God because God has not done what God has promised. When Israel trusted in God, they were delivered from their enemies—this is the God of Israel living up to the promises God has made!

When God does not protect the people, when outsiders can mock because their prayers remain unanswered, when God's beloved Son is hung on a cross to die, then God has forsaken.

This is why we must cultivate the radical act of lament within the people of God. To feel forsaken by God is to be in a place where God has not acted as God has promised. The only mechanism for righting this situation is for the people of God to stand together and demand of God that God act according to divine character.

By placing such cries within the book of Psalms, the Bible teaches us that we discover part of our corporate identity in siding with the forsaken of the world and crying out to God for rescue. In this, we embody the saving faithfulness of Christ who sided with the forsaken in being himself forsaken on the cross.

God of our salvation, show yourself faithful by saving those who are mocked and even killed for trusting in you. Amen.

Never underestimate the power of the past. In ways that we often are not even aware of, the past shapes our understanding of the present and our hopes and fears about the future. We connect the dots between the past and the present, telling stories that make sense of how our lives (or the world) hold together. But sometimes the stories don't work out as we would expect. Sometimes the hopeful pursuits of our life are derailed; sometimes a life of promise is cut short.

Psalm 22 expresses the expectation that the God known in grace, care, and salvation is the God who will be present in the same way yet again. The God who brought us into this world, the God who saved us from the powers of sin and death in the life of Jesus, is the God to whom we now look for deliverance.

Lament involves more than complaints to God about life's being off kilter. Lament is complaining to God that life is off kilter because God has not been as consistent in living up to the standards of loving care that God has set.

In lament we lay bare before our Great Caretaker the places where the people of the earth suffer and die—and therefore need divine intervention. In lament we call to God from the midst of the darkness. We bring God into the suffering and injustice, and we demand an answer.

The strange reality seeping its way through lament is this: We not only have a calling to proclaim God's good news to the world; we also have a calling to proclaim the world's bad news to God. These are perhaps the two greatest tools God has given us to participate in the great project to make all things new.

Father, you have shown us in the life, death, and resurrection of Jesus that there is no length to which you will not go to save and deliver your people. Open your eyes to the pain of the dying, the abused, the trafficked, the lonely, the sick; show yourself to them and the world as the God of all comfort. Amen.

This week, Job and the writer of Psalm 22 have come before God boldly. They have come more boldly than most of us would dare. We are too aware of our own hearts. We are too aware of the ways we have fallen short.

Hebrews provides some vindication of this caution. The word of God is living and active—scripture is personified as an agent that has the power to sort out our fidelity to God from our self-preserving faithlessness. It has the power to summon us to perseverance right at the point where we are ready to quit.

But Hebrews and Job actually proceed from the same starting point. Job knows that if only he can get an audience with God, God will have to vindicate him. Why? Because God knows everything. Hebrews also tells us that God sees everything. We must give an account before God.

One crucial difference exists between these writers, however. While Job cannot get the ear of God to save his life, the writer of Hebrews knows uninterrupted access into the very throne room of God. As the great story of God continues to unfold, there appears the Living Redeemer who sits at God's right hand with one particular task. He intercedes for the saints, for us, according to God's will.

This week we have been called to lament by Job and by the Psalms. We cry out to God in times of distress because we know that God will hear. Moreover, Jesus, who ensures we will be heard, himself has spoken the words of lament that we have read in Psalm 22—and has been answered by God the Father through the resurrection from the dead.

Lament is a great act of faith. It is prayers to a God who we believe can and will act because this God gives life to the dead.

God who hears, even when we know our shortcomings, give us faith to cry out, knowing that you will hear us because of the perfection of your resurrected Son, our Lord. Amen.

Job and Psalm 22 reflect the cries of the confident. But sometimes our darkness is more our own doing. The living and active sword of God's word calls us to faithfulness; it calls us to endurance; and it shows us the ways in which we have failed.

At times, the heaviness we experience is less a matter of injustice than the just chastisement of a father who disciplines those whom he loves. Since we will have to give an account to God for what we have done, our experiences of pain and suffering can remind us of our need to cling to God's love and that of our neighbors.

The message of Hebrews paints a magnificent portrait of grace. Immediately after holding up before us the inescapable eye of the God to whom we must give an account, the letter reissues the invitation to approach the throne of God—not as a judgment bench but as a throne of grace and a source of help. Crying out and lamenting before God, seeking help and deliverance and justice—these are not simply the postures of the righteous who demand that God repay in kind; they are also the postures of the sinners who demand that God repay in Christ.

Whether as champions of justice or as petitioners who desire grace, we come before God in time of need. In both cases we require God's intervention to transform this world so that God's kingdom will come, God's will will be done on earth as it is in heaven.

We can be pulled away from our faith in different directions. Whether frustrated with God or frustrated with self, the same, transformative offer of help is extended to us by the crucified and risen Christ who knows our suffering and the triumph over it, who knows our weakness and temptation and also the life without sin.

Father in heaven, draw us to your light whatever the cause of our darkness, and allow us to find in you grace to help in times of need. Amen.

If we ever wish to come face-to-face with where our day-in, day-out lives demonstrate how far we are from the kingdom of God, we can do no better than listening to what Jesus has to say about money. If we were shocked by the particular demand Jesus laid on the rich man to sell his possessions, we will find ourselves even more troubled when Jesus turns the earlier story into a general principle.

In the twenty-first century, we are all embedded in a worldly kingdom whose standard of justice is not equality or democracy or liberty but the acquisition of wealth. From a young age we are formed to be wealth producers or, more importantly, consumers who produce wealth for others. Ours is a world, across numerous cultures, that strives above all else to show signs of wealth (even if what these signs truly signal is crippling debt). We strive for good-paying jobs, for high-paying opportunities out of college. We appoint people to church leadership who have attained these ends that we hold most dear.

Each act of complicity in the belief system of capitalism is a potential denial of the kingdom of God. Defensively we reinterpret Jesus' words. Surely he can't mean us! Surely those of us who live in cities with hundreds of churches can't be the least likely to inherit the kingdom! Surely our success within the system we were born into signals God's great favor!

But Jesus keeps repeating: It is hard for the wealthy to enter God's reign. You could more easily cram a camel through a needle's eye than cram one person of wealth through the gates of God's kingdom. Our only hope lies in God's overcoming this impossibility through God's gift of grace.

God, we have worshiped before the gods of wealth that have promised us life. Free us from the chains that bind us, that we will know the true wealth that pours out from your holy presence. Amen.

Following Jesus calls us into what can be a harsh reality. It's a calling to give up all that we have and all that we think we are. It's a calling to rethink how we value the world around us and the things for which we pour out our lives.

When we weigh the cost of discipleship and the insistence that we leave houses and siblings and parents and sources of income for Jesus' sake, we all too easily envision a life alone. Western people have transferred our deeply individualistic way of viewing and interacting with the world to our understanding of Christianity. But Jesus reminds us that our thoughts of "going it alone" are not God's thoughts about the Christian life.

God provides us with a new family—the family of those who, like us, have chosen to forgo the world's way of reckoning family, of accumulating wealth, of attaining long-term security. Church is not simply supposed to be the place to which we head off on Sunday morning. It is supposed to be the community that makes possible our obedience to the impossible calling of Jesus.

The gospel faces all sorts of challenges today from those who claim to follow Jesus. Some of the most severe, however, are not acts of moral failing but the day-to-day tasks of the church to create a community with an alternative value system that makes itself known in the riches of self-giving love.

Are we the kind of people who can be family for those who have left family for Jesus' sake? Can we be the kind of people who can create an alternative economy so that the pursuit of wealth no longer defines us as persons or as the people of God?

Father, draw our lives into a new way of being that demonstrates to the world that your kingdom is the greatest source of life. Make us agents of self-giving love that will make possible for others the obedience that comes with accepting Jesus' call to follow him. Amen.

The Limits of Human Power

OCTOBER 11–17, 2021 • DIANA L. HYNSON

SCRIPTURE OVERVIEW: At this point in Job's story, God has heard questions from Job and long-winded moralizing by three of Job's friends, who have pronounced that his misfortunes are divine judgment. Now God has heard enough and declares that God's perspective is superior to theirs. God has been there from the beginning, as the psalmist reiterates, so no one should claim to know God's mind or speak on God's behalf. Even Jesus, the divine Son of God, yields to his heavenly Father. Hebrews tells us that Jesus made appeals to God as the ultimate high priest and thereby became the source of salvation for those who obey him. In the Gospel reading, Jesus specifies that his approaching act of submission and service will allow him to become a ransom for us.

QUESTIONS AND SUGGESTIONS FOR REFLECTION

- Read Job 38:1-7, 34-41. How do you continue to hold on to belief in God's goodness when you are in a period of anguish?
- Read Psalm 104:1-9, 24, 35c. How do you share in the creativity of God?
- Read Hebrews 5:1-10. In what ways does the understanding of Jesus' willing vulnerability while serving as high priest affect the way you interact with others?
- Read Mark 10:35-45. Where do you see genuine examples of servant leadership in your community?

Retired United Methodist member who attends Annville (PA) UMC; served in local churches, as an editor of resources for church school, and as a leader in teacher/leader development; enjoying a return to the choir and loves puttering in small construction and fix-it projects at home.

THANKSGIVING DAY, CANADA

"Sin in haste; repent at leisure" is a common theme in our Old Testament history. Things are going so well; then because of thoughtlessness, greed, envy, complacency, stupidity, or any manner of other poor behavior, it all falls apart.

The people of Israel were called to be a holy people, those in a coveted position of favor and love with the supreme God. Ever since Creation, humankind has been heir to this relationship. All we have to do is cooperate! Then we expect life to be good.

But when we don't cooperate, things are not so good, even downright awful. Joel begins with the lament by God that the people have caused the ruin of the country. He calls them to repent, put on sackcloth, lament, fast, and worship. How many times had they been in this position? Why could they not learn from God's teaching and guidance? All, it seems certain, is lost.

Does any of this feel familiar? Has poor judgment ever cost you a promotion (or a job)? Selfishness or thoughtlessness cost you a special relationship? Worship of money, position, or power cost you the ability to see the blessings and beauty of the smaller things in life? Is all lost?

Joel tells us NO! He reminds us to rejoice and be glad, for the Lord does great things! We have tremendous spiritual power as the heirs of Israel and as the body of Christ. It's never too late to turn toward God. Joel's images of refreshing rain, full harvests, food aplenty assure us that God has abundant blessings awaiting us when we turn again to the One who has ultimate power. Then we "shall know that [God] is in [our] midst" and just as importantly, that God's "people shall never again be put to shame."

Gracious God, help me to be in right relationship with you, the source of all great power and all good things, and to give you my endless thanksgiving and praise. Amen.

The psalmist almost sounds as if he is in love! What grandeur there is in the lofty images describing the height and depth and width of God's magnificent creation: the vast stretch of the heavens, fire and flame as messengers, boundaries so broad that neither mountain nor valley can cross.

When we love someone or something, we tend to use superlative terms to describe what is beloved. Clearly the psalmist loves God and is giving due praise and reverence to the Almighty. God is wiser than we are, stronger than we are, much bigger than we are, more creative than we are, far more powerful than we are. God is worthy of our praise and thanks, and it is only right that we should offer it. This is how our relationship to God should be.

The foundation of a contemplative and faithful life is to love God first, then to love all else—including the very people, things, experiences, and practices that we desperately don't love and don't even *want* to love. It is in our power to love even what we don't presently love.

Just as God gives unstintingly of God's self to us, we are called in that boundless love to love just as actively and thoroughly as God loves. Having been created in God's image, we are imbued with something of God's power and creativity ourselves, and that is not something to be hoarded.

What would your life look like if you were "clothed with honor and majesty" in God's service? What would your legacy of personal discipleship be if your witness spread as if with "fire and flame"? What would others learn of God from you if your speech and demeanor reflected the love of God that the psalmist showed in his superlative testimony?

O Creator God, how wonderful and manifold are all your works! Draw me so into love with you that I give you my all in service and devotion. Amen.

The psalmist's testimony (Psalm 104) demonstrates a humble recognition of God's boundless love and power. Joel offers a historical example of calamity when we try to seize power and fail to love God without reservation. The story of Job illustrates that life is not so simple as "love God, everything is good; sin against God, all is lost." We come to the end of the story, after Job has been tested by the Adversary and then endured a series of "consolations" and accusations by his friends. They were stuck on the retributive model of sin and righteousness mentioned above.

In a series of "If I had . . . " statements, Job agrees that, if true, these claims would be proof of sin. But he hasn't done those things; and because of his innocent suffering, Job demands justice from God. (Be careful what you wish for!) What he receives instead probably feels like a pointed put-down to his demand.

"Who is this that darkens counsel by words without knowledge?" God, speaking with great power (from a whirlwind), asks a series of questions that Job is too humbled to answer directly. "Where were you when I laid the foundation of the earth?" "Do you know the measurement of the universe?" [Obviously not.] God reminds Job that humans do not possess full divine power and knowledge. We have limits, and it's good to remember them.

Does this mean that God doesn't care what happens to us? No, the Psalms are full of complaints and pleas just like Job's. God wants justice and reconciliation for all of creation. So what does it mean? Perhaps that as a people called to be holy, we realize that these lofty goals set by God are not something we can create for ourselves, sustain for ourselves, or know fully ourselves. We need God's light and counsel.

Loving God, hear my cries and complaints, and enable me to see the justice and reconciliation possible within your power and love. Amen.

In yesterday's reading, God spoke to Job from the whirlwind with a pointed question about the limits of Job's wisdom, as compared to the vastness of God's character and limitless knowledge. Today's passage is a continuation of that exchange between Job and God, this time shifting slightly to ask yet more rhetorical questions about whether Job is able to do all the powerful things God is able to do.

Reading between the lines, we might imagine this commentary with Job's feeble answers interjected. Can you call forth floods with just a command? [Well, no.] Can you cause lightning to strike or count all the clouds? [Well, no.] Do you have provisions enough to feed all the wild creatures? [Well, no.] These questions continue for another three chapters. Poor Job must have felt horribly puny by the end of that interrogation.

But is that the point? Yes, our power to be and do what God is and does is indeed puny in comparison; and we do well to remember that we are dependent on God, not the other way around. Job confesses, "I know that you can do all things, and that no purpose of yours can be thwarted. . . . I had heard of you by the hearing of the ear, but now my eye sees you" (Job 42:2-3).

There, Job captures the essence of our lesson: "I thought I knew, but now, with more intimate experience and insight, I have taken into my soul ("my eye sees") how truly awesome you are. I am content to be your creature and to enjoy the blessings of your goodness and benevolence." Here is a healthy understanding of the limits of our power before God. By placing ourselves wholly in God's care, we have tremendous power to conform as we can to the image of God.

Loving God, help me to understand the paradox that in surrendering I find wisdom and power in you. Amen.

Were James and John not listening? Jesus had just predicted in grim and specific terms what he expected to happen to him when they reached Jerusalem. Perhaps they just caught the last few words, "After three days he [Jesus, the Son of Man] will rise again" (v. 34). Yeah, we like the "rise again" part!

Apparently, they missed the part about being mocked, spit upon, flogged, and killed because James and John ask Jesus to grant them positions of supreme significance "in your glory." Jesus understands that they don't understand. "Are you able," he asks, "to endure what I will endure?" [Oh, yes!] "Well, you will endure these things, but you may get more mocking and flogging than glory." We might hear the echo of God's word to Job: "Who is this who darkens counsel without knowledge?"

Their takeaway may have been to realize they would get the hard work and the accompanying punishments to go with it, without necessarily gaining the glory. Hmm. What's wrong with that picture? Seeking power without understanding the obligations and responsibilities that go with it is dangerous business. We may get more than we bargain for. Still, Jesus does not contradict their claim of readiness. He will depend on their bold promise to follow in his footsteps in the days and years to come. And they do.

How often do we request responsibilities we aren't prepared for, or conversely, refuse responsibilities for which we are equipped? How often do we want the praise and recognition but hope for someone else to do the heavy lifting for us?

Notice how patient Jesus is with this request from James and John. He does not rebuke; rather, he encourages and redirects them. In the crucial work of discipleship and kingdom building, this is our model.

Empowering Lord, give me strength to be up to the task of discipleship and to remain steadfast in the face of opposition and difficulty. Amen.

James and John are not yet ready. They have not learned the hard lesson of forgoing desires and delusions of grandeur for the Christlike role of servanthood.

When the other disciples hear of their outrageous request for power and glory, they are angry. We might guess why. Do they already understand the lesson that the brothers did not yet grasp? [Probably not.] Are they holding the brothers accountable for reckless desires? [Perhaps.] Or are they annoyed that these two have asked outright for powers and honors they would have preferred to have themselves? [Could be.]

Again, with gentle patience, Jesus defuses the situation with more guidance and redirection. Though they have had three years of first-hand exposure to Jesus' power, the disciples are still stuck in old notions of power as strength over, as strength against, as governance of, as "I'm up; you're down."

No, Jesus says; that's not it. A kingdom of love does not have tyrants. Servanthood, not force, is the driving power in this new era. Greatness is measured in what you give away, not in what you grab for yourself. What have you seen me take, and what have you seen me give? I am about to give up my last breath—for love of you, not to seize the throne.

Had you been among the Twelve, what might have you thought? Would you declare yourself ready for whatever demands faith placed upon you? Would you happily accept a "secondary" role as servant rather than ruler? Would you resent or welcome the idea of relinquishing your personal desires to God rather than pursuing them as you wish?

Understanding the paradox of receiving by giving away is at the root of understanding God's power and how to participate in the faithful use of that power.

Gracious God, teach me the lessons of humble servanthood, and prepare me for a life of devotion to Christ's work. Amen.

The Limits of Human Power

In the scriptures for this past week, God spoke through the prophet Joel, the psalmist, the whirlwind, and Jesus (God incarnate). Today, we have the witness of this cosmic yet earthly God and how God's power works on behalf of humankind.

Hebrews tells us that Jesus was assigned the role of high priest, not to glorify himself but because God designated him. He offered up prayers and supplications for himself while in the flesh; learned obedience through suffering; was perfected; and thus is the source of eternal salvation for all who obey him.

The identity of high priest is not something Jesus claimed of himself in the Gospels, though the high priest is responsible for the holiness and wellbeing of the community. (See Leviticus 10:8-11.) The Gospels do not suggest that Jesus had to be perfected through suffering. They do portray his human anguish and petition to be delivered from that suffering and show his perfect obedience by enduring it.

Consider the characteristics of the "mortal" high priest: to offer gifts and sacrifices for sins and to deal gently with the ignorant and wayward. The high priest does not presume but acts because of God's call. Each of us, by God's power and by the example of Jesus Christ, is capable of and called to such a role.

What might you do better or differently if you viewed yourself as a humble agent of God to deal gently with the ignorant and wayward? What would change if you were to offer "gifts and sacrifices" for sin (if only for your own)? How might you act differently if you kept at the front of your mind that you are subject to weakness—and may also yourself be the ignorant or wayward person? What might be the response of others if you consistently demonstrated this kind of servanthood?

Gracious God, guide me to seek the Christian perfection that is possible through perfect submission to your will. Amen.

Liberation

OCTOBER 18–24, 2021 • STEPHANE BROOKS

SCRIPTURE OVERVIEW: Sometimes we can look back and see why challenging things happened to us, but this is not always the case. Job never fully understood his story but finally submitted his life to God in humility. In Job's case, God restored with abundance. The psalmist also rejoices that although the righteous may suffer, God brings ultimate restoration. The reading from Hebrews continues celebrating Christ's role as the compassionate high priest. Unlike human high priests, who serve only for a time, Christ remains our priest forever. A man without sight in Jericho knows of Jesus' compassion and cries out for it, despite attempts to silence him. He asks Jesus for mercy, physical healing in his case, and Jesus grants his request because the man has displayed great faith.

QUESTIONS AND SUGGESTIONS FOR REFLECTION

- Read Job 42:1-6, 10-17. What are your happy and unhappy endings? How do you acknowledge both?
- Read Psalm 34:1-8, 19-22. How does God deliver you from your fears? Recall a recent experience of this.
- Read Hebrews 7:23-28. What distinction do you draw between sacrifice and offering?
- Read Mark 10:46-52. How do you respond to Jesus' question, "What do you want me to do for you?"

International Director of Emmaus Ministries at The Upper Room; ordained clergy; married to Claudine and father of Stephanie, Sophia, and Charisse.

Coming from a small Caribbean island, I find that the opportunity to take long, uninterrupted drives is one of the things I enjoy about living in the United States. For me, these drives offer an opportunity to step back from the many situations I'm facing, relax, and receive new insight before reengaging. They are liberating experiences.

In the Bible, the theme of liberation is found from cover to cover. Early on, God is the one who, through human instruments, sets the Israelites free from bondage. Liberation is found in the Gospel of Luke when Emmanuel—God incarnate—reads revolutionary words from the prophet Isaiah and states, "Today this scripture has been fulfilled in your hearing" (Luke 4:21). Liberation is found in the book of Revelation which, among other things, is believed to be God's great message of hope to oppressed believers.

Today's text from Psalm 34 reminds us again of God's desire to see God's people set free—to liberate them from belittling situations, systems, spiritual forces, and thoughts—to enable them to live meaningful and purposeful lives. When we think of this psalm written by David, who experienced miraculous deliverance at God's hands, these words invite us as Christians to seek to remain planted by the streams of living water that are found in Jesus Christ, the Savior of the world.

Lord, day after day, grant me the desire to remain in your way and to lean on you for all things. Amen.

The background to Psalm 34 is an unusual and quite amusing story. In First Samuel 21:10-15, while David is fleeing his archenemy King Saul, David goes to Achish king of Gath, another deadly enemy. Unfortunately, Achish's servants recognize him, and David's only way to escape the situation is to feign madness by acting strangely and dribbling at his mouth. Pretty soon, because of David's supposed madness, he is dismissed by Achish, thus freeing him to go his way.

On its own, this is a pretty funny anecdote that might cause us to smile at our human ability to wiggle ourselves out of almost any circumstance. In today's reading though, having reflected on his experience, David deepens our understanding of the event.

He does not attribute his deliverance from danger to his cleverness or his acting skills. Rather, he places God at the center of the event. David acknowledges that while he might have had the presence of mind to put on an act, it was God who softened Achish's heart, thus causing him to change his mind about David. And so it is from this place of certainty and assurance of God's safekeeping of those who trust in God that David extends an invitation to steer away from all self-centeredness and all belief in self-sufficiency, in order to taste and see how good God—the liberator—really is.

Reflect on a time when you were delivered from a dangerous situation. How was God present in that situation? Consider writing your own psalm of praise for God's deliverance.

Sometimes, as a result of our limitations, our understanding of God and the ways of God become blurred. Amidst life and its realities, our dim vision then results in prolonged periods of desolation. The book of Job opens with a brief background to the events that were to come. Following a few details about Job's relationship with God and his social status, we come to a conversation between God and Satan that ends with a decision to examine the depth of Job's commitment to God. The ensuing chapters—more than thirty of them—are mainly attempts by Job and his friends to make sense of the hardships that suddenly befall this God-fearing man.

As the conversation evolves, Job's world is increasingly turned upside down. He is confused. In the middle of Job's pain and sorrow, while appealing to God for an audience, he accuses God of creating a chaotic world—one in which it seems as if righteousness is no longer rewarded and evil goes unpunished. In response to Job's accusation, God follows a line of questioning that results in today's words for reflection: "Surely I spoke of things I did not understand, things too wonderful for me to know . . . My ears had heard of you but now my eyes have seen you" (NIV). With this divine intervention, Job not only gets his desired audience with God but also comes to the realization that God's creation is beautifully ordered. This encounter with God and Job's renewed vision of God lead him from desolation to consolation. He now knows that human beings are not at the center of God's creation. We each have a divine calling to play an active role in God's world, but God remains in control of God's creation. There is freedom in knowing that truth.

Lord, help me always to be mindful of my place in your creation. Amen.

As the audition of witnesses began, a young political leader was taken into pretrial detention. His alleged crime: making government-owned property available and affordable to a certain section of the population, 90 percent of whom previously lived in rented apartments. His real crime: performing a seemingly small act that had the potential to make a huge difference for families who lived with the effects of generational poverty.

In today's reading, we see Jesus performing a small act with huge consequences as he and his disciples move through Jericho. By now Jesus' reputation has grown, and he is highly sought-after. In this scene, he is surrounded by a huge crowd. In the midst of the cacophony, a desperate Bartimaeus cries out. He is blind; and, in that time and culture, he has no way of supporting himself or his family. He desperately wants his situation to change. Yet when he cries out for help, there is a popular attempt to intimidate him and leave him in his present condition. Fortunately for Bartimaeus, Jesus hears and pays attention. Jesus invites him to draw nearer and asks about his need. With a trusting heart, Bartimaeus shares his deepest concern—and he is set free from his blindness. Jesus gives him new life.

There is a clear connection between faith and deliverance. There is also a clear indication of the importance of individual or institutional channels of God's grace. What if the invitation in this story—to individual Christians and the institutions they represent—is to go beyond introducing and inviting people to faith in a sanitized Jesus? What if we are invited to be visible, attentive, and genuine channels of God's grace to the dispossessed? What if we are to meet them in their situations and journey with them to new spiritual depth and long-lasting freedom from the physical dispossession that oftentimes underlies a multitude of ills? What if?

How are you, or the institution you represent, making a difference in the life of the dispossessed?

Liberation 351

Some years ago, my family doctor recommended that I see a psychologist. To my great surprise and joy, by the end of the third session with the psychologist, we had gotten to the troublesome issue that had been impacting me physically. The renewal I experienced in the following weeks was so great that I gave serious thought to taking up studies in psychology. Similarly, reflective response to the liberating grace of God often leads to a desire to partner with God in setting others free.

This is what we see in our reading for today as Bartimaeus responds to his deliverance from blindness. He "followed Jesus along the road," and what a road this was! Indeed, five chapters later Mark tells us that Jesus was judged and, though found innocent, was handed over to those who meant him no good. He was then nailed to a cross on which he died a horrible death. What a road this was for Bartimaeus who had just come from darkness to light! It really shouldn't surprise us, though. When God sets us free, we have an urge to set others free. And sometimes we find ourselves doing so at great cost.

Our response to God's liberating grace leads us to strange places. May we graciously remain open to this reality, for even in those places, God is with us.

> *Liberating God, grant that I may never take your goodness for granted. As you set us free, increase our desire to set others free and continue to prepare us for our contribution to your work. Amen.*

Further revelation of God usually results in God's being stripped of our human-imposed limitations. It also leads to God's creation finding new life and availing itself to the renewed call to be in partnership with God, transforming the world and bringing freedom to others.

In today's scripture, we read of a Job who has been in God's presence and now knows without a shadow of a doubt that his Redeemer lives and stands upon the earth. From this place of certainty, Job is able to come alive, trust, and regain pleasure in life.

Without fear, Job avails himself to be used by God in new ways. He is first called to be a priest to those friends who had spent countless hours theologizing instead of encouraging him during his time of distress. Probably most of all, as one who was dispossessed, Job is called to be a model of courage with a willingness to start all over again, entrusting all things to the God of whom he has a renewed understanding. Then, as one who has known the pain of losing his children, Job is called to fearlessly reengage in parenthood, this time with an understanding that God also deeply loves and cares for daughters and sons. With this renewed understanding of God, Job radically turns the cultural norms of his world upside down by granting an inheritance to his daughters as well as his sons.

Reflect on what this new status would have meant for Job's daughters. What cultural norms is God calling you to view in a different way and to question? How will you respond?

Today is the day God brings good news to the poor, proclaims release to the captives, gives sight to the blind, and sets the oppressed free. And so shall we."* These are the concluding words of the companion litany to The United Methodist Church's Social Creed.

These words come on the heels of affirmations of God's concern and desire for the well-being of all of humanity—the rich, the poor, workers, families, nations. The creed, which is meant to be continually available to individual believers and emphasized regularly in every local church in my denomination, is a potent reminder that the transformation of the human heart is not an end in itself. Indeed, the complete salvation that is found in Jesus Christ involves much more than a renewal of the human intent, attitude, and disposition.

As John Wesley hinted, holiness of heart and the holiness of life that plays itself out in renewed behavior, conduct, and visibility, are intimately linked. The latter comes in reflective response to God's incredible grace. It plays itself out in transformative practices and, in turn, fuels ongoing growth in the likeness of Christ. As God continues to invite us to join in God's transformative work through today's reading, God reminds us that those who join God through Christ—the Oone who saves completely—are themselves set free and empowered to carry out this mission both efficiently and effectively.

---

*The Book of Discipline of The United Methodist Church–2016. Copyright © 2016 by The United Methodist Publishing House, Nashville, TN.

Here I am, Lord. Use me to your glory. Amen.

Embrace the New

OCTOBER 25–31, 2021 • CHARITY M. KIREGYERA

SCRIPTURE OVERVIEW: Ruth and Psalm 146 share a thematic connection. Ruth is a foreigner who decides to follow the God of the Israelites, and the psalmist praises God for being the trustworthy God who cares about the poor, the oppressed, and the foreigner. In Ruth, Boaz will demonstrate this kind of care for her. The New Testament readings focus on sacrifice. Hebrews teaches us that Christ was both the greatest high priest and the eternal sacrifice. A scribe in Mark receives praise from Jesus, for he understands that the sacrificial system is less weighty than the act of loving one's neighbor. Ruth and this scribe are examples of those, named and anonymous, who have come before us in the faith.

QUESTIONS AND SUGGESTIONS FOR REFLECTION

- Read Ruth 1:1-18. When have you left the familiar behind to set out into the unknown? Where did you experience God's presence and help in that situation?
- Read Psalm 146. When have you witnessed God at work in the world in a way that gave you hope about an otherwise seemingly hopeless situation?
- Read Hebrews 9:11-14. How does the redemption offered in Christ's death free you to worship the living God? What form does your worship take?
- Read Mark 12:28-34. What does it mean to you to love your neighbor as you love yourself? How do you act on that commandment in your everyday life?

Minister of Kyonyo Pentecostal Assemblies of God in Western Uganda.

In today's scripture, we read that the Lord Jesus came as a high priest of "the good things that are now already here" (NIV). Some earlier texts say "the good things that are to come."

Christ ministers in a tabernacle that is not made by human hands but by God.

The sanctuary where Jesus is serving is heaven itself. "For Christ did not enter a sanctuary made with human hands that was only a copy of the true one; he entered into heaven itself, now to appear for us in God's presence" (Heb. 9:24, NIV).

God instructed Moses to make a tabernacle with the Holy of Holies as a model of heaven. Under the old covenant, only the High Priest could gain access to the mercy seat—and then only once a year, on the Day of Atonement. (See Leviticus 16:2.)

However, when Jesus, the New Testament High Priest, died on the cross he opened the door of heaven to us. We, whom Jesus has made priests of the New Covenant, have the freedom to enter into God's presence any day and any time. Furthermore, Jesus not only saved us but continues to intercede for us. (See Hebrews 7:25.)

Jesus understands and sympathizes with our human weaknesses. Scripture tells us that he was tempted in every way that we are, though he did not sin. (See Hebrews 4:15.)

Therefore, in our failures and weaknesses, we do not need to worry that Christ will reject us or cast us away. Quite the opposite, in fact! Instead of rejecting us, Christ invites us to come boldly to the throne of God. It is there that grace is freely offered to believers for all the issues we face in life.

We can put our trust in the new high priestly office of Christ, who is the assurance of the New Covenant and the divine promise that the Covenant is true and eternal.

What a gift Christ has given—that we may come boldly to God's throne of grace and there find help in our times of need! (See Hebrews 4:16.)

The blood of Christ described in today's reading refers not simply to the bodily fluid but to the whole atoning, sacrificial work of Christ in his death.

The death of Jesus Christ did for us, as those who live in the New Covenant, what animal sacrifices did not and could not do for those who lived under the old covenant—take away sins.

The sacrifices of the old covenant did not remove the offerers' guilt or provide them with full forgiveness for their sins. It was only symbolic of something else that ultimately would bring full forgiveness—the blood of Jesus Christ.

The animal sacrifices of the Old Testament merely covered sins. And the constant repetition of these rituals was a reminder of how inadequate they were. In the New Covenant, through the blood of Jesus, our sins are removed, forgiven, and forgotten. (See Matthew 26:27-28.)

In our Christian walk, we sometimes stumble and fall. This happens to all of us; and when it does we experience feelings of guilt. Our consciences accuse us. But when we sincerely repent of the wrong we have done, the blood of Jesus cleanses us from all unrighteousness.

Let us embrace the new chance of full forgiveness and live free from guilt.

"Therefore, brothers and sisters, since we have confidence to enter the Most Holy Place by the blood of Jesus, by a new and living way opened for us through the curtain, that is, his body . . . let us draw near to God with a sincere heart and with the full assurance that faith brings" (Heb. 10:19-20, 22, NIV).

When Naomi decides to return to her homeland of Judah, she insists that her widowed daughters-in-law, Ruth and Orpah, go back to their mothers' houses. She spells out the reason. Naomi is too old to produce more sons who could later become husbands to Ruth and Orpah.

Though both women had wanted to stay with their mother-in-law, Orpah realizes the logic in Naomi's warning and kisses Naomi goodbye. But Ruth chooses, in spite of the negative outlook, to cling to Naomi. She will not leave her mother-in-law or return to her mother's house. Instead, she will belong to Naomi's people and, best of all, embrace Naomi's God—the God of Israel.

Like Ruth and Orpah, we too face difficult choices. In those moments, we are often tempted to give up on what we always believed about God's goodness, mercy, love, and faithfulness. We are tempted to go back—at least in our minds—to think, *Nothing good will come my way again, at least not as good as what I had before. There's no hope. Maybe God doesn't love me after all.*

But from Ruth's story we learn what to do when hard times hit: cling to God, who does not change whether times are good or bad. God is able to turn negative situations around, to turn our mourning into dancing, as David testifies in Psalm 30:11.

In the end, Ruth's choice of the God of Israel is greatly rewarded. Ruth marries again, and she and Boaz produce Obed, one of the ancestors of Jesus Christ. (See Matthew 1:5.)

God, help me to choose to embrace the new things that lead me to your unseen blessings. Amen.

Abimeleck, his wife, Naomi, and their two sons go to live in Moab. Actually they are "escaping death" in the form of famine because there is food in Moab while there is none in Judah.

But in time, Naomi's husband dies, followed by her two sons. Moab becomes "a land of the dead" for her—a dead husband, dead sons, and a dead god called Chemosh. (See 1 Kings 11:17.) Even her relationship with her daughters-in-law, Ruth and Orpah, appears dead as the two younger women are expected to stay in Moab while Naomi plans to return to Judah.

In the meantime, Naomi hears that the famine in Judah is over. God has visited God's people. Naomi chooses not to continue living in "the land of the dead." She chooses to leave behind what she cannot resurrect and instead to focus on and head for a fresh start. She chooses to embrace the new reality of her life. She sets out on the road that will bring her back to Judah where there is a fresh promise of God's provision.

We too experience death in many different situations: the death of a loved one, the disruption of a cherished relationship, the end of a once satisfying career, a betrayal by someone we once trusted.

However much we loved or were attached to anything or any person, they are no more. Choosing to cling to it will only cause us to lose our zeal, perhaps eventually even our desire to go on living. It is wise to choose to embrace the new reality and move past what we can't resurrect, as Paul reminds us, "Forgetting what is behind and straining toward what is ahead, I press on" (Phil. 3:13-14, NIV).

Help me, Lord, to leave behind what I cannot resurrect. Amen.

Journeying to the Promised Land, the Jews encounter many challenges. In the wilderness of Shur, they find no water. At Marah, the water is bitter. In the Desert of Sin, they find no food. (See Exodus 15:22-24; 16:1-3.)

In all these situations, God's people murmur and complain. How quickly they forget the misery of their bondage in Egypt! How soon they lose the sense of joy they felt when God delivered them from their enemies!

As it was for those ancient people, it is easy for us to resort to complaining when things don't turn out well for us. But in today's scripture we see that the psalmist makes a commitment to praise the Lord, to sing praises to God, throughout life, no matter the circumstances, And we can learn to do the same.

God wants us to offer praise both when we see God's victory and before we see it, when we are still in the midst of our trials.

God was pleased when King Jehoshaphat and his people praised God for answering them. (See 2 Chronicles 20.) In fact, when they began to praise God, God ambushed their enemies which resulted in these enemies turning on one another and finishing off themselves. In Acts, we see Paul and Silas who—after being beaten and thrown into the jail, their bodies aching and their feet fastened in stocks—"were praying and singing hymns to God, and prisoners were listening to them" (Acts 16:25). And while they were praying and singing hymns, the foundations of the prison shook, the doors were opened, and all of the prisoners' chains fell off. Furthermore, this miraculous occurrence led the jailer and all of his household to become believers.

We all face times when things are going the wrong way for us. When we do, let us embrace the "new" but old wisdom of praising God in every circumstance.

Lord, I know that you are pleased when I praise you. Help me to commit to praising you at all times and in all situations. Amen.

The psalmist tells us not to misplace our trust by putting it in human beings whose thoughts and plans end when they die. Instead, the psalmist tells us to put our trust in the God of Jacob, the One who "made heaven and earth, the sea, and all that is in them: who keeps truth for ever" (NIV).

In these ancient times, different nations each had their own god. The god of the Moabites was called Chemosh. The one of the Ammonites was called Molech. The Zidonians' god was called Ashtoreth (1 Kings 11:5, 7), and the god of the Philistines was called Dagon (Judges 16:23).

But all these gods were mere works of mortals' hands which could be burned, stolen, damaged, and even destroyed completely. This is not true of the God of Jacob, who is the creator of all things and cannot be destroyed. In fact, God does not change. (See Malachi 3:6.)

For many people in Paul's day, the belly had become their god. (See Philippians 3:19.) We too in our materialistic world need to avoid the danger of embracing the new gods—new in comparison to the Ancient of Days, the Alpha and Omega, the Creator God.

If we are not watchful, money or possessions or power can become our gods. Putting our trust in these or any other created things is futile; they cannot save us or give us peace. But the God of Jacob is a Rock, a Savior, a Deliverer, and a Healer. Those who worship other gods worship them in vain. The Lord says, "My people have forgotten me, they burn incense to worthless idols" (Jer. 18:15, NIV).

"Who is a God like you, who pardons sin and forgives the transgression of the remnant of his inheritance? You do not stay angry forever but delight to show mercy" (Mic. 7:18, NIV).

Jesus teaches that loving God and loving one's neighbor as oneself are the greatest commandments and that, indeed, "All the Law and the Prophets hang on these two commandments" (Matt. 22:40, NIV).

Likewise, James says that loving one's neighbor as one loves oneself is the royal law. "If you really keep the royal law found in Scripture, 'Love your neighbor as yourself,' you are doing right" (James 2:8, NIV). James is not advocating some kind of emotional affection for oneself. Rather the command is to pursue the spiritual health and physical wellbeing of one's neighbor (all within the sphere of our influence) with the same intensity and concern as we naturally do for ourselves.

In Jesus' parable of the good Samaritan, he explains who our neighbor is. (See Luke 10:29-37.) Priests are ministers at the altar; they teach people the laws of God. Levites are charged with the care of the tabernacle and the Temple. So the priest and Levite, who passed by the injured man, are "Temple people," religious authorities. But they show more concern for the routines, rituals, and forms of their religion than for a person who is in dire need of help. They lack internal godliness and obedience to God's truth.

The Samaritan, who is not a "Temple person," is the one who fulfills the royal law by caring for the injured man.

In our busy world, we too need to avoid being mere "church people," going to and rushing out of church without ever interacting with people whose lives intersect with ours, finding no time to show active concern for those whose needs we could meet. God calls us, instead, to love and care for our neighbors as we love and care for ourselves.

Let us embrace Jesus' new commandment to love one another as Jesus has loved us. (See John 13:34.)

Our Hearts' Desires

NOVEMBER 1–7, 2021 • AIMEE MOISO

SCRIPTURE OVERVIEW: Ruth's story forms part of the background of the family of Jesus. The son of Ruth and Boaz, Obed, is David's grandfather. The women of Bethlehem rejoice with Naomi at the birth of her grandson, and the psalmist declares that children are a blessing from God. In the scriptures, children are spoken of only as a blessing, never as a liability (unlike some narratives in our culture). The writer of Hebrews builds upon the eternal nature of Christ's sacrifice, proclaiming that his death was sufficient once for all. In Mark, Jesus warns his disciples not to be fooled by appearances. Those who put on a big show of piety do not impress God. God wants us instead to give from the heart, even if no one but God sees.

QUESTIONS AND SUGGESTIONS FOR REFLECTION

- Read Ruth 3:1-5; 4:13-17. Who are the people in your community who lack the basic provisions for a safe and healthy life? How do you try to help meet their needs?
- Read Psalm 127. In what ways do you invite God to be part of your work?
- Read Hebrews 9:24-28. When have you eagerly waited for something? How did that feel?
- Read Mark 12:38-44. How do you practice generosity in the way you allocate your resources and time?

Minister in the Presbyterian Church (USA); holds a PhD in homiletics and liturgics from Vanderbilt University; interested in ecumenical connections across the Christian tradition, gardening, and baking.

ALL SAINTS' DAY

This week of devotions begins with All Saints' Day, a day of thanksgiving for the lives of those in the family of faith who have come before us, and a celebration of the company of ordinary saints, past and present, who walk with us. In many churches, All Saints' Day is a bittersweet recounting of those who have died in the past year, a remembering of those no longer present. Almost every year as I hear the calling of that roll, I think poignantly, *I wonder who will not be with us this time next year.*

The text from Isaiah 25 speaks deeply to the desires of the heart that are caught up in All Saints' Day: honest gratitude for the lives of those we have loved, unspoken and unresolved parts of our relationships, bitter grief at being separated from one another, and a wrenching longing to one day be together again. On the mountain of the Lord, all peoples will gather at a feast, says Isaiah. The shadows around us and the divisions among us will dissipate. Disgrace, sorrow, and even death will vanish.

It is striking that on that day and on that mountain, the people proclaim, "*This* is our God . . . *this* is the Lord for whom we have waited" (emphasis added). It is as if God is finally recognized as True because this God is the one who is able to enact this salvation—a salvation not only from grief and loss, but from human division and separation. Our petty squabbles, our buried heartaches, and our most evil transgressions are all reversed in a moment of feasting. God is known by the power to bring to pass the deepest desires of our hearts; and in that transformation we know that this reconciliatory, deathless feast is our hearts' desire, and our salvation.

Thank you, God, for understanding our hearts' desires and being the God of our salvation. Amen.

Scholars note that the book of Ruth is notoriously difficult to translate into English in ways that capture the layers of symbolism and meaning. Not hard to translate, however, is Naomi and Ruth's need to find security and well-being. Both are widows with no male heirs, which is the biblical equivalent of an unarmed protagonist running from a dragon along the edge of a precipice. Though in preceding verses Ruth and Naomi have received kindness from Boaz and have been able to glean some grain, their situation remains desperate.

The Hebrew word for *widow* suggests someone who is unable to speak, unable to advocate on her own behalf. Rather than stay silent, however, Naomi speaks an all-too-human truth: "We need security if we're going to be well." Naomi and Ruth may not be able to lobby publicly in the courts of justice, but perhaps they can more subtly persuade Boaz, their kinsman, to take responsibility.

Naomi's words are a reminder that we all long for security and well-being and that we are often driven to great lengths to achieve them. What a universal and human experience! We need look no further than to store shelves emptied of bread, milk, and toilet paper in times of disaster to see evidence of our shared desire for protection and provision in times of anxiety and need.

Recognizing our common desire for well-being and security is also an opportunity to deepen our empathy and love for others. When refugees from other shores seek escape from war, or when someone down on their luck asks for spare change, we can choose to see their hopes and fears as something with which we can identify. Being able to acknowledge the commonality we share with others—such as our common need for safety and well-being—helps us to respond with compassion and recognition rather than fear or contempt.

Jesus, open our hearts so that we can see ourselves—and you— in our neighbors. Amen.

In this text from Ruth, all that Naomi has hoped for has happened. Naomi's daughter-in-law Ruth is now the wife of Boaz, and she has given birth to a boy. The arrival of a male next-of-kin in a patriarchal society means there is now someone who will take care of them. The women of the village celebrate and give praise to God; the security and well-being for which Naomi prayed and planned have come to pass.

This makes it all the more interesting and curious that the village women specifically proclaim that Ruth is more important to Naomi than seven sons. Given that much of the story has been focused on Naomi and Ruth finding security as sonless widows, it might seem natural that Obed, the prayed-for son, would be the sole focus at the end of the story—perhaps especially since Obed is in the lineage of David, from whose house Jesus will be born. Instead, the story circles back around to the love shared between Ruth and Naomi, which is where the story began. (See Ruth 1:16-18.) Their relationship has led to their salvation in a very tangible way—through a marriage and the birth of a child who can care for them. But it appears that the relationship they share with each other is even more important.

As the old saying goes, "Money can't buy happiness." Perhaps for Ruth and Naomi, something similar has happened. Security and well-being were critical for their survival, of course; and they are overjoyed to no longer live in the anxiety of a hand-to-mouth existence. Still, even in their most desperate moments, they had each other—and perhaps because of that, they found the strength to persevere and to keep faith. In the midst of their wretched circumstances, they had been given the gift of their close bond, and that gift became as precious as everything else for which they longed.

Holy God, help us to be gifts of love and solidarity in all that we face together. Amen.

I completed my PhD in the middle of the school year, and frequently afterwards I was asked, "Are you going to walk?" This is academia-speak for, "Are you planning to participate in graduation ceremonies in May?" Often, any hesitance in my response was greeted with a wholehearted, "Oh, you should! You've earned it!" Of course, to participate in graduation, I would need a robe—and not just any robe: an approved-gold-with-black-doctoral-stripes-and-the-uiversity-logo robe. Academic robes are not cheap, even to rent for a day; and the higher the degree you've earned, the more expensive they are. For many of us, though, donning robes and hoods is a precious moment that completes the arduous academic journey we've taken.

The scribes in this Mark text were scholars of the law, and their robes and privileged seats were marks of honor. But Jesus points out that with honor and privilege can come detachment—a sense of no longer being interconnected with others because of achievements or knowledge. When we become distanced or disconnected from other people, we begin to make excuses for the privileges afforded to some and not others, and to justify benefits for some at the expense of the rest. For the scribes, the biting critique is that they enact their duties for appearances rather than out of devotion to God. They have lost sight of the very purpose of their study.

Graduations are one of the rare times many of us wear robes. The fancy garb, the ceremony, and the general (and musical) pomp and circumstance are all part of a grand celebration of accomplishment. It is not wrong to honor hard work and academic success. But this text from Mark suggests that our love of the trappings of honor and ceremony can become distorted into forms of hierarchy and segregation that stand against love of God and our neighbors.

Gracious One, teach us to honor you and one another in all we do. Amen.

Humans have a complicated relationship with the idea of control. Sayings such as, "He's totally out of control" or admonitions to "Get control of yourself!" give the impression that we are supposed to take charge, be organized, stay calm, and do what needs to be done. Conversely, the first step in many 12-step recovery programs is to admit our lack of control. Meanwhile, being too tightly wound leads to accusations that we are "control freaks."

Psalm 127 reads like a response to folks caught in the latter category. Maybe people building the house or guarding the city aren't "control freaks," but they seem to have an unrealistic sense of their own ability to determine outcomes. Rising early and going to bed late, they labor in vain—because, the psalmist says, it is God who is in charge.

The psalmist's message, however, is not quite so simple or literal. Leaving building material in a vacant lot and waiting for the Lord to build the house is likely to be a futile effort. It reminds me of high school friends who didn't study for a math exam but instead prayed that God would help them pass because "God is in control." I wanted to say, "Yes, but God also gave you a brain and a math textbook and a teacher so you'd learn this stuff for the exam."

Psalm 127 speaks to the deep human desire—and temptation—to ascribe to ourselves more power than we actually possess, and to take credit for more than we deserve. But the psalm is not an excuse to wash our hands of responsibility. Instead we are called to a balance: of toil and rest, of work and discernment, of gratitude and accountability. We have work to do, but we attend to it within a world God has created for our good, and for the good of those with whom we share it.

Holy Creator, grant us wisdom, courage, and balance in all we face. Amen.

The story of the widow and the two coins often makes its way into sermons during church fundraising campaigns, where the woman's generosity is praised because of her complete devotion. I've always wondered why preachers didn't focus on rich people contributing large sums, which would seem a more effective stewardship message. But as this text has been interpreted over time, many have seen Jesus' words as an affirmation of the widow's sacrifice, and perhaps that's why she's become the hero.

In fact, all Jesus does is point out a fact: As a portion of overall income, the widow—who had little to begin with—has contributed all she had. In verse 40, Jesus denounces those who "devour widows' houses," which is an apparent reference to injustice borne by widows. For this reason, some commentators argue that Jesus' words condemn a system in which someone who has so little feels so obligated—or desperate—to give her last penny. But the Gospel writer doesn't explain any giver's motivations. All in the story give to the treasury, some out of their abundance and some out of their poverty.

We are left with a dramatic portrait of the scene: all those people passing by the treasury to make their offerings. Maybe the wealthier people were laughing and joking with one another as they easily made their gifts. Maybe they saw the widow but weren't sure how to respond. Was she hunched over, shuffling forward to make her offering? Did others make way for her to pass, lowering their voices in awkwardness or shame? Did they rush forward to help when her shawl slipped from her shoulders? Did she meet their eyes, and would they meet hers? Did a moment of human connection pass between them?

What did each of them long for in that moment, that moment of seeing each other face-to-face?

Brother Jesus, help us see your face in all those we meet. Amen.

In the New Revised Standard Version, Hebrews 9:28 says Christ is coming to save those who are "eagerly" waiting for him. The New International Version just says they are "waiting," but doesn't specify in what spirit. The Living Bible says "eagerly and patiently." No specific adjective appears in the Greek. It is the verb itself that implies the mood of the waiting, and different translators have made choices about what to emphasize.

I can't think of a time when my experience of waiting could be described with only one adjective. Waiting for something—especially something good—can be done patiently, yes. But much more often when waiting we may find ourselves *im*patient, not to mention restless, calm, excited, agitated, distracted, watchful, fidgety, thrilled, eager. As a child waiting for Christmas to come, I rolled through all these feelings and more in the course of a few hours. Each week between lighting the next Advent candle seemed to take a lifetime.

As an adult, however, the season of Advent seems to arrive quickly and then just barrels right along. I rarely feel impatient during Advent because I barely have time to feel like I'm waiting. I feel more like I'm holding up both hands and saying, "Slow down! I want to enjoy preparing for the coming of Jesus!"

Awaiting the second arrival of Jesus is not quite the same as preparing for a twenty-first century Christmas holiday. But this 2,000+ year season of waiting is also a time of living in this world, of seeking God in that which happens here and now, and of finding meaning in this anticipation time. The hoped-for coming of a Messiah who will bring salvation to all is something for which we also wait with multiple feelings—joy and hope, of course, but also confusion and grief, distraction and excitement, doubt and trust. May all our heart's longings find their home in the One who comes.

Come, Lord Jesus, and hold us fast until that day. Amen.

Perseverance

NOVEMBER 8–14, 2021 • DEVONNA R. ALLISON

SCRIPTURE OVERVIEW: The inability to have a child brings pain to many today, and this was equally true in ancient times. In that context it was sometimes even worse, for Peninnah openly ridicules Hannah for being unable to conceive. But as a result of Hannah's desperate, heartfelt prayer, God blesses her with a son, Samuel, who will become a powerful prophet. Hannah then rejoices in a God who exalts the poor and needy. Hannah provides an example of the boldness with which we also can approach God now because of Christ's sacrifice. The destruction of Jerusalem is the focus of the passage in Mark. Jesus here predicts the demolition of the Temple and the city, which the Romans executed in 70 CE.

QUESTIONS AND SUGGESTIONS FOR REFLECTION

- Read 1 Samuel 1:4-20. How do you persist in prayer when your prayer seems unanswered for a long time?
- Read 1 Samuel 2:1-10. How do you express your joy and thanks when God answers your prayer?
- Read Hebrews 10:11-25. What helps you to persevere in the practice of your faith?
- Read Mark 13:1-8. What signs make you anxious about the future? What helps you to hold on to hope?

Freelance Christian writer, speaker, and Marine Corps veteran who attends Christ Community Church in Ocala, FL.

In 1914, the explorer Earnest Shackleton set out on his ship, the *Endurance*, with a crew of twenty-seven men, headed for the bottom of the earth. Their mission was to be the first to cross the Antarctic continent on land. However, their ship became trapped, crushed in polar pack ice, leaving them stranded.

Though Shackleton and his crew didn't achieve their goal, the real story of this expedition is their survival after the loss of their ship. The crew was forced to abandon the *Endurance*, salvaging only the supplies they could carry. For two years, the men overcame numerous life-threatening challenges before facilitating their own rescue. Remarkably—some might say miraculously—not a single life was lost. The crew's survival was undeniably due to Shackleton's extraordinary leadership and ability to keep his men organized, motivated, and encouraged.

When the men returned home to England in 1916, despite the expedition's failure to achieve its goal, all but four of the crew were awarded their country's Polar Medal in recognition of their heroic survival.

The four who were not awarded the Polar Medal were not recognized at the insistence of Earnest Shackleton who said they had fallen short in the fulfillment of their responsibilities. How sad to have survived such an ordeal and fail to be rewarded!

Though I am uncertain of the religious affiliations of Shackleton's men, I know they exhibited a principle that is essential to our journey as Christians and the one we will be exploring this week—perseverance. They did not quit or give up on their faith in their leader, despite extreme hardships, or they would not have survived. We can be encouraged and challenged by their example and by today's reading to persevere in our own lives.

Lord Jesus, help us to be your faithful followers, persevering in faith, prayers, and praise. When we become discouraged, help us to look to you for the strength to continue. Amen.

In today's reading, Jesus and his disciples visit the Temple in Jerusalem. At the time it was 500 years old, but the Temple was still a marvel of ancient industry. One of the disciples exclaims over it to Jesus, who in turn warns that nothing endures; change and destruction are inevitable in this world. Within 100 years, the beautiful Temple would lie in ruins; and Christ's followers would be suffering terrible persecution. Jesus' lesson that day was that despite severe trials, our faith can endure when we follow and lean on the Author of our faith.

Just as the Temple was the physical symbol of the Jewish faith, the ship the *Endurance* was the symbol of Earnest Shackleton's expedition to Antarctica. At the time it was the strongest ship ever built, and Shackleton was so confident in the ship that he christened it the *Endurance* after his family motto: "Through endurance we conquer." Just as the disciples could not imagine the Temple lying in ruins, Shackleton's crew could never foresee their ship crushed like an eggshell in the jaws of polar ice. Each group, the disciples and Shackleton's crew, had to rally their will to survive in the face of devastation, and they had to place full confidence in their leaders' ability to bring them through.

Our finances, our relationships, our health, our reputations—all are vulnerable to destruction. But what about our faith? The nightly news reports horrific crimes, wars, natural disasters, and humanitarian crises. We can throw our hands up in despair. Or we can invest in our faith by persevering in confidence in our Savior. Jesus encouraged us with these words, "Do not be alarmed; this must take place."

Believing is a choice. Despite outward circumstances, we can choose to believe in God and God's care for this world.

Could you persevere if the thing you hold dearest were destroyed? We can be supremely confident in God's faithfulness. "Let us hold fast to the confession of our hope without wavering, for he who has promised is faithful" (Heb. 10:23).

Has it ever occurred to you that nothing new has ever occurred to God? We can take comfort in the knowledge that God has no new revelations, no sudden insights, no lapses in attention or judgment. God is aware of all that is before us and encourages us, through scripture, to stand fast, to persevere in the one mainstay of our lives—our faith.

There was a stowaway aboard Ernest Shackleton's ship. Eighteen-year-old Perce Blackborow hid onboard the *Endurance* for three days before being discovered at sea. Shackleton was outraged at the young man's presence and scolded him vigorously before declaring that on such expeditions, stowaways were the first ones eaten should the crew fall on hard times. Blackborow retorted good naturedly, "They'd get a lot more meat off you, sir," and won the famous explorer over.* The young man not only became a valued member of the crew, he was given the honor of being the first one to embark onto dry land on the crew's way to being saved. When the time came, he was awarded the Polar Expedition Medal along with "legitimate" crew members. He was no longer a stowaway.

It takes courage to grow. It takes courage to continue in the face of defeat or rebuke. It takes determination to imagine yourself other than what you've always been. As Christians we are continuously encouraged to grow and evolve in our faith. We have never "arrived." There's always room to stretch and expand our lives in Christ.

---

*Roland Huntford, *Shackleton*, (New York: Carroll and Graf Publishers, 1998), 384.

> *How are you challenging yourself to grow in Christ? Do you make the most of the opportunities that present themselves? How can you continue to develop and grow? Ask God today to show you where and how God is calling you to grow in your faith.*

With the sinking of the *Endurance*, Shackleton's crew knew their expedition had failed. As long as the ship remained upright, they could probably muster some hope that they could at the very least return home. But once the ship was swallowed by the sea, their final link to home and safety was gone. They could no longer entertain ideas of returning the way they had come.

Today's reading gives us a graphic depiction of the anguish of disappointed hopes. Hannah was bereft at the withholding of her heart's desire, a son. She suffered misunderstanding and judgment from her husband for her grief and was mocked by his other wife. Even Eli, the priest in the Temple, mistook Hannah's anguished prayer for drunkenness. Still, Hannah continued in her prayers; she recognized there was One who could give her what she most longed for.

We don't know how long Hannah prayed for Samuel, but we know it was years; and we know that the wait took a toll on Hannah. Waiting can be discouraging and disheartening. I think, however, that the longer we wait for something, the sweeter it is when it finally arrives.

We may face discouragement in our prayers and wonder, *Does God hear me?* But delay is not necessarily denial. It takes courage, faith, and continued hope to persevere in prayer. Shackleton's crew was rescued after two years of desperate struggle for survival. Hannah's years of faithful prayer were rewarded with the blessing she most desired—the birth of her son, Samuel, who was called by God to be a prophet and a judge over Israel.

Perseverance and prayer go hand-in-hand.

We are wise to remember that prayer is not a monologue; it is a dialogue. It is a time of communion between us and God. Are we listening? Pause in your prayer time today and listen with your heart in quiet contemplation. Is what you desire God's desire as well? If it is, can you find rest in God's timing?

Unanswered prayer is one of the biggest challenges we can face as Christians. It can be intensely discouraging. Think of Hannah as you reread this portion of her story. Hannah's torment at the delay of her heart's desire was genuine and powerful. Perhaps you can relate. Have you ever faced a dilemma that had no earthly solution? Maybe you are facing just such a challenge today.

Take heart! Remember that Hannah did not pray once for a child and find a baby in the crib the next morning. Even after Hannah finally conceived, there was a nine-month wait before she held her baby in her arms.

We can assume that as Hannah waited for her baby she made preparations for him. I know that each time I was an expectant mother, as I waited I got things ready. I happily daydreamed of my child's future and even prayed for his or her salvation. Waiting need not be a stagnant time.

My point is that God's timing is perfect. As we persevere in prayer and wait on God, let our prayers be mixed with praise and a spirit of happy anticipation. There have been times when I felt worse after praying. In hindsight, I see that those were times when I was simply rehearsing my fears before God without acknowledging God's sovereignty.

The Lord wants us to find strength, hope, and encouragement in our prayers. Let's take our example from the Lord's Prayer. As we pray this prayer today and reflect on its familiar words, may we look for the elements of praise and hope.

"Our Father which art in heaven, Hallowed be thy name. Thy kingdom come. Thy will be done in earth, as it is in heaven. Give us this day our daily bread. And forgive us our debts, as we forgive our debtors. And lead us not into temptation, but deliver us from evil: For thine is the kingdom, and the power, and the glory, for ever. Amen (Matt. 6:9-13, KJV.)

The last two days we have concentrated on Hannah in her agony. In today's reading we see Hannah in her glory! She praises God for answering her prayers, recognizes God's faithfulness, and honors her promise, even though it must have cost her dearly to see Samuel go. Hannah was faithful to give credit where credit was due; the Lord received her praise and honor. For ten verses Hannah, by the Holy Spirit, recognizes the power of God to deliver, strengthen, judge, and provide. She recognizes God's ability to raise up or put down all earthly matters, including life itself.

Hannah is in a position to mourn in First Samuel, chapter 2. After all, she had just delivered her long-desired son to Eli at the Temple. Instead of grieving the loss of the boy she loves so well and for whom she prayed for so long, she perseveres in praising God for giving Samuel to her in the first place.

Think back to our story of the expedition of the *Endurance.* After the crew was rescued from their two-year ordeal, they were hailed as heroes. Some of the crew members published memoirs of their journey; some were in demand as speakers. Some of the crew joined other polar expeditions, and some served in World War I. I'm sure they all faced other trials in their lives after the *Endurance*; but I think, like Hannah, they would remember for the rest of their lives their life's greatest deliverance.

Reflect today on the great deliverance we have received in Christ from eternal separation from God our Maker. When we repent of our sin and recognize our need for a Savior, we can receive him along with help for the present and eternal life. Remembering the miraculous redemption that is ours in Christ, let's faithfully offer our praise every day.

Perseverance isn't always a good thing. Sometimes we persevere in bad habits or in behaviors that do not benefit us. Stubbornness, pride, anger, resentment, unforgiveness—all these bitter pills can poison our souls and lead to loss. Loss of what? Loss of joy, loss of peace, loss of relationship with God and our fellow Christians. Our forgiveness in Christ is not a license to continue in sin; it should spur us on, as Hebrews 10:14 says, as we become holy.

We don't strive against sin in order to be forgiven. We strive against personal sin *because* we are forgiven, and Revelation 22:12 tells us clearly that Jesus is coming soon.

Let us recall one more time the crew of Earnest Shackleton's expedition. They were all rescued, but they were not all rewarded. Four men—hardy, strong, and experienced—lost their opportunity to receive a high honor upon their return to civilization. As we noted earlier, Shackleton said the four men had fallen short in the fulfillment of their duties and responsibilities. All four, at one time or another, failed to recognize Shackleton's leadership, thereby putting everyone else at risk.

Did Shackleton's crew struggle to survive for two years so that they could one day stand before the king of England and receive a medal? Of course not! Neither do we serve the Lord day by day with future rewards in mind. But the scriptures make it clear that if we faithfully persevere in following Christ, we will surely receive an eternal reward. (See Matthew 16:27-28.)

Reflect today on whether there is anything that is hindering your growth in Christ—perhaps a harmful habit or minor rebellion, a favorite resentment, or a spirit of resistance. Ask God to help you let go of whatever it is so that you may continue to grow in faith.

Righteous Rule

NOVEMBER 15–21, 2021 • BRITNEY WINN LEE

SCRIPTURE OVERVIEW: Second Samuel records the final words of David. David takes comfort in the covenant that God has made with his family, which must be continued by kings who will honor God and rule justly. The psalmist sings of this same covenant with David's family and the same necessity to follow God's decrees in order to rule well. Revelation opens with a vision of Jesus Christ, the fulfillment of the Davidic covenant, the King to rule over all kings for all time. Many expected Jesus to set up a political kingdom. Yet in John, Jesus tells Pilate that his kingdom is not an earthly one. This week let us thank God that the kingdom is based not on the exercise of power but on Jesus' example of serving others.

QUESTIONS AND SUGGESTIONS FOR REFLECTION

- Read 2 Samuel 23:1-7. What characteristics would you include in a description of a just leader? Where do you see those characteristics in world leaders today?
- Read Psalm 132:1-18. What is your vision of Paradise? Who will be seated at the table with you?
- Read Revelation 1:4b-8. How do you bear witness to the "Alpha and the Omega"?
- Read John 18:33-37. What is your understanding of what it means to live in God's kingdom?

Community arts director living in Shreveport, LA, with her designer husband and big-hearted son; author of *Deconstructed Do-Gooder: A Memoir About Learning Mercy the Hard Way* (Cascade, 2019) and *The Boy with Big, Big Feelings* (Beaming Books, 2019); editor of *Rally: Communal Prayers for Lovers of Jesus and Justice* (Fresh Air Books, 2020).

Power—like water, like fire, like crowds, like promises—walks a fine line between restoration and destruction. Given to someone who is not committed to the common good, power can be abused and weaponized, especially against those who navigate the world in the margins. We see this in dictatorships or oppressive theologies. If leveraged and shared, power can be a tool of kingdom-building resistance; it can call us out of the margins and into movements that uphold the dignity of all people. We see this in grassroots efforts for justice and in the old spirituals of the oppressed.

In today's scripture, King David's last words regard this difference in power. One who rules with justice, David says, is like the sun that bursts over the horizon at daybreak. That person brings hope and growth and works all things toward goodness after darkness. But unjust rulers are cast aside like thorns. Thorns are designed to protect the plant, not to invite the harvest. Thorns here can symbolize a self-preservation by those in power who end up being unapproachable and ultimately tossed out, left alone.

In our places of power, it is important to ask ourselves what about our leadership and privilege is perpetuating self-preservation and what is bringing about hope and growth through justice. Are the words we are saying (or leaving unsaid), the decisions we are making, and the people we are supporting attuned to the common good and considerate of the marginalized? Or are they leading us down a path of fear which will inevitably leave us disconnected and alone? Power is not intrinsically bad, but it is not something to be accepted and wielded without thought or conscience. Consider who your power is prioritizing today.

Omnipotent God, within the power and privilege we have normalized in our lives, call to our conscience the places where we are not considering the common good. Lead us out of fear and into perfect love. Amen.

We live in an era of deconstructing authority—spiritual, political, and societal. Some of this is the result of generations nursed on the education of critical thinking. Most of it is the result of a progressively globalized existence now entirely entrenched in the "world wild web." Many who are over forty can remember a time when information, news, and morals were distributed by the encyclopedia, the newspaper, and the local pastor. Now, with so many sources for fact-checking and comparison, it is almost impossible to take anything at face value.

This is not necessarily negative as much as it is just the reality of where we are now. Historically, major and important shifts in culture have followed seasons of authority deconstruction. But with this bucking of authority, it can be difficult for modern readers to wrap their minds around the idea of Jesus as the ruler of the kings of the earth or seated on a throne. After all, we have seen kingdom-rulers and throne-sitters do terrible things from their positions of power. How do we separate what we've known and experienced at the hands of power-abusers from the way Christ is portrayed in the language of the New Testament?

I try to consider in these instances that the kingdom of God is for all people. The throne of God governs in favor of the last and the least. The cabinet of God is made up of those who need one another. The crown of God is a symbol of shared pain and sacrifice for others. The motorcade of God was a borrowed donkey. The platform of God invites the government to rest upon God's shoulders. The rank of God is Prince of Peace. And the reign of God is co-creation with the world that God loves forever and ever. May we take time today to remember and recognize that the rule of God is love.

Holy King, who entered this world in meekness and vulnerability, help us rest in the faithfulness of your great love for us, that we may feel safe to be citizens of your good kingdom. Amen.

Can you remember a moment when you felt truly seen? There are few instances as sacred as feeling seen, known, and loved for who you are, who you have been, and who you will be. I can recall a handful of moments when it felt as if someone sincerely bore witness to who I am on the very base level of my identity. Each of these moments was incredibly humanizing and holy. On the other hand, there are few things more dehumanizing than not being seen—being misunderstood, unknown, and unloved. I would wager that acts of hate and exploitation are more easily carried out when we have mastered ways of not seeing one another for who we are in the story of God.

Our screens, labels, and camps enable "othering." Our insistence on surrounding ourselves with people who look, spend, and vote like us permits exclusion and oppression. But efforts to get close, pay attention, and listen to one another can produce a people who recognize divinity in the person in front of them and who are willing to be seen by those who once harmed them.

This scripture says that "every eye will see him, even those who pierced him." Much had to be in place for God's creation to find Jesus so unrecognizable that people were willing to torment and murder him. Yet the environment into which God entered humanity was one of puppet politics and distorted religious rule. People were divided and outraged. Money was power, and power was for a select few. These distractions created fertile ground for missing God, even to the extent of murdering God. Yet there will come a time when Christ returns and will be seen by all, even those who missed him in devastating ways. This passage reminds us to sort through our distractions to truly see God in those with whom we come in contact and to leave room through forgiveness to be seen by those who once missed seeing God in us.

Meditate today on the words "My enemy is a child of God," that you may see Christ in all.

In moments in his ministry, Jesus answers a question with another question. If we weren't talking about God incarnate, we could dismiss this as conversation filler or procrastinating banter. Or we could consider that there is holy strategy behind Jesus' interactions that steer away from direct answers and toward prompts that cause people to consider and self-reflect.

My four-year-old, who truly hates naps and therefore frequently fights his morning drop-offs at our children's center, often demands, "Why do I have to go to school?"

I could answer, "Because I said so," and sometimes I do. But this response is a conversation stopper. It enforces the notion that his world is dictated by outside forces, which might cause him to resist even more. So sometimes I reply, "Why do you have to go to school? You tell me." This is a conversation starter, a cue for reflection, and an invitation for growth. That's the idea, at least.

And while my child's school drop-offs and Jesus' interaction with Pilate have very little in common, I am reminded of the sacred power of responding with a question rather than a decided answer. In this story, Jesus has all the power. We know that as readers and followers reflecting back into history. But Jesus chooses not to interact with this leader of the law in a way that halts the conversation and causes Pilate to write Jesus off. Instead, he invites Pilate, even in this dire moment, to go inward. "Is that your idea, or are you just regurgitating what you've heard?" (AP).

From Jesus we can learn that it is more important to invite others (even our enemies) into moments of reflection and growth than it is to demand an understanding, maybe especially at times when we feel we have all the answers.

Jesus, the next time we are faced with a question meant to challenge our faith and ethics or defame our character and intentions, guide us into responses that further the conversation and betterment of all. Amen.

Iwas nineteen when I first began to question what was meant by the terminology *kingdom of God*. I remember sitting on the couches of the student union building at my college talking through it with a trusted friend. It had taken me up until that point, but I was finally starting to wonder if there was more to understanding all these Christian sayings that flew about our sermon and prayer spaces so often loosely and generically.

What did it mean to say *Lord*? What did it mean to say *King*? What did it mean for my actual life to live in and for the kingdom of God and not just have it be a part of the language and culture of Sunday mornings and small groups?

My subsequent journey with New Monasticism (and the practice of implementing monastic wisdom into a modern context, especially in regard to faith and justice) realized many of these phrases for me. If *Lord* referenced the one to whom I looked for guidance and indication of purpose and morality, then Jesus was not fully Lord if he was not Lord over my finances and my relationships with my neighbors, over how I shared my possessions and who I would invite into my home. I was not living in and for the backwards kingdom of God if my daily, sometimes hourly, decisions were not bent toward those whom Jesus said would inherit said kingdom: the poor, the hungry, the meek, and the mourners.

"My kingdom is from another place," Jesus says (AP). But he also instructs us to pray to the Creator, "Your kingdom come. Your will be done, on earth as it is in heaven" (Matt. 6:10). God's kingdom is both here and on its way. May we ask ourselves today what we mean by *Lord* and *kingdom* and what we're willing to let that inform in our actual lives.

Holy Spirit, challenge us to take our words and our prayers to a different level. Help us to question whether our language matches the practical application of our faith in our lives. Amen.

Before I left the house when I was a child, my mother would echo the advice of her mother: "Remember who you are." This meant that as I journeyed I should check my decisions and intentions by holding them up to my heart and making sure they matched. "Don't get away from yourself," her words suggested. "I know you. And you know you. Live in that truth."

The rhythm of the story of God is one of exodus and homecoming. From the moment the first humans leave the garden to the prophesied reunion of every bowed knee and confessing tongue, people of faith have been roaming and returning. Is this a symptom that we are "prone to wander," as the hymn says? (UMH, no. 400). Possibly. Is it a mimicking of creation's tempo—the coming and going like beach-side waves, full moons, and heart beats? Maybe. Whatever accounts for it, there is a theme in our faith to remember, to recall, to return.

The word *remember* is mentioned in scripture around 166 times. God tells people to remember the covenant, remember the sabbath, remember commands and monumental days, remember your history, remember the former things, remember the words of Jesus, and that the Lord is our God. And God remembers Rachel and the promises made with Abraham and Jacob, remembers dedicated servants and the offspring of the faithful, remembers the great love for humanity, to be merciful, and to show kindness, remembers David, and remembers you and me.

To remember in scripture is to come home to what is true. Remembering is really about the relationship that is acknowledged and edified when we are called back to the truth of who and whose we are. Spend time today allowing God to recall within you the truth about yourself in Christ Jesus, and then spend some time recalling to God the truth about God.

Holy Parent, you remember me. And I remember you. Let us live this next moment in that truth. Amen.

REIGN OF CHRIST

Sometimes, when I get lost in analytically dissecting my theology by wondering if following this faith is good, I remember that God did not have to make a home among us. Wouldn't it be logical for an all-powerful Creator and ruler of the universe to remain distant from its work or, at least, not embedded in it?

As an artist and writer, I know what it means to create something that absorbs your blood, sweat, tears, and time, only to disdain it and cast it aside. But the Good Creator loved the world so much that God made it a home. This is such good news to me! It is a testimony to the worth of humanity and of the world, as well as an invitation for us to humble ourselves and make homes in vulnerable places.

God, through Jesus, relocated into the world in order to fully experience, relate, express, invite, and demonstrate what it means to love unto death, what it means for death not to be the end. This is so personable, kind, intimate, and inspiring! The One who made everything put the divine self in the middle of everything to teach us that we are loved and that we can love, that we are not alone in our suffering or in our restoration.

Christ, whose holiness far surpasses human comprehension, entered our reality as a brown-skinned refugee who experienced homelessness and discrimination before ultimately being executed by the state. Jesus made a home not only among God's creation but among its pain and loss. He related to people on the deepest levels—where our loss and hope live—so that we may be compelled to do the same through holy relocation and homemaking among the last and the least. Out of this reality comes the reign of Christ: informed by the human experience in which he chose to live and love.

Thank you for making your home among us, God. Show me where you are calling me to relocate my life so that I can relate to those in need at the deep level of their loss and hope. Amen.

LOVE Is Coming

NOVEMBER 22–28, 2021 • DOUGLAS RUFFLE

SCRIPTURE OVERVIEW: As we prepare our hearts for Advent, the celebration of Jesus' first coming, we remember in Jeremiah that the birth of Jesus has a deep background, a background rooted in God's promise to David. Psalm 25, traditionally credited to David, speaks of God's faithfulness to those who follow the paths of the Lord. David asks God to teach him to follow God's paths even more closely. The New Testament readings actually point us toward Jesus' second coming. Paul encourages the Thessalonians to excel in holiness and love while they wait. In Luke, Jesus discusses the coming of the kingdom in a passage that some find confusing. We note that he focuses not on the exact time frame of the arrival of the kingdom but on our need to be alert.

QUESTIONS AND SUGGESTIONS FOR REFLECTION

- Read Jeremiah 33:14-16. How have you experienced the promises of God in your life?
- Read Psalm 25:1-10. How has the Lord taught you and led you in the path of your life?
- Read 1 Thessalonians 3:9-13. Is there a faith community for which you pray in joy? How else do you express your gratitude for that community?
- Read Luke 21:25-36. How are you approaching Advent this year? What will you do to prepare your heart?

Director of Community Engagement and Church Planting Resources/Path 1 at Discipleship Ministries; author of *A Missionary Mindset: What Church Planters Need to Know to Reach Their Community—Lessons from E. Stanley Jones* (2016).

Jeremiah's message to the people of Israel gave a vision of hope in the midst of troubled times. We know about troubled times. We will never forget the quarantining, fear, illnesses, and death during the COVID-19 pandemic of 2020. While the troubled times that Jeremiah spoke into were not dealing with a pandemic, it nevertheless referenced extremely difficult days. During his time of prophecy, Israel was under the political domination of outsiders—Assyria and Babylon. Jeremiah knew that his people yearned for a time of safety and one that was free from fear.

The twentieth-century missionary and evangelist E. Stanley Jones believed that every human seeks to live under a just and good order. Moreover, every human being yearns for a just and good leader. Jones said that we have both in the message and the messenger of the gospel. The message is God's reign and the messenger-leader is Jesus Christ. As we enter the season of Advent, we come upon the time when the yearnings that Jones spoke about take center stage in our life as Christians. Jeremiah served as a prophet for its announcement: "The time is coming, declares the LORD, when I will fulfill my gracious promise with the people of Israel and Judah" (CEB).

Jeremiah envisioned a day when a leader "will do what is just and right in the land." His vision transcended the geographical boundaries put in place by human beings and spoke to a new realm led by a new leader, to God's coming reign, and the birth of Jesus.

Gracious and loving God, in times of trouble and despair, we seek your guiding hand to lead us toward a future with hope. Help us prepare our hearts and minds this coming Advent season so that we can become instruments of Jesus' love and leadership in the world. Amen.

This week's devotions carry the title of "LOVE Is Coming." We mentioned yesterday that every human being desires a good and just leader and to live in a political order that is also good and just. These two yearnings give us the first two letters of our acronym LOVE: Leader and Order. The leader we seek is found in the person of Jesus. The order we desire is found within God's reign inaugurated by Jesus with his presence on earth, his ministry, his death and resurrection.

"The time is coming," writes Jeremiah. The time is coming when a righteous branch from the line of David will do what is just and right. Jeremiah anticipated the coming of Jesus, this LOVE incarnate, who shows us "the way, the truth, and the life" (John 14:6, CEB). Despite living under the rule of Assyria and Babylon, Jeremiah can see a better future, a better day, one that will be characterized by justice and righteousness in the land. "In those days," writes Jeremiah, "Judah will be saved and Jerusalem will live in safety. And this is what will be called: The LORD Is Our Righteousness" (CEB).

Do we not also long for a day when our land will be known for justice and righteousness? Do we not long to live in safety with our families, our neighbors, our fellow citizens? Jeremiah says that God's promise to "raise up a righteous branch from David's line" is a gracious promise—that is, a promise for each of us flowing out of the love of God and the God of love. This gracious promise comes without price—it is freely given because it forms part of God's divine plan for humanity.

LOVE is coming this Advent, O Lord. We know that love comes in the birth of Jesus who continues to show us the way, the truth, and the life. Help us to prepare. Amen.

Psalm 25 is one of many psalms attributed to David. Psalms "of David" were not necessarily written by the shepherd king. Their designation as belonging to David is more an indication that they were to be recited in public worship. In this psalm, verse four expresses its central message: "Make me to know your ways, O LORD; teach me your paths." As we enter into the season of Advent, we are on a path of preparation. We reflect on the meaning that Jesus' birth has for our lives. We want to know Jesus' ways. We want to immerse ourselves in Jesus' teachings. We want to walk a pathway of a life worthy of Jesus—a life imbued with his love.

The selected verses from Psalm 25 conclude with this affirmation, "All the paths of the LORD are steadfast love and faithfulness, for those who keep his covenant and his decrees." Echoing the words of Jeremiah, the psalmists's words are a gracious promise that by keeping covenant with God, our pathway will be characterized by steadfast love and faithfulness. The theme "LOVE Is Coming" returns in this psalm. The promise of love calls for faithfulness.

Love is coming in the birth of the One who will show us how to live life to its fullest. It is a life where love is central to our identity and our relationships with others. When asked how Christianity might take root in India, Mahatma Gandhi once told E. Stanley Jones, "Emphasize love and make it your working force, for love is central in Christianity."* Love is coming, and Advent is our time to prepare for it, to live into it, and to make it our life force.

E. Stanley Jones, *Gandhi: Portrayal of a Friend*, (Nashville, TN: Abingdon Press, 1948), 51.

Gracious and loving God, guide us in our pathway of preparation for the birth of Jesus into our lives all over again. Amen.

THANKSGIVING DAY, USA

In this week when we are preparing for the LOVE that is coming, for the season of Advent, those of us who live in the United States pause for a day of Thanksgiving. This has always been my favorite holiday of the year. Throughout my life, Thanksgiving Day has been a time for family gatherings, great food, great conversation, and, at least during my younger years, a game of football among family members after the big meal.

What better way to give thanks to God than to celebrate the close ties of family and friends! My son has been part of a tradition going on ten years now of celebrating "Friendsgiving" among people whose families live far away but who can enjoy a family-like gathering among friends.

Thanksgiving reminds us of the things in life that are truly important. In the scripture passage for today, Jesus reminds us of what is ultimately important. Jesus knows how we humans can worry about everyday things: food, shelter, clothing. All these are important to us and important to God. But Jesus doesn't want us to worry about them because worrying won't help. Instead, Jesus invites us to put our trust in God. Such focus on God's faithfulness makes all the difference in the world for how we think and relate to others and to our everyday needs. Jesus wants us to strive first for what we have been referring to this week as the *O* in LOVE: Order, the reign of God, sometimes referred to as the kingdom of God or the kingdom of heaven. Jesus says that if we strive first for the reign of God and God's righteousness—if we make following God's commandments and Jesus' example the first priority in the way we live our lives— "All these things will be given to you as well."

O Lord, help us to focus on what is truly important: your reign. In Jesus' name. Amen.

Paul, in this letter to the Thessalonians, expresses his love and care for the people. He expresses admiration for their faithfulness to the gospel amid adversity. Paul was forced to flee from Thessalonica, being accused of false teaching by leaders of the synagogue. The members of this new faith community were "Godfearers"—non-Jews who worshiped with Jews in their synagogue. Paul's letter told them he missed them and loved them deeply. He prays that the Lord Jesus "make you increase and abound in love for one another and for all, just as we abound in love for you." He also urged them to grow in faith: "May [the Lord] so strengthen your hearts in holiness that you may be blameless before our God and Father at the coming of our Lord Jesus with all his saints."

The theme of LOVE works its way once again into our reading. Yesterday's devotion underscored the *O* in LOVE, that is, the Order or reign of God that Jesus inaugurated with his presence on earth. Today's reading highlights how Jesus is seen as the *L* in our acronym: its Leader, the one who increases love, the one who strengthens hearts for holiness. As we continue our preparation for Advent and the coming again of Jesus, let us give thanks for the great love of God in and through Jesus that sustains our faith communities and urges each of us on to maturity in our faith.

We haven't forgotten the last two letters of our LOVE acronym. We will turn to them tomorrow and Sunday. We are mindful from today's reading that the anticipated "coming of the Lord with all his saints" was not a fearful looking to the future. It was filled with a message of love for members of the household of God.

Lord Jesus, lead us to a greater, more mature understanding of your way. Amen.

The early Christians living at the time of Luke's writing know troubled times. They have experienced persecution for their beliefs in Jesus. They fear for their lives, as fellow believers—like the apostle Paul—have been jailed or martyred. The signs that portend Jesus' second coming turn the tables. Now the people will "faint from fear and foreboding of what is coming upon the world." But what is distressing news to the world is good news to the persecuted followers of Jesus. Echoing words from the Old Testament prophet Daniel—"I suddenly saw one like a human being coming with the heavenly clouds" (Dan. 7:13, CEB)—Luke says that the followers of Jesus "'will see the Son of Man coming in a cloud' with power and great glory." Thus, to the faithful, Luke says it is time to "stand up and raise your heads because your redemption is drawing near."

Your redemption is near. You followers of Jesus will end up victorious. Herein we have the *V* of our acronym LOVE. We have a leader in Jesus; we have an order in God's reign; and we have Victory through the redemption that comes from being a faithful follower of the Lord. It is a message to stay the course of faith. It is a message not to lose heart during troubling times that may be personal or may come from the circumstances of the world around us, such as wars, economic collapse, or pandemics.

In our preparations for Advent then, we are invited to remember that "LOVE is coming" in the birth of the long-expected One. We are invited to remain faithful to the leadership of Jesus and to choose to live in the order he brings to the world. Therein is our victory.

Guide our steps of preparation, O God, as we anticipate the coming of Jesus into our hearts and lives. Amen.

FIRST SUNDAY OF ADVENT

Luke is writing to Gentile believers. These were the followers of Jesus who, though not born into Judaism, nevertheless participated in synagogue worship. These "Godfearers" also represent the fact that faith in Jesus opens up faith in God to all people. As the apostle Paul wrote, "There is no longer Jew or Greek, there is no longer slave or free, there is no longer male and female; for all of you are one in Christ Jesus. And if you belong to Christ, then you are Abraham's offspring, heirs according to the promise" (Gal. 3:28-29). The God of Abraham and Sarah, Moses and Miriam, Jacob and Rachel, is fully available to all people. The LOVE that is coming in the birth of Jesus is a love for everyone. Thus, the *E* of our acronym stands for Everyone.

Luke encourages his readers to stay alert. He reminds them to not allow the present, troubled times to weigh them down and cause them to be distracted by worry. "Be alert at all times, praying that you may have the strength to escape all these things that will take place, and to stand before the Son of Man."

Jesus encourages our every step through life. Even in times that are shaky, Jesus beckons us to follow his lead (Leader), to enter his way of being (Order), to know that redemption is near through faith in him (Victory), and that this invitation is open to all (Everyone). LOVE is coming. It is coming through the actions of God who sends his Son to live among us so that we will know a life worth living—filling each day with activity that is meaningful and imbued with the love of God and the God of love, not just for ourselves but for others as we serve in Jesus' name.

Guide our steps through this season of Advent, O God, so that the love we know in Jesus becomes the love we share with others. Amen.

Being the Righteous

NOVEMBER 29–DECEMBER 5, 2021 • LINDA FURTADO

SCRIPTURE OVERVIEW: The prophet Malachi speaks of a future day when God's messenger will come to prepare the way for the Lord. The Lord will then purify the people and restore proper worship of God. Christians believe that John the Baptizer was this messenger, preparing the way for Christ. In Luke 1, the Holy Spirit fills Zechariah, John's father, who proclaims that the fulfillment of God's promises to their descendants has begun. Luke continues the story of John in chapter 3, describing John's ministry of calling people to repentance. They need to prepare the way of the Lord in their own hearts, thus fulfilling Malachi's prophecy. Paul in Philippians focuses not on the advent of Christ but on the ongoing power of Christ's presence to make us blameless and righteous in God's sight.

QUESTIONS AND SUGGESTIONS FOR REFLECTION

- Read Malachi 3:1-4. How have you encountered the refiner's fire? What was your experience?
- Read Luke 1:68-79. In what ways have you experienced God's tender mercy in your life?
- Read Philippians 1:3-11. How do you make expressing your gratitude for others a daily habit?
- Read Luke 3:1-6. How are you preparing the way of the Lord? What crooked paths are you helping to make straight?

Ministry leader and educator, wife, and mother of three daughters; member of Belmont United Methodist Church in Nashville, TN, and founder of www. MinistersHelper.com.

In this reading, "the LORD whom you are seeking" (CEB) is said to be like both the heavenly embodiment of the purifier as well as the agents of purification in and of themselves. This Lord—Jesus—is beyond comparison in power and ability, as well as deeply engaged in the needs that we have as people in need of purification.

This embodiment of our Lord is the source of our hope as Christians. It is by God's grace that we are justified so that righteousness may be made real within us. I imagine God as a parent saying, "This will hurt me more than it hurts you," as discipline is administered to help shape a child for the child's future good. None of us likes to be corrected, but what if we open ourselves to allow God's power to influence us? After all, it is only God who can mold us into newness of life for divine and righteous purposes.

When we receive Christ into our lives and come face-to-face with our Lord, we must accept the reality of our imperfections and offer to God our suffering in the woundedness of such knowledge. In doing so, we then become refineable into the purest nature possible for each of us. We make ourselves open to being cleansed and shaped for our unique calls to follow Christ. God can cleanse us so deeply that mind, body, and spirit become like the finest materials that earth has to offer—yet better because we "will belong to the LORD, presenting a righteous offering" (CEB) of ourselves.

God, guide us closer to perfection so that our minds find clarity, our bodies are healthier by your grace, the spirit within reflects the depths of your presence, and others near and far know you through us. Give us the courage to come face-to-face with our past, knowing that the present and future in Christ are full of hope for a good and righteous way of living. Amen.

Many will come to know Christ in a way that is sudden, as if the messenger were coming for the very first time. Senses will be awakened. Awareness of the reality of God is likely to overwhelm even the formerly faithful who are now back in community with Christ's church. This grace-laden process makes the scripture real. God's righteous desires for the people of God will begin to take root with one refining act and cleansing moment after another.

Even when the beginning rush of the reality of Christ seems like more than we can receive, there is a sense of delight available to us. When we give up shaping ourselves, we become open to God's resting with us and working through us. Yet how do we move forward from the euphoria of knowing and experiencing the initial benefits of God's sanctifying grace? What does it take to go from that moment to a sustainable endurance of a long-term commitment to Christ? What disciplines will keep us on the path of righteousness? What reinforcement will remind us to stay in the hands of the Divine even when it is not comfortable?

The scripture gives us insight and hope. While we may not be able to define all of the ways that grace abounds in our day-to-day experience, we can trust that God is working, cleansing, refining, and purifying us. We can practice our faith and join in this work by means such as prayer and worship. It is not that we should attempt to be the cause of our own transformation, for that is the work of God. But through our intentional engagement, we make way for God to inspire and influence the next, best steps toward our purification.

Thank you, Lord, for helping us think differently, move daily with purpose, and pray without ceasing. May we follow your call to support one another in being the community of faith. In Jesus' name. Amen.

Zechariah's song of prophecy following the birth of his son, John the Baptist—who will prepare the way for Jesus—praises God for the deliverance from enemies that will allow God's people to live without fear.

When pain is linked to power that causes harm, it often invades every aspect of our lives. The experience of pain can become so familiar that we might begin to think of despair as the natural state of things. Whether harm is caused by those intentionally wishing us ill or by beloved followers of Christ revealing their imperfections, God promises to deliver us because God's power is a source of only good. There is no hardship that can overshadow or fear that can oppress in the midst of God's love and light.

God provides grace abounding in love, care, and forgiveness. Through an extended season of shifts and changes toward perfection in Christ, we can be formed into servants of God because we know the source of such saving grace. When we choose to step into God's covenantal relationship, we can achieve a peace which frees us from our past and provides hope for our future.

If it were possible for us to be completely self-sufficient, to bring about light in darkness, visibility to faults, and direction to the most righteous way—then there would be no incentive to grow in faith. But, as Zechariah says, it is because of God's great compassion that light breaks upon us. Then, just as a seed planted in the ground, we can grow toward the light. And just as root systems give trees the ability to support one another in the darkness of the earth while their branches stretch toward the light of the sun, so we are the connected community of faith, sharing the benefits of knowing Christ both for all to see and across the depths of our own being.

God, abide in us so that we might have peace of mind, rest in our weariness, faith through it all, connections with your people, and trust as we receive your direction. Amen.

God promised that salvation is ours, a gift that is completely available to God's faithful people. Zechariah looks ahead to the coming of the Savior who would be proclaimed by Zechariah's son, John the Baptist. But as we look back on the nature of the redemptive act of Jesus Christ, a gift covered with pain and beyond comparison, it is no wonder that we cling to the promises and saving grace of God. There is no symbol or expression of love that we can offer one another that matches God's gift to us. Yet we can reflect those gifts of transformation such as salvation, mercy, forgiveness, and compassion.

Part of being people after God's desires is choosing to serve as the presence others need, stretching ourselves to love in ways that reflect God's love. When we choose to serve the relational and spiritual needs of others, we receive God's power and operate without fear. Just as a child offers a beloved toy to an adult whose heart seems to be hurting, we can offer what is precious of ourselves with a heart for those in need. Just as God promises saving grace, we can give sacrificially as bearers of God's good news.

The power within us is worth our focused attention as we strive to live in ways that are holy, whether in our normal daily activities or in profound seasons of transformation. Although pretend-care for the toys of a child may seem like the work of a child, it is also an opportunity to practice how to receive, express thanksgiving, and pass on to others such kindness. The moments we have with our children, our neighbors, and our closest loved ones are opportunities to practice what we say and believe every time we focus our attention on God.

May we never think too lightly as God teaches us through children. May we embody Christ, listen to the Spirit, connect with others, and take focused time apart to reflect on what God is doing in and around us. Amen.

Being the Righteous   399

Imagine the difference between a life deeply rooted in prayer and such a life without prayer. One prayer after another and across the seasons of our lives, we grow in a clearer understanding that God is active and present through the power of prayer.

As followers of Christ, we are uniquely created people, ever developing into more and more faithful children of God. In our life of prayer, we can find the divine within and around us. Paul's letter to the Philippians is itself a prayer of thanksgiving in which the apostle reveals to the people his heart as outwardly expressed before God. Whatever our writing, speaking, singing, dancing before the Lord, we are also privy to the opportunity to offer such expressions.

God's grace justifies us to be level and centered, in position to be sharers and receivers of all that is holy and righteous. So then our prayers take on a new sensibility. As people afforded the gift of life that comes through the saving grace of Christ, we are poised to celebrate rather than dwell in worry or fear that we are not enough. Our praying for others, our words of thanksgiving, and our commitment to live within the love and righteous aims of Christ enhance the power of God at work within us. God tames the challenges that fear creates and emboldens in us the power of love.

What better manner to give glory and praise to God than through our prayers? How better to highlight and value Christian community than by lifting others by name and sharing our joys with one another and with God? Open letters give us a window into stories of which we might not otherwise be aware.

God, may we be so open, so bold in our love, so frank in our appreciation, that our words lift off the pages of our lives and impact the world in our sharing and witness. Amen.

There is something fascinating and inspiring about hearing words clearly and powerfully shared. Here John is without doubt as he cries out in the wilderness into that "region of the Jordan River" (CEB). He is determined and passionate as he proclaims that everyone needs the work of salvation.

It is easy to lose sight of what bold and holy righteousness looks like today and to become complacent about how and where we share the good news. It takes people of faith to encourage others to come to know what genuine Christian experience is all about. To inspire others to live in the righteousness of Christ may require some of us to participate in church meetings, serve in worship, or call a prayer line. For others, those traditional means may not represent the most engaging path for revealing the presence and love of Christ, so they serve in other ways.

Without attention to the needs of those on the receiving end of our words, we will fail at following John's lead. Too often Christians try to inspire without knowing the culture or understanding the background of those to whom they are speaking. We must remember that the wilderness in the regions of our present day are different, so our voices need new and exciting words and images to offer while we remain rooted in the gospel. There is unending joy to be spread, just as there is eternal truth to be told. This life in Christ is not an easy life, but it is a fulfilling life. People need honesty which touches the already-present realities rather than hiding the challenges we must face. For those we reach, our passion must be evident from our first encounter to the last.

Lord, teach us, guide us, and press our hearts so that we may be creative witnesses who offer hope-filled inspiration to all as we "prepare the way for the Lord." Amen.

SECOND SUNDAY OF ADVENT

John aims for his message to reach all people, putting no limits on who should hear him and carrying every expectation that his testimony will bear fruit.

As he takes to the region a message for all of humanity, his actions seem audacious, even today. We are in a world designed to make communication across oceans as simple as a call or instant message. Even so, the idea of reaching all people is challenging and feels impossible for many of us. What will it take to get over our assumptions regarding who will listen and to stretch our voices beyond the comfort of faith communities and friend networks? How can we become so excited, so inspired, so moved to tell the good news that we persist despite the odds?

It may be that we must engage by faith in our own cries out of the wilderness spaces of our lives. But what does it mean to cry out? Should we cry, shout, whisper, sing, or pause in silence? Just as Jesus comes through the pain of childbirth, announcements of angels, and leaps in wombs, so we can be attentive to place and time. Discernment of how to share the good news is not easy work, but what if we listen more intently for our unique gifts and unique circumstances before we spread the good news?

We must remember that the desire of John for all people to see God at work has not changed. But many methods, people, and places are different today. It helps to know that no matter how hard we try, even John knew that everyone not everyone will open themselves to receive this good news. Still, our call is to faithfully proclaim it.

Lord, grow excitement within us as we anticipate the coming Christ. Help us to focus on the One who brings the stories and lessons full circle. Inspire us by the life that makes new life possible, and connect us anew through the newness of life that Advent brings. Amen.

Rejoice in the Lord Always

DECEMBER 6–12, 2021 • JEAN CLAUDE MASUKA MALEKA

SCRIPTURE OVERVIEW: Reviewing the scripture passages for this week, the hymn title "Rejoice, Give Thanks and Sing" might come to mind. The writers of this week's texts advise us to do all these things. At this time of year, these responses often seem to come naturally for many of us. The prophet Zephaniah exhorts his audience to sing aloud and rejoice. The prophet Isaiah calls on the people of Judah to "give thanks to the LORD." In the letter to the Philippians, Paul advises his audience to "rejoice in the Lord always." The tone of the Luke passage for this week is more somber; through the words of John the Baptist, Luke challenges his audience to maintain right relationships with God and humanity. Taken together, these passages provide a number of life lessons.

QUESTIONS AND SUGGESTIONS FOR REFLECTION

- Read Zephaniah 3:14-20. Recall a time when you have experienced joy in the midst of trouble. Give thanks to God for your joy.
- Read Isaiah 12:2-6. How does your trust in God enable you to overcome fear?
- Read Philippians 4:4-7. Are you able to release your worries to God when you pray, or do you tend to hold on to the worry even after you have prayed about it?
- Read Luke 3:7-18. Where in your life are you being nudged to do the right thing? How will you respond?

From the Southern Congo Annual Conference of The United Methodist Church, currently serving as a global missionary assigned to Evangelism and Church Planting in Cote d'Ivoire.

The prophecy of Zephaniah reveals God's faithfulness to God's people. The prophet had predicted the coming wrath of God upon the people because of their sin. But Zephaniah ends the dire warnings which precede today's reading with great promise for the future, a time when God will rule in the midst of the people. Soon after, there was a national revival under King Josiah. Judah had lived wickedly for more years under King Manasseh and King Amon, so Zephaniah urges the people to repent. The nation is filled with idolatry, selfishness, and immorality.

The sins that were found in Judah at the time of Zephaniah's prophecy are the same ones that tempt us today: disobeying God, resisting correction, failing to trust in God, or simply not having any desire to learn about God. Many today still neither seek God's blessing nor fear God's wrath. But if we do not care about the things of God, or if we believe that we can continue in sin without consequences, we are headed for judgment.

Even though there is judgment for sin, however, God is faithful to each person who turns to Jesus Christ in faith. In Jesus, God has taken away our judgment and cast out our enemy. God is able to save, protect, and bless. We are able to rejoice by being in Jesus Christ, who can bring us the same restoration as God did for Judah. The presence of Christ is the symbol of hope, love of God, joy, and peace to the world because whoever believes in him will be saved.

This Advent season provides an opportunity for each of us to prepare our hearts and repent of our sins. God is faithful, and we need not fear. There is no more punishment for those who believe in Jesus Christ as Lord and Savior. Rejoice then! In Christ we have eternal life!

Lord, thank you for sending Jesus Christ for my salvation and for the salvation of all who repent. Give me joy and peace in my heart today. Amen.

Our God, who loves all of humanity and indeed all of creation, is One who restores. After seeing the sufferings and sorrow of the Israelites, God promises them restoration. In exile, they were not able to worship God as they previously had done. They were not able to celebrate their religious events in Jerusalem. But the prophecy of Zephaniah brings hope of a bright future to the people. There is an assurance of better things to come. God is coming to bring peace and to establish harmony.

In our lives, we often face difficult challenges. In this life, no one escapes such trials. At times we may despair and wonder if we will find a solution to our problems. But we should always remember the presence of God with us. In God, there is peace and unity. God's Son, Jesus, is coming to restore our lives and to give joy to humankind. Whoever trusts and obeys Christ as Lord and Savior will experience restoration of the soul. This is true regardless of our circumstances—even those who are in the hospital or in prison and feeling very far from or even excluded from their faith community. There is nowhere that God is not present! Just as God, through the prophet, promised restoration to God's exiled children in Babylon, God also wants to restore all those who today hear God's voice calling them to return home.

Lord Jesus Christ, you came to redeem us from sin. Help us to understand that you are the only way for our humanity to be restored. Give us joy, peace, and the will to remain always in your hands. Amen.

The prophet Isaiah announces God's deliverance of the remnant of the children of Israel from their captivity. This deliverance touches on all aspects of life—spiritual, physical, economic, and social. The prophet instructs the people to celebrate and to sing of the joy of their deliverance—their salvation.

Likewise, God's gift of Jesus Christ to the world is to bring that complete deliverance to God's people. What a joy it is to know that God sent Jesus—"Emmanuel, which means, God is with us" (Matt. 1:23)—and that Jesus has come to bring another form of deliverance: forgiveness of our sins. Now, "everyone who calls on the name of the LORD shall be saved" (Joel 2:32 and quoted by Luke in Acts 2:21).

In African culture, when someone is singing songs of joy it means something wonderful has happened in the life of that person. To sing songs of joy is to recognize what the Lord has done in our lives. This Advent season invites us to recognize God's presence among us with a thankful heart, to celebrate and adore the presence of Jesus Christ, who is the source of our deliverance. During this season, let us meditate on what Christ has done and is doing in our lives and on what he will be able to do in the future. And in response, let us sing our songs of joy!

Thank you, God, for your deliverance and for teaching us to rejoice in you, even in difficult times. No matter what challenges we face, we know that you are always with us. Give us strength when we feel alone. In the name of Jesus Christ. Amen.

The apostle Paul instructs the Philippians to rejoice in the Lord. This kind of rejoicing is really the angels' song of gladness. Paul exhorts his friends who share in the work of spreading the gospel to rejoice in the Lord *always*. Yes, they face many challenges and tribulations as followers of Christ, and certainly Paul knows this. But they are to continue to rejoice.

Being able to rejoice regardless of our circumstances is one good example of what life in Christ means. Whatever situation we face—good or bad—we are able to rejoice in the Lord because, as the Bible tells us, "The joy of the Lord is your strength" (Neh. 8:10).

This Advent season brings celebration and happiness for many, but many others experience great sadness. Whether one is grieving the death of a loved one, experiencing loneliness, dealing with serious illness, facing financial difficulties, or even spending the season isolated in prison, it is still possible to rejoice in the Lord Jesus Christ.

Christ was sent to the world for our sake and for the sake of all people. That is plenty of reason to rejoice, regardless of our circumstances! He is the source of our strength and the solution to any troubles we may face. When we rejoice in the Lord, it is for both our own sake and for the sake of others. Those who look at our lives and see our joy—despite our challenges—may be inspired also to follow Jesus Christ, who is the source of our joy. We can feel confident, too, that our rejoicing in the Lord is also for Christ's sake because we know that he is always pleased when we honor him!

Dear Lord, source of my joy, help me to rejoice in you always because you are the answer to all the challenges of my life. Strengthen my faith and my trust in you each day. Amen.

In today's reading, the apostle Paul extols the Philippians to show their gentleness to all people. He also encourages them in their discipline of prayer. Their prayers, supplications, and requests should be directed to God, Paul tells them. Only God can respond to our prayers, and we can trust that God knows us completely and knows what is best for us in all situations.

This passage also talks about the peace of God, a peace which is beyond all human understanding. It is God's peace that will guard the hearts and minds of Philippians through Christ Jesus. Is there anything more desirable for a guarding presence than the peace—the *shalom*—of God?

God's peace is different from the way most of us typically think of peace, which often tends to be merely about the absence of war or hostilities. This way of thinking represents only a very narrow definition of peace. But in Ephesians 2:14 we learn that Christ Jesus is our peace. That means that the presence of Jesus Christ in the world is breaking down the dividing walls of hostility among people, creating a new humanity, and bringing harmony among different tribes and ethnicities. God's faithful love acts for peace in our world.

Let us trust in Jesus Christ the Prince of Peace in whatever situation we may face in our lives today and in the days to come. And let us trust him not only to give us the peace which passes understanding but also to teach us the best ways to work for peace in our world.

Dear Lord Jesus Christ, you are the source of peace in the world. Give me peace in my heart this day, that I may be able to share it with others. Amen.

The message of John the Baptist was directed at all classes in the Pharisaic society. The people in the audience of John's message were proud of being descendants of Abraham, but John knew that their hearts were very far from God. They thought that because they were children of Abraham they had no need for repentance. Their attitude was wrong, which is why John exhorts his listeners to bear fruits worthy of repentance.

Often today, many people take pride in having been raised by Christian parents, or perhaps even in being the children of pastors, as if this heritage alone were enough to ensure their salvation. They fail to look at their personal relationship with God. It is a wonderful thing to have a family heritage of faith, but the faith of our parents is not enough! God wants each of us to cultivate a personal relationship with Jesus Christ, who is the way of life each of us must choose for ourselves.

Whoever trusts in and obeys Jesus Christ will bear in his or her life the fruits John speaks of. And what are the fruits? John gave us examples: If we have two coats (or more), we are to find someone who has no coat and give one or more of ours away; if we have more than enough food, we are to offer life-sustaining food to someone who is hungry—maybe constantly hungry. These and other acts of compassion are a vital part of what it means to be a follower of Jesus Christ.

God knows our failings and our sins. That is why, in love, God sent Jesus to save those who turn from their own way to follow in Jesus' footsteps. And as we follow, we learn who Jesus is and how we are to bear fruit for the kingdom of God.

Dear Lord, thank you for knowing who I am and for inspiring me to turn away from my sins. Help me this day to bear fruits worthy of repentance. Amen.

THIRD SUNDAY OF ADVENT

John the Baptist is preaching the good news of Jesus Christ. Because of the success of John's mission, people are wondering if John himself is the promised one. But, no. John says he is not the Messiah. He assures people that the Messiah will work with authority and will judge and baptize with the Holy Spirit and with fire. The preaching of John is clear, trenchant, practical, and fearless. The truth of it pierces everyone in his audience, and it is an example for all who seek to preach the good news.

Today we seldom hear sermons which are as fearless and passionate as John's. Do we even want to hear this kind of message? More often it seems that we want our preachers to deliver only what we want to hear. We usually prefer that they not make us too uncomfortable. After all, who wants to hear about the chaff burned with unquenchable fire!

The true Messiah—the One for whom John prepared the way—is Jesus Christ, our Savior and Lord. We know that whoever believes in him will receive everlasting life. (See John 3:16.) Some people come to Jesus expecting material blessings rather than to have their spiritual needs met. But Jesus himself instructed us to seek first the kingdom of God. (See Matthew 6:33.) And this kingdom work doesn't always bring comfort in the traditional sense.

This Advent season, let us continue to look for Christ's presence, his coming into all the circumstances of our lives. As Messiah, he comes to free us from whatever weakens or imprisons us. Let us give thanks then for Christ Jesus, the everlasting source of our healing and freedom!

Lord Jesus, give us the courage and passion to proclaim and to live out the good news of the salvation we have in you. Amen.

God with a Body

DECEMBER 13–19, 2021 • HANNAH E. SHANKS

SCRIPTURE OVERVIEW: As Christians we understand that our faith is rooted in the ongoing story of God's faithfulness to God's people. Micah celebrates this story, prophesying that the true king of Israel will one day come from the small village of Bethlehem, Jesus' birthplace. Luke features women prominently throughout his Gospel. The two readings from Luke this week highlight the prophetic insights of Elizabeth and Mary. Mary visits Elizabeth, who is pregnant with John, God's messenger. After Elizabeth identifies Mary as the mother of the Lord, Mary breaks into song, understanding that her story is tied to the fulfillment of God's promises going back to Abraham. Little does she know that her son will one day offer his body as a sacrifice for all, as Hebrews tells us.

QUESTIONS AND SUGGESTIONS FOR REFLECTION

- Read Micah 5:2-5a. What small beginnings have yielded great results in your life?
- Read Psalm 80:1-7. What is your song of praise to God today? How will you share it?
- Read Hebrews 10:5-10. How does your body help you to experience God?
- Read Luke 1:39-55. How has God spoken to you through a joyous meeting with another person?

Writer, storyteller, and professor living in St. Louis, MO; author of *This Is My Body: Embracing the Messiness of Faith and Motherhood* (Fresh Air Books) which focuses on embodiment, incarnation, and Communion.

The turn toward Advent is a difficult turn to make. We issue this ancient call to contemplation at the same time we receive calls for year-end reports, charity solicitations, academic finals, and holiday parties. We are called to pause at the same time we may want to numb ourselves with activity, evading the grief of a holiday season post-divorce, job loss, illness, or death.

Today's psalm bids us pause and consider what, precisely, we are waiting for. Or really, whom we are waiting for. This psalm is an invitation to envision what restoration may look like. As we focus on the coming birth of Christ, the light of the world, we are asked today to imagine what that light may reveal and how those revelations may be restored.

Take a moment today to rewrite this psalm in your own words. Name God in the way that feels appropriate to your place. In verse 1, the psalmist names God "Shepherd" and asks God to stir up might to save them. What aspect of God are you most close to right now? Guardian? Mother? Comforter? Mystery? Author? Dreamer? What action do you most need God to take?

Once you have written your response, speak aloud the psalmist's refrain: Restore us, O God, let your face shine, that we may be saved.

This plea, this asking for God's face to shine is a plea for God to be recognized in our midst, a heartfelt cry for God to show up in the ways we most need. Consider your needs and where you are looking for God's face.

God of the forgotten, the scorned, the aching.
God of the hustling, the harried, the frayed.
Find us where we are, and draw us close to you.
Give us eyes to see and recognize your shining face,
And all that your presence would heal and restore,
That we may be saved. Amen.

Bodies are important to God.

It can be easy to overlook the embodied nature of our God's story, especially during this season. Our eyes turn to the ethereal, heavenly messengers, to the ancient voices passed down in our hymns: "O Come, O Come, Emmanuel." But at its heart, this is a story about how the God of the Ages came down to be Emmanuel, God with Us.

God with a body.

The Incarnation is the story of God's taking on the fullness of our human vulnerability. God in a fetal body, vulnerable to every factor and disease that harms God's own human creation. God in a child's body, completely dependent on God's own creation. God in a body, experiencing disease, discomfort, loss. Today's scripture reminds us that God's plan wasn't for us to make endless sacrifices and offerings—it was to be with us. And this still is God's greatest desire: to be with us, wholly and without reservation, with nothing standing between. Enfleshed. Embodied.

Many of us are very practiced at distancing ourselves from our bodies. We are overworked and underslept. We might frequently ignore cues of hunger, illness, or discomfort in pursuit of something "more important." But it is God on High who values our bodies, took on a body, found wisdom and teaching in its needs and wants. May this scripture lesson remind us that there is value in our created bodies and that in embracing and learning from our created selves, we may find God there.

Take a few moments today for embodied prayer. This might be through breathing, stretching, dancing, or a run. Where have you been ignoring or downplaying the signals you get from your body? What do you need to feel at ease and joyful in your created, God-given body today?

During this season, prophecy can feel extraordinarily close, just at the tips of our fingers. We can marvel at a child in a manger. We can relate to the struggle of breathing through pain as something new is born.

Our congregations are full of people who know, down to their bones, what labor and birth feel like. Our congregations are full of people who know the kind of suffering, sacrifice, loss and joy that are present in this holy season of expectation surrounding the birth of Christ. But likewise our congregations are full of people longing for that knowledge, but feeling shut out. Through miscarriage or loss, illness or lack of a partner, there are many for whom this season of waiting and birthing language is difficult and complicated.

But we are not without wisdom, and we are not without hope.

As we speak to our Christian family during this time of expectation, as we talk of labor and birth and baby Jesus, let us not forget that these are words and experiences etched in flesh, in the deepest desires of our hearts. Let us attend to the many labors of love that bring forth our common life together, and let us make room for the wisdom of the birthing and mothering bodies in our midst, whatever form they may take.

God of the laboring, God of the loss,
God of danger and birth,
Bring forth in us now a new hope.
Though it may start small and fragile,
Help us to nurture it well.
Give us ears to hear from those gasping for life,
And shape us into midwives for your world to come. Amen.

In this beautiful, powerful passage, we witness something great. Here, two of the first named prophets of the New Testament greet each other, rejoicing in the work God is doing in their midst. Mary and Elizabeth are most often lauded for their works of motherhood. Mary is most often spoken of in terms of her virginity, while Elizabeth is focused on in her "barrenness" leading up to her pregnancy with John. Both of these common signifiers brush past the vibrancy of these women as they appear in our scriptures, inviting us to flatten them and gloss past their full character.

In the New Testament, Mary and Elizabeth are the first to know of God's audacious, scandalous, world-upending plan. In response, both cry out in songs of praise, blessings on their journey toward birth and God's coming work. They prophesy to the nature of God and the coming Christ. They know deep within themselves the truth of what God has done for them. They can recognize what God has done in the life of the other, and share joy in the anticipation of what will come.

Many of us are not used to hearing Mary and Elizabeth described as prophets, or as heroes engaged in dangerous work. But just as other biblical heroes made great proclamations of faith and set their lives on the line, so too did Mary and Elizabeth. Their faith and recognition are constant examples to us. Rather than defining them by their sexual status or proximity to parenthood or hemming them into sanitized visions of saintly, unattainable motherhood, we can hear Mary and Elizabeth call us into God's revolutionary world—one of great risk but also of great, leaping joy.

God, make us like Elizabeth. Let us shout in a loud voice when a blessing walks into our midst and take notice when something within us leaps with recognition of your divine presence. Amen.

Often when we focus on Mary, we tend to zero in on her youth, obedience, and chastity. All of this is, of course, part of Mary's story. But it can be simple to resign Mary to the part of a background character in the "Baby Jesus" story.

But Luke 1 is, without doubt, the Mary story. What she says is powerful—a statement steeped in the prophetic tradition, too bold for someone so young, too radical for someone meek and obedient, too haughty for an unwed teen mother's lips. Here, Mary speaks for herself and for all of God's chosen people —the humble, the hungry, the poor. Far from a quiet, demure mother, blurred in the background of a creche, Mary instead provides a sneak peek of what we will come to expect from her Son. She speaks with authority, even though none was given to her by the power establishment.

Mary the God-bearer calls to us all. A pregnant, unmarried young woman who most would wish to write off, who by now may have endured whispered slurs, shame, and innuendo. Her story was unbelievable, and she knew it. Rather than let others shame her out of what God was working in her, she shouted it from the rooftops. This week, let us pray in the form and spirit of Mary. Let us proclaim with confidence what God has done for us.

My soul magnifies the Lord,
My spirit rejoices in God, my Savior.
For God has been mindful of . . .

Name what God has done for you or what you wish to have restored. Call upon God's upside-down mercies, where those left wanting are filled and the wealthy are freed from their possessions. Remember the long line of God's mercies that have brought you to this moment.

During this season, it's common to hear Mark Lowry's popular Christmas song "Mary, Did You Know?" It may appear on the radio, in the Christmas cantata, or on a favorite holiday album. It is beautiful and moving. But it begs the question— what *did* Mary know of her work in God's plan? While we can never know Mary's mind, we can imagine what Mary knew and take our cues from her.

Mary would've known that pregnancy and childbirth were dangerous and that women did not always survive. She was promised that her son would be called the son of the Most High, but she was not promised that she would survive the birth. Mary's engagement (and likewise, her stability and safety in the world) were reliant on her status as a virgin. Mary knew the child in her womb would be born an Israelite Jew in an occupied Roman state, that he would encounter danger and hardship because of who he was—and who he wasn't. Mary knew that in Roman occupied territory, Caesar was God and proclaiming otherwise was an act of sedition. Mary knew all these things, and still she said yes to God. Still she proclaimed God's goodness at the top of her voice.

This week, let us use this scripture to remind ourselves of what Mary knew and ask ourselves whether we would be willing to do as she did. Can we risk ourselves and our lives in order for God's world to be birthed? Can we face head-on the trouble that comes from going against patriarchy and authority? Can we understand the political trouble the gospel can cause and still proclaim it anyway?

God, you asked Mary, and Mary said yes, without safety or guarantee. And in her risk, she found great joy. Bless us today with what Mary knew—that your presence is worth the trouble. Amen.

God with a Body

FOURTH SUNDAY OF ADVENT

Bodies are important to God because they are sites of healing, transformation, touch, and comfort. Nobody—no body—is disqualified from the work of God-bearing.

As Mary bore Jesus into the world, so must we. For as this scripture in Hebrews reminds us, God's plan has always been a body. Now, as Christ's body in the world, it is up to the church to embody that plan. It is up to you and me to fulfill that promise. We are reminded here that we are made holy through Jesus' work in our midst.

We are all called to the work of birthing God's new world, of nurturing the hope of restoration, of bringing forth life and light through the labor pains that come with it. If we look for the wisdom of our created, holy bodies, that wisdom may bring us closer to our holy Creator. We will see it in the caress of a caregiver's hand, in the elbow offered to steady a swaying companion, in the gaze of compassion that follows the moment when a loved one divulges something held close in their heart. This is not to say that this embodied work is easy. We must consider, too, the bleeding of birth, the sleeplessness of round-the-clock care, and the pain that comes from watching loved ones struggle. But the body of Christ—our individual bodies and the church's collective body—has been Plan A for God all along. We serve as God-bearers never in spite of but always because of who we are. A body, prepared for God.

God, thank you for my body. Help me to honor the wisdom in my body. Thank you for the chance to be a God-bearer. Amen.

Waiting for a Different Kind of King

DECEMBER 20–26, 2021 • D. L. MAYFIELD

SCRIPTURE OVERVIEW: The boy Samuel worshiped and served God from a young age. He grows in stature and favor, the same description that will later be applied to the young Jesus in this week's reading from Luke. The psalmist praises God for raising up a "horn" for the people. This "horn" is referred to elsewhere in the Psalms as being the True King from the line of David, identified later by Luke (1:69) as Jesus. Paul encourages the Colossians to let love rule in their community and to praise God with songs and hymns (such as the Psalms). The additional readings for this special week focus our minds on the Advent of the Lord, the amazing truth that "the Word became flesh and lived among us" (John 1:14), as the prophets had prophesied long ago.

QUESTIONS AND SUGGESTIONS FOR REFLECTION

- Read Isaiah 9:2-7. Where in your world do you see darkness? What lies within your power to dispel it?
- Read Psalm 148. How do you experience God's creations worshiping and praising God? How do you join in that worship?
- Read Colossians 3:12-17. How are you clothing yourself with love during this season?
- Read Luke 2:1-20. In what ways do you hold and ponder the story of Christ's birth in your heart?

Writer and neighbor who lives in Portland, OR, whose most recent book is *The Myth of the American Dream: Reflections on Affluence, Autonomy, Safety, and Power.*

Advent is about the pain and surprising hope of waiting. We see it everywhere in scripture—including in the story of Hannah in First Samuel. We see it in her inability to conceive a child, in her prayer praising God and promising to dedicate her child to service, and in the way God rewarded her obedience with Samuel. It feels like a perfect ending to a clean-cut story, but this is not what Advent is. In First Samuel 2 we read that Hannah went to the Temple for the yearly sacrifice and to visit her son; and she brought a little robe she had made for him. This reminds me of how young Samuel is and how cruel the separation from his mother must be. I feel pain in these sentences, even in the context of Hannah's admirable courage and faith.

Hannah kept her promise to God, and throughout the centuries she has been held up as a model woman. But she also makes the tiny robe as her own act of defiance, her own reminder to herself, to Samuel, to the priest Eli, and to God. Hannah is reminding everyone that she is connected to Samuel, by birth and blood and by the trauma of letting him go. In this I see how Hannah echoes another woman who centuries later would also be asked to give up a son in return for the promise of blessing, a blessing for all people.

Hannah knows the ache of a light shining in the darkness, of receiving a miracle and also having to give it up far before she is ready. She knows what it is like to wait for a promise. And I believe Hannah transcends the transactional ways that many of us approach God. She has faith enough to voice her sadness in the midst of the miracle of life.

God, in this season of waiting for all things to be made new, let us know you are with us in our struggles, in our pain, in our miracles, and in everything in between. Amen.

There is an old story about St. Francis and a wolf that terrorized a small town. Eventually, through the power of God, Francis convinces the wolf to stop attacking people. According to the story, the wolf then lives peacefully among the townspeople for two years, When the wolf dies, the people bury it, mourning and venerating the wolf as a sign of God's power. Psalm 148 reminds me of this story—raising the question of who gets to praise and give glory to God. *Everyone*, says the psalmist! The very youngest to the very oldest among us, the heavens and the angels, and the sky itself—all offer praise to the Creator.

It sounds lovely, until we think more deeply about it. Shouldn't only the good and safe things be counted as creatures of God—brother moon and sister sun, as St. Francis used to wax so eloquently about? But what about the wolves? What about sea monsters? What about those creatures which slither and creep across the ground, the spiders hiding in dark corners, the storms that rip apart buildings, the floods which decimate landscapes, the large and looming animals which strike fear in our hearts? The Lord God made them all, and the one common thread is that the wildness of creation all praises God in the end.

The scriptures recognize that humans are linked to creation by this bond—that we are created. We burst forth from the same Being that gave us sea turtles and hailstorms and Jesus Christ, the Messiah raised up to save us all. Can I think of a wolf changing its ways or a storm praising God? Not quite, but I can envision a creator God who will not abandon any of God's creations. We are interconnected with the birds and the beasts and the skies above, not to exploit or to control them but to continue to learn the old song of praise that has surrounded and will continue to surround this earth as long as God deems necessary.

God, in this season of winter and darkness, help me to praise you alongside creation, even the parts I don't understand. I trust in your wild and wonderful ways. Amen.

Like any good Christian girl, I have heard the refrain often: As God's people we are to clothe ourselves in humility, meekness, compassion, kindness, and patience. I have said I wanted to do this, but it soon became clear that my heart and the hearts of others were oriented in a different direction. Often I heard fearful whispers that our culture was growing more godless, that the church was losing the battle, that we had to fight for our rights to our religion and ways of being in the world.

I realized that many of my fellow Christians wanted to be in power—to use it for good, of course. We wanted influence because we wanted to spread the love of God. Did Jesus do this? Or did he come in the meekest way possible? Didn't he have to constantly subvert those around him who wished that he would take power with force and enact God's will on everyone?

Jesus came clothed in meekness and humility—born to people who were poor, revealed first not to kings but to poor shepherds. Jesus relied on the compassion, kindness, and patience of others around him as he grew. And when I look at the Gospels, I see Jesus leaving a trail of confused religious folks in his wake, people who longed to be good but who found themselves deeply disturbed at the good news of this wandering prophet who called God his very dear Father. I see a death on a cross, a crucifixion by an empire, that does not look very peaceful at all.

Jesus did not stay the meek and mild baby in a manger that we often see this time of year. But as he grew up he still embodied the hallmarks of the kingdom of God, which included subverting the norms of power and influence and religiously inspired hierarchies. Jesus brought a peace which ended up getting him killed. It's a sobering thought today, as it was for those in the early church.

God, as we seek to be meek like your Son, help us learn to relinquish the values we have been taught to love: power, influence, respect, and money. Amen.

Is peace the absence of conflict? Or is it something more? When Jesus said, "Blessed are the peacemakers" (Matt. 5:9) it was in the context of his praising those who are often maligned by the world. Being people who pursue true peace—justice for all and a world where everyone flourishes—means that we will get into trouble with those who benefit from the status quo. We see this in Jesus' life and in the lives of the early Christians.

Paul urges the small groups of believers huddled together in houses to let the peace of Christ dwell in their hearts—to sing and to remember the good works of God, to praise, to teach, and to admonish one another. In this way, they practice true peace: life as Jesus lived his life—in community with other people, thanking God for the blessings of the days, and being strengthened to confront the works of evil in the world.

How can we start to cultivate a desire for Christlike love in our hearts? And how can we start to live into the duty of being peacemakers in a world full of injustice? Perhaps the answer lies partly in Paul's letter. Perhaps we need one another to be able to fulfill this work. We need to gather together, to read and sing and laugh and cry. We need to eat food and tell stories. We need to gather together in any way we can in order to truly live out the life and message of Jesus. We need one another in order to start to see the kingdom of God be born into our world.

As Christmas Day approaches, let us think about how we can be a part of bringing true peace in our communities. We look from the birth of Jesus ahead to his death, and we know that we were never promised this road would be easy. But together, the duty of being peacemakers becomes a community undertaking, and we know we shall never be alone on this journey.

God, create in me a desire to see justice in my own home, neighborhood, city, and country. Thank you for the witness of Christians throughout the centuries who have shown us the way of peace. Help us to walk boldly in that same direction. Amen.

CHRISTMAS EVE

My mother is a tutor at an elementary school, whose students include many immigrants and refugees. (In this small school there are twenty-nine languages spoken.) Every day my mom asks her students a simple question. One day she asked a seven-year-old from Afghanistan what he liked about living in the U.S. *No war*, he carefully scrawled on his paper.

I think about this boy and his family, who are struggling to make it here in their new country. They face many barriers, but they no longer face the specter of war all around. It reminds me of Isaiah's prophecy that the people who have lived in darkness will see a great light and that "all the boots of the tramping warriors and all the garments rolled in blood shall be burned as fuel for the fire."

It has taken relationship with refugees to help unpack new meanings for me in the story of Jesus, who knew what it was like to flee violence and dictators. Advent songs about the Wonderful Counselor, almighty God, Everlasting Father, Prince of Peace, did not mean all that much to me—a girl who grew up safe and comfortable, my religion the majority, never having to leave my home to escape persecution. But the richness of the good promises of God have continued to grow for me as I have worked with refugee populations over the past decade and a half. As the stories of displacement around our world grow and as more of them have found their way into my ears, the miracle of the kingdom that Jesus came to announce starts to take my breath away. This is a world I long to live in! And it is one I am learning to yearn for more and more with each passing year, with each story of displacement that comes my way.

Reread Isaiah 9:2-7. Which good news leaps out the most to you? How do you see God's kingdom coming even now in the midst of increased global conflict?

CHRISTMAS DAY

Christmas Day is the day we celebrate the birth of the Son of God. We focus on God becoming flesh in the most humble and vulnerable form imaginable. We celebrate the tiny baby who grew up to declare that God's blessing was so much bigger and more extravagant than people would want to believe. We meditate on a baby who was not born in a palace, who opted out of hierarchy from the first moment possible. Think of the nativity scenes we set up in our homes, images of humble stables as a hallmark of Christian celebrations. We mark that the angels appeared to shepherds—peasants—and ignored the kings. We put up figures of donkeys and horses and sheep (and in my house, a little cat), both to lure children into the story but also to connect to scriptures of old. The whole earth, down to the smallest animal, rejoiced at the birth of Christ.

Today we do not celebrate just the birth of a baby but the birth of a baby who was born into a specific place and context, who had brown skin, and who grew up a poor Jewish man—the minority in a place governed by rulers who oppressed him and his people economically. We have a hope in a God who will restore all things lost, who suffered and was always drawn to those who had been cast aside by society.

Jesus didn't come to tell people to be better, to behave in a way that was more pleasing. He didn't even come to tell people to believe in God—most everyone already did in that day and age. Instead, Jesus came to embody who God was—an everlastingly good Father who desperately longs for real relationship with us all.

All the sad and wild things of the earth, everything meek and humble, was drawn to Jesus—the night of his birth and the rest of his life. And Jesus had good news for all of them, for all of us. May we be able to receive it this day!

When my son was few weeks old he became very sick with what the doctors thought might be meningitis. Those few days in the hospital broke something in me. I determined that as his mother, I would never let anything bad happen to him again. Months later, I realized the foolishness of my thoughts; but they made sense at the time. Mothers, like anyone who loves another, wish we could control the world to protect our people. The tragedy is that we can't, but often we try to distract ourselves from this fact or persuade ourselves that we have at least some control.

Jesus remains the example of what it means to fully surrender oneself to a life lived for God. Even as a teenager he was teaching those around him. Luke 2 tells the story of Jesus in the Temple during Passover, the festival to commemorate the time God overcame the power of Pharaoh. Jesus is in the thick of the festivities, so much so that he stays behind, unnoticed, to remain in the Temple and learn about God.

His good news—his time of sitting and learning, of growing in wisdom and stature—feels like bad news to his mother. Mary, who already knows the shadow of a hard and holy life is on her son, struggles to understand. Her anxiety foreshadows the grief that will be not just hers but that of Mary Magdalene, Jesus' disciples, and countless other followers when he is executed by the Roman empire.

Babies and children remind us of the fragility of life. They point out how much our desire to control is only an illusion. Jesus in the Temple is already teaching his parents what it is like to move throughout the world when God is your very good Father. It is a life not beholden to typical structures of power. It is a life free from the fear of having to control it all.

Teach me, O God, to learn to give back to you what is not mine to control. Be with me in the grief of unknowing, and give me the faith to listen to those who are following your voice. Amen.

The Joy of Restoration

DECEMBER 27–31, 2021 • MEMORY CHIKOSI

SCRIPTURE OVERVIEW: The readings for this week are full of praise for God's gift of Jesus Christ and an emphasis on human helplessness apart from God. Jeremiah portrays an exiled people's despair turning to joy at their restoration. The psalmist proclaims God's power to protect and provide for God's people, and Paul's letter to the Ephesians explains that God's will from the beginning has been for our adoption as God's children through Christ. Praise and thanksgiving to God are the common and appropriate responses to all these mighty acts of God.

QUESTIONS AND SUGGESTIONS FOR REFLECTION

- Read Jeremiah 31:7-14. How have you been restored by God's kindness?
- Read Psalm 147:12-20. In what ways have you experienced God strengthening and restoring you?
- Read Ephesians 1:3-14. How do you set your hope on Christ? How do you live differently because of that hope?

Elder in The United Methodist Church in the Zimbabwe Episcopal Area; holds a master's degree in Theological Studies; United Theological College lecturer and chaplain; Amazing Grace circuit associate pastor.

The scripture reading for today falls within a section (chapters 30-31) that foretells the beautiful vision of the restoration that God plans for the exiled people of Israel. Jeremiah announces that God will restore the land of Judah and Israel from captivity amidst shouts of joy. The prophet goes on to say that people from all walks of life—the blind, the lame, women with children, and those in labor—will be liberated from every tyrant and will return home.

Our God is a God of dependable love and care. God will never fail to keep promises or fail to fulfill the divine plans. Just as God promised to save and comfort Judah and Israel's exiles from their oppressors, God has the same kindness for us and can guide us in our own difficult trials. With God, we will not stumble even though our paths may be rough. The God who was the Father to Israel is also our Father. Just like Ephraim, we are God's sons and daughters.

God has good plans for our well-being—strategies to protect and prosper us. When we repent, worship, pray, and praise God—when we search for and seek our Creator with all our hearts—God will hear us, redeem us, and grant us a glorious future with hope. The plans and promises of God never fail. This is our everlasting joy!

For all the pain and bruises we experience as a people, Lord, reconstruct, purify, and grant us the capacity to experience your leading and full restoration. Amen.

The goodness of God brings comfort and joy to God's people. As Jeremiah continues celebrating restoration, he focuses on recovery of lost stock. Through Jeremiah, God promises to end the people's suffering, to comfort them, and to restore their joy by granting them a blessed future. God promises to rebuild and purify the people and that they will never be destroyed again.

New life will be experienced as the people who were scattered, along with the wheat, wine, and oil that were depleted, and the sheep and the cattle, will all flourish again like watered gardens. This promise of restoration happens even before people have put in any of their own effort beyond obedience.

Despite the transgressions of the people, this passage shows that God took Israel as a model nation to exemplify God's love and forgiveness toward all humanity. Therefore, God will do the same for us. The grace of God is abundant for all people. God continues to plan to liberate those who obey the Lord. With constant and everlasting loving-kindness, God will restore God's broken people. Even when we are experiencing extreme hardships and oppression, God will water our lives like gardens, give us rest, and comfort us. Furthermore, God will forgive us and restore our happiness. Our former sorrow will be no more. The Lord will transform our sin-sick souls and make them alive again.

As God looked on God's people Israel, God had mercy on them because they were being oppressed by "hands too strong for [them]." When we are in bondage to forces too strong for us, God in mercy is ready to restore our joy and to gratify our souls with abundance.

Gracious Lord, ever-loving and forgiving God, I yearn for your goodness and mercy. Turn my mourning into joy. Amen.

The Joy of Restoration

Psalm 147 speaks words of comfort to the people of Israel and exhorts them to praise God for God's power. God's understanding is unlimited, and our Creator rejoices in those who trust in the Lord's loving-kindness in any situation. The psalmist assures the people that God's power is greater than anything else on earth. God is never overwhelmed by upheaval or by any circumstance we may face.

The security of people's habitation, blessing of children within, peace on the land, and plenty of good food are part of God's divine provisions. In a world that faces many catastrophes—wars, poverty, life-threatening diseases, and natural disasters—the psalmist affirms that God is the comforter and the provider of all our needs. God is the defender and peace-builder. God heals the brokenhearted and binds their emotional wounds, as well as their physical and spiritual wounds.

One very real question becomes: How does God accomplish these acts of healing and restoration? What is our role in being coworkers with God, offering our talents, gifts, and substance so that lives are healed and restored.

The God of Jacob, Moses, Miriam, Esther, and Isaac is the God who reconstitutes and recovers what has been lost. Our response is to love God, to follow God's commands, and to have faith and hope in God's mercy. God is the creator and sustainer of life. As God's people, we are to humble ourselves before God who delights in those who fear God and grants them provision and peace. We need not doubt God's ability. Instead, we commit our lives to God and offer our praises for God's acts of salvation.

Lord of mercy, my helper, protector, and comforter, give me serenity in all things, and show me how best to offer you my praise. Amen.

Ephesians 1 opens with Paul announcing peace and the grace of God to the believers in Ephesus. He describes God's spiritual blessing on humanity in Jesus' name. The text makes clear that the spiritual blessings are the everlasting purpose of God. God"'s will has always been that God's people remain holy and blameless before their Creator. Paul emphasizes God's relationship with humanity, the traits of that relationship, and what it means to be adopted in God's kingdom. In this relationship, God's role is to show loving care for God's people. Our obligation as believers is to obey God and to offer our praise for God's gift of grace.

Today's reading expresses that God created us to be God's people, a church serving others and praising God. As God's people, we have to pursue God's perpetual redemptive purpose. Jesus Christ, the agent of redemption and the mediator of God's grace, is our guide.

We understand the purpose of God to bless God's people through the love of Christ whose sacrifice on the cross made us free from the power of sin. Through Christ, the grace of God transforms our inner being. Christ makes known the mysterious will of God, and our responsibility as believers is to proclaim this mystery. Christ, who is the gospel and who is the spiritual blessing to all people, assembles and unites the people of God as one holy church. As Christ's church we offer our praise of God and witness to the word of God. God's spiritual blessings sustain us in hardships as we await the time when God will "bring unity to all things" under Christ" (NIV).

Loving God, help me understand your everlasting purpose of uniting all things in the church of Jesus Christ. Amen.

Paul explains to the believers in Ephesus that God is in control today, tomorrow, and forever. The apostle explains that God has a plan to adopt each person in Jesus Christ and encourages the Ephesians to surrender themselves to God's perfect will and find new life in Christ.

We often wonder how we can know God's will for our life. God planned to send Jesus to live on earth in order to gather all things from heaven and earth in Christ. God's plan for the church is everlasting. The church becomes the tool of our inward transformation and redemption by God. God desires countless blessings for us and intervenes in our life experiences through the Holy Spirit.

We are created in God's image so that we have a close relationship with our Creator. The responsibility of a faithful and obedient church is to serve God and to praise God's beauty revealed in Christ. All who are baptized by the Holy Spirit and have received inner transformation are incorporated into the church, destined and appointed for God's work.

The church has been granted a vital place in the divine creation, a place where God is served and praised, the proper role of all believers. Additionally, when we read that we are to "live for the praise of his glory," we know that we have servant work to do. Very simply, we praise God best by loving and caring for God's people. God's plan is made absolute by the work of the Holy Spirit within us, and God approves us as children of God. Thus, we continue to trust and have faith and hope in God, no matter what trials we may experience.

God, help us to be part of your persuasive and gracious plan to treat the transgressions of your people with your grace. We want to learn how better to be instruments of your grace so that you may bring healing to a troubled world. Amen.

The Revised Common Lectionary* for 2021
Year B – Advent / Christmas Year C
(Disciplines Edition)

January 1–3
Jeremiah 31:7-14
Psalm 147:12-20
Ephesians 1:3-14
John 1:1-18

> **New Year's Day**
> Ecclesiastes 3:1-13
> Psalm 8
> Revelation 21:1-6a
> Matthew 25:31-46

January 4–10
BAPTISM OF THE LORD
Genesis 1:1-5
Psalm 29
Acts 19:1-7
Mark 1:4-11

> **January 6**
> EPIPHANY
> *(may be used for Sunday, Jan. 10)*
> Isaiah 60:1-6
> Psalm 72:1-7, 10-14
> Ephesians 3:1-12
> Matthew 2:1-12

January 11–17
1 Samuel 3:1-20
Psalm 139:1-6, 13-18
1 Corinthians 6:12-20
John 1:43-51

January 18–24
Jonah 3:1-5, 10
Psalm 62:5-12
1 Corinthians 7:29-31
Mark 1:14-20

January 25–31
Deuteronomy 18:15-20
Psalm 111
1 Corinthians 8:1-13
Mark 1:21-28

February 1–7
Isaiah 40:21-31
Psalm 147:1-11, 20c
1 Corinthians 9:16-23
Mark 1:29-39

February 8–14
TRANSFIGURATION
2 Kings 2:1-12
Psalm 50:1-6
2 Corinthians 4:3-6
Mark 9:2-9

February 15–21
FIRST SUNDAY IN LENT
Genesis 9:8-17
Psalm 25:1-10
1 Peter 3:18-22
Mark 1:9-15

February 17
ASH WEDNESDAY
Joel 2:1-2, 12-17 (*or* Isaiah 58:1-12)
Psalm 51:1–17
2 Corinthians 5:20b–6:10
Matthew 6:1-6, 16-21

February 22–28
SECOND SUNDAY IN LENT
Genesis 17:1-7, 15-16
Psalm 22:23-31
Romans 4:13-25
Mark 8:31-38 *or* Mark 9:2-9

March 1–7
THIRD SUNDAY IN LENT
Exodus 20:1-17
Psalm 19
1 Corinthians 1:18-25
John 2:13-22

March 8–14
FOURTH SUNDAY IN LENT
Numbers 21:4-9
Psalm 107:1-3, 17-22
Ephesians 2:1-10
John 3:14-21

March 15–21
FIFTH SUNDAY IN LENT
Jeremiah 31:31-34
Psalm 51:1-12
(*or* Psalm 119:9-16)
Hebrews 5:5-10
John 12:20-33

March 22–28
PALM/PASSION SUNDAY
Liturgy of the Palms
Mark 11:1-11, 15-18
(*or* John 12:12-16)
Psalm 118:1-2, 19-29

Liturgy of the Passion
Isaiah 50:4-9a
Psalm 31:9-16
Philippians 2:5-11
Mark 14:1–15:47
  (*or* Mark 15:1-47)

March 29–April 4
HOLY WEEK

HOLY MONDAY
Isaiah 42:1-9
Psalm 36:5-11
Hebrews 9:11-15
John 12:1-11
HOLY TUESDAY
Isaiah 49:1-7
Psalm 71:1-14
1 Corinthians 1:18-31
John 12:20-36
HOLY WEDNESDAY
Isaiah 50:4-9a
Psalm 70
Hebrews 12:1-3
John 13:21-32
MAUNDY THURSDAY
Exodus 12:1-14
Psalm 116:1-2, 12-19
1 Corinthians 11:23-26
John 13:1-17, 31b-35
GOOD FRIDAY
Isaiah 52:13–53:12
Psalm 22
Hebrews 10:16-25
John 18:1–19:42

HOLY SATURDAY
Easter Vigil
Exodus 14:10-31
Isaiah 55:1-11
Psalm 114
Romans 6:3-11
Mark 16:1-8
EASTER SUNDAY (APRIL 4)
Acts 10:34-43
Psalm 118:1-2, 14-24
1 Corinthians 15:1-11
John 20:1-18
   (*or* Mark 16:1-8)

April 5–11
Acts 4:32-35
Psalm 133
1 John 1:1–2:2
John 20:19-31

April 12–18
Acts 3:12-19
Psalm 4
1 John 3:1-7
Luke 24:36*b*-48

April 19–25
Acts 4:5-12
Psalm 23
1 John 3:16-24
John 10:11-18

April 26–May 2
Acts 8:26-40
Psalm 22:25-31
1 John 4:7-21
John 15:1-8

May 3–9
Acts 10:44-48
Psalm 98
1 John 5:1-6
John 15:9-17

May 10–16
Acts 1:15-17, 21-26
Psalm 1
1 John 5:9-13
John 17:6-19

May 13
ASCENSION DAY
Acts 1:1-11
Psalm 47
Ephesians 1:15-23
Luke 24:44-53

May 17–23
PENTECOST
Acts 2:1-21
Psalm 104:24-34, 35b
Romans 8:22-27
John 15:26-27; 16:4b-15

May 24–30
TRINITY
Isaiah 6:1-8
Psalm 29
Romans 8:12-17
John 3:1-17

May 31–June 6
1 Samuel 8:4-20
Psalm 138
2 Corinthians 4:13–5:1
Mark 3:20-35

June 7–13
1 Samuel 15:34–16:13
Psalm 20
2 Corinthians 5:6-17
Mark 4:26-34

June 14–20
1 Samuel 17:1a, 4-11, 19-23,
  32-49
Psalm 9:9-20
2 Corinthians 6:1-13
Mark 4:35-41

June 21–27
2 Samuel 1:1, 17-27
Psalm 130
2 Corinthians 8:7-15
Mark 5:21-43

June 28–July 4
2 Samuel 5:1-5, 9-10
Psalm 48
2 Corinthians 12:2-10
Mark 6:1-13

July 5–11
2 Samuel 6:1-5, 12b-19
Psalm 24
Ephesians 1:3-14
Mark 6:14-29

July 12–18
2 Samuel 7:1-14a
Psalm 89:20-37
Ephesians 2:11-22
Mark 6:30-34, 53-56

July 19–25
2 Samuel 11:1-15
Psalm 14
Ephesians 3:14-21
John 6:1-21

July 26–August 1
2 Samuel 11:26–12:13a
Psalm 51:1-12
Ephesians 4:1-16
John 6:24-35

August 2–8
2 Samuel 18:5-9, 15, 31-33
Psalm 34:1-8
Ephesians 4:25–5:2
John 6:35, 41-51

August 9–15
1 Kings 2:10-12; 3:3-14
Psalm 111
Ephesians 5:15-20
John 6:51-58

August 16–22
1 Kings 8:1, 6, 10-11, 22-30,
  41-43
Psalm 84
Ephesians 6:10-20
John 6:56-69

August 23–29
Song of Solomon 2:8-13
Psalm 45:1-2, 6-9
James 1:17-27
Mark 7:1-8, 14-15, 21-23

August 30–September 5
Proverbs 22:1-2, 8-9, 22-23
Psalm 125
James 2:1-17
Mark 7:24-37

September 6–12
Proverbs 1:20-33
Psalm 19
James 3:1-12
Mark 8:27-38

September 13–19
Proverbs 31:10-31
Psalm 1
James 3:13–4:3, 7-8a
Mark 9:30-37

September 20–26
Esther 7:1-6, 9-10; 9:20-22
Psalm 124
James 5:13-20
Mark 9:38-50

September 27–October 3
Job 1:1; 2:1-10
Psalm 26
Hebrews 1:1-4; 2:5-12
Mark 10:2-16

October 4–10
Job 23:1-9, 16-17
Psalm 22:1-15
Hebrews 4:12-16
Mark 10:17-31

October 11–17
Job 38:1-7, 34-41
Psalm 104:1-9, 24, 35c
Hebrews 5:1-10
Mark 10:35-45

October 11
Thanksgiving Day, Canada
Joel 2:21-27
Psalm 126
1 Timothy 2:1-7
Matthew 6:25-33

October 18–24
Job 42:1-6, 10-17
Psalm 34:1-8, 19-22
Hebrews 7:23-28
Mark 10:46-52

October 25–31
Ruth 1:1-18
Psalm 146
Hebrews 9:11-14
Mark 12:28-34

November 1–7
Ruth 3:1-5; 4:13-17
Psalm 127
Hebrews 9:24-28
Mark 12:38-44

November 1
All Saints Day
Isaiah 25:6-9
Psalm 24
Revelation 21:1-6a
John 11:32-44

November 8–14
1 Samuel 1:4-20
1 Samuel 2:1-10
Hebrews 10:11-25
Mark 13:1-8

November 15–21
The Reign of Christ
2 Samuel 23:1-7
Psalm 132:1-18
Revelation 1:4b-8
John 18:33-37

November 22–28
FIRST SUNDAY OF ADVENT
Jeremiah 33:14-16
Psalm 25:1-10
1 Thessalonians 3:9-13
Luke 21:25-36

> **November 25**
> THANKSGIVING DAY, USA
> Joel 2:21-27
> Psalm 126
> 1 Timothy 2:1-7
> Matthew 6:25-33

November 29–December 5
SECOND SUNDAY OF ADVENT
Malachi 3:1-4
Luke 1:68-79
Philippians 1:3-11
Luke 3:1-6

December 6–12
THIRD SUNDAY OF ADVENT
Zephaniah 3:14-20
Isaiah 12:2-6
Philippians 4:4-7
Luke 3:7-18

December 13–19
FOURTH SUNDAY OF ADVENT
Micah 5:2-5a
Luke 1:46-55
  (*or* Psalm 80:1-7)
Hebrews 10:5-10
Luke 1:39-55

December 20–26
FIRST SUNDAY AFTER
CHRISTMAS
  1 Samuel 2:18-20, 26
  Psalm 148
  Colossians 3:12-17
  Luke 2:41-52

December 24
CHRISTMAS EVE
Isaiah 9:2-7
Psalm 96
Titus 2:11-14
Luke 2:1-20

December 25
CHRISTMAS DAY
Isaiah 52:7-10
Psalm 98
Hebrews 1:1-12
John 1:1-14

December 27–31
SECOND SUNDAY AFTER
CHRISTMAS
Jeremiah 31:7-14
Psalm 147:12-20
Ephesians 1:3-14
John 1:1-18

A Guide to Daily Prayer

These prayers imply worship time with a group; feel free to adapt the plural pronouns for personal use.

MORNING PRAYER

In the morning, O LORD, you hear my voice;
> in the morning I lay my requests before you
> and wait in expectation.

—Psalm 5:3

Gathering and Silence

Call to Praise and Prayer
> God said: Let there be light; and there was light.
> And God saw that the light was good.

Psalm 63:2-6
> God, my God, you I crave;
> my soul thirsts for you,
> my body aches for you
> like a dry and weary land.
> > Let me gaze on you in your temple:
> > a Vision of strength and glory
> > Your love is better than life,
> > my speech is full of praise.
> > I give you a lifetime of worship,
> > my hands raised in your name.
> > I feast at a rich table,
> > my lips sing of your glory.

Prayer of Thanksgiving

We praise you with joy, loving God, for your grace is better than life itself. You have sustained us through the darkness: and you bless us with life in this new day. In the shadow of your wings we sing for joy and bless your holy name. Amen.

Scripture Reading

Silence

Prayers of the People

The Lord's Prayer (see Midday Prayer for text)

Blessing

May the light of your mercy shine brightly on all who walk in your presence today, O Lord.

I will extol the LORD at all times;
   God's praise will always be on my lips.
                    —Psalm 34:1

Gathering and Silence

Call to Praise and Prayer

   O LORD, my Savior, teach me your ways.
      My hope is in you all day long.

Prayer of Thanksgiving

   God of mercy, we acknowledge this midday pause
   of refreshment as one of your many generous gifts.
   Look kindly upon our work this day; may it be made
   perfect in your time. May our purpose and prayers
   be pleasing to you. This we ask through Christ our
   Lord. Amen.

Scripture Reading

Silence

Prayers of the People

The Lord's Prayer (ecumenical text)
   Our Father in heaven,
      hallowed be your name,
      your kingdom come,
      your will be done,
      on earth as in heaven.

Give us today our daily bread.
Forgive us our sins as we forgive
    those who sin against us.
Save us from the time of trial,
    and deliver us from evil.
For the kingdom, the power, and the glory
    are yours, now and forever. Amen.

Blessing

Strong is the love embracing us, faithful the Lord from morning to night.

My soul finds rest in God alone;
my salvation comes from God.
—Psalm 62:1

Gathering and Silence

Call to Praise and Prayer

From the rising of the sun to its setting,
let the name of the LORD be praised.

Psalm 134

Bless the Lord,
all who serve in God's house,
who stand watch
throughout the night.

Lift up your hands
in the holy place
and bless the Lord.

And may God,
the maker of earth and sky,
bless you from Zion.

Prayer of Thanksgiving

Sovereign God, you have been our help during the day and you promise to be with us at night. Receive this prayer as a sign of our trust in you. Save us from all evil, keep us from all harm, and guide us in your way. We belong to you, Lord. Protect us by the power of your name. In Jesus Christ we pray. Amen.

Scripture Reading

Silence

Prayers of the People

The Lord's Prayer (see Midday Prayer for text)

Blessing

May your unfailing love rest upon us, O LORD, even as we hope in you.

This Guide to Daily Prayer was compiled from scripture and other resources by Rueben P. Job and then adapted by the Pathways Center for Spiritual Leadership while under the direction of Marjorie J. Thompson.